Friends for Life, Friends for Death

Friends for
Life,
Friends for
Death

James A. Pritchett

University of Virginia Press
CHARLOTTESVILLE AND LONDON

University of Virginia Press
© 2007 by the Rector and Visitors of the University of Virginia
All rights reserved
Printed in the United States of America on acid-free paper

First published 2007

1 3 5 7 9 8 6 4 2

Library of Congress Cataloging-in-Publication Data

Pritchett, James Anthony.
    Friends for life, friends for death : cohorts and consciousness among the Lunda-
Ndembu / James A. Pritchett.
        p.   cm.
    Includes bibliographical references and index.
    ISBN-13: 978-0-8139-2624-7 (cloth : alk. paper)
    1. Ndembu (African people) 2. Male friendship—Zambia. I. Title.
DT3058.N44P74 2007
305.896'393—dc22

2006033613

To my mother
Myrtle E. Angel
and in loving memory of
Joseph L. Angel
(1930–1997)

Contents

Illustrations follow page 90

Preface

The book that follows was conceived in the mid-1980s during the initial stages of my Ph.D. dissertation research in the rural Mwinilunga District of northwestern Zambia. Thoughts about its form emerged in response to the overwhelming feeling of incompetence that enveloped me at that time. I had prepared well for fieldwork, so I thought, by reading every known anthropological account of the region. I knew much about local forms of social organization, belief systems, subsistence practices, and ceremonial life. Yet, somehow that information provided me with little comfort or guidance in ordinary interactions with the people who now made up my social world. Indeed, my bundle of anthropological facts appeared to exist in a realm utterly separate from the realities of day-to-day life in Zambia. I felt no more at ease, no more capable of responding properly to quotidian events than perhaps the most ill-informed traveler. Certainly I was well aware that it was not the job of anthropologists to produce tourist guides for the uninitiated. Our goals were much more lofty. To us fell the task of delving deeply into a society, to explore the unfolding relationship between the eternal and the contingent, to disentangle symbol from substance, to seek out the complex layers of meaning embedded in social discourse. But was it really necessary to encase anthropological insights in theoretical frameworks and rhetorical styles that actually camouflaged the tone and tenor of daily life? Could not analytical rigor be achieved without distancing oneself from the sights and sounds, the smell, taste, and feel of the lived-in world? I promised myself that my first ethnography would be different. I would strive to capture the immediacy of daily life, the raw sensorium of a culture that was not my own.

Back home in Cambridge, Massachusetts, I immediately broke that promise. First in pursuit of approval from my college advisors, later in pursuit of a career, I wrote in ways primarily meant to demonstrate my command of the tools of my discipline, endeavoring to be accepted into the fold of gainfully employed academic anthropologists. I paid homage to the founders of the field. I carefully crammed my thoughts into widely recognizable anthropological categories. I built my arguments through the meticulous arrangement of standard theoretical blocks. That which did not fit the conventional schema, such as scenes from everyday life, vignettes of social indeterminacy, or moments of spontaneous creativity or outright invention remained as raw journal entries, notes scattered in the margins of more polished text or multicolored Post-its precariously clinging to my office wall.

This book gathers up that scattered material, moving it from the margins to center stage with the faith that collectively such material has its own powerful story to tell. I hope that story flows here unencumbered by excessive academic jargon and largely unhampered by theoretical musings, aiming instead for a clarity of exposition and an immediacy of emotions that will enmesh the reader in a more vivid sensation of being there. It has not been easy to forsake the comforting embrace of academic purity, indeed to write as if academic disciplines did not matter at all. Here one will find a text that contains bits and pieces of ethnography, history, philosophy, theology, political science, economics, and literature. Yet, most assuredly it is fully none of these.

The courage to move in this novel direction was provided by the daily inspiration of a unique working environment: the African Studies Center at Boston University. The physical space that constitutes the center is constantly awash in interdisciplinary thinking. Over morning coffee, at the weekly brown-bag seminar, and in spontaneous hallway gatherings, conversations flow across academic boundaries as if they did not exist. Anthropologists debate economists about the impact of a recent piece of political legislation in Nigeria. Historians and theologians confer on readings for a jointly taught course on missionaries in Southern Africa. Linguists and curriculum development specialists deliberate over the usage of vernacular languages in adult literacy programs in Niger. Graduate students routinely construct research projects that bring faculty from diverse departments into productive interaction. Among the faculty and fellows of the center whom I must dearly thank for intellectual sustenance and encouragement over the years are Barbara Brown, Edouard Bustin, John Harris, Jean Hay, John Hutchison, Patrick Seyon, Parker Shipton, Irene Staehelin, Diana Wylie, and most especially the long-term director of the African Studies Center, James C. McCann. Joanne Hart, whose personal touch is on everything the center does, is also deserving of special mention. Africana librarians Gretchen Walsh, David Westley, and Loumona Petroff staff one of the most comprehensive and accessible Africana libraries in the country. Their work was central to the research process at every stage.

Thanks are also due my colleagues in the Anthropology Department at Boston University for their kind indulgences and patience with a project that proceeded at a glacial pace. Thomas Barfield and Robert Weller, in particular, and perhaps unknowingly, gave wonderful words of support that uplifted me precisely when I was most deeply discouraged. Thanks, likewise, to Wyatt MacGaffey (Haverford College). Without his seminal contributions to our understanding of Central

African social, political, and economic processes my own work would have been greatly impoverished. Without his personal support at key moments my original manuscript might never have been transformed into this monograph.

As I have noted frequently elsewhere, in my many visits to Mwinilunga, Zambia (summer 1982, March 1984–December 1986, and the summers of 1993, 1994, 1998, 2000 and 2004), I relied on the assistance of far more people than I could possibly mention here by name. The many neighbors and friends in Chifunga village alone who contributed daily to my survival by teaching me the local language, helping me build shelter, showing me how to fish and farm, and how to avoid illness would make quite a long list. The many more who made up the daily procession of people curious about my research, and who informally served as my teachers, translators, interpreters, informants, and confidants would number in the hundreds. A collective thanks, however, would be woefully inadequate. Some individuals simply must be mentioned by name. They include Senior Chief Kanongesha Silas and his subordinate chiefs: the Ikelenge, the Nyakaseya, the Mwiniyilamba, and the Chibwika, who along with the government officials of the Mwinilunga District gave me complete freedom of movement throughout Lunda territory. Senior Headman Isaac Nkemba (the Chifunga), who treated me as a son and who, along with Jake Smart Ndumba, Chitambala (Kabubu), Tebalu, Chimwasu, Izenzi, and the other *akulumpi* (elders), guided me through a wealth of esoteric material and whose constant attention to my education gave local legitimacy to my efforts to learn Lunda culture. Noah, Miri, Speedwell, Greenford, and Rupert Kataloshi adopted me as a brother and thereby provided me with a publicly identifiable position in the local system of kinship reckoning. Special thanks must go to Yeta, Ifezia, Sombia, Mrs. Nkemba, Hilda, Ester, Dorothy, Betty, and the other women of Chifunga village who with conspiratorial winks and whispered commentary told me far more about the female world than might have been publicly permissible.

Also deserving of special thanks for their sincere friendship at all times and special assistance at key moments are the Franciscan friars Joe, Louis, Efisio, Werner, Fritz, Pete, Terrance, and Pio, as well as the ever-changing array of Catholic sisters at Lwawu mission and Mwinilunga Boma.

Ilse Mwanza, then the affiliate officer at what was the Institute for African Studies at the University of Zambia must also be singled out for special thanks. Without her efforts this project would never have gotten off the ground; without her sustained interest it would have been greatly impoverished.

I must also gratefully acknowledge the Wenner-Gren Society for Anthropological Research, the Harvard Sheldon Fund, the Ford Foundation, and the College of Arts and Sciences, the Department of Anthropology and the African Studies Center at Boston University for their financial contributions to this project.

But the real stars of this story, and the ones to whom I owe the most profound thanks, are Elias Kangasa, Noah Kataloshi, Gabriel Katoka, Stone Mafulo, Kapala Sakuumba, as well as Peter Lambacasa, Noah Waylesi, Godfrey, Tobias, Jah, Ndumba, Josayi, Shimishi, Kakoma, Kalenga, Wishmeli, Kamau, Yowanu, Jacksoni, Jampari, Charles, Teddy, Joseph, Benson, Anthony, Sebe, Vincent, and all the other *wubwambu* who provided me with friendship and constant companionship while endeavoring against all odds to mold me into a reasonable semblance of a competent adult male member of Lunda society.

With all the assistance I have received over the years there should be no excuse for errors of fact or analysis. Nevertheless, they will invariably occur, and I alone must take full responsibility.

Friends for Life, Friends for Death

Introduction

The aim of this book is to transport the reader to a place few have ever heard of, to examine the lives of people few will ever meet. This vicarious journey is headed to the Central African plateau for an extended visit among the Lunda-Ndembu of northwestern Zambia.[1] It would be disingenuous to claim that the Lunda-Ndembu are one of Africa's most interesting people. Indeed, visually they are rather drab, dressed mostly in well-worn secondhand clothes donated by foreign missionaries. Their villages are often hodgepodges of mud, bamboo, and grass huts of varying shapes, in differing states of ill repair. Neither their art nor their music can be counted among Africa's grandest traditions, having been virtually abandoned by the Lunda-Ndembu in favor of the aesthetic production of neighboring peoples. Their philosophical musings about gods, ancestors, and the metaphysical domain lack the informative elegance and centuries-old certitude often found elsewhere. And their forms of governance, modes of social organization, and ritual enactments vary in no significant way from those of adjacent peoples. The Lunda-Ndembu are just plain folks. Yet, perhaps plainness can be a benefit. Perhaps the humanness of the Lunda-Ndembu can assume center stage in this text, stepping out from the shadow of exotica that far too often dominates the tales of Africa, cloaking the fact that we humans, wherever we may reside, are all far more alike than we are different.

South Central Africa

Even the most imaginative among us might find it difficult to bridge the proverbial six degrees of separation between the Lunda and ourselves. Yet before our journey to the Central African plateau commences, it needs to be made absolutely clear that the Lunda-Ndembu do not exist in a timeless void, or in some mythical time outside of time, or in a world apart from our own. They are fellow participants in a grand globalizing process in which political, economic, and social acts in one part of our planet can have powerful repercussions in other parts. We all breathe the same air, drink the same water, and attempt to stave off the same diseases. We shall collectively overcome or collectively succumb to the forces that threaten the survival of our species, forces that range from environmental pollution to overpopulation to the seemingly insatiable passion for making war. It is impossible to fully understand any place in the world without understanding its place in the world.

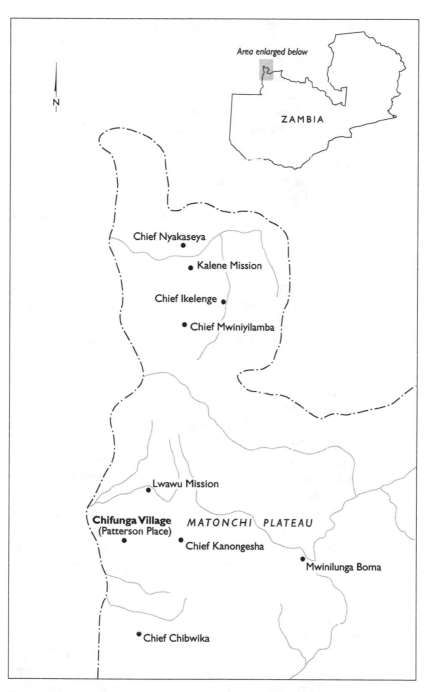

Lunda-Ndembu Territory

By way of example, the nation-state in which the Lunda-Ndembu find themselves embedded, Zambia, has but a single highly developed economic sector, the production of copper. Historically, as much as 90 percent of annual government revenue has been derived from the export of this metal. During the first decade of Zambia's independence from Britain, 1964–74, the world market price of copper was quite high. The United States was engaged in a war in Vietnam, littering that country with tons of copper-encased bullets and bombs. And with an economy buoyed by that war, America was also experiencing its biggest housing construction boom in history, with the concomitant need for massive amounts of copper pipes for plumbing. Indeed, the world market voraciously gobbled up all the copper Zambia could export, paying ever-higher rates to stimulate further production.[2] The Zambian government, in turn, endeavored to put the windfall to good social use, promising its citizenry programs of universal free education and health care. Schools and clinics sprouted upon the landscape like mushrooms after a rainfall, even in the most distant reaches of the country. Networks of roads, railways, and telecommunications reached out to the most isolated villager. A sense of hope saturated the Zambian psyche. The future looked golden. It was a time when even midlevel workers in the copper mines could wear tailored suits and look forward to purchasing an automobile someday. Zambia seemed genuinely poised to make the leap from middle-income "third world" country to genuine "first world" status. In 1969 its per capita GDP was twice that of Egypt and three times that of Kenya, higher even than Brazil, Malaysia, South Korea, and Turkey.[3]

In the mid-1970s the bubble burst. The Vietnam War came to an end. The housing industry saw a wholesale shift to the use of polyvinyl chloride (PVC) piping rather than copper. Global demand for the metal plummeted, as did its price. Simultaneously the world witnessed the maturation of the Organization of the Petroleum Exporting Countries (OPEC), the oil cartel that flexed its newfound muscle and sent the price of oil skyward. Landlocked and totally dependent on imported oil, the copper equation in Zambia began to produce negative numbers. The cost of mining and smelting copper now exceeded its selling price. For the next two decades Zambia continued to produce copper at a loss, accumulating massive foreign debt and bringing to a screeching halt the government's grand social vision. Personal dreams were dashed as nearly everyone, urban and rural, experienced a precipitous drop in standard of living. James Ferguson in *Expectations of Modernity* (1999) eloquently addressed the utter despair that accompanied the Zambian collapse, seeing it not only as an economic crisis but also a crisis of meaning, an erosion of peoples' ability to imbue life with significance and dignity. Unlike Ferguson's text, however, this book is not really an ethnography of the social experience of decline. Rather, the purpose for outlining the scenario above was to provoke several questions that frame the narrative that follows. Certainly the example makes manifest global connectedness—the interrelatedness of cause and effect, actions and reactions everywhere on this planet. But hopefully it leads one to also ponder the improbability that any Lunda-Ndembu individual ever considered the impact of a war in Indochina on the quality of his or her daily life. And what is the likelihood that any Lunda-Ndembu ever manifested angst at the possible invention of a white water-insoluble thermoplastic resin for use as plumbing pipe? Furthermore, in designing long-term strategies for a secure future did any Lunda-Ndembu factor in the charismatic appeal and organizational savvy of a Saudi Arabian oil minister in uniting petroleum-producing countries? Probably not. Yet decisions still had to be made, goals had to be set, tactics had to be employed. Even in the absence of perfect knowledge people must plug the available facts into some interpretive framework and conjure up what they hope are appropriate responses to quotidian contingencies.

In short, people act on what they *think* is happening rather than on what is necessarily *actually* happening. They do not live their lives on high with the analytical overview and scholarly hindsight of the historian or the anthropologist. Rather, people live their lives midstream, forced to quickly negotiate the rapids, eddies, and whirlpools of life, often with little time for extended investigation or deep introspection. Nor can people always perceive what lies around the next bend or beyond the next hill, let alone the potential impact of actions taken half a world away. Decisions must be made quickly. Preexisting notions and past experiences shape responses to unexpected and novel circumstances. Thus, in attempting to understand unfolding events, an analysis of social memory often needs to take precedence over the analysis of empirical reality. This text, accordingly, aims to go beyond a simple retelling of what has happened to the Lunda-Ndembu in favor of speculations about why. In short, it is a journey in search of consciousness—that mysterious black box deep within each individual, where events, incidents, and the contingencies of life go in, and strategies and tactics come out. The journey is also in many ways a return to one of anthropology's original imperatives: explorations into the nature of social cohesion. What are the fundamental forces that hold a society together? What makes the individuals within any particular society feel more related, connected, and akin to one another than they do to members of some other society? What are the relationships between the basic social units and the totality? Under what conditions do things change, and under what conditions do things remain the same?

To Victor Turner (1920–1983) we owe an especially great debt of gratitude. His four books and dozens of articles on the Lunda-Ndembu lifestyle based on his 1950s research set the stage for much that follows in this text. Without his contribution I would have but a feeble base from which to launch my own assertions. For many Turner will best be remembered as the foremost representative of the

Manchester School of Thought. However, within a decade of publishing his first volume on the Lunda-Ndembu, Turner would not only break free of his structuralist moorings but would begin to challenge restrictive intellectual paradigms more broadly. Frederick Turner provides a vivid description of Victor Turner as an intellectual prophet perpetually wandering across disciplinary boundaries as if they did not exist, conversing easily with the elders of each domain of knowledge in their own language, only to be seen moments later, several disciplinary fields away, engaged in new conversations.

> He showed again and again that the answer to a problem in one field usually lay in plain view in another; he sometimes acted as if one field actually interpenetrated another or even lay superimposed upon it, so that, as it were, one could be in two places at once. . . . He refused to acknowledge the distinction between researcher and object of study, and recruited gifted native informants as collaborators, guides, or even research directors (as in his essay on Muchona the Hornet). One of the essential properties of the old model was that the researcher is more conscious and aware than the object of research; Turner often assumed precisely the opposite. (F. Turner, "Hyperion to a Satyr," 150)

Meticulous, interdisciplinary, person-centered research is surely one of Victor Turner's most lasting legacies. Yet perhaps his greatest insight was that reflexivity is not just a feature of the postmodernist predicament but is the normal condition of humans everywhere:

> There never were any innocent unconscious savages, living in a state of unreflective and instinctive harmony. We human beings are all and always sophisticated, conscious, capable of laughter at our own institutions, inventing our lives collectively as we go on, playing games, performing our own being. This is our specialization as animals, our nature. The true naivety is the naivety of modern or postmodern intellectuals who believe that they are the inventors of social criticism, existential insecurity and metaperspectives. (F. Turner, "Hyperion to a Satyr," 156)

Victor Turner's collective body of work is full of paradox. Early Turner was a quintessential champion of structure. He explicated the structure of ritual (separation, transition or liminality, reincorporation). He laid out the structure of conflict (breach, crisis, redress, reintegration or recognition of schism). He explored the structure of symbols (from ideological pole to sensory pole) and the structure of symbolic analysis (expert exegesis, operational meaning, and positional meaning). Yet, later Turner gave us anti-structure, liminality that dissolved structure, and liminoids who lived perpetually outside of structure. Turner breathed new life into structural functionalism by setting structures in motion. Yet he also gave us notions of culture as protean, liquid, free flowing with spirit and charisma, rather than rigid categories saturated with preexisting social imperatives. While Turner, on the one hand, saw rituals, symbols, and myths as wondrous forms of human expression, on the other he warned us of their capacity to ossify and make routine, to camouflage the true seed of culture that lay somewhere beneath these casings. It was Turner who placed "lived experience" on a par with kinship, ritual, and social structure as a necessary focus of anthropological inquiry. Indeed, his early experimentation with "social dramas" would ultimately blossom into a full-blown "anthropology of experience." He noted that lived experience, as thought and desire, as word and image, is the primary reality. Social scientists have long given too much weight to verbalization at the expense of visualization, to behavior at the expense of experience. Experience includes not only actions and feelings but also reflections about those actions and feelings. It is self-referential.

Victor Turner never returned to Zambia physically subsequent to his arrival at these remarkable conclusions. Nor did he revisit his field notes intellectually to construct for us a portrait of the Lunda-Ndembu as, noted above, a people sophisticated, conscious, capable of laughter at their own institutions, inventing their lives collectively as they went on, playing games, performing their own being. It is in response to Turner's encouragement that lived experience as actions, feelings, and associated reflections need to be the focus of anthropological inquiry that this present volume was produced. It is as a complement and corrective to Turner's many excellent structure-focused treatments of Lunda-Ndembu social processes that I offer the reader this more people-centered text.

This volume, for the most part, is about consciousness. Yet, rather than being about the individual consciousnesses that make up a collection of people, it is an exploration into the collective consciousness of a group of individuals. The group is a set of male friends who live in separate villages located within a few miles of one another on the Central African plateau, in and around Chifunga village, in the northwestern corner of Zambia. The selection of this entity as the principal focus represents an analytical compromise. On the one hand, to speak of the Lunda-Ndembu as a whole is (1) to speak at a level of generality that camouflages much of the internal social dynamism and variation in individual comportment, or (2) to speak to such an extent about dynamism and variation as to leave insufficient space to richly illustrate discernable patterns, or (3) to speak for such a length about both of the above as to probably exceed the limit of most readers' patience. Yet to focus on individuals is not only to provoke questions about representativeness but also to miss one of the key points about the construction of consciousness among the Lunda-Ndembu; that is, individuals invariably go through life constructing notions of self and others as part of, and in tandem with, social groups.

Lunda-Ndembu society possesses nothing comparable to the formal institution of age grades that characterize most East African pastoral societies. Nevertheless Lunda individuals, particularly males, travel through life firmly encased in clearly defined and enduring social cliques that are subsets of age-based cohort groups. Cliques are self-selected collections of friends who present themselves to the larger society as cohesive and undifferentiated status groupings. Within the clique, members do compete vigorously with one another for special acknowledgment of individual skills, capacities, and accomplishments. Indeed, members of a clique may be internally ranked on a wide range of scales. But to outsiders the clique presents a united front, an entity endeavoring to surpass in fame and recognition other cliques among its cohort. Cliques devote a great deal of time and attention to cultivating elements of style as visible markers of their separate identity embedded within their larger identities as members of cohort, village, and lineage groups. Modes of dress, formulaic greetings, music, dance and food preferences, and even subsistence strategies are carefully elaborated over time to serve as public manifestations of membership in particular cliques.

Clique members are constantly engaged in the process of mutually witnessing and mutually fabricating one another's lives. Being of roughly the same age is fundamental to clique relations. Sharing age means going through biological transitions and sociological stages collectively. It means jointly discovering and devising responses to life's ever-unfolding mysteries. Clique members confront crises and reveal vulnerabilities to one another that may remain hidden from family members. Mutual witnessing in societies based on orality, rather than literacy, is stocked with utilitarian value. Clique members are the embodied chroniclers of one another's lives. They can verify each other's land claims, vouch for ownership of domestic stock bred or purchased, validate debts accrued and loans repaid. Clique members are living confirmation of challenges met and transcended, of plans conceived and actualized, of promises made and fulfilled. That such relationships are asked to negotiate some of life's rockiest social terrain surely leads to tension and strain at times. But the value of those relationships is evident in their longevity, their stability of personnel, and the aggregate energy devoted to accommodating and adjusting to individual personalities in the effort to forge intragroup solidarity.

To be nestled deeply within a clique is to be ideally situated to view lived experience as actions, feelings, and associated reflections. From this analytical perspective one can see people engaged in long-term relations with other people around things that matter and things that do not, while simultaneously interacting with inherited structures in ways that bring a shared consciousness into being. Focusing on a group helps to overcome the limitations of individual experience by directing our attention toward collective representations, that is, the expressions, performances, objectifications, and texts that are transmitted through a widely shared cultural repertoire of meanings. Thus, although individuals will appear in the text that follows, some by name and others by pseudonym, this is not essentially a story about individuals. This is an attempt to map out life at the level of the clique, to abstract out those processes that are reflective and constitutive of group identity, to keep our analytical gaze on the points of intersection where individual stories merge, contribute to, and are transformed by the shared repertoire of meanings.

The selection of friendship as a site of consciousness construction will also stand as a corrective to classical ethnographies of rural Africa that have tended to focus on ascribed rather than achieved status. Anthropologists working in urban Africa have demonstrated a fair amount of creativity in noting the importance of self-selected groupings such as welfare societies, unions, and other occupationally based assemblages, cultural and performing arts groups, revolving credit associations, and even sports clubs. But when the anthropological eye returns its gaze to rural Africa, it reverts to old habits of isolating kin and clans, lineages and age grades, households and villages, as the most meaningful units in people's lives. Ascribed features invariably prevail to the noticeable absence of achieved statuses in the rural world.

In matters concerning the vital status of friendship in society perhaps anthropologists have been too strongly influenced by those in sociology. For the latter, friendship has been viewed most often as a tool for identity formation among youth, a structure that facilitates the movement of individuals from exclusive attachment to family toward the assumption of larger social roles, or as an escape from rigidly defined social positions or undesirable social constraints. The adolescent peer group, for example, is widely recognized as an absolute necessity for successful maturation. G. S. Hall (*Adolescence*) assumed that its age-specific features were behavioral consequences of physiological drives. He emphasized the Sturm und Drang of adolescence, the emotional turbulence beginning at puberty that would inevitably be outgrown when the person moved into full adulthood in the early twenties. Because the social and psychological characteristics of adolescence have a physiological basis, he argued that an adolescent stage is an inescapable feature of human development everywhere. Psychoanalysts have added that adolescence is a time when childhood conflicts are resolved and persons learn to control sexual and aggressive impulses. Developmental psychologists have directed our focus to adolescence as a time of cognitive reorganization, severance of early emotional ties to parents, and experimentation with adult social roles.

> By no means does the peer group supplant the family as a socializing agent; rather, it coexists with the family as a structure that allows for intense interaction outside the family, for the organization of activities that affect the community, and for jockeying for status in settings relatively free from adult intervention. Within the peer group, adolescents can try out the social activities and maneuverings of adulthood while still sheltered by their families. The peer group gives them the opportunity to experiment while their subordinate age status gives them license to do so without being taken too seriously. (Schlegel and Barry, *Adolescence*, 9)

There is widespread agreement across disciplines that the successful transition to adulthood is manifested by the waning power of the adolescent peer group over the individual and the concomitant movement toward dyadic friendships. Adult social worlds are supposedly composed of collocations of discretely defined, one-on-one relationships between best friends, lovers, or spouses. Children, by contrast, move about in a crowd. The sociological literature on polyadic friendships that persist into adulthood is thus mostly about criminal gangs, religious cults, and other groupings said to be composed of anti-social and dysfunctional individuals.[4] Furthermore, some such as Robert Paine propose that true friendship itself can be found only in certain types of societies. Friendship as personal and private and with characteristics such as autonomy, unpredictability, and terminality tend to be found in technologically advanced and complex societies.[5] Paine believed that for those encased in societies where efficient and dispassionate bureaucracies regulate most social interactions, friendships provide one of the few opportunities for individuals to personalize their world. Indeed, he suggested that one of the charming attractions of friendships in complex societies is that they remain unstructured in comparison with the other aspects of people's lives. Ralph Linton, by contrast, proposed that the above scenario was more aptly characteristic of social groupings at the opposite end of the spectrum.[6] In societies organized around kinship, where everything from political and economic rank to appropriate social comportment is determined by one's position within a matrix of lineal and affinal kin, friendship is the "way out." It provides an emotional release from the daily stress of role-playing. Anthropologists H. H. Driberg ("'Best Friend' among the Didanga") and Raymond Firth ("Bond Friendship in Tikopia") both speak of friendship's unique function in abridging and mitigating the otherwise restrictive categories that would narrow the social reach of individuals in the relevant societies. In all cases friendship is a reaction against structure or an emotional adjunct to structure rather than being actually constitutive of structure as herein proposed.

Lunda-Ndembu males do not outgrow the need or the desire to be firmly em bedded in peer groups. Such groups do not exist outside of structure but are structures unto themselves that shape both individual personalities and larger social processes. David Livingstone (*Missionary Travels and Researches*), Silva Porto ("Novas Jornadas de Silva Porto"), Mellend (*In Witch-Bound Africa*), and C. M. N. White (*Outline of Luvale Social*) each commented on the presence and seeming permanence of adult male friendship ties in Central Africa. These travelers noted the geographical reach and the instrumental efficacy of friendships as their own guides and porters used such links to secure provisions, hospitality, and the range of timely information needed for safe passage across the plateau. Friendship has apparently long been important in Central Africa, but in a context of rapid social change it takes on added importance. When the political and economic systems of old are crumbling, when new powers attempt to impose their will, when it is evident that the past provides little insight into the future, and the accumulated wisdom of the elders offers few solutions to the problems of the day, the clique and the cohort group assume even greater potency as sites where new contingencies are processed, consciousness fashioned, and strategies deployed.

Mannheim ("Problem of Generations"), Riley et al. (*Aging and Society*), and Elder (*Children of the Great Depression*) have alerted us to the "cohort effect": that behavior is due not to abiding norms or patterns but rather to conditions specific to a particular time. There is thus the need to "cohortify" the history of consciousness through more detailed examinations of the life experiences of particular cliques within sets of cohorts. Accordingly in this text we follow a group of Lunda-Ndembu males, here called Amabwambu (friends), through time, through political and economic transformations, through the ever-changing relationship between rural-urban social, political, and economic dynamics, through changing matrices of constraints and opportunities, and through changing styles of personal presentation. Every clique is unique in certain respects. The major point in favor of selecting this particular group for extensive ethnographic treatment is my long-term relationship with them. Through sheer happenstance, I met and received hospitality from several members of this group during my initial three-month visit to Mwinilunga in the summer of 1982. While undertaking an extended period of field research from 1984 to 1987 I was again befriended by members of this group. They helped me construct the buildings that would constitute my village, patiently teaching me how to mold and stack adobe bricks, how to make rope from bark fiber, how to lash together a bamboo frame for roofing, and how to affix watertight grass thatching. Later they would be my language instructors, my social etiquette coaches, my guides to local hunting and fishing techniques, my partners in figuring out the meaning and the appropriate responses to a host of novel situations. We were constantly in the company of one another, sometimes around the clock for days on end. We ate, slept, bathed, laughed, cried, and mourned the death of mutual friends together. Our wives even gave birth and looked after one another's children together. Because I was the widely known, uniquely tall, and sole African American guy in the entirety of the Mwinilunga District of Zambia, my affiliation with the group became one of its most distinctive symbols. Admittedly my close association with Amabwambu tempered my perspectives on Lunda-Ndembu culture and style, and surely I disproportionately heard and absorbed their view of the larger world. But hopefully that will be the strength of this ethnography. I can provide the intimacy of details that would have been muted by the traditional focus on the group as a whole. Ideally, I would have liked to have been able to compare and contrast male and female cohorts' reactions to the same historical contingencies. Unfortunately, as a male I lacked the ability to establish the required level of intimacy with my confederates' female counterparts to do justice to the enterprise. Lunda-Ndembu society is highly segregated by gender. The division of labor and the prevailing notions of propriety are such that husbands spend little time publicly with their wives, brothers spend little time with sisters, and even fathers spend little time with daughters. A male anthropologist lurking about, attempting to investigate the world of any group of women, would thus produce palpable tension, perhaps threatening his relationship with the community as a whole. I therefore aim for richness of exposition of the chosen male world in hope that someday one better situated than I can produce the complementary ethnography of the female world.

This book deliberately avoids the tone, structure, and rhetorical style that readers have come to expect from ethnographic texts. Indeed, as one early reader rightly noted, this manuscript has taken little pain to properly situate itself within the contemporary constellation of anthropological theory. It has not taken advantage of a wealth of opportunities to directly connect itself to the prevailing discourse on social memory and consciousness, or the literature on social capital and wealth-in-people. It makes no mention of the utility of Foucault's notion of episteme or Ian Hacking's concept of styles of reasoning. It turns a blind eye to Barth on boundaries, as well as Bourdieu on habitus. Yet, no disrespect is intended by this author. The aim instead is to present a story that can be read at many levels. The theoretically sophisticated reader will hopefully find much that is thought provoking, that critiques or confirms theoretical notions elaborated elsewhere. And those more interested in cultural practice will hopefully find the vicarious experience provided here more enjoyable when not simultaneously assaulted by needless professional jargon. Nevertheless, the text attempts to achieve age-old anthropological objectives: figuring out the who, what, and why of the existence of an "other." Who are the Lunda-Ndembu? What kinds of activities and relations sustain their existence? And why, from their own perspective, is their existence meaningful and worthy of being sustained? Numerous African groups have proverbs that claim that the world is like a masked figure dancing. To see it properly, one needs to move about and view it from every angle. This volume is simply one more angle to add to our already variegated view of Central African processes. It is meant to complement rather than replace more conventional ethnographies of the Lunda-Ndembu. Life everywhere consists of disjointed strands of events, encounters, undertakings, outcomes, and realizations that no two individuals combine in quite the same way. Yet this is a search for shared elements of a consciousness constructed and embodied by a group of Central African males.

The text that follows is divided into two parts. The first half examines Amabwambu's vicarious experience with the world, and orientation toward the world, through stories heard from their grandfathers (*ankaka*) and fathers (*ataata*). The second half represents a compilation of Amabwambu's own direct experience in the world. The historical digressions contained within are not meant to be comprehensive, stand-alone, thorough-going accounts of the area in question but are the bits and pieces of the past that are remembered and that continue to influence tactics and strategies in the present. I examine the cohort group as a principal site for receiving and analyzing information from and about the world and a place where strategies are hatched, tested, and applied on the world. Over the last century the discipline of anthropology has moved successively from a focus on the evolution of cultural differences to uncovering the structure and function of social organization to mapping consciousness over time, mediated by class, gender, and ethnicity. I hopefully the reader will find this exercise a welcome continuation of that tradition.

Part One

1

Tales of the *Ankaka*
Muzungu, Missions, and Border Commissions (1906–1924)

Introduction

Between grandparents (*ankaka*) and grandchildren is a relationship unique in its social, existential and even architectural implications.[1] Grandparents are friends, confidantes, and tutors who help grandchildren navigate through life's rocky social terrain, who help allay the anxiety of transition from one social plateau to another. In an oral society, where knowledge is most often embodied rather than transcribed, grandparents are deep text, heavy tomes saturated with the group's esoteric and exoteric experiences. Grandparents are the preferred advisors on everything from the mundane and banal to the arcane and intimate. Sex education, for example, is often part of grandparents' domain. When a child is considered too old to sleep with parents, he or she is sent to sleep with a grandparent. Grandparents and grandchildren are permitted to speak openly about sexual matters and may even witness each other's sexual activities. The interaction between grandparents and grandchildren is, in many respects, the very model of intimate egalitarian relations. Often referred to by the Lunda as *wusensi* (joking relationship), it is one in which the formal rules that guide social behavior may be suspended. *Wusensi* may tease one another shamelessly, saying anything they please without inciting anger. They may freely borrow possessions without first seeking permission and may call upon one another for assistance with the certainty that it will be forthcoming. So strong is this bond that a married couple wishing to move from a parent's village cannot necessarily expect their own children to willingly join them. If children are old enough to choose, they may indeed choose to remain with grandparents.

From another perspective, grandparent-grandchild relations represent a curious merging of the linear and the cyclical, the hierarchical and the egalitarian. Clearly, the age and experiential gap between grandparents and grandchildren are so great as to make hierarchy undeniable. But the gap is also too great to make competition tenable. The mutual dependence of each on the other, economically, socially, and even metaphysically, blurs the lines of power, creating the friendliest and most open of relationships. Lunda philosophies traditionally revolve around the notion of life as an unbroken chain of linked individuals. The multitude of the living, the many more who have died, and the countless number yet to be born all form a single community. Notions of hierarchy, social responsibility, and moral obligation include them all. The grandparent-grandchild relationship not only represents the end points of the world of the living, but through the incipient reproductive capacity of the latter and the nearness of the former to the world of the ancestors, the relationship also symbolizes the widest reach of the moral community. It embodies hope fulfilled and promise to be realized. The symbolic centrality and encompassing capacity of this relationship can be observed whenever individuals are called upon to formally address any large group where myriad social positions are present. The wide array of relational terminology that could be employed in such situations invariably merge instead into a dyad; *nkaka* and *mwizukulu* (grandparent and grandchild). The customary salutation and concluding remark to any audience is *Mwani vude! Ankaka nazukulu!* (Greetings to the grandparents and the grandchildren!).

Lunda ancestral spirits occasionally reach out to the living from the metaphysical realm by manifesting their presence in a favorite grandchild.[2] Oddly, that presence leads to lingering and debilitating illness, unameliorable by either traditional or modern medical procedures. The most frequent antecedents of this transcendental phenomenon are (1) the failure of a kinsperson to fulfill a specific promise made to the afflicting spirit while she or he was alive, (2) family members appearing to have forgotten the departed one, performing none of the expected public acts of remembrance, and (3) family members behaving improperly toward one another, with feuding, fighting, lack of sharing and cooperation being most often cited as the kind of activity that forces a spirit to show its displeasure by afflicting a member of that family with illness. Particularly in these latter two cases, a person may be afflicted not for some individual transgression of his or her own, but rather is selected as a surrogate to suffer on behalf of the entire group. It is said that a grandchild may be chosen for three reasons: the ill health of a widely loved young one grabs the attention of a lineage more quickly and more resolutely than the similar ill health of a more elderly member; it is believed that the intensity of terrestrial grandparent-grandchild relationships facilitates the process of spiritual linkage; and memories of particular grandparent-grandchild relationships help the group to narrow down and identify the potential angry spirits, and thereby more quickly ascertain the relevant transgression and remedy.

The Lunda say that a person suffering from spirit-induced illness has been *kwata* (caught or grasped) by the spirit. Yet, the verb *kwata* also connotes transformative and creative qualities. Indeed, it contains shades of geniture. For example, to *kwata mwana* (to "catch" a baby) is the most common way of referring to childbirth. Similarly, to be caught by a spirit, although painful, is a form of rebirth. The selected individual becomes a channel of communication between the physical and metaphysical worlds and also stands to gain powerful curative abilities, particularly to treat others tormented with spirit-induced illnesses. Rituals abound for adjusting these metaphysical grandparent–corporeal grandchild relations. Currently, at least once a month a public ritual enactment takes place within easy walking distance of the Chifunga village clique.

Children are frequently named after a grandparent, living or dead, as a sign of respect and reverence, to signal in the most profound way possible the desire for the continuing presence of that grandparent in the daily lives of kin. Naming is an activity shot through with power in more ways than can be elaborated here. The Lunda lexicon, for example, contains the verb *kutena*, which means to mention a person or thing by its proper name. It suggests that uttering an appellation has the power to evoke, to entice the presence of, or to conjure into being the essence of an individual or thing. The most potent exemplification of this capacity is *kanfunti,* a person born immediately after the death of another member of the family, of the same sex, particularly a grandparent. It literally means: the one who has returned as a little one (from the verb *kufunta,* to return, and the diminutive, *ka*). Such individuals are immediately given the name of the recently deceased. Yet, it remains unclear whether the naming process lures the newly liberated spirit into the young body or merely acknowledges the spirit's inevitable presence. Not only do the Lunda possess inchoate notions about this peculiarly direct form of reincarnation, but their lore also contains a good deal of esoterica about ways that living grandparents, through naming and the manipulation of substances, can prepare their favorite grandchild to receive their own spirit after death. Few today, however, recognize this as appropriate behavior.

The relationship between generations is given spatial representation in the layout of villages. Members of the senior generation build their houses together in one hemisphere of a circle, facing their descendants in the adjacent generations in the other half of the circle. Grandchildren old enough to have their own house would build in their grandparents' half of the circle. Traditionally, village leadership moved down the line of men in the senior genealogical generation before passing over to the line of brothers and cousins in the next generation. Although conceptually power can be seen to pass in stages down the line of descent, and then laterally out to the edge of male kin branches, spatially it can be seen to spiral seamlessly around the center of the more traditionally organized villages. Grandparent and grandchild, alternate loops of the same circle, opposite but equal, are separated by the greatest social distance yet are existentially conjoined. The easygoing alliance of alternate generations contrasts mightily with and can dampen the antagonism between adjacent generations. In many respects, the grandparent-grandchild relationship is a social glue that binds lineal and affinal fragments into cohesive long-lasting and multidimensional residential clusters. That relationship also mediates time and space, linking villages near and far, uniting the living with the dead.

Kankinza: Variable Age and Validating Tales

The eldest of the grandparents to exert significant influence on Amabwambu, our Chifunga village clique, would have come of age in the early decades of the twentieth century. It may be instructive to note, however, that Senior Headman Kankinza (the Chifunga) who died in 1984 was said to have already been an elderly headman when the British South Africa Company (BSAC) arrived in 1906 to seize the territory they would initially call Lunda and later Mwinilunga District.[3] Even in the 1980s it was said that Kankinza had in his possession a registration card issued by the BSAC shortly after their arrival listing him as 109 years old at that time. Yet, some of the most senior elders claimed that Kankinza had lied about his age, actually pushing it downward, lest the British think he was too old to continue to rule. Word had supposedly reached Mwinilunga from the south that the British had a propensity for younger, more pliant chiefs. These elders claimed that Kankinza was far closer to 250 years old at his death. None of the members of Amabwambu had ever actually seen such a document with their own eyes, but they had grown up in a world in which the senior genealogical generation stood united in asserting personal knowledge of the truth of this tale. The assertion itself was, in some respects, meant to authenticate the legitimacy of one's membership in the senior cohort.

Age is the dominant idiom for expressing relationships between people. Yet, in truth, age is not an absolute phenomenon among the Lunda. Birthdays are the subject of neither public nor private elaboration. Few people seem to know or care to reveal even the precise year in which they were born. Age is a relative matter. One is either *kanzi* or *mukulumpi* (junior or senior) to another person. One's clique or cohort group is either *kanzi* or *mukulumpi* to another clique or cohort group. Imprecision is useful, however. It adds a degree of flexibility to an otherwise rigidly ascribed system of hierarchical reckoning. Through secrecy and revelation, selectively remembering and forgetting, individuals can actually gain or lose age vis-à-vis other individuals.

Age has traditionally been a shorthand for talking about social ranking, which is the summation of a complex array of ascribed and achieved qualities including industriousness, wealth, knowledge, comportment, social utility, experience, and so forth. Yet age and social mastery do not necessarily proceed in lockstep. Individuals can vary greatly in their pace of achievement and in the separate foci of their productive efforts. Some individuals work harder, take on adult responsibilities earlier, contribute to group life more substantially, and thereby command respect and positions of authority sooner. Other individuals may mature more slowly, be content to remain dependent longer, go through maturation rituals later, postpone marriage and childrearing, and be reluctant to ever assume leadership. Furthermore, even equally hardworking individuals may have nevertheless mastered vastly different elements within the social array of success. Reducing this complex calculus to a single variable, age, is the quintessential Lunda game. Among the Lunda, to gain respect is a coterminous concept with to gain age. It can be seen as an attempt to tame and mitigate, through submersion and displacement, the fervent competition, particularly among men, for social prestige. It transforms an achievement-based system of ranking, saturated with elements of contingency, uncertainty, and potential instability into a system seemingly based on the orderly passage of time. Heaping age on successful individuals is a way of ritualizing and naturalizing the fluid outcome of purposive human behavior by enveloping it in a widely shared rhetoric of morally sanctioned constancy.[4]

Claiming age—that is to say, constructing scenarios to increase one's age—is the favorite pastime of many Lunda males. Kankinza was evidently the master of this game. But gaining age is a social act that may come with a price. For some it may require residing at a distance from kin and cohorts, who have firm notions about one's age, in order to facilitate the projection of a more senior mien. Even under the best of circumstances, gaining age requires the active cooperation of a validating group. More often than not this means dragging some of one's cohorts up the hierarchy as well.

Cohort groups coalesce around supposed shared participation in certain experiences that may exist only as stories to younger generations. Flexibility of reckoning age allows a wide chronological range of people to participate in the same story and thus be socially acknowledged as members of the same cohort group. When we speak, therefore, of the *ankaka,* the collective grandparents of Chifunga, we are referring to the group of individuals who have made successful claims to be included in the senior genealogical generation of the area. This generation, in theory at least, has unique powers to shape its own history and, therefore, to control its own legacy and validate moral status, due to the absence of oversight by an ascendant generation. Listening to tales of the grandparents was one of the few ways of gaining experience of worlds beyond one's immediate temporal and geographical reach. Thus, when the grandparents spoke, the grandchildren listened. The tales they heard, and the people they heard them from, no doubt provided some of the earliest threads of vicarious experience out of which the current tapestry of consciousness is woven.

Tales Remembered, Tales Embodied

Lunda oral tradition is chock-full of proverbs, riddles, maxims, jokes, and poetry. Lunda history, however, is most fully encapsulated in etiological myths, genealogies, countless hero tales, and personal recollections.[5] Throughout the width and breadth of Lundaland one can, for example, still hear versions of a creation myth about the high god Nzambi, who brought into being the sun, moon, and stars, the earth, sky, and water, and the inhabitants of each.

On the edge of the great forest, it is said, Nzambi created and placed the original two humans, Nyamuntu and Samuntu (Mrs. and Mr. Person).[6] They each had their own separate little house from which they would depart every morning to spend the day laboring in separate gardens. They would return each evening, prepare their individual meals, and retire to their own beds. They were two identical and sexless beings, undifferentiable by biology or culture, innate characteristics or acquired habits. They lived parallel lives, virtually always within eyesight of one another, yet never cooperating in productive tasks, never sharing leisurely moments, and never even exchanging casual greetings. It is said that Samuntu became increasingly frustrated by the endless cycles of solitary activities. He (if Samuntu can be so designated at this point) was tormented by the loneliness and haunted by disturbing existential questions: what is the purpose of life? Why had Nzambi created two of his type? Why did the two never interact? Did Nzambi have a plan for them? Growing anxiety compelled Samuntu to seek out answers. Thus, he trekked seven days and seven nights to reach the center of the great forest where Nzambi dwelled. There he talked with Nzambi about his bewilderment, his confusion of purpose. He asked, "Why have you made Nyamuntu and me when we have nothing to do with one another? We are identical in every way, in thought and deed, and thus have nothing to say or share with one another." Nzambi listened patiently, thought for a while, and then went away. Upon returning he announced that he had an idea. In his outstretched hands were two differently shaped sex organs. He told Samuntu to select one, affix it between his legs, and carry the other back to Nyamuntu. Samuntu was utterly per-

plexed. What are these ugly things? What have they to do with the problem? Which one should he select? Nzambi simply repeated his instructions: "take one, and give the other to Nyamuntu." Samuntu started the seven-day homeward trek carrying the two strangely shaped organs, unable to decide between them. On the third day he finally selected the long cylindrical one and continued carrying the other. On the final night Samuntu placed the organ intended for Nyamuntu in the fork of a tree, as he had done each of the previous evenings. But in the morning he departed without it. Some versions of this tale say he simply forgot it. Others say he was offended by its smell and deliberately left it behind. In any event, he returned to his little house and his usual round of activities. Nyamuntu, however, immediately noticed that Samuntu now had an appendage that she (if Nyamuntu can be so designated at this point) did not have. Angrily she walked seven days and seven nights to reach the center of the great forest where Nzambi dwelled. "Samuntu and I have always been equal in every way," she intoned. "Why now have you given him something that you have not given me." Nzambi explained that he had actually given Samuntu two organs, and that one was intended for Nyamuntu. But Nyamuntu assured Nzambi that she had neither seen nor heard anything of a second organ. "I am disappointed with Samuntu," said Nzambi. "Nevertheless, I will make a new organ for you." But first Nzambi needed to know which organ Samuntu had selected. "It was a long cylindrical thing," said Nyamuntu. Nzambi left, and after a short while returned and handed Nyamuntu something that resembled a beautiful wild orchid of flesh. "But this in no way resembles Samuntu's thing," complained Nyamuntu. "Trust me," said Nzambi. "Simply affix it between your legs and return home." Seven days and seven nights later, Samuntu spots Nyamuntu with her new thing. His body becomes inflamed with passion, his own thing begins to grow, and in a flash he realizes the nature of Nzambi's divine plan. But Nyamuntu rebuffs all Samuntu's overtures, reminding him of the organ he had left behind. "Go fuck the forked tree," she screams at him. Utterly dejected, Samuntu hiked seven days and seven nights to reach the center of the great forest where Nzambi dwelled. He apologized profusely for not following instructions, for not trusting in Nzambi's wisdom. He begged forgiveness and received it. Clearly, Nzambi was well aware of the foibles and frailties of his own creation. Nzambi thus revealed a new plan and handed Samuntu a fox. Seven days and seven nights later Samuntu arrives home. He releases the fox, which immediately jumps through Nyamuntu's window, pounces on her bed, bares his fangs, and growls fiercely. Nyamuntu manages to bolt out the door and reach Samuntu's house. Terrified, sweating, barely coherent, Nyamuntu tries to describe the horrible creature that had nearly eaten her alive. But Samuntu calmly assures her that she is now safe. He is more than capable of protecting her from any four-legged creature. They spent the night together and got to know one another quite well. In the morning Nyamuntu again becomes anxious. What if that fanged creature is still out there? "Don't worry," *said Samuntu, "the creature is nocturnal, it will rest until nightfall." "Well then, can I spend the night with you again," pleaded Nyamuntu. "I'll fix dinner for you." "OK," said Samuntu, "I'll try to pick up some special food for us in the forest."*

Tales such as the above are rich in material for fireside musing. Not only are they wickedly entertaining, but they also set the stage for local debates about human genesis, the original state of existence, the various compacts between God and his creations, and the ontological status of women and men. Such tales have enticed generations of young minds to ponder deeply, to scrutinize intensely each episode for relevant meaning. For example, what are the implications of an original genderless couple performing identical tasks? Why were humans capable of convincing God to modify the original state of being? Was Samuntu's initial indecision about sex selection meant to emphasize the arbitrariness of division by gender? Are males more inherently interested in female sexuality than in their personality? In giving Samuntu the fox, did Nzambi decree or otherwise bring into being a special association between males and the forest domain? Did females seal their own destiny by offering to prepare food in return for male protection? And, of course, one must wonder, why was it Samuntu rather than Nyamuntu that first expressed dissatisfaction with the human lot?

Each era, each generation, indeed, each individual fireside discussion, may lend its own exegetical spin to the oral tradition. Each hermeneutic exercise may produce unique interpretations, may tease out different intrinsic lessons. Yet it appears, to this author at least, that there is broad acceptance and even internalization of the Nzambi, Nyamuntu, and Samuntu tale as the founding charter of the Lunda people. The ubiquitous recitation, unpacking, and decoding of this tale, in turn, leads to persistent engagement with certain sets of ideas and regular immersion in particular frames of interpretation. In other words, such tales are an integral part of consciousness construction. As we shall see throughout this text, Lunda seem to be constantly confronting and working through the relationship between oppositions, between similarities and differences. For example, notions of autonomy and incorporation, individual freedom and social embeddedness, are recurring themes in fireside discourse. In certain contexts autonomy is a concept akin to freedom, power, and ascendancy. In others it connotes loneliness, isolation, and ineffectualness. Nyamuntu and Samuntu were originally the epitome of autonomy. They were independent and answerable to no one, free to pursue their daily rounds of activities unconstrained by anyone. Yet, from another perspective, it was an autonomy enforced by the lack of differentiation, a sameness of body and mind that mediated against complementarity and thus narrowed the possible areas of cooperation. The emergence of biological differences first made new forms of physical interaction possible and then eased the way for the original couple to rethink domestic relations and labor allocation. If Nyamuntu cooked for both, then Samuntu could spend extra time seeking out the rewards of the forest. For Nyamuntu's favors Samuntu was willing to assume higher risk-productive strategies. Thus, sameness can be equated with blandness and needless duplication, whereas diversity can perhaps lead to exciting and more efficient interdependent action.

Lunda oral traditions are saturated with suppositions about the complementarity of oppositions, indeed the actual necessity for opposites to exist within the same philosophical frame of reference. The hunter and the headman, for example, are two archetypes that illustrate this tendency. Celebrated big game hunters are invariably solitary personae, spending days alone in the deep forest. The image is of a person more at home in quiet verdant splendor than in the midst of noisy village life. The headman, on the other hand, is sociability personified. He is at the heart of every celebration, the epicenter of every dispute. The image is of one constantly surrounded by people, offering advice here, consolation there, ever ready with the right words and actions to smooth the rough edges of daily village life. In Lunda lore, big game hunters are consummate explorers, ferocious killers, and clearers of space. They convert the wild into the tamed, the natural into the cultural. They are the ideal founders of new villages and even new dynastic realms. They can provision the village with meat and forest products and protect it from enemies. But they lack the nurturing and sustaining qualities of the headman, the diplomatic tact to mediate day-to-day social conflicts that rupture the social fabric. Hunter and headman; opposite but equal. The presence of each is vital to the establishment and maintenance of village life. Hunter and headman; founder and sustainer, polar opposites in an existential configuration that necessarily encompasses extremes. Thus, as we proceed, we notice that Lunda consciousness is never framed by a simple dyadic linkage between cause and effect, nor a linear exposition moving from point A to point B. Rather, the Lunda live in a conceptual world that is complex and expansive, a world that domesticates contradictions through embodiment rather than avoidance. Yet, how could it be otherwise? In a world without ugliness, how could one identify beauty; without evil, how could one demonstrate righteousness?

There are also divergent myths describing the emergence, evolution, and expansion of a Lunda empire out of a constellation of competing polities. Most versions agree, nevertheless, that the sheer size of the empire and the quantity and quality of its productive capacity attracted much attention from the Indian Ocean trade network from perhaps as early as the twelfth century A.D. and the Atlantic world from the sixteenth century onward. Indeed, throughout much of the sixteenth to eighteenth centuries, the Lunda Empire was a major point of overlap between these two great global trading systems, a place where the terms of trade and the terms of trust influenced the flow of goods on nearly every continent.[7] Similarly, widespread tales agree that after a long period of profiting successively from the slave, ivory, and rubber trades, the Lunda Empire imploded during the nineteenth century as waves of fear, suspicion, and outright terror swept across the Central African plateau. The Lunda capital itself was overrun by better-armed Chokwe people from the west during the 1880s, and the Lunda broke up into small bands, relying on their hunting and gathering expertise to survive during this troubled time.

Within these widely shared grand traditions exist tales specific to certain Lunda lineages or segments. Jealously guarded and carefully remembered, these tales link clusters of living individuals to significant historical events, perhaps justifying some contemporary claim to place or privilege. The Chifunga tradition of our Amabwambu clique, for example, asserts its central role in the formation of the Kanongesha Lunda polity on the upper Zambezi during the 1700s. The first Chief Chifunga, Ipepa, was supposedly a man with remarkable magical powers, without whose assistance Paramount Chief Kanongesha might never have defeated the autochthonous Mbwela, the original inhabitants of Mwinilunga.[8] For his special service Ipepa was allowed to marry the Kanongesha's sister. Thus every succeeding Kanongesha and Chifunga address one other as *ishaku*, in-laws of the same generation, a relationship that implies a great deal more parity in prestige than their colonially inherited titles of Senior Chief and Senior Headman.

These etiological tales are often presented with a great deal of solemnity, each episode retold in well-rehearsed formulaic fashion. They are important devices for structuring relationships among individuals, lineages, and even polities. They establish the most generic bases for the integration of social fragments into cohesive units. But the tales from lived experiences are told with far more spontaneity, vigor, and passion. They are also told more frequently and in more varied settings. They are the stuff not of mythical time, or times outside of time, but personally experienced time within the world. These tales leave their imprint not only on the memory but also on the conditioned reflexes and studied responses to the contingencies of daily life. The tales of the grandparents, varied in so many respects, are nevertheless dominated by a single motif: the coming of Muzungu, the white man.

Muzungu: From Phantasms to Familiar Faces

By the beginning of the twentieth century, European products were well known throughout Central Africa, having been circulating there in increasing quantity for over three hundred years. European peoples, however, were much less well known. Few of them had ventured into the interior of Africa before the eighteenth century.[9] Tales about the comings and goings of Europeans on the west coast of Africa, among BaKongo and Ndongo peoples, were initially the exclusive province of the Pombeiros. These offspring, generally of Portuguese fathers and African mothers, were legendary travelers, some of whom literally crisscrossed the African continent from coast to coast several times during their lives. Later representative of this group, such as P. J. Baptista and Amaro Jose, left us journals, written in Portuguese, lush in details about the daily lives of Central African peoples during the late eighteenth and early nineteenth centuries.[10] In the complexity of their own identities, in an area of uniquely protean ethnic formation, the Pombeiros quite literally embodied the interface between the African and European worlds. They were instrumental in setting the terms of trade and the terms of trust that would structure African-European relations during the initial centuries of contact.

As the Atlantic world increasingly emerged as a distinct social and economic construct after the seventeenth century, its eastern arm reached into Lunda territory via an African-controlled commercial caravan system. Portuguese goods, in particular, were transported principally from the port city of Benguela up to the Angola plateau of Bihe by members of coastal groups such as the Bailunda. But the people around Bihe initially exercised a monopoly on the transport of goods beyond that point. From Bihe, caravans of up to two thousand people would set out on journeys lasting a year or more. These itinerant cities of merchants, carriers, and artisans of all types followed well-known circuits, setting up camp for weeks at a time, buying and selling goods and services throughout the length and breadth of the Central African plateau. The legend of Bihean caravan leaders spread far over the interior. Many of these "Black Portuguese" became fabulously wealthy, amassed tremendous followings, and surrounded themselves with the accoutrements of the European world of their business partners.[11] Many became fluent in the Portuguese language, took on Portuguese names, Portuguese dress, and, at times, exaggerated Portuguese manners and social etiquette. This style, in fact, became their social marker in the interior, symbolizing the authenticity of their connections to the Portuguese and hence the genuineness of the products they peddled. But while the Biheans specialized in mediating the gap between European and African commercial spheres, they also excelled in tactics designed to keep coastal Europeans and interior Africans physically separated. As middlemen, they profited by controlling the flow of information as much as by controlling the flow of commodities. To the Europeans they delivered tales of an interior filled with fierce tribes, inhospitable terrain, vicious animals, and incurable diseases. To interior Africans they delivered tales of Europeans as uniquely dangerous creatures. They were witches supreme, who not only consumed human livers, as African witches were known to do, but who possessed the power to actually process human beings into a range of useful products. They could turn African bodies into oil, flesh into meat, skin into leather, brains into cheese, bone ash into gunpowder, and blood into wine. Europeans were said to be full of knowledge, to possess strange contraptions, to produce rain or drought at will, and to spread terrifying diseases with the glance of an eye. They were kings of the sea, white-skinned, straight-haired water creatures with the power to walk upright on land, and they would surely seize African territory if given half a chance.[12] Stories circulated throughout Central Africa about the need for special metaphysical protection in order to safely deal with Europeans and their products. There arose a professional guild that specialized in charms and rituals to fortify those engaging in business with Europeans and to decontaminate the products and restrain the destructive capacity of persons of European origin. No trade caravan was complete without its own traveling *nganga,* medicine man, charged with taming the dangerous forces inherent in the process of bringing the African and European worlds in contact with one another. They traveled throughout Central Africa dispensing their highly sought-out secrets, for a dear price. Although Lunda legends mention the exploits of a few local adventurers who traveled to the coast, tales of the returnees tended to complement rather than contradict the accumulated evidence of Muzungu strangeness.[13]

The nineteenth century brought limited but increasing opportunities for the people of Central Africa to gain firsthand experience with Muzungu. Exploration and survey parties, royal emissaries, and agents of governmental, religious, and commercial enterprises passed through Central Africa, variously attempting to sign treaties, cultivate allies, chart physical space, catalogue animal, plant, and mineral resources, explore marketing capacity, and assess the proselytizing potential and the quality of souls to be saved. The more well-known European expeditions into the region included those of Joao Vicente da Cruz (1815), Joaquim Rodriques Graca (1846), Saturnino de Sousa Machado (1850), Francisco de Salles Ferriera (1850), David Livingstone (1853–56 and 1858–63), V. L. Cameron (1875), Paul Pogge and Anton Lux (1875), Otto Schutt (1877), Serpa Pinto (1878), Félix António Gomes Capello and Roberto Ivens (1877–80), and Max Buchner (1878–81). Few of these visitors, however, remained long in any one place.[14] Thus they provided local Africans with only the briefest glimpse of the European body and the faintest inklings of the European mind. Nevertheless, it is clear from the reports of these same early travelers that Africans were tremendously interested in every aspect of European personhood, possessions, and productive capacities. Central Africans became famous for their creativity in slowing down European parties moving across the plateau in order to better scrutinize their wares, substantively engage their personnel, and establish social connections as a bases for, or a complement to, trading relations. Tactics ranged from overwhelming travelers with elaborate displays of hospitality enticing them to stay longer to entrapping them in petty offenses requiring their presence at extended judicial proceedings to assuring them of the pending availability of some highly prized product or causing delay by misdirection or feigning ignorance of the way forward.

As the twentieth century approached, however, a new type of European joined the Central African mix. Differing in aims and motivations from their military and mercantile counterparts, these Europeans were not on their way somewhere else but were seeking to settle in the region. They built clusters of strange dwellings, undertook novel activities, and inserted themselves in the daily lives of Africans in the most curious of ways. It is here that the tales of the grandparents begin in earnest, with the most famous of the new European settlers: Ndotolu, or Walter Fisher the missionary doctor.[15]

Ndotolu and Kalene Hill Hospital

The dean of European missionary-explorers, David Livingstone, made several well-known journeys to and through Lunda country.[16] On the lecture circuit back home in Scotland and elsewhere in Europe, he spoke glowingly of the commercial and Christianizing potential of the area. Frederick Stanley Arnot, a neighbor of the Livingstone family in Hamilton, Scotland, was one of the first to take up the challenge. He retraced Livingstone's footsteps through the interior of Africa, exploring more intensely some adjacent areas, establishing his own mission stations at King Lewanika's court in Barotseland in 1882–83, and at Msidi's capital in Katanga in 1885.[17] Walter Fisher, the man who would become known as Ndotolu (the doctor), was born and raised in Greenwich, England. Missionaries on leave frequently visited its municipal halls and private homes giving talks, enlivened with Magic Lantern slides, about the far-flung reaches of the world. Such presentations generally ended with appeals for money and fresh recruits to support particular causes. Fisher, upon attending a presentation by Arnot, decided at age twenty-two to commit his life to missionary and medical work in Central Africa. Fisher had been raised as a "Plym," a member of the religious community originally known as the Plymouth Brethren, later to become the CMML, Christian Missions in Many Lands. They were devout Christians who preferred simplicity of worship, shedding traditional accretions of ritual and directing their lives according to a literal interpretation of the Bible. They were fervently anti–High Church, whether it be Catholic or Anglican, stressing the individual nature of salvation and the attendant individual responsibility for spreading Christianity.[18] Fisher, having prepared himself for mission work by studying medicine and surgery, complemented by carpentry, leatherwork, cobbling, and basic dentistry, set sail for Africa with Arnot in 1889. He arrived on the Angolan coast, working first on the Bihe plateau before moving inland to build a mission station at the Kazombo capital of Chief-tainess Nyakatolo of the Luvale, the western neighbors of Kanongesha's Lunda.

Initial African resistance to Fisher's medical practice evaporated when he was able to cure the cheftainess of a painful and lingering illness that none of her own medical or spiritual specialists had been able to alleviate. News of Fisher's powers spread rapidly throughout the plateau. Soon he would develop a vaccine locally to prevent smallpox and would perform the first painless surgeries in Central Africa through the pioneering use of chloroform as an anesthesia. Ndotolu quickly attained legendary status. His small station was constantly inundated with treat-ment seekers across a wide geographical and ethnic spectrum. Likewise, a seces-sion of European missionaries would come and go from that station over the next few years. Some were intending to remain in Angola, some were pushing on in-land to work in the Congo or Northern Rhodesia. Few, if any, would escape the ravages of malaria and other tropical diseases while at Kazombo. After marrying Anna Darling, a Brethren missionary in her own right, and having eight children, two of whom died of tropical diseases, Fisher sought out a healthier locale for the next stage of his Central African dream. He was determined to build a modern hospital complex, suitable not just for African patients, but for the increasing number of European missionary families as well. Several factors informed his choice. First, Angola was becoming a less hospitable place for the Brethren to live and work. Portuguese authorities were beginning to insist that all schooling of Africans be in Portuguese rather than African vernacular or other European lan-guages. Furthermore, the Portuguese had a clear preference for the spread of Catholicism over other religions.[19] The Brethren, as both foreigners and non-Catholics, came under increasing scrutiny. Second, Brethren leader F. S. Arnot had explored the hills near the source of the Zambezi River years earlier, just across the border in Northern Rhodesia. He had identified a particular place he called Border Craig, later Kalene Hill, as a uniquely healthy location for a mission. The hill, at an elevation of five thousand feet, offered amazing vistas of three colonial territories, British, Angolan, and Belgian. Known for its cool crisp breezes, the hill was believed to be relatively free of mosquitoes and thus less "malarious." Fisher conducted experiments, examining the spleen of local children. Lower incidence of enlargement added scientific confirmation to the belief that malaria was less prevalent at Kalene. Third, the Lunda of that region had often visited Fisher dur-ing his tenure at Kazombo, bringing him food and gifts as offerings of thanks for his supposed role in freeing one of their enslaved kin who was being badly treated by her Luvale master. These Lunda, in fact, invited Fisher to resettle in their area.

In January of 1905 Fisher and family moved from the Portuguese-controlled ter-ritory of Chieftainess Nyakatolo to the nominally British-held territory of Chief

Ikelenge in Northern Rhodesia.[20] Fisher obtained a grant of land from the British South Africa Company administrator of northwestern Rhodesia, Robert T. Coryndon, staking out a level site on top of the hill, between rock outcroppings, with plenty of room for the buildings he had in mind. The family initially lived in a three-room Lunda-style house, with clay walls and a thatched roof, and took their meals in an attached open-air veranda. Cooking was done in a separate clay and thatch structure adjacent to the house. Walter and Anna Fisher spent their days overseeing the digging of foundations and the making of bricks, doors, and window frames. Possessing a generous supply of trade goods, such as cloth, beads, iron tools, and utensils, they were able to hire ample local labor to move the project forward at a rapid pace. Several months into their new lives at Kalene Hill, however, tragedy struck. It was the cold dry season, a time when the temperature regularly dipped toward the freezing point. Night frost was not uncommon. Some of the Fishers' domestic staff routinely slept huddled around a fire in the kitchen. One night a spark ignited the grass roof. Flames jumped to the main house. The roof caved in just as the Fisher family escaped with only the nightclothes they were wearing. Ammunition exploded, creating quite a scene as flames consumed all the Fishers' personal belongings, equipment intended for the new hospital, and trade goods set aside to pay workers. The flames, however, did not consume Walter Fisher's dream. Two days later a European prospecting team passing through Kalene gave the Fishers blankets, clothing, and food. European missionaries stationed in Angola and the Congo made pilgrimages to Kalene Hill bringing all the surplus goods they could bear to part with. Friends and associates from overseas, upon hearing of the tragedy, quickly set about raising fresh funds, sending gifts in kind to enable the Fishers to pay workers to continue building. To the Lunda, Ndotolu was clearly a very big chief who received tribute on an unimaginable scale, from followers spanning incomprehensible distances.

As the hospital complex began to take shape, and European nurses and medical practitioners began to arrive at Kalene, Fisher increasingly spent the twilight hours on the hilltop, searching the horizon for pillars of smoke in order to pinpoint the location of unfamiliar pockets of people. Central Africa in the early 1900s was still aflame with fear of the slave trade. Although many Europeans residing in the metropole harbored the belief that the traffic in human bodies had long been abolished, their compatriots in Africa continued the evil trade under a variety of guises. Angolan coffee plantations were worked almost exclusively with slave labor. The Congo Free State had agents scouring even the Rhodesian countryside, buying slaves at a price of £30 each to serve as colonial soldiers. Whether the Africans were called *colonials* or *free contract labor* or simply *ticketed individuals* with spurious agreements, the question of their ownership was clear, and their lack of power to renegotiate the terms of their deployment no less so. Hence, as a defensive measure, some Lunda lived nervously in small bands, hunting and gathering, ever ready to flee at the first sign of suspicious activity. Others lived in stockaded villages, surrounded by high fences of heavy tree trunks set deeply into circular earthworks. The sole entrance was often through a single tunnel over-hung by a portcullis of timber, guarded by an axeman ready to chop off uninvited heads. Such was the fear of marauding slave raiders in the early 1900s. Yet Walter Fisher would track down these villages, fearlessly enter the tunnel, attempt to make friends, and persuade the sick to come to his new hospital for treatment. His bravery added to his legendary status.

The ever-expanding colony of Europeans at Kalene must have presented the lo-cal Lunda with quite a curious spectacle: a continual parade of ladies dressed in corsets and crinolines arriving in *tipoya* (hammocks) hoisted aloft by African porters from the coast; men sweating profusely in stiff white collars, wool jackets, ties, and wide-brimmed hats. Fisher made known his apprehension about many of these new European recruits, most of whom had few skills to offer, had little knowledge of Africa, and made only faint attempts to learn local languages.[21] On the one hand, Fisher himself was very much a product of his times. He believed that urging Africans to emulate Western culture, as a system of values, social eti-quette, and aesthetic frameworks, was an essential part of leading Africans toward adopting Christianity as a philosophical system. European recruits were, thus, ex-pected to be models of European probity and preeminence. To let down the side in either demeanor or decorum was unacceptable. Fisher, for example, was always the perfect British gentleman in his woolen underwear and starched white shirt.

The standard mission diet was a local adaptation of the European fantasy of tropical dining at its best: tea, spices, wheat flour, buckwheat and groundnut cakes sweetened with honey and fruits, pineapples, bananas, guavas, mangoes, granadillas, and citrus eaten with thick sour milk like yogurt. The mission kept its own flock of sheep and goats, as well as cows, pigs, and chickens. There was plenty of fish to be had from the nearby rivers and plenty of mushrooms and berries from the forest. Fisher's wife Anna grew vegetables, smoked and pickled pork, and made jellies and jam. The most pampered citizen from the British Isles would have felt right at home, excited by the comfortable familiarity yet exotic diver-gences that Kalene could offer its guests. In years to come it would be de rigueur for all Europeans passing through this part of Central Africa to divert to Kalene Hill, to recreate, and to refortify themselves against the alienating and disorient-ing effects of the African physical and social landscape. For Europeans in Central Africa, Kalene was home base, the local font of memories of a distant place, an op-portunity to fully immerse themselves in the substance and style of the best of Eu-ropean civilization.

Yet concomitantly, Fisher recognized that effective proselytizing was synonymous with effective communications. God can be approached in any language. People can be more quickly and completely converted to Christianity if the
word of God arrives in their own tongue. Fluency in local languages should, there
fore, be neither optional nor exceptional, but the essential aim of every missionary. Translating the Bible into Lunda was assumed to be the unique calling of the
Brethren. Fisher's own children would grow to embody that sentiment. His two
older sons in particular, Singleton and ffolliott, were cared for by African nurses
as babies, were in the constant company of African servants as toddlers, and
played in the villages with their African counterparts as youth. Singleton and ffolliott grew to be as comfortable conversing in Lunda as they would be in the English language. The boys' experiences were fundamental to deciphering the intricacies of Lunda alliteration, tonality, and noun classes. Singleton, in fact, would
produce the first Lunda-Ndembu grammar in 1919, a text second in importance
only to the Bible among missionaries. In revised form it is still in classroom use as
contemporary Lunda grapple with the complex structure of their own language.[22]

Singleton and ffolliott, in return, provided the Lunda with a unique learning
opportunity. Here for the first time were Muzungu not as conquering warriors
armed to the teeth or wonderful wizards, masters of medical mysteries, but rather
as vulnerable little creatures, totally helpless, differing from Lunda babies mainly
in the color of their skin and the texture of their hair. There was nothing magical
about their birth and maturation. They were born neither spitting fire nor citing
prophecy. They cried a lot, got sick from time to time, needed constant guidance
and occasional discipline. The very ordinariness of the Fisher kids was a revelation in itself. The experience of having two Europeans grow to adulthood in the
village, in full view of all, did more to humanize Muzungu than all the preaching,
teaching, and healing of their elders combined. Singleton and ffolliott, those mis-
chievous Fisher boys, would become legends in their own right as "Sin" and
"Folly." The details of their childhood exploits are retold to this day. Singleton
would most directly follow in his father's footsteps, becoming a missionary doctor in the Congo; ffolliott, after serving and being wounded in World War I, would
start a cattle ranch at the foot of Kalene Hill, open the first retail store in the area,
and sponsor and provide the land for Sakeji School, an elite institution for the
children of missionaries throughout Central Africa.

Some Brethren missionaries were moderately successful at attracting financial aid for their overseas activities from family, friends, and supporters back
home. But the Brethren movement, in general, lacked a wealthy central mission
society capable of providing consistent and predictable funding for African evan-
gelizing. Thus each mission station was individually responsible for its own economic vitality. From the beginning, each pursued a diverse array of economic

strategies, including cash cropping, cattle rearing, the export of honey, wax, and other tropical commodities, craft production, and trade in local consumer goods. By 1930 nearly one hundred Europeans lived in northwestern Zambia: doctors, nurses, teachers, farmers, and craftspeople of every ilk. An integrated network of Brethren mission stations, farms, and bible study groups would become a pervasive and deeply embedded part of the local milieu. The Brethren's capacity to hire large amounts of local labor and pay attractive wages historically rivaled that of subsequent colonial and postcolonial governments.

While mission stations absorbed much local talent, they also reinvigorated, retrained, and reoriented much of the local labor force. Foreign missionaries were a primary font of innovation, often experimenting with novel crops, the viability of new technologies, and the marketing of nontraditional commodities. Africans picked up, extended, and successfully modified some of these experiments. When a system of taxation was introduced in 1913, throngs of individuals flocked to the half-dozen or so major mission stations seeking jobs that would allow them to avoid the vagaries of a migrant labor system aimed at directing Lunda labor toward the plantations of Southern Rhodesia and the mines of South Africa. A mission elite emerged whose history is less well documented than that of the "Boma Class" in Central Africa, but whose impact was no less significant.[23] The mission elite consisted of those who managed to secure full-time positions as cooks, houseboys, launderers, gardeners, lorry and tractor drivers, carpenters, mechanics, bricklayers, supervisors of casual laborers, or lay religious leaders on whom the missionaries depended heavily in pursuit of their ecumenical objectives. With the new economic imperative of taxation, Lunda dependence on the success of mission enterprises became more deeply entrenched, the connections between Africans and Europeans more inextricably bound. The Fishers, it is often said, are as African as mosquitoes and honey bees, as annoying and as welcomed. For those born today, the Fisher clan is simply an everyday part of life in Mwinilunga. Only the grandparents can claim to speak with authority about the origins of the Fishers. The impact of the Fishers on local consciousness, however, is embodied by all.

The Souls of White Folks

The story of the Fishers is a story about the changing existential and phenomenological status of Muzungu. At Kalene Mission, Africans learned that Europeans were human. They entered the world like any other people and passed away when their time was up. Along the way they ate and slept, laughed and wept, endured periods of illness, and grew frail with age. They were rather unremarkable as physical specimens, being neither particularly strong nor particularly swift. Their strange utterances turned out to be ordinary language that could easily be picked

up by the facile minds of youth. Their remarkable deeds were the result of accumulated knowledge based on inductive and deductive reasoning, rather than
the product of supernatural powers. The European life cycle so paralleled that of
Africans that it became natural to assume that the European afterlife might not
differ substantially either. The Lunda traditionally believed that spirits of the dead
remained in the areas they frequented during life. Their happiness was contingent
upon the performance of symbolic acts that acknowledged their contributions to
and continued association with the world of the living. The frequent mention of
their deeds and exploits, propitiating them at mealtimes, and passing on their
names to children were the standard means of honoring the deceased. Spirits in-
sufficiently venerated would vent their wrath via disease and misfortune. Social
relationships developed in life continued on into the afterlife. The binding nature
of promises and obligations do not cease with death. As the numbers of Europeans living and dying in Mwinilunga expanded, so too their presumed numbers
in the local metaphysical realm. Thus, important questions arose. Who should be
responsible for appeasing European spirits? What form should acts of remembrance take? Can Africans suffer when European spirits are displeased? How is the
presence of European spirits to be revealed, represented, and mediated? The answers to these questions were vital. Clearly the requirements of the dead strongly
influence strategies for dealing with the living.

For a time, the appearance of any new disease in Mwinilunga was attributed
by some Lunda to the European presence. In most cases the mode of transmission
was rather straightforward. Various influenza outbreaks, for example, could be
traced directly to concurrent influxes of Europeans or the return of locals from
European territories. The great influenza pandemic of 1918–20 had a particularly
pernicious impact on Central Africa. In Mwinilunga it was mostly associated with
the decommission and sudden return of hundreds of locals who had supported
the British in World War One as transport carriers. The war ended in November
1918, and much of the Mwinilunga contingent reached home the following
month. According to local reports, between December 1918 and March 1919 nearly
every African in Mwinilunga District came down with the flu, and there were five
hundred deaths reported.[24] Yet, it is believed that hundreds more died and were
simply buried by kin without contacting district officials. Anna Fisher, Walter's
wife, writes in her diary of the difficulty of returning to Kalene Hill from a trip to
Europe in 1918. She managed to survive a German torpedo attack on her ship, was
rescued from a lifeboat on the high sea clutching her two children, and returned
to England. There she was delayed for months due to the inability of any shipping
line to muster sufficient crew not infected with the flu. Deterred until after the
Armistice, and finally returning by way of Angola, Anna wrote of observing a trail
of death, a line of corpses rotting in the bush from the African coast all the way to

Kalene Hills, victims of influenza. Whole villages in places were hors de combat.[25] In November of 1922 a fresh outbreak of influenza hit Mwinilunga. This time a group of Lunda migrant workers returning from tours of duty in Elisabethville (now Lubumbashi) and Kambove in the Belgian Congo were thought responsible. Mwinilunga was also plagued by sporadic outbreaks of smallpox until the massive vaccination campaign of August 1954. Yet neither influenza nor smallpox was ever linked in local consciousness with witchcraft or ancestral affliction. Rather it was thought "to come to you in the air from Europeans."

There remained, however, several categories of disease believed to be caused by angry European spirits. Slow-progressing, debilitating afflictions such as tuberculosis and perhaps new strands of venereal disease were the most likely suspects. At least two new rituals, Tukuka and Masandu, emerged to appease European spirits causing illness. As Victor Turner noted in the early 1950s:

> These two rituals are becoming very popular and are often performed for persons suffering from tuberculosis. The shades (spirits) who cause the disease are said to be those of Europeans or of members of other tribes like the Lwena and part of the treatment consists of giving the patient European foods, served by a 'houseboy', miming European dancing in couples, wearing European dress, and singing up-to-date songs such as "We are going in an airplane to Lumwana." (V. Turner, *Forest of Symbols*, 15)

Chieftainess Nyakatolo provides another early example of the psychosocial integration of Europeans into the African metaphysical world. This formidable Luvale leader, whose illness provided Fisher that most valuable opportunity to demonstrate his medical prowess, requested in her waning years that the fourth Fisher baby be given her name. The Fishers complied, calling her Katolo, or Tolo for short. Some years later another local chieftainess asked that the seventh Fisher child be given her name. Again, the Fishers complied, calling that daughter Chilombo. It is not clear if they realized the supposed power of naming among the Lunda. As noted earlier, to name something or someone is more than attaching a passive label. Naming is a constitutive or transformative act. It is participation in constructing the essential character of a thing. Some Lunda believed that to give a child one's own name toward the end of one's life is part of the process of preparing a *kanfunti*, a vessel for one's return. It is a way of readying a body in which to reincarnate by infusing that body with a bit of one's self. The situation is rife with irony; Nyakatolo, famous for selling enslaved Lunda to the Portuguese, reincarnated as the daughter of an anti-slavery missionary doctor. Nevertheless, it is a remarkably powerful statement about the presumed transcendental equality, compatibility, and even transmutability between European and African bodies and souls.

The Kalene enterprise also brought new explanatory frameworks and knowledge systems to Mwinilunga. First and foremost, mission success in the area of medicine validated the existence of whole new categories of disease. Traditional African medical practitioners tended to conceal their knowledge. The logic underpinning their diagnostic practices, the manufacture of their potions, and particularly their techniques for mediating between the worlds of the living and the dead were their personal possession. Traditional healers were paid for efficacy, not for the revelation of their esoterica. Patients could be content if a treatment worked. Why and how it worked was none of their business. Fisher, however, was quite different. Not only did he practice his medicine in full view of all, but unlike traditional healers, he took on apprentices free of charge. Kalene became, in essence, a teaching hospital where generations of Africans would train as physicians' assistants, nurses, midwives, and laboratory technicians. At Kalene they would be introduced to Western epistemology. They would work side-by-side with Fisher as he drew blood, placed it under a microscope, and identified the exact parasitic microbe responsible for particular illnesses. Africans were present when Fisher took the infected blood of smallpox victims and created a concoction, a vaccine that would effectively protect others from contracting the disease. Fisher's research clearly demonstrated the relationship between certain pathological manifestations and the existence of microscopic creatures in the blood. He popularized injections as the preferred method of attacking those creatures and thereby restoring health. Within a few years of Fisher's arrival in Mwinilunga even traditional healers were experimenting with the direct infusion of medicine into the blood stream.

Perhaps more important than Kalene's influence on Lunda medical styles was its impact on medical thought. Certain lingering diseases formerly attributed to the intervention of angry ancestors had been undeniably cured by Fisher's injections. New debates inevitably arose. What is the relationship between ancestors and microorganisms? Are microorganisms perhaps agents of the ancestors' will, akin to *tuyebela,* the class of evil creatures that do the nefarious deeds demanded of them by witches? Is Fisher's medicine stronger than that of local healers? Is Fisher himself more powerful than the ancestors? Ultimately, those categories of diseases caused by microorganisms and those caused by angry European ancestors would join, rather than replace the existing Lunda world of pathology-inducing forces, increasing the difficulty of identifying causality and thus complicating the process of building a consensus for therapeutic action. In some respects the traditional treatment-seeking sequence was lengthened. Previously that sequence entailed, first, treating patients with combinations of herbs commonly found around farms, fields, and villages, prepared with knowledge held within the household. Most of the aches and pains of daily life could be successfully managed at this level. If not, the more powerful remedies of professional herbalists would be sought out. Only if an illness persisted for some time would metaphysical rather than organic causes be suspected. A diviner would be consulted, and exorcistic rituals might be enacted. In the post-Kalene world the treatment sequence has additional stages. After homemade and professional herbal remedies have been tried without success, most individuals resolve to try clinic medicine before entertaining the possibility of metaphysical involvement. Should pharmaceutical drugs likewise prove unsuccessful, then increased participation in Christian church or other European-inspired rituals may constitute the first appeal to the spirit world. Only as a last resort will some proceed to consult a diviner and organize a traditional exorcism. Such rituals can be quite costly, time-consuming, and socially constraining, placing a host of onerous taboos on those even tangentially related to the patient in question. It has become increasingly difficult to mobilize a consensus and amass the resources necessary to sponsor a curing ritual until family members are convinced that the efficacy of all other therapeutic approaches has been tried and exhausted. Curing rituals still occur. But the frequency has dropped precipitously throughout the twentieth century.

Symbols and Substance of a Shared Creator

As the name *Ndotolu* suggests, Fisher was most widely known for being the doctor. His medical cures and his painless surgery no doubt boggled the mind. But Fisher was first and foremost a missionary. Healing bodies was simply a device for gaining access to souls. The Brethren seized every opportunity to publicly announce their faith, to spread their version of God's tenets, and to bring Africans into the Christian fold. Patients were enjoined to pray before receiving treatment, subjected to frequent sermons while convalescing, and enticed to attend Bible study groups upon recovery. The multitude of jobs that the mission station generated went primarily to Christian converts. Schooling was a special privilege reserved for the most pious. Foreign-born missionaries quite literally saw themselves as Christian soldiers engaged in a great war against the forces of evil and ignorance, witchcraft and superstition. There was no room for compromise or equivocation. Traditional beliefs were an anathema to all things Christian, an affront to all things civilized.

To the Lunda, however, Christianity and traditionally held beliefs were overlapping and interlocking epistemologies. Clearly, there were points of divergence. Yet, the points of convergence seemed more numerous and more salient. Both systems acknowledged an entity named Nzambi as the high god. The Europeans, thus it was assumed, were not attempting to introduce a new deity, but rather were bringing novel information about the age-old Lunda high god. Conversion to Christianity could be framed as acceptance of the missionaries' belief that Nzambi was benevolent and responsive to prayers, in contradistinction to traditional images of the high god as distant and disengaged. Conversion required few other modifications in belief. Indeed, Christianity as a broad complex of principles and practices had much to command the attention of the local population. It resonated loudly with Lunda consciousness at both an aesthetic and an emotional level. It was a religion whose basic instruments, a holy book and a set of rituals, were open and accessible to all. Lunda engagement with the metaphysical world had long centered on taming its nefarious aspects through divination and revelation.[26] That which is hidden is always dangerous. Revelatory practices that uncover the hidden and bring its evil aspects into full view subdue that power, transforming the harmful into the harmless, and perhaps even the helpful. Christianity was attractive precisely because it had no hidden aspects. Everything, including the very will of God itself, was accessible to all—sometimes through direct literate engagement with the Bible, other times through aural engagement with sermons, and still other times through personal engagement via prayer. The Bible, particularly the Old Testament, is stylistically similar to Lunda oral traditions. It utilized techniques locally acknowledged as valid for justifying authority. The Bible is saturated with genealogies linking the people of its time to primordial processes. It confirms the existence of an original couple and expands on their covenant with their maker. The Bible also locates ethnolinguistic divisions among humans in a Lunda-like tale of a collapsing tower. It is replete with stories of invisible beings, angels, devils, ancestor spirits, and even a holy ghost that regularly interacts with the living. In no way did Christianity contradict Lunda notions about a metaphysical world filled with disembodied spirits with the capacity to enter the world of the living and cause illness and social unrest. Thus, rather than transforming Lunda beliefs, Christianity became an additional weapon in the local arsenal for engaging the spirit world and for combating nefarious forces. Christians could appeal directly to the high god for relief from spirit-caused afflictions as well as make traditional appeals to the particular ancestor thought more directly responsible for the extant illness.

Although the Lunda seem to have had little difficulty merging the substance of tradition and Christianity, mediating the symbolic distance between the two was a different and far more difficult matter. The European view of an apocalyptic struggle between good and evil required clearly drawn lines between "us" and "them," between allies and enemies.[27] Symbols as markers of identity and affiliation had to be overt and unambiguous. The sides were deliberately kept distinct. Conversion to Christianity had to have more than intellectual, philosophical, or emotional implications. It had to have its outward material and behavior concomitants as well. Lunda Christian converts, for example, were encouraged to broadcast their new status through residential architecture. Christians built square or rectangular houses rather than the traditional round dwelling. Christians used Kimberley bricks—molded sun-dried clay blocks, stacked using a mortar of fresh clay. Traditional houses were made by spreading wet clay directly over bamboo latticework. Christians were supposed to eschew eating with the fingers, favoring instead the use of European utensils. Good Christians used English, no matter how poorly, somehow managing to infuse God, Jesus, or biblical themes into the most prosaic conversation. European clothing, no matter how tattered, was a Christian symbol preferred over the traditional loincloth, no matter how elegant. Finally, and perhaps most importantly, the monogamous Christian family became the quintessential expression of adherence to the new faith.

The slow but steady adoption of Christian symbolism, perhaps even more so than its substance, profoundly affected Lunda social organization. The heavy investment of time and money required to build a Kimberley brick house, and its durability in comparison with the earlier style, served as a powerful disincentive for residential mobility that characterized the pre-Kalene era. Monogamy and a declining divorce ratio also slowed the movement of individuals between villages. The desire, if not the necessity, to speak English led to an increased focus on social and economic strategies for accessing schooling. The desirability of European clothing, utensils, and other aesthetic expressions led to changing notions of labor and commodity values. The terms of trade tilted in favor of imported goods.[28] Thus, the rising tide of European products required an exponential growth in the production of African trade goods. Notions of appropriate labor allocation were modified in accordance with local desire for cash to purchase the accouterments of new lifestyles.

It would be an egregious error of the highest order to attempt to reduce the intricate and multifaceted interaction of Lunda and European missionaries in Mwinilunga to a dyadic search for cause and effect, stimulus and change in local consciousness. Bits and pieces of consciousness may occasionally present themselves as a seemingly cohesive ideology, usually as strategic responses to specific historical challenges. But more often than not, consciousness is a mass of ill-defined and ill-understood ideas and impressions, feelings and attitudes whose connective logic remains out of reach even to the individual who has embodied them. The analytical possibilities in Mwinilunga are further complicated by the fact that the Brethren were but briefly the sole gatekeepers to the European world. Another set of Muzungu began to arrive a year after Walter Fisher moved to Kalene Hill. These were the officers and soldiers of the Royal Charter Company awarded a monopoly on exercising governmental functions and directing economic and social development in Northern Rhodesia: the British South Africa Company of Cecil Rhodes.

Bellis and the Company: Staking Claim to Borders and Bodies

The British government of the late nineteenth century has been described as a reluctant participant in the affairs of Central Africa. With no established trade or proven mineral reserves the area was not deemed essential to British imperial interests and thus was considered unworthy of investment from the public treasury. The northward movement of European settlers and miners out of South Africa was organized and financed by private capital, particularly that of Cecil Rhodes—politician, gold and diamond magnate, and perhaps the world's richest individual at that time. Rhodes, with enthusiastic backing from London financiers, founded the British South Africa Company (BSAC) in October 1889 as an instrument to move forward his master vision of a string of British-controlled territories in Africa stretching from the Cape to Cairo.[29] His more immediate goal, however, was the search for a "Second Rand" on the Zimbabwe plateau, a gold-producing region he hoped would rival the vast Transvaal goldfields of South Africa. The Charter allowed Rhodes to establish his claim and exclude his rivals from moving north of the Limpopo River in Southern Africa. The British citizenry, in return, would receive three new colonies free of charge; Nyasaland (Malawi) and two named after Rhodes, Northern and Southern Rhodesia. Initially Rhodes had even sought to forestall the claim of the Belgian king, Leopold II, to the Katanga region of southern Congo. He dispatched his own agents to both assess the mineral wealth and to negotiate treaties with paramount chiefs in the area. A coalition of British interests, however, who had long supported Leopold II, was quite comfortable with the king's arrangements for free trade in the Congo and thus refused to support Rhodes's machination. Subsequently Rhodes would float a plan to merge the BSAC with a Belgian counterpart, the Katanga Company, and to share mining revenue. This plan too was thwarted. Despite such setbacks, Rhodes would remain an influential player in shaping the economic destiny of Katanga, a region whose mining potential had long excited his imagination. In 1899 Rhodes had granted his partner, Robert Williams of the Tanganyika Concessions Company, the rights to prospect in Northern Rhodesia. After much closed-door intrigue, Williams would emerge in 1900 with the rights to prospect and finance mines in the Congo as well. From 1906 through the 1930s Williams would also be integrally involved in the development and management of the Katanga mining amalgamation, the Union Miniere du Haut-Katanga. With these arrangements securely in place, and with international recognition of his control of the territory between the Zambezi River and Katanga, Rhodes turned most of his attention to the embryonic mining and settler colony of Southern Rhodesia. According to BSAC policy, Northern Rhodesia was deemed unsuitable for European settlement, nor would the Company permit the development of economic activities in Northern

Rhodesia that might challenge the economic viability of the nascent commercial sector in Southern Rhodesia. Instead, Northern Rhodesia would become a supplier of labor to the mines, farms, and factories of its southern neighbors.

Compared to other regions of Northern Rhodesia, BSAC administration established its presence relatively late among the Lunda. Although the line drawn at the Conference of Berlin (1884–85) separating Portuguese Angola from its British neighbor to the east may have been sufficiently clear on paper, the line's actual location on the ground was less obvious. After extended and at times acrimonious debate, the exact coordinates of the border were determined by the King of Italy Arbitration and announced on September 12, 1906. Prior to this point, the nearest BSAC administrative post (*boma*) to Lunda territory was at Kasempa, over three hundred kilometers to the southeast of Kalene Hill.[30] E. A. Copeman was in charge, and it is said that he spent most of his time chasing local slave traders called Mumbari, exhibiting little interests in the territory to his northwest. C. H. S. Bellis, acting tax collector at Kasempa, was appointed official in charge of the new Lunda District on April 1, 1907. He arrived in Mwinilunga to begin building his *boma* on May 29, 1907. On his first constituency tour to introduce Company rule to the Lunda and to explain the new political dispensation, he was shot at point-blank range by a local headman named Kasanza, who was incensed at Bellis's claim to authority. Bellis barely survived this encounter, requiring nearly a year and a half of hospital convalescence. He returned to Mwinilunga as native commissioner on August 23, 1909, lasting barely two years before constant debilitating illnesses cut short his tenure in Africa. He died of sleeping sickness in London in 1917. Interestingly, in May of that same year, Kasanza, the man who had shot Bellis, voluntarily returned from Angola, where he had been hiding for nine years, gave himself up to BSAC authorities, and promptly died of natural causes a few days later. Local lore has it that Kasanza knew he was about to die and returned solely to better position his soon-to-be-liberated spirit to torment the British for forcing him from his home. Such is the nature of the written and oral accounts of the Lunda's initial encounter with the British South Africa Company.

> In Western Europe the eighteenth century marks not only the dawn of the age of nationalism but the dusk of religious modes of thought. The century of the Enlightenment, of rationalist secularism, brought with it its own modern darkness. With the ebbing of religious belief, the suffering which belief in part composed did not disappear. Disintegration of paradise: nothing makes fatality more arbitrary. Absurdity of salvation: nothing makes another style of continuity more necessary. What then was required was a secular transformation of fatality into continuity, contingency

into meaning . . . few things were (are) better suited to this end than an idea of nation. (Anderson, *Imagined Communities*, 11)

As Anderson and others have noted, the unquestioned legitimacy of sacral monarchy was increasingly contested in Western Europe after the seventeenth century. Over time, vertically linked subjects recast themselves as horizontally linked citizens endowed with inalienable rights that superseded or stood outside royal prerogative. Everywhere kingdoms, principalities, duchies, and dukedoms receded and reemerged as nation-states. Although the majority of the world's political systems continued to be dynastic regimes up to the beginning of the twentieth century, most were by then fortified with notions of nationhood. The modern state is conceptually a collection of people linked by a primordial past, sharing a common tongue, and governed in the present by a uniform judicial code fully and evenly operative over every square inch of a legally demarcated territory. By contrast, in the older monarchical model, states were defined by their center of power, be it court, castle, or cathedral, with the power of the state diminishing with distance from the center. Borders were porous and indistinct. Polities faded imperceptibly into one another. In the nineteenth century Europe was still in the process of structurally moving away from this latter model even as the attempted imposition of the nation state concept on colonial subjects became a defining characteristic of Europe's imperial project.

The Lunda political imagination held more in common with older European notions. On the one hand, the extent of a particular chiefdom might be delineated in broad geographical terms: this river, that side of the valley, those hilltops. Yet in reality, relationships rather than geography defined a chiefdom. Connections to people rather than space defined one's political status. Giving tribute, for example, was the clearest statement of one's political affiliation. It affirms in no uncertain terms that one was part of the tribute receivers' realm. One has demonstrated one's allegiance. One was thus entitled to the privileges of political affiliation, be they unencumbered access to land for cropping and grazing, resources from the forest to build villages, access to the group's healers to sustain health of kin, and, equally important, protection from the demands of other chiefs. Polities in Africa were mutable and often dynamic collections of linked individuals—rarely, if ever, static alignments of land. Rather than territory identifying people, people gave a territory its identity.

The Lunda are well known for their fluid and frequent movement across the landscape, as individuals, as kin and cohort groups, as villages and chiefdoms. Indeed, Central African history is replete with examples of even large-scale polities migrating vast distances, seeking fresher soils for cropping, greener pastures for grazing, greater proximity to trade routes, or escape from disease, political tur-moil, or other constraints on dynastic ambitions.[31] Polities were not infrequently interspersed and even interwoven at their margins. In these interstitial regions it was not at all uncommon to find cases where individuals within the same village owed allegiance to different chieftaincies, spoke different languages, and even practiced differing sets of ethnic traditions.

The coming of the British South Africa Company provoked an immense amount of tension at every level of Lunda society. Yet the Company viewed its own actions in a more benign light. Its initial objectives, it thought, were simple, straightforward, and relatively unobtrusive. BSAC officers would register extant villages and conduct a population census to assess the labor potential, ascertain the size and complexity of administrative subunits needed, and, importantly, identify local chiefs to incorporate into the administrative apparatus. Failure to recognize the profound implications of these acts almost cost the first BSAC ad-ministrator his life.

To the east, in the vicinity of the Kabompo River, the Lunda were considerably intermarried with the neighboring Kaonde. To the south Lunda and Luvale people and villages were virtually indistinguishable. To the north and west Lunda villages flowed seamlessly into Belgian and Portuguese territories. To presume an exclusive and linear relationship between person, village, chief, and tribe was to constrain residential flexibility, economic possibility, and leadership opportunity. The early literature on this period, written and oral, is dominated by two motifs. First, there are endless tales of angry chiefs complaining of subjects being stolen by the BSAC or other chiefs. The surviving district records of Mwinilunga pre-sent a portrait of colonial offices and officers beleaguered day and night by chiefs demanding modifications in the number of loyal villages assigned to their do-main or a reassessment of their personal hierarchical ranking vis-à-vis other chiefs.[32] The second motif is of the Company's utter frustration with Lunda move-ment. Individuals refused to stay put in their registered villages, and in some cases, entire villages refused to stay within British territory, disappearing overnight into the Congo or Angola. These dynamics were animated by individual fear of losing rank and resources under the new political regime, as well as by individual at-tempts to capitalize on British ignorance to alter old political alignments to per-sonal advantage. Many a spurious claim to title and territory arose in those early days. Fireside intrigue against old foes or coalition building with trusted allies was the order of the day. As the Company's plan for administrative subunits came increasingly into focus, so too did the stakes surrounding the identification of chiefs, the enumeration of subjects, and the delineation of territories.

From the beginning, the Kanongesha was recognized by the Company as the reigning paramount chief of all the Lunda in Mwinilunga. The record initially speaks of him as friendly, fine looking, and intelligent. After the introduction of taxation, however, which he roundly resisted, the Kanongesha is portrayed as considerably less amicable. Increasingly his name is associated with suspicions of slave trading, murder, and witchcraft. Nevertheless, his preeminence remains undisputed. His powers may have been mitigated at times but never abrogated. The Kanongesha was traditionally assisted by up to a dozen subchiefs of more or less equal rank, widely dispersed throughout the northwest with oscillating and overlapping territories. The British clearly had no intention of utilizing so many chiefs to rule a population of scarcely twenty thousand. Thus, winnowing out the surplus chiefs would be a constant theme that reverberates to this present day. Subchief Ikelenge, who ruled the area around Kalene Hill, was an early and enduring favorite among BSAC officials and missionaries alike. He was a staunch supporter of the Brethren, satisfying most of their needs for land and labor. He sent many of his young followers to the mission for schooling and even mandated literacy as a prerequisite for all his successors. To the Company, he was the model citizen, leading by example, always the first to pay his taxes, always trumpeting the benefits of civilization to be gained by cooperating with the Company.

Few of the other subchiefs elicited any emotion from the Company other than contempt. Subchief Mwinilunga, whose capital village in the center of the district was by chance chosen as the site for BSAC headquarters and who thus lent his name to the entire district, was despised for fleeing to Angola with all his followers upon the introduction of taxation in 1913. Although he would later negotiate a return, neither he nor any of his successors would ever again be afforded the opportunity to participate in district administration at any level. Subchief Ntambo in the extreme west and subchief Chirumbo in the extreme southwest, whether by coordination or coincidence, developed distinctly similar styles. Each moved his capital village to within a hundred yards of the Angolan border. Each attracted a huge following who sought to evade taxes and labor impressment by fading across the border in advance of any Company visit. Subchief Mukangala and his followers played the same game on the northeastern border with Congo. All three subchiefs were tolerated in the early years while the Company gained its bearing in the new district. All three, however, would ultimately be decommissioned, despite the extended protestation of Kanongesha, Ikelenge, and the remaining subchiefs. It would take two decades to arrive at a stable system of local indirect rule composed of five chiefs with clearly delineated and immutable boundaries. Those chiefs, formally recognized to this day, include Kanongesha in the center, Ikelenge, Mwiniyilamba and Nyakaseya ruling the heavily populated north, and Chibwika overseeing the sparsely peopled south. Those first two decades were characterized by constant political parry and riposte, convention and subversion, ploy and counterploy. Above all else, one thing would become clear to the Lunda:

borders are serious, perhaps even sacred business to the Europeans. If the ongoing exercise of dividing Mwinilunga into subunits did not sufficiently make that
point, the ferment of activity associated with two border commissions most certainly would.

The set of European-drawn lines that distinguished between Portuguese, Belgian, and British territories in Central Africa subjected the Lunda to a tripartite
division, in theory separating the Kanongesha Lunda from their kin in Angola
and the Congo. In truth, however, there were few visual markers to distinguish
one territory from the other. Savanna woodlands and craggy hills spread evenly
across borders. Dry season grass fires raced indiscriminately from one territory to
the next. In the rainy season small streams changed their courses, meandering first
in one territory and then the other. That neither colonial power placed a high priority on developing this region and thus stationed relatively few troops further contributed to the porosity of borders. Traditional Lunda patterns of movement initially continued unabated. Hunting and fishing expeditions, wild honey and berry
collection, family visits, and even cross-border romances proceeded with little regard for BSAC statements about imaginary lines on the ground and the need to
stay within them. Besides, one could always feign ignorance if apprehended on
the wrong side of an imperceptible divide. The few soldiers posted to the region
faced a difficult and dangerous task. In attempting to police peripatetic people
and barely discernible borders, one runs the risk of confrontation with hostile or
simply confused foreign troops holding different notions about where particular
people and borders belonged. The solution to curtailing this potential for international conflict was simple. A line of clearly visible markers had to be installed. The
joint Anglo-Portuguese Boundary Commission was established with a mandate
to set up a series of stone beacons definitively marking the Angolan–Northern
Rhodesian border. Concomitantly, a joint Anglo-Belgian Boundary Commission
was establish to do likewise along the Congo–Northern Rhodesian divide.

For two years, 1912–14, teams of European surveyors and African laborers
cleared bush, took measurements, and set up beacons. That period is well remembered in oral tradition as a time of profound fear and anxiety. Initial BSAC
efforts at recruiting African labor for the project met with little success. When
the company began forcefully impressing labor and marching hundreds of men
north toward the Congo, locals were certain that their kin were being sold into
slavery. The length of stay away from home only contributed to this view, sending much of Mwinilunga's population fleeing into the bush. Shortening the tour
of duty, rotating labor more frequently, and effectively publicizing the level of
wages offered allayed this first fear and drew people back to the villages. Yet, questions remained. Who were these new white men with crates of maps and ma-
chines, scopes and chains, feverishly measuring all day, calculating by lantern well

into the night? For some, this profusion of activity, with its concealed meanings, smacked of witchcraft. And what of those white beacons being set up at all prominent points of the country? Were they likewise tools of European witchcraft? Would harm befall those who touched them or otherwise transgressed their limits? The somber mood of these Europeans, the pervasive sense of urgency, the explosion of anger that ensued from even the tiniest error gave the whole project a menacing aura. These Europeans were odd. They drew lines through space, rather than with space. Their lines were often straight in areas where nothing else was straight. The countryside rolled, the rivers meandered, the escarpment fell off in places. But the lines that European drew continued on and on as if nothing else mattered, as if they alone possessed the power to define space, and to define the people within that space. This, of course, was the abiding fear of Lunda laborers, that their cooperation with the commissions was contributing to their own conquest and containment.

Fear is a funny thing, however. It can evaporate as quickly as it precipitates. That which is mysterious and terrifying one moment can rapidly become the banal and utilitarian the next. In less than a single generation European notions of borders and nationhood moved from novel concept to fear-provoking possibility to strategic tool widely manipulated throughout Central Africa. By 1930 a second round of boundary commissions had to be assembled to resurvey the lines marked by the first in 1912–14. Lunda villagers had become adept at moving the beacons in their own favor to improve access to water or good soil and to include relatives' villages in the same territory as their own. They had become equally adept at moving their bodies for comparative advantage, for accessing the best and avoiding the worse of the three colonial powers staking claim to their region. They came to realize that borders were indeed sacred things to the Europeans. Borders had the power to compel and repel, subdue and subvert, imprison and protect. In selecting to reside on a particular side of a border, one was simultaneously submitting to one set of forces and assuming protection from another. And the closer one resided to a border, the greater one's flexibility in balancing the oscillating relationship between coercive force and paternalistic protection.

Straddling borders, dancing across imaginary lines of power, and repositioning bodies dominated early-twentieth-century Mwinilunga. Individuals fearful or apprehensive of colonial intentions might quietly maintain separate residences in neighboring colonies, shifting with the approach of census takers or labor recruiters. Chiefs concerned for the long-term security of their title might endeavor to increase the flow of people out of rivals' assigned territory into their own through rumors of witchcraft or offers of protection. Even BSAC officials regularly attempted to attract famous Lunda senior chiefs from across the border in Congo and Angola to set up residence in Mwinilunga instead.[33] Appeals could be accompanied by offers of cash, titles, land, freedom from labor impressment, and so forth. The coming of BSAC rule led to drastic changes in the demographic spread of people across the Mwinilunga landscape. More importantly, however, was the rapid change in political consciousness, conflating in local imagination the relationship between lines and loyalty, lines and social obligation, lines and political authority.

One-Eyed Mac: Mangling Bodies and Breaking Spirits

In order for the grand scheme of colonialism to unfold as designed—that is, the acceptance of imperial claims, the redefinition of space, and the reconfiguration of social relations—many smaller, messier, but indispensable plans had to be enacted along the way. G. A. MacGregor was the kind of creature that colonialism produced to move forward its less glamorous, more immediate agenda. BSAC records show MacGregor's tenure as district commissioner to be so brief that he might seem little more than a historical footnote. But "Mac," or "Jacksoni" as Lunda would come to remember him, did the dirty, back-breaking, spirit-crushing work of pacification. It was his job to show the locals the unadorned reality of the shift in power. Mac was specifically the kind of man the company sent in when the natives had done the inexcusable: demonstrated a total lack of fear and actually attacked a white man. Mac was the replacement for Bellis, the retribution for his shooting. Every horrendous deed imaginable, and some utterly inconceivable, were associated with Mac's reign. He had a widespread reputation for murder, kidnapping, burning old people alive in their huts, raping extremely young girls, mutilating young boys, destroying crops, wiping out entire villages, sending thousands fleeing into the bush. For light amusement he enjoyed smacking chiefs around in front of their subjects. With too few troops to manifest a continuous presence in the daily lives of people, Mac relied instead on random, arbitrary, and extreme violence. His name lives on as the epitome of terror.

The late nineteenth and early twentieth centuries were, indeed, an age of furious movement. Africa was saturated with parties of Europeans ever in motion, stumbling over one another, exploring terrain, cataloguing flora and fauna, mapping rivers and mountains, surveying native populations, assaying mineral distribution, asserting control, and regularly demonstrating the technological basis on which those assertions of control were made. The common denominator of these varying mandates was a threefold need for a dependable supply of labor: labor to carry things, labor to build roads and way stations, and labor to produce surplus food to feed the other laborers yanked from their agricultural existence. The tale of MacGregor is essentially a tale of labor control, of readying a population to fulfill the labor demands of a European agenda. Mac provided both the push and the pull toward the new labor market. He systematically destroyed alternative outlets for local labor. He personally regulated, banned, or simply intimidated out of existence any suprasubsistence activity, including blacksmithing, crafts production, alcohol brewing, herbal preparation, hunting and fishing, honey gathering, and salt panning. As a complementary force Mac would raze any village that did not immediately fulfill his request for labor.

Kasanza's bullet had quickly reduced the first BSAC administrator, Bellis, to the status of mere mortal, and a rather unimposing mortal at that. But Mac was a different character altogether. The stories surrounding him suggest a warrior unmatched in bravery, a wizard unmatched in potency. Oral tradition to this day, for example, speaks of a time when MacGregor caught a lion by the tongue when it sprang on him. One of his messengers attacked the lion with a stick, giving MacGregor time to reach his gun and finish off the Lion. Lions, elephants, antelope, people; Mac was a killing machine. Mac also had one glass eye that became a legend in its own right. It is said that he would place his glass eye on a post to watch that workmen did not loaf in his absence. The most courageous workers would creep up and put a hat over the eye.

Men such as Mac were both products and producers of ethnic stereotypes that would become ever more deeply entrenched in British colonial administrative lore. The Zulu, the Ndebele, the Bemba, and other groups with better established martial traditions, who most forcefully resisted the colonial incursion, would ultimately be reckoned as "superior" peoples. They were presumed to be more noble, indeed, more like the British themselves. Peace with them could be an honorable affair. Greater trust would be extended to "superior" groups to manage their own lives. Groups such as the Lunda, however, who responded to the colonial presence by retreating from military confrontation altogether, were deemed weak and deceitful. Such groups were seen as less honest, less likely to respect and abide by the terms of a peace agreement. They were, therefore, subjected to more direct, intrusive, and forceful management.[34] The Lunda came to be known as having an inborn distaste for work, would desert their duties at any opportunity, and thus could not be trusted. Furthermore, they were thought to have inferior physique, bones, and stamina, and only with a firm hand could one get a good day's work out of them. Mac's extra firm hand with the Lunda, however, was probably more constitutive than confirmation of this belief. He terrorized the population beyond any capacity to meaningfully cooperate.

Tales of Mac's sadistic behavior reached BSAC headquarters. In 1909 the Company sent a Major Hodson to conduct a surprise investigation of the Mwinilunga operation.[35] Hodson wrote that he found Mac and his assistant, J. M. Pound living under deplorable conditions. They had been reduced to doing their own cooking and cleaning, for no native would willingly stay under the same roof with

Mac for any amount of money. Hodson concluded that MacGregor was a man of uncertain temper and his administration was a failure. He was excessively harsh with the natives and had difficulty getting carriers to go on tour without assistance from Kalene Mission. Even his police messengers and personal servants had deserted him. But most tragically, vast numbers of natives had fled into Angola and Congo. Others were said to have taken to living in the bush like animals, eating wild fruit and honey. Both Mac and Pound were immediately recalled. MacGregor was asked to submit his resignation. Two years later, in June of 1912, the Company made the grand mistake of reposting Pound to Mwinilunga. Memories of his association with MacGregor were still fresh. Indeed, Pound's own violent temper had earned him the Lunda nickname Kusaloka: the pot on the edge of boiling over. When taxation was formally introduced the following year, people immediately fled again in great numbers across the borders. Veteran colonial officer F. H. Melland was sent from his post in Kaonde territory, to the east, to head up an investigation into the reasons for the mass exodus. Melland met with people who remained and others who had been enticed back to testify before his commission. Out of these hearings emerged the general conclusion that proximate causes were no doubt a hatred of taxes and forced labor, fear and suspicion of the Boundary Commission, and the overall intimidating manners of BSAC police patrolling the countryside. Yet, it was believed that the deeper problem was that the Lunda were a timid, shy, and nervous people, probably traumatized by a century of slave raiding and attacks from Chokwe and Luvale from the west. In short, they spook easily. If this population was to be kept in Mwinilunga, available for British rather than Portuguese or Belgian labor needs, the Company would have to provide some inducements. Melland devised a seven-point plan of incentives.

1. Taxpayers could import gun power for their own use
2. Taxpayers could visit friends in Congo without pass
3. Taxpayers could collect and sell rubber
4. Road work must not be compulsory
5. Big villages would not be insisted upon
6. Boma would give 10 British Shillings for a full load of grain
7. Second wives would not be taxed[36]

Melland's package would seem to suggest awareness of a set of local problems far more complex and wide-ranging than that of easily frightened natives, reluctant to their pay taxes. His incentives are a clear response to pervasive concerns about constraints on economic opportunities, reduced residential flexibility, unfair commodity prices, unwanted interference in domestic matters, outright brutality, and a host of quality of life issues. Despite Melland's reputation for understanding the native mind, all but number 7 of his recommendations were rejected. The Company expressed a willingness to live with African anger. Indeed, they acknowledged that Africans had good cause to hate the Company. As Commander Hazell noted in his response to Melland's report, the native question in Mwinilunga was essentially the labor question: "Administration means labor. A decent house must be built rather than a grass hut. Roads must be built rather than winding paths through the bush. Gardens must be cultivated, where the natives prefer nature to take care of their needs through wild fruit and honey. Most importantly, they must leave home for a month or two to earn the wherewithal to pay their annual tax. Anger was to be expected and contained, but not appeased."[37] Ultimately, Lunda who fled the district would learn what perhaps the Company already knew. Portuguese and Belgian authorities were making even more onerous demands on their colonial subjects. Major British concessions would be unnecessary. Slowly, family groups began to return to Mwinilunga. Some hid in the bush until found and coaxed out by BSAC messengers. Small units were amalgamated into larger villages. Slowly life returned to a semblance of normality. The Company may have feigned embarrassment at Mac's administration, but he had done his job well. Now that the natives were well aware how bad things could be, even slightly less oppressive conditions seemed a blessing. Mac had been the bad cop, but he effectively set the stage for the good cop, Bruce Miller.

Bruce Miller: Routinizing the New Regime (1914–1924)

Frederick Vernon Bruce Miller was sent to Mwinilunga as commissioner in 1914, hard on the heels of J. M. Pound, the taxation fiasco, and the Melland Report. Bruce Miller would come to be rated by Dr. Walter Fisher as the best commissioner ever for dealing fairly and squarely with the Africans. They confided in him, and ultimately that helped move forward all European projects, sacred and secular.[38] While Mac lives on in Lunda lore as evil incarnate, Bruce Miller is remembered as the epitome of honesty and compassion. In truth, the two may not have been such radically different individuals. Both were Company men through and through, risking their lives daily for Company aims. But Bruce Miller was wildly successful at getting locals to go along with the Company agenda. Mac was not. Perhaps Bruce Miller did have a better eye for detail, for the nuances of native life in the bush. For example, Mac had seen the constant clamor of the Lunda for access to guns, powder, and the right to hunt, as well as the clandestine cross-border trade in weapons, as a significant threat to European safety and environmental sustainability. Violently disarming Africans and curtailing the weapons trade was his highest priority. Bruce Miller, on the other hand, came to a different realization. The environment presented far more dangers to the Lunda than the

Lunda presented to the environment. Although the Lunda may have feared and despised the Europeans, in truth the greatest threat to Lunda livelihood and physical safety was marauding animals. Mwinilunga was a territory dense with game. An entire year's crop of millet or sorghum could be wiped out in a single night by a herd of hungry elephants, or more slowly by the daily appearance of antelope and bush pigs. Lions and leopards, following their natural prey, had no aversion to dining on domestic stock or even the stock keepers. Indeed, reports of humans falling victim to animal predation were a regular feature of life in early-twentieth-century Mwinilunga.[39] Thus, Africans were not conspiring to amass precision weapons for a political uprising. Rather, in many cases, they were simply seeking powder for old flintlock muzzle-loaders to clear their gardens and villages of four-legged aggressors. In the absence of that capacity, investing family labor in crop production was not always deemed wise. This in turn aggravated the European search for surplus food to feed conscripted labor.

Company records portray Bruce Miller as a uniquely enlightened individual who made the brilliant tactical decision to redirect police activities away from intimidating villagers to protecting them. The BSAC force took up the task of driving animals away from productive agricultural regions, thereby creating additional incentives for Africans to leave the forest and resettle in larger villages more firmly under Company control. Lunda oral tradition, however, credits the *ankaka* (the grandparents) with sufficient discernment of the intersection of local and European interests and sufficient insight into the workings of the European mind to influence, orient, and direct Bruce Miller's actions far more effectively than Mac's. The *ankaka* led Bruce Miller, bit by bit, to a fuller understanding of Lunda needs and perceptions, offering their cooperation as reward for his comprehension. Bruce Miller, of course, had to demonstrate his worthiness of their consideration, and this he did in magnificent fashion. As is common in Lunda lore, the quickest route to kingly treatment among men is through a successful confrontation with the most kingly of beasts. Mac had survived his encounter. Bruce Miller would now do likewise. While personally leading his troops in pursuit of a lion that had taken to preying on cattle in the area, Bruce Miller was seriously mauled. He managed to shoot and kill the lion, but suffered horrendous injuries. He was carried unconscious, bleeding profusely, for 60 miles to Kalene Hill where Walter Fisher set his bones, gave him transfusions, and performed the locally unknown procedure of skin grafts, cushioning the pain with chloroform. Bruce Miller's full recovery propelled his reputation skyward. That he had suffered such injuries protecting local domestic stock made him all the more worthy of veneration. Equally important, on March 14, 1917, Bruce Miller would marry Tolo, the now grown third daughter of Fisher who had been named after the Luvale queen.

The uncanny parallel between Bruce Miller's unfolding life story and the standard Central African tale of dynastic formation did not go unnoticed by the local folk. Lunda, Luvale, Kaonde, Chokwe, Mbunda, and most other peoples on the plateau possess an extensive repertoire of stories about a hunter from afar who is injured performing some extraordinary feat and who then is nursed back to health and given the local chief's sister or daughter in marriage. He becomes the titular head of a new dynasty and leads the polity to greater glory. Indeed, many Lunda had long seen Fisher as a chief among white men. Company officials appeared to bring him tribute frequently, seek out his advice, and beg his assistance in managing the affairs of the district. Many Lunda likewise took tribute to Fisher, hoping he in turn would protect them from demands of the Company. Bruce Miller's strategic marriage, thus, solidified his position as a legitimate and perhaps even divinely ordained leader among Europeans, worthy of African respect. His elevation heralded the dawn of better times.

Bruce Miller's mandate from the Company, however, was not to buoy African spirits but to harness African bodies. The failure of Mac and his protégé J. M. Pound was due largely to their overdependence on capricious violence and wanton destruction. Such tactics may ably demonstrate the futility of resistance to colonial rule, but they offered insufficient reward for full compliance. Arbitrary and unpredictable labor impressment constrains the development of a stable and willing workforce. Yet, BSAC philosophy held that African aversion to labor was due to contentment with a life of dependence on nature's bounty. Force was thus a necessary tool for driving Africans into labor markets. History shows, however, that the Lunda have rarely been content with nature's bounty. They had long been accustomed to working hard, taking risks, investing capital, generating surpluses, and seeking out commercial relations with those who could bring them the best in global offerings.[40] Lunda history is replete with examples of an almost fanatical pursuit of novel imported items. This was in no way a rejection of local cultural production but was rather a manifestation of the longstanding tradition of symbolically demonstrating one's connection with and mastery of the outside world as a prerequisite to local power. The possession of imported commodities, in short, gave one an aura of worldliness that increased one's prestige and concomitantly the size of one's local following. The scale, scope, and longevity of the Central African caravan system are the greatest demonstrations of local productive capacity, attracting as it did thousands of merchants and carriers up to the plateau annually. Merchants on both the Atlantic and Indian Ocean coasts were well apprised of Lunda appetite for cloth dyed in the latest European and Asian designs, Chinese pottery, utensils, jewelry, glass beads, guns, alcohol, and, especially, any commodity or contraption that infrequently circulated in the region. Merchants could also rest assured that Lunda would have stockpiled sufficient food to feed any size caravan and amassed ample items of value to pay for imports: ivory, worked copper, honey, beeswax, rubber, raffia cloth, oils and spices, and, at certain historical moments, slaves.

As the remnants of the old Central African caravan system faded farther from memory and the goods that flowed across the plateau were increasingly available only for European currencies, Africans were indeed prepared to work for those currencies. The problem with Mac's and Pound's approach to labor management was that it prevented Africans from systematically planning their own engagement with the labor market, from rationally allocating their time among the competing needs of family subsistence, community obligations, and surplus accumulation. Under Bruce Miller, Lunda gained a clearer vision of the colonial project, along with a more stable environment in which to wrestle with its demands. Under Mac and Pound, locals could only react. Now, under Bruce Miller, they had the information necessary to strategically act.

The 1913 tax introduced in Mwinilunga was of a variety called a hut tax. The Company had borrowed the term *sonka* from Northeastern Rhodesia as their standard appellation for taxation.[41] Unfortunately, among the Lunda that word seemed a derivation on their own term, *sonkola,* to be impaled. A taxable hut was defined by the company as the principal residence of an owner, his wife, and children. Untaxable huts typically contained either a set of young boys too old to sleep with parents, or one or more elderly individuals, perhaps assisted by a young niece or nephew. A polygamous male might try to place his second wife with an elderly person to avoid being assessed for a second hut. The tax was pegged at 10 shillings per year and would remain fixed at this rate for the next two decades. Correspondingly, the basic wage paid to African labor in the district was pegged at 10 shillings per month. By way of contrast, native commissioners at the time made £20–30 (400–600 shillings) per month. The Company estimated that Mwinilunga contained roughly two thousand taxable huts that could collectively produce an annual revenue of £1,000. Employment options were initially quite limited, diversifying over time. With the exception of work at mission stations, most jobs required the worker to leave his home village for the term of employment.

When tax was imposed in 1913, the two boundary commissions operating in Mwinilunga had a constant need for carriers, primarily because of the high rate of desertion. They paid 10 shillings per month and provided all the workers' food. When the commissions left in 1914 the principle market for labor shifted to the copper mines in Lubumbashi (Congo) at 15 shillings per month. But this option was unpopular, first, because one had to sign on for a six-month term, quite a long period to withdraw one's labor from the village economy, and, second, because the work itself was exceedingly dangerous. In 1915, for example, 325 Lunda men went to the mines; 22 died, and their families received no compensation.[42] Using Rhodes's investment in the Katanga mines as leverage, the BSAC managed to ne-

gotiate a benefit package for Northern Rhodesian labor that included a payment
of 20 shillings to family members in the event of death. Mine owners complained
that Lunda simply did not have the physique for mining and thus died too easily.
In 1916, there were 400 Lunda who were recruited as war carriers, ferrying supplies to the British front with Germany in Tanganyika. This work was far more
popular than the Lubumbashi mines. It paid 48 shillings for a four-month contract, and relatives would be compensated 40 shillings in the event of death. The
following year 500 more Lunda were recruited for war transport, under the same
conditions as above, but the route this time was to Kabinda on the Atlantic coast
of Angola. In 1918 an additional 600 war transport jobs were available.[43]

As early as 1910 the BSAC had established an African Messenger Corp to ferry
information and supplies between the network of Company stations and substa-
tions. There was a constant flow of directives from the center to the periphery, a
reverse tide of reports and documents from distant outposts to Company headquarters, and the constant movement of commodities and equipment from areas
of plenty to those of scarcity. Messengers were housed in barracks, fed well, and
clothed in uniforms of khaki shirts and shorts, prominent leather belts, and red
caps. They were kept busy cleaning and gardening when not traveling and were
paid in accordance with distance covered. Records from 1917 show that a short trip
up to Kalene Hill and back paid 3 shillings.[44] A three-hundred-mile roundtrip
from Mwinilunga Boma to regional headquarters at Kasempa would have netted
a messenger 14 shillings. A roundtrip to the Katanga mines paid 18–20 shillings.
And a trip to the National Headquarters at Broken Hill was worth 40 shillings. On
average, messengers received 1 shilling, 3 pence per 25 miles covered, plus a food
allowance, call *poso*. Wages remained relatively constant over time, but *poso* would
be adjusted to reflect seasonal fluctuations and regional shortages. In general,
messengers would receive their *poso* in advance and would be expected to purchase their own food along the route. Records reveal constant problems with the
Messenger Corp, however. With their uniforms as symbols of authority, a few
shillings *poso* in their pockets in areas where currency was usually scarce, and au-
thorization to travel great distances unsupervised, many messengers yielded to
temptation and exploited the system shamelessly. Some coerced food from local
villagers, spending their *poso* instead on alcohol and other vices. Some would
linger in towns, seeking opportunities for business and pleasure. Few messengers
lasted long, most being dismissed for neglect of duty, drunkenness, desertion,
and, especially, adultery.

Despite European expression of concern about Lunda physique and stamina,
the Lunda nevertheless found themselves with ever-increasing employment options. By the early 1920s labor recruiters from throughout Central and Southern
Africa were active in Mwinilunga. In 1921 alone the Rhodesian Native Labour

Board (RNLB) recruited 19 Lunda to work on Northern Rhodesian farms and another 31 to work on Southern Rhodesian farms. A BSAC-authorized agent, F. W. Yates, recruited 300 workers to South Africa. Roughly 500 more went to the Katanga mines. Additionally, 292 were hired as traveling workers on projects within the district, 183 as hut builders to house the Company's African workers, 54 as full-time road workers, and 72 as gardeners and herders, overseeing the Company's expanding agricultural operation. The Messenger Corp comprised 73 individuals that year. Another 34 were hired by the Company for miscellaneous duties. In total 1,558 workers are accounted for on district records, in an area with an estimated 2,000 taxable huts.[45] The suggested penalty for tax default was five weeks in jail, followed by a reprieve from that year's tax burden and a strong warning to begin preparing for next year's tax. Yet, the record shows few defaulters. At this point the tax compliance ratio in Mwinilunga compares favorably with that of any other region of Northern or Southern Rhodesia. By the late 1920s, even Walter Fisher's son ffolliott had acquired a recruiter's license, attempting to capitalize on the per head fee paid by the Congo mines for African labor.

One should be reluctant to refer to these as boom times. The redirection of so much African labor away from the village economy toward European profit-making enterprises cannot be declared a good thing. History would later show that male wages did little to stem the forces that impoverished the lives of women and children left behind. But local memories, particularly elderly male memories of these times, are quite favorable. One well-remembered incident, indicating the attractiveness of Mwinilunga at that time, concerns the battle for the local title of Kanongesha. As noted earlier, the line dividing Northern Rhodesia from Angola bisected Kanongesha territory, leaving many of his previous subjects under Portuguese rule. A separate Kanongeshaship emerged on the Angolan side of the border. That Kanongesha had periodically asserted his own suzerainty over all the Lunda, including those in British territory. But eyeing the relative prosperity of Mwinilunga in 1921, he negotiated a deal with British authorities to cross the border and receive their formal recognition of his ascendancy over their own less well liked Kanongesha. A veritable flood of Angolan Lunda would follow in the next few years.

This rapid expansion of available labor attracted the attention of some less than scrupulous Europeans. Some grabbed for title to as much land as the Company would allow, set up plantations, and hired African labor for less than a penny a day, deducting the cost of food and work clothing from that already ridiculously low wage. Shades of slavery returned as floggings again became routine for minor infractions, and Company soldiers were called upon to enforce the sanctity of labor contracts by chasing down and returning workers who had deserted. Those most remembered for their brutality include Mr. Frykberg, who had acquired

4,000 acres in Mwinilungua as early as 1914, and who attempted to greatly expand his holdings in the early 1920s by filing a request for an additional 43,000 acres.[46] The Company would only approve 20,000 acres. Additionally, Kenneth Patterson and his wife, who are featured prominently in the next chapter, managed to have 3,000 acres pegged and approved in December of 1922, paying only 3½ shillings per acre. Also conspicuous on the list of despised white farmers is ffolliott Fisher, who had lied about his age and enlisted in the British army at age seventeen during the First World War. He was wounded three times, discharged with a badly mangled leg, and thereafter walked on crutches. Upon his return to Mwinilunga, he sought out level land for farming and herding rather than the hilly land his father had at Kalene. In 1921, Chief Ikelenge, longtime friend of the Fisher family, gave ffolliott 3,000 acres of level and highly fertile land along the Sakeji stream, free of charge. He then bought an additional 3,000 adjoining acres from the colonial office, first without the knowledge and later against the wishes of Chief Ikelenge. In a court case brought by Ikelenge, the Company magistrate ordered ffolliott to pay £20 compensation to the chief for his deceitful behavior. The chief had wanted £50. In accordance with Lunda tradition, ffolliott also gave the chief a white chicken to cool his anger. It is said that the chief accepted the chicken but remained angry.

Conclusion

The information in the accounts above and their retelling in village settings would rarely, if ever, parallel the literary conventions utilized here by this author. They crop up not in the form of conventional tales per se, with standardized episodes and commonly acknowledged beginnings, middles, and ends. Rather, they issue forth as fragmented commentary, casual mentionings, and sporadic allusions to aspects of the lives and times of universally known characters who have come to represent archetypes, moral types, and object lessons. Often they are utterly de-temporalized. Acts and incidents that formed part of one character's story may be attributed to another. MacGregor, for example, came to symbolize all that was evil about colonial overrule. He was the archetype of the bad European. The despised acts of succeeding commissioners are often projected back in time and attributed to Mac instead. Conversely, Bruce Miller was the good European trapped in an evil system not of his own making. He was known for his love of the people, and any vaguely remembered good act by any long forgotten commissioner might ultimately be attributed to Bruce Miller. Singleton Fisher epitomized the good son, following in his father's footsteps by becoming a missionary doctor in rural Congo, whereas ffolliott Fisher showed that even European sons could go astray, with a life of shady deals, deceptive practices, recruiting local labor for dangerous jobs on the mines in Congo, land grabbing, underpaying workers, and so forth.

Accuracy is not the point of these mentionings. First, they mark time. "Before Fisher came" or "after MacGregor left" or "during the time of Bruce Miller" are all locally acceptable ways of dating historical moments. Second, these tales mark transition—from local to global, from autonomous to incorporated, from tradition to modernity. Third, they validate membership. Those with direct rather than vicarious experience of the above processes, socially acknowledged, constitute the *ankaka*, the senior genealogical generation.

Although European wares had been circulating on the Central African plateau since the sixteenth century, the physical attributes of the commodities themselves barely hinted at the social formations from which those products emanated. European social structure, labor relations, land tenure, philosophical musings, and theological leanings would remain largely a mystery to the Lunda until the early twentieth century. Although the Lunda were famous travelers, none of the peoples they encountered in their peripatetic ways possessed such curious notions of land, politics, and labor control as the Europeans. Nor could any Central African society exert such overwhelming force on others or dare to devise such ambitious plans. And although "might" does not necessary make "right," it can often compel compliance, in a host of ways, to a variety of things. The act of compliance, in turn, sets up its own debates, within and between subjected individuals, which is in itself a powerful force for change. In the final analysis, the deepest and most long-lasting impact of the coming of Muzungu should probably not be measured in terms of bodies battered, kingdoms crushed, or land appropriated. Rather, the wrenching apart of the preexisting social fabric, the straining beyond repair of old relationships, and the act of rendering meaningless old relied-upon truths have damaged African societies in ways not yet fully comprehended or, worse yet, remedied.

The *ankaka's* tales about Muzungu harness, tame, present, and represent the dramatic changes experienced by that elderly generation. For today's younger generations, however, the stories are little more than interesting background to the contemporary state of things. They may entertain, but they do not shock. How could they? They do not stand out in sharp relief against some alternative reality. They are the only reality. For the youth, tales of the Muzungu do not rise up to challenge some countervailing perspective on the world. Rather, they provide meaningful insight into a fairly uncontested view of the past and its residue in the present. More often than not, Lunda youth, like youth everywhere, listen to tales of the elder, nod, feign disinterest, or shrug their shoulders as if to say, "I've heard it all before." But, later, when those same youth can be overheard referring to someone or some action as the "Mac" or the "Bruce Miller," the "Fisher" or the "Frykberg," then it becomes clear that they have indeed heard well.

2

The World of *Ataata*

Insects and (In)animate Objects (1924–1948)

The *ataata* (fathers) of our Chifunga clique were born, for the most part, in the 1920s and 1930s, a time when the rapid transitions and strange juxtapositions of the previous decades were becoming significantly more comprehensible. Sets of people from a distant world, long known primarily for its conveyance of novel commodities, had appeared from over the horizon. These Europeans first dispensed gifts to those who converted to their way of thinking and meted out marvelous cures for troubling ailments, new technologies for using the land more effectively, and the tool of literacy to engage the word of God. It was a bargain difficult to resist. But hard on the heels of this first group came their compatriots, seizing land and labor and seemingly reinstituting the system of slavery that the first group railed against so vehemently. The *ankaka* (grandfather) generation had been caught off guard. Confused, bewildered, and outright terrified, they spent a good portion of their lives running hither and yon, seeking sanctuary or solitude, answers or antidotes to the multidimensional tragedy that had befallen them. In the blinking of an eye they had been forced to accept new power relations and political arrangements and had been immersed in a new economic system and territorial alignment. Their chiefs were insulted, their traditions maligned, and their ancestors blasphemed. Most importantly, perhaps, they had to confront the reality that neither their chiefs, traditions, nor ancestors were sufficiently powerful to alter the new reality or even provide convincing interpretations and social directions. The combined toll of this massive disorientation and disparagement on the Lunda psyche and soul is barely hinted at in either the oral or written history. The contemporary anthropological literature would speak of the Lunda experience as one of cultural trauma, expecting an inevitable elevation in their rates of alcoholism, domestic abuse, suicides, and other destructive behaviors.[1] We know much of how the Lunda responded to colonialism with their bodies. We hear much less of how their spirits fared.

In 1924 the British Colonial Office assumed direct control of Northern Rhodesia as the British government rescinded the BSAC charter. The reasons for this change are many and complex, having been extensively debated elsewhere.[2] But clearly most stakeholders in Northern Rhodesia's future at that time were discontented with the status quo. The expanding European population grew increasingly hostile toward the BSAC for its appalling lack of support for their basic needs, such as labor, transport, farming inputs, veterinary services, marketing facilities, and, especially, education for their young. By 1924, for example, there were an estimated six hundred school-age European children in Northern Rhodesia, less than half of whom were being formally schooled. The Company reluctantly spent barely £6,000 on European education that year, receiving nearly £1,000 in return through the school fees it charged.[3] African education, for the most part left totally dependent on the generosity of missionaries, in some cases exceeded in quality that provided European youth by the Company. This state of affairs fed into a uniquely Southern African "Degenerationist discourse" and a pervasive fear of encroaching "Poor Whiteism."[4] In the absence of protection provided by a thorough-going immersion in European learning, values, customs, and commodities, the African environment, it was believed, literally had the capacity to drag poor Europeans down a notch or two on the evolutionary ladder. Poverty could trigger genetic drift that rendered Europeans incrementally more apelike, more African-like. The rapid intergenerational Africanization of Europeans was said to be most pronounced among poor Afrikaner families in South Africa. But it was a persistent threat to Europeans everywhere residing long-term under the tropical sun. This and other fears set Northern Rhodesian settlers clamoring for increased participation in governance. Most advocated the northward extension of the Southern Rhodesian Settler Council system, with its mix of elected and appointed officials and its acknowledgment of settlers as partners in constructing colonial policy.

The BSAC agenda, however, had long been clear. The search for minerals was the number one priority. The nurturing and cultivating of a European presence in Northern Rhodesia was not even ranked a distant second.[5] The nascent European settler community was seen by some officers as diluting and detracting from Company efforts in the south, increasing the cost of administration in the north, and offering no discernible benefit in return. Additionally, the mining sector had yet to turn a profit in Northern Rhodesia, adding little to company coffers even after decades of mapping, sampling, and assaying. Furthermore, the Company was still smarting from the responsibilities and expenditures it was forced to assume during World War I for protecting the colony from German invasion. Indeed, at one point German African forces under Paul von Lettow-Vorbeck from Tanganyika advanced on BSAC headquarters at Broken Hill. The approach was halted only by the timely signing of the Armistice in Europe in November 1918.

Britain, for its part, was growing increasingly weary of the succession of scandals, investigations, and horrific reports of Company behavior in Northern Rhodesia. Company treatment of African labor was an offense to liberal British sensibilities, and the wholesale destruction of African lifestyles was an affront to British notions of indirect rule. In a deal with little international fanfare, the Company was allowed to retain some mineral rights, but the charter was revoked, and formal management of Northern Rhodesia was moved into the colonial office. This change would appear to have meant very little, initially. Indeed, many Company officials simply moved directly into the colonial service, retaining their old positions, as well as their old attitudes, animosities, and administrative procedures. In Mwinilunga, Bruce Miller would remain on board as commissioner for another five years.[6]

Yet, serious changes were afoot, both in and outside the colonial office, whose major impact would reveal itself in years to come. First, the colonial office would devise plans to set Northern Rhodesia on a track of autonomous development. No longer would it be considered a labor reserve for the benefit of others, but rather a territory with its own unique array of possibilities that merited exploration and promotion. Slowly at first, accelerating after World War II, Northern Rhodesia would indeed become a global force in copper mining.[7] Second, in years to come, the European farming community would be greatly expanded through the dispensation of cheap land and loans, supported through subsidies and extension services, and protected from African competition through the award of monopolies on provisioning the massive mining industry.[8] Third, to compete with the more highly developed enterprises and labor markets to the south, Northern Rhodesian mines and farms were encouraged to focus on worker stability and productivity by offering higher pay, more comprehensive benefits, longer term contracts, and increased training opportunities. In short, a labor philosophy emerged that supported the creation of a class of skilled permanent workers, rather than continued reliance on cycles of migrants.[9] Fourth, Britain rededicated itself to the principles of indirect rule by rapidly expanding avenues of African participation in day-to-day administration.[10] Last, it should be noted that even the explanation given locally for the change from Company to Crown rule took on a sui generis existence, compelling action and underpinning African behavior for decades to come. Colonial answers to African questions tended to eschew subtlety or complexity in favor of childlike declarative statements with little room for alternative or competing interpretations. The residents of Mwinilunga, for example, were simply told that the Company has been bad. The King of England was stepping in to prevent further mistreatment. And, henceforth the Lunda would be direct subjects of the king, rather than his vassal Cecil Rhodes. Over time, however, the Lunda were able to imbue these simple statements with breadth of meaning and intensity of passion that would astound and confound their colonial administrators. The Lunda were positively jubilant at the idea of becoming "direct" subjects of the British monarch. It was almost as if the term itself could transport one immediately to Buckingham Palace, endow one with rights to an audience with his majesty, and bestow upon one all the goodness and glory of the imperial realm. Perhaps this is the clearest reflection of a people historically traumatized, whose psyches have been so shattered that they now revel in even the smallest acknowledgment of their humanity. That this most powerful of all kings, as the Lunda were fond of saying, was aware of their existence and that he was moved by compassion for their wretched condition became a local source of pride. It should be noted, however, that Lunda beliefs about the relationship between subjects and sovereign are perhaps less asymmetrical and more mutually constitutive than the European corollary. It is through public adoration and tribute that people make a leader strong, rather than the strength of the leader necessarily compelling adoration and tribute. Subjects and sovereign are each a product of the power of the other. It was thus an honor to be chosen to share in and contribute to the grandeur of the British monarchy. The Lunda fascination with British royalty would reach a fever pitch with the elevation of Elizabeth II to the throne in 1952. Lunda took great delight in telling or hearing stories of the queen. They spoke knowingly of her latest endeavors, saved pictures of her from magazines, collected cheap copies of royal memorabilia, and expressed their loyalty by walking long distances to see any member of the queen's family visiting Zambia or to catch a brief glimpse of her in old newsreels shown in urban movie houses.[11] As we shall see, the Lunda will thrust to the fore their supposed special relationship with the queen as a shield against future colonial abuse, assuming that she would swiftly punish their abusers if only she were made aware of their actions. Petitions to the queen and appeals in the name of the queen join the local repertoire of tactical responses to individual or collective administrative misdeed. The Lunda will fight against racial discrimination and the imposition of the Colour Bar in Northern Rhodesia, as well as the 1953–64 merger with Southern Rhodesia and Nyasaland, citing them as actions that run counter to the queen's wishes.[12]

As we return this tale to the Lunda world of the 1920s, place must be acknowledged as the surest determinant of social possibilities. The *ankaka* (grand-father) generation had been geographically dispersed, moving frequently and widely throughout Lunda territory, crossing borders between Northern Rhodesia, Angola, and the Belgian Congo. The *ataata* (fathers) of our focal group, however, are all members of the cluster of villages collectively called Chifunga, on or near Matonchi Plateau, in Senior Chief Kanongesha's personal territory, in central-western Mwinilunga. This generation would pioneer three contrasting strategies for lives embedded within the newly imposed economic framework. Their corresponding lifestyles would vary radically. Yet in some ways their divergent experiences would lead toward similarities of consciousness. One group spent the better part of their lives on the plateau. A second group migrated to South Africa (particularly Cape Town) returning as elderly men. The third group spent their lives oscillating back and forth between the plateau and bouts of contract labor in the Congo, the Copperbelt, district headquarters, mission stations, and anywhere else they could secure money for taxes and the new consumer goods that moved quickly from the category of luxury to staple in the rural economy.

Those Who Stayed

For Lunda living in the north of the district, economic life after 1906 centered on the Fishers. Walter Fisher's expanding hospital compound at Kalene Hill represented the region's most diverse assemblage of African laborers: carpenters, brick-layers, mechanics, and craftspeople of all sorts: cooks, cleaners, launderers, and seamstresses. Kalene was also a teaching hospital where Africans were trained and employed as nurses, midwives, chemists, microscopists, and attendants. From 1919 onward, ffolliott Fisher's farm was, likewise, an expansive labor-intensive operation requiring hundreds of farmhands and herders. Also, ffolliott established the largest wholesale and retail trade operation in Mwinilunga, employing African buyers, clerks, accountants, stockers, and carriers. Various Brethren missionaries had offered classes to a limited number of students, European and African, since 1906. Gradually the Brethren would open a boarding school at Sakeji Stream, near ffolliott's farm, and a whole network of village schools would follow. These establishments would train and hire African teachers and attendants. Each missionary family also required domestic servants, gardeners, watchmen, drivers, and, in some cases, nannies. Training and employment options in the north were thus comparatively abundant.

Fifty meandering miles to the southeast of Kalene Hill, two to three days' walk over rough terrain, lies Mwinilunga Boma. As noted earlier, this center of colonial administration offered hundreds of positions in the carrier and messenger corps and to laborers in road and public works, station building and maintenance, and agriculture and herding. The *boma* was also home base for a detachment of African soldiers known as the Barotse Native Police (BNP). But such troops were not re-cruited from among those they were called upon to police. After the enactment of the Native Authority Ordinance of 1929, the five recognized Mwinilunga chiefs would become more formally employed in the district's administration. Addi-tionally, an array of other positions would be created and opened up to African employment: court clerks, treasurers, assessors, local police, and, later, skilled councilors in the areas of education, health, agriculture, veterinary, fish and game management, and public works.

A two-day walk south of Kalene, and a full day and a half west of the *boma* lies Chifunga village on Matonchi Plateau. Once proudly located in the center of Chief Kanongesha's traditional heartland, Chifunga village up to 1922 found itself on the margins. Like the entire district, it was situated on the edge of three com-peting European economic spheres and was deemed not particularly valuable to either. Furthermore, within the district, it was situated on the periphery of new centers of economic activity. Matonchi was too distant from Kalene to benefit from jobs and educational opportunities sustained by the Brethren presence. Re-moteness from the *boma* was a problem as well. Yet, it was Chifunga villagers' lack of access to instruction in English literacy, biblical knowledge, and European comportment that perhaps rendered the social distance to European centers even more unbridgeable than the physical distance. Things would change radically, however, in 1922. Muzungu would finally arrive at Matonchi in the form of Mr. and Mrs. Kenneth Patterson from England. Lives of the *ataata* would come to be structured, made interpretable, and, at times, totally dominated by the exploits of the Pattersons. They were Muzungu, Europe, and colonialism personified. They were all that was foreign, novel, strange, frightening, attractive, incomprehensible, powerful, and now governing.

Just who or what the Pattersons were before arriving in Northern Rhodesia was either never fully known or poorly transmitted to subsequent generations. The latter would seem unlikely considering the amount of time and attention lo-cals devoted to examining every kernel of information about the Pattersons. Ac-counts referring to their background are absent from available Company and colonial records, which continues to give rise to much speculation among con-temporary missionaries. Some say they heard Kenneth Patterson was a pilot in the Royal Air Force during World War I, was wounded in action, and came out to the colony to recuperate. Others suggest that he was involved in some scandal or that he was the black sheep of a well-to-do family and had thus been sent away to pro-tect the family from further embarrassment. Colonial territories were well known as dumping grounds for "remittance men," those who would stay away from home in exchange for regular installments of cash. Speculations abound, but no definitive account exists.

Mrs. Patterson, in a letter to a friend, did leave a few details of her and Kenneth's initial encounter with Africa.[13] They left England in February 1921 accompanied by a European man who claimed extensive Africa experience and who would serve as their guide. They boarded a ship destined for Lobito, Angola, the starting point of a railway heading inland. The ship was forced into quarantine in Luanda, 250 miles north of Lobito, in response to an outbreak of bubonic plague. The Pattersons and companion were allowed to disembark and remain as guests of the British consul. Months later when the quarantine was lifted they all proceeded to Lobito and loaded their belongings on to the "Rack," a train that was able to climb up the steep escarpment by the use of two engines, one pushing and one pulling. They traveled as far east as the city of Chinguar on the Bihe Plateau, the last railway stop in those days, still a distance of over 500 miles from Northern Rhodesia. They had brought out a light Ford truck but soon realized it was unsuitable for the terrain ahead. Deserted at this point by their European companion, they nevertheless decided to continue eastward alone. They sold the truck, bought a Scotch cart and eight oxen, hired a young boy from Damaraland (Namibia) who knew how to drive oxen and a young "Cape Coloured" to act as servant, and set off to cross Africa, knowing nothing of what lay ahead.[14] After surviving ten months of broken cart wheels, misdirection, hunger, debilitating illness and potentially lethal fevers, the Pattersons reached a Plymouth Brethren Mission at Kavungu, Angola, now only 100 miles away from Northern Rhodesia. After a period of convalescence the Pattersons were ready to proceed again. Upon hearing that Northern Rhodesia had placed a ban on the entry of Angolan cattle to prevent the spread of disease, the Pattersons sold the scotch cart and oxen, hired African carriers instead, and headed east. But soon their food ran out, their workers deserted, illness struck, and they wandered about aimlessly until discovered by some Brethren servants sent to look for them. Emaciated and utterly disoriented, they were carried by hammock to Kalene Mission, where Ndotolu's medicine and Anna Fisher's home cooking slowly brought them back to health.

The Pattersons chose not to settle among the cluster of Europeans in the north of the district, but rather headed south forty miles and staked out a site on the sparsely populated Matonchi Plateau. Nearly two years after having left England, they received formal approval for a claim of 3,000 acres in December of 1922. The Pattersons' rationale for choosing the plateau remains unclear, joining their origins as a topic of speculation. Some speak of Mrs. Patterson's love of the landscape, especially the spectacular sunsets observable from the western edge of the plateau, which jutted sharply upward two hundred feet above the plains below. Others suggest the site fit Mr. Patterson's plans best. The well-watered grassland at the foot of the plateau that stretched all the way to the Angolan border was teeming in the 1920s with zebra, buffalo, duiker, kudu, eland, and even elephants year round. Perhaps it was the vision of countless grazing ungulates that led

Mr. Patterson to believe that this was ideal country for cattle ranching. The plateau edge, however, was populated with lions. It was the perfect perch from which to keep an eye on future meals below. They had to be cleared out.

Some of the earliest stories of Mr. Patterson describe his exploits as Jaha Mutupa, the lion killer. But he didn't stop with the lions. He was also determined to clear the plains of all animals that might compete with the cattle he intended to install. Indeed, he is remembered as the perpetuator of carnage on an unimaginable and unforgivable scale. Lunda notions of manhood are inextricably bound to the concept of *wubinda* (huntsmanship). To be called *chibodi* (one without hunting skills) ranks among the gravest insults. Most occupants of the Lunda pantheon of heroes and the founders of dynasties were hunters of note. Elderly headmen and kindly old village councilors cling tenaciously to honorific titles that hearken back to their hunting days. Nearly all Lunda rituals are saturated with hunter symbolism. And when an ancestor wishes to grab the attention of a living male relative, or a sorcerer wishes to best a rival, they first *kasa wubinda* (tie up his hunting prowess). Through success in hunting, even the lowliest born can gain praise, acquire a following, and rise up the ranks of leadership. Yet, still the Lunda viewed Mr. Patterson's actions with horror. The scale of killing was unprecedented, aimed neither at acquiring victuals nor veneration. Not only was Mr. Patterson compared to the sadistic MacGregor, he was likened to a demon unleashing an assault on nature itself. The antelope he decimated represented a major source of local protein, a means of income, as well as a method of attaining manhood. Indeed, it was as if Patterson meant to deny all future Lunda males the possibility of entering manhood. His was a hunt to end all hunts. The land was awash with blood; the air constantly filled with the sound of gunshots as Mr. Patterson shot virtually everything on four legs, clearing the way for cattle.

Soon cattle would arrive from the north, probably purchased from around Mutshatsha in southern Congo, and Mr. Patterson set about hiring and training a crew of herders. Yet, he refused to arm his cowboys, leaving them vulnerable to attack from the occasional marauding lion coming up from the forest to the south. Some workers would die; others would desert. Few developed any abiding sympathy for Mr. Patterson or his projects.

To complement cattle rearing on the plains, Mr. Patterson experimented with a novel array of crops on the top and sides of the plateau. He tried tobacco, wheat, cotton, coffee and tea, hiring locals to dig furrows and rows and to plant and weed these unfamiliar plants. He molded the landscape in ways never before seen. He hired teams of young men to haul large stones and boulders from the valley below to create dozens of stone walls running perpendicular to the slope of the plateau. Women were hired to hoe up, back-fill, and level the ground behind each wall, creating terraces. Here Patterson planted hundreds of mango, orange, and other fruit trees whose pollen-laden blossoms attracted hordes of bees that would, in turn, allow him to experiment with honey and wax extraction.

The succession of houses that the Pattersons had built were architectural marvels for their time. Although constructed mostly of local materials, baked anthill-clay bricks and straw-thatched roofs over bamboo frames, they were little more than stylistic nods to African sensibilities. The main house was huge, dwarfing everything previously built in the area. An elevated front porch supported by tall heavy tree trunks created the impression of a classical Greek portico with Ionic columns, a style so beloved by wealthy Victorians. A grand circular driveway completed the image. The house had solid heavy lockable doors throughout, windows with imported glass panes, and a host of features few Africans had ever seen. One of the house's most talked about attributes was a cistern built on a twenty-foot tower at the back of the house, connected to a series of pipes that made indoor plumbing possible. A smaller version was built at the outhouse to create a flushable toilet. Much African labor was expended each day climbing ladders and lugging buckets of water skyward to keep both systems fully functioning.

The house was filled with rugged tools, precision instruments, fine china, utensils, and pots and pans of varying shapes, composition, and utility. As construction on the Central African railway inched ever closer to Northern Rhodesia, it brought an increasing number of parcels for the Pattersons, keeping them well stocked with the latest fads and fashions and the newest gadgets and gismos emanating from Europe. The Patterson Place on Matonchi joined the ranks of famous European stations in Central Africa. Convoys of vehicles snaking their way to and from the plateau became a common sight. Grand parties and picnics were held for missionaries, mining engineers, farmers, and government officials. Dinner was always an elegant affair: platter after platter of succulent meats, sweet treats, and imported delicacies. Guests sat in straight-back chairs, dined on a massive table with a lace cloth, and used individual place settings of highly polished silver. For Africans accustomed to sitting shoulder to shoulder in tight circles on goat-skin stools, hunched over a large bowl or two of food, placed at best on a straw mat, witnessing a Patterson affair provided an overabundance of material for the next village palaver. The price of admission to a Patterson affair was simply being European. Tea was served every afternoon, stronger beverages at sundown. As provisions continued to arrive at the Patterson place, hospitality offered by the Brethren at Kalene or the military government at the Mwinilunga Boma appeared ever more austere in comparison.

As gracious as the Pattersons may have been toward their European guests, toward Africans they are remembered as having been mean, spiteful, and petty. Mr. Patterson, in particular, appeared to take great delight in acts of outright cruelty. Again, comparisons to MacGregor were apt to crop up. From the very beginning Mr. Patterson demonstrated little desire for African friendship, little concern for African advice, and absolutely no need of African approval. He arrived suddenly from a place no one knew, staked out land, and built fences by rights no one understood. He quickly demolished or burned down any African house or garden found to be within his granted territory—and he pointed his gun and threatened to shoot all who protested. Although, traditional Lunda land tenure granted individuals reasonably secure rights of residence and cultivation on specific pieces of land, it in no way restricted the movement of others across that land. Freedom of passage across the landscape was a fundamental right. Yet, Mr. Patterson rejected such notions. Any African caught crossing his land without express permission would be soundly beaten.

Tales from up north were of little assistance to those at Matonchi in comprehending Mr. Patterson's behavior or penetrating his motives. Unlike the Brethren at Kalene, who heaped benefits on those Africans most able to emulate European appearance and practices, Mr. Patterson had a particular disdain for such individuals. Africans were little better than trained monkeys, he was noted to have said often, and they should remain as such. Kicking and caning, for example, were his automatic responses to meeting an African wearing European-style long trousers. Worse treatment yet was meted out to any African who dared cross his land wearing European shoes.

Residents around Matonchi felt helpless in the face of Mr. Patterson's onslaught. He acted as a law unto himself, denigrating and marginalizing even Senior Chief Kanongesha. Recourse to other whites yielded no relief. For some reason, even the otherwise well-thought-of Bruce Miller turned a deaf ear to complaints about Patterson, confirming in the minds of many that Mr. Patterson was now the biggest of the Muzungu big men. His reign of terror, backed by his itchy trigger finger, produced a mass exodus away from the plateau. Yet, the *ataata* of our focal group are precisely those who chose to remain. Why? A range of reasons, simple and complex, could be put forward. In truth, however, it is difficult to deduce motives eighty years after the fact, especially when filtered through as many layers of interpretation. The simplest and most straightforward assumption is that the *ataata* represent the group most desirous of cash employment, most infused with a deep sense of fatalism, and clearly a bit intrigued by the whole experience. They realized that life with Patterson would be rough. But life everywhere had a bitter edge in those days. District governmental agencies were notorious for corporeal punishment, flogging workers for even minor misdeeds. Jobs in the Congo mines were incredibly dangerous; deaths were frequent. And those first Lunda who had migrated to Southern Rhodesia and South Africa had yet to return to report on the labor situation in those places. Patterson had literally hundreds of jobs to offer: herders, houseboys, cooks, cleaners, launderers, laborers, craftsmen, carriers, messengers, and mechanics. Although he is remembered for being miserly, paying his basic workers a penny a day, the 1920s is also remembered as a time when one could purchase a singlet and a pair of short pants for five pennies. One's tax obligation could be met in as little as four months. Patterson had rows of worker houses built so that essential staff would be nearby and available around the clock. Workers, nevertheless, were still able to maintain contact with family and loved ones back in the village. Most simply remained in the villages and walked to work each day. All could dedicate their off-hours to the traditional pleasures of socializing, drinking, attending rituals—a far cry better than the presumed drudgery of life in the city, on mines, or distant plantations.

The Pattersons tended to hire young workers, apparently believing that old Africans, like proverbial "old dogs" could not learn new tricks. In doing so, they created the first local class of young big men on Matonchi. Each worker became famous in his, and more rarely her, own right. Each was highly sought after for information on the Pattersons, intimate insights into their personal habits and predilections, as well as assessments of European manners and mores more broadly. The job counseling that African workers could provide, their capacity to explain the duties and requirements of new occupational categories for which the Pattersons were willing to pay cash, was a valuable asset to the area at large. Advanced or individual notification of job openings, a few words of recommendations, and hints on approach and presentation became the most valuable stock in trade of a Patterson employee.

A style emerged at Matonchi, the origin of which is not fully remembered. The most famous of the new-style big men, those with steady income from Patterson employment, became known far and wide by their self-effacing nicknames. Men such as Chuula (frog), Izenzi (cricket), Mupumpi (beetle) and Chitombu (lizard) were the giants of their time. Young Chitambala, for example, who was selected by Mrs. Patterson as her personal servant, became famous as Kububu (bug). He would spend thirty years as her constant companion. Bug was, without a doubt, the single most famous of the Patterson employees and the most trusted local authority on all things European. Bug became quite wealthy by local standards, using his salary to construct a spacious house that borrowed many architectural features from the Patterson's place. Much of his money, however, was used to enhance his position within the Lunda traditional world. He was a major sponsor of local rituals. He married a half-dozen women over the course of his lifetime and assembled a large following. But Bug never produced any children. Nevertheless, generations of youth would gain jobs and education through the graces of his recommendation and later through his donations of cash for school fees. He would assist many in assembling bridewealth. In a metaphorical sense, bug would become the father of many Lunda who resided on Matonchi Plateau.

The style would change over time, as younger employees become known by their function around the Patterson Place: Taawalu (towel) the butler who stood in the corner during meals with a towel draped over one arm, Tebalu (table) the bus-boy responsible for setting and clearing the dinning table, Naife (knife) the cook's assistant most often assigned to slice, dice, and trim food in preparation for the pot. This would be a surprisingly long-lived group. Many were still alive, telling their tales well into the 1990s.

The Pattersons left deep imprints on the social organization and thought of generations of Matonchi Plateau dwellers. Indeed, as we shall see, their impact reverberates down to this present day. In short, they occasioned a massive demographic shift as individuals and entire villages deserted the area. Others moved inward toward the margins of Patterson property to witness more closely unfolding events, to better position themselves to secure employment, or to be first in line to sell the Pattersons any goods or services they might require. The Pattersons influenced prevailing aesthetics in a wide range of areas, including clothing preferences, personal presentation, dietary habits, hygienic standards, and architectural style. An African elite began to build larger and sturdier houses, stocked with more furniture than previously thought desirable. Individuals increasingly experimented with forks, knives, and spoons rather than eating solely with fingers. European articles became a standard part of every bridewealth package.

Matonchi was seen as a center of sophistication exceeding in every aspect Kalene and the Boma. By attracting the full range of the expatriate community to their household, the Pattersons brought the outside world near enough for Lunda inspection. To be from Matonchi was to be chic, to be endowed with an air of modernity. Even today the *ataata* still talk of the time when they could travel across the landscape fully aware that they would be well received, laden with hospitality, plied with the best of food and drink in any village they approached. Their stock of stories about the Pattersons was far more valuable even than cash.

In an odd way, the fear and anxiety provoked by the Pattersons was perhaps reconciled, mitigated, and counterpoised by their entertainment value. The Pattersons were fun. Fun to think about, to talk about, to imitate, and to ridicule. The Lunda composed stories, songs, poems, and riddles based on the Pattersons' deeds. Youth, in particular, excelled at improvising skits around the fire about Muzungu, with the Pattersons figuring prominently. A standard theme was the humorous contrast between the way Europeans and Africans did the most basic of things. "Africans walk like this," a narrator might say as his confederate glides by with a smooth, elegant, well-balanced gait. "Muzungu walk like this," he then intones as the village clown rambles into view with jerky motions, head bobbing out of control, and ultimately trips over a barely visible twig, in Charlie Chaplinesque fashion. Another widely known skit compared the daily rhythms of work: "Africans wake up early, go straight to the field, work up a sweat, go bathe in the stream, then home to eat. Muzungu sleep late, take hot bath, eat hot breakfast, sweat, then call 'lazy' African to do his work." Even plays about comparative toilet behavior and sexual practices are well represented in the local repertoire. Some plays are of great age, passed along with pride but reinvigorated by each generation with the addition of contemporary flourishes.

Even the unknown did not escape elaboration. That the Pattersons, for example, never produced children was a constant topic of speculation. One set of handed-down stories had Mr. Patterson engaged in numerous sexual escapades with young African women. That there were no known pregnancies is presented as proof of Mr. Patterson's impotency or sterility. From this premise extends one proposed rationale for his violent impulses. Anger over his inability to produce life, it was said, manifested itself in his drive to destroy life. Opportunities to kill in Europe subsided with the end of the Great War. Thus, Patterson was attracted to Africa as a place where Muzungu could kill at will, on a vast scale. Jealousy of African fertility-cum-masculinity explained his propensity to humiliate African males through physical assault and psychological emasculation by assigning them women's work within his household.

Some rejected this interpretation, believing, rather, that Patterson found African women, if not all women, disgusting. They deny that there is any evidence to the contrary. Rather than being best understood as a distraught human being, Patterson was best understood as a rather normal but ambitious nonhuman. Consistent with Lunda belief, he was a selfish *muloji* (witch/sorcerer) who simply preferred to "keep his blood to himself" and to consume as much flesh and blood of others as possible to build up his own power.[15]

Mrs. Patterson's sexuality was likewise dissected around village campfires. Some suggested that Bug had had relations with her. Perhaps she was a witch who had consumed both Bug's and Mr. Patterson's fertility. Or perhaps she was fertile and simply had the misfortune of attracting sterile men. Perhaps she hated children and was content with her sex life. Probably no one knew for sure, but speculating about Muzungu sex lives was a game open to all.

Women's memories of Mrs. Patterson tend to be harsh. She was remembered as a lazy woman who lived a life of leisure, while increasing the workload of African women by occupying their menfolk with work more properly her own. Interestingly, although many aspects of European customs and habits were fun to experiment with or were good symbolic material to play with to demonstrate one's mastery over foreign things, the same cannot be said of Pattersonesque gender relations. Not even the wealthiest of local men seemed to have embraced the "wife-on-a-pedestal" model. Nor is there any evidence of local women lobbying for such treatment.

The *ankaka* (grandfather) generation who knew Bellis, Ndotolu, One-Eyed Mac, J. M. Pound, and Bruce Miller, or who had grown up with stories about them, would, no doubt, have developed expansive notions about the variability of personality types among Europeans. They could have simply viewed Mr. Patterson as a Mac type, without his personal set of flaws and foibles calling into question the finer qualities of men such as Fisher and Bruce Miller. The fathers, however, whose first experience of any sort with Europeans came via interaction with the Pattersons might have initially been more inclined to stereotype and generalize. Yet, over time, this would change as the Patterson house staff—men such as Bug, Towel, and Table—would have ample opportunity to intimately view the behavior of diverse Europeans visiting the Pattersons. And anything the house staff observed, deduced, surmised, or merely conjectured would fuel the fire of curious speculation about the nature of Muzungu and the accommodation their presence required.

When Kenneth Patterson died on May 20, 1950, he was buried in an above-ground stone crypt on his favorite spot for viewing the sunset on the western edge of the plateau. During the 1960s, when the entire British Empire was shocked by the so-called Mau Mau revolt in Kenya, Mrs. Patterson for some reason came to believe that Africans around Matonchi might be tempted to dig up her husband's bones to make a kind of anti-European juju, or magical substances, as was supposedly the case in Kenya. The fact that the crypt had remained untouched for over a decade did not allay her angst. She had the bones exhumed and cremated. Whether this act reflected late life paranoia or a well-founded fear of African animosity issuing forth from decades of ill treatment is not clear. In any case, the event seemed not to have poisoned her relationship with or loyalty to Bug. After returning to England, Mrs. Patterson and then her estate continued to send regular remittances to him up to the end of his life in 1990. Again, there was much local speculation as to why this was the case. In any event, it served mostly to augment Bug's legendary status, to give more power to his stories, and to confirm his mastery of an age and a set of processes that sent lesser men fleeing.

Those Who Left: Mr. Jake and Isaac Nkemba

Rumors about Lunda unsuitability for hard work had gained sufficient credence by the mid-1920s to begin slowing the rate of labor recruitment in Mwinilunga. By 1930 it had stopped altogether as both Congo and Northern Rhodesian mine operators were in agreement that the death rate of Lunda workers was disproportionately high compared to other groups. Mine officials in Northern Rhodesia were, in fact, settling on the Bemba as their preferred ethnic group. The initial language of mine communication was Fanagalo, or kitchen-kaffir, a blend of Zulu,

English, and Afrikaans that had originated in nineteenth-century South Africa and then spread northward. Its vocabulary was quite limited and its syntax underdeveloped. It was primarily a collection of declarative statements and responses suitable for master-servant relations characterized by command and obedience. Over time, the Bemba language would come to replace Fanagalo as the lingua franca on the Northern Rhodesian mines. The inadequacies of Fanagalo, however, had contributed to an era of fluid identity, ethnic de-emphases, or "detribalization" as the colonials termed it.[16] Unrelated to local languages, devoid of local cultural markers, and easily mastered, Fanagalo opened the door to mining employment to all. With Bemba hegemony, things changed. Bemba gatekeepers could readily ascertain by accent where an individual was from, or most certainly where an individual was not from. With ample clan and kinsmen waiting in line for employment, Bemba supervisors had no incentive to support non-Bemba efforts to enter the mines. The message was clear: Lunda need not apply.

The Lunda fared poorly, as well, in other sectors of the Northern Rhodesia urban labor market. Their reputation for ready flight from domination and for desertion of duty followed them to town. They were declared too sneaky and irresponsible for domestic work, perhaps the second largest urban job category. Nor could they be trusted to effectively manage a master's cash or commodities, thus closing them out of the burgeoning retail and wholesale trade sectors. Northern Rhodesian urban stereotypes would ultimately hold that Lunda were only good for digging graves, hauling garbage, and emptying night soil jars. Town life was rarely a pleasant experience for Lunda, and hence relatively few would settle there permanently. Lunda urban networks would remain underdeveloped, in a vicious cycle, making the transition for subsequent arrivals all the more difficult.

Stories had reached Matonchi Plateau about plantation work in Southern Rhodesia and about the massive expansion of mines and port facilities in South Africa during the interwar years. Under contracts with the WNLA (Witwatersrand Native Labour Agency) and the RNLB (Rhodesian Native Labour Board), a few scores of Mwinilunga residents had headed south in the early 1920s. In general, the experiences they recounted upon return bordered on the horrific. Yet an expanding cache of details was being assembled that would serve later migrants well. Locals were apprised of the various routes south, with the consensus being that traveling east first via the Copperbelt was best. That route led initially through the territory of the Akosa chief Sailunga, a classificatory brother of the Kanongesha, where Lunda received excellent hospitality. The next ethnic group encountered would be the Kaonde, who were *wusensi,* joking cousins of the Lunda. Among them one could, in theory at least, demand or simply take sustenance as needed without resistance. In reality, however, Lunda would accentuate the odds of being amicably received by traveling well stocked with smoke-dried *chituba,* succulent cane rat. This most highly prized of all meats in Central Africa was particularly plentiful in Lunda country. No sensible traveler was ready for departure without first amassing a couple dozen *chituba*, dried, pressed flat, stacked like pancakes and tied up with bamboo and bark fiber. Any host along the way would gladly provide a night's lodging and a few days' food in exchange for one *chituba*.

Subsequently one would enter Bemba territory, where unfortunately Lunda needed to keep a low profile. Here one intersected the line-of-rail, a series of roads and railways heading south all the way to South Africa. A good deal of attention was focused on the types of work Lunda could secure, services they could offer, and strategies they could employ from this point onward. Some migrants had acknowledged their Lunda-ness and accepted any dirty job offered long enough to buy a ticket south. Others claimed to have literally walked the entire distance to South Africa. Most, however, proceeded in stages, walking a bit, hitching rides wherever possible, stopping and working a spell when the opportunity presented itself.

The issue of identity would remain a cause for concern. Being Lunda offered travelers few advantages, while saddling them with a host of liabilities, some economic, some psychological. Ultimately, sometime in the 1930s, Lunda migrants in Southern Africa would become Shangaan. Shangaan, or Tshangana, was initially a term that referred to a Tsonga-speaking people in Mozambique under Chief Soshangane, some of whom crossed over to work in South African mines around the beginning of the twentieth century.[17] Increasingly the term would be expanded to include all Mozambican mineworkers in South Africa, regardless of background. Distance traveled from home and the hopelessness of conditions left behind created an image of Shangaan desperation. They rapidly gained a reputation for taking on the hardest and most dangerous underground jobs and were thus in high demand by mine operators. Over time, camaraderie forged out of shared peril in an environment of ethnically segregated work teams and housing breathed life into the Shangaan identity. Shangaan welfare and funeral societies emerged, followed by dance societies. Later, a Shangaan petty bourgeoisie developed in South Africa and serve as the backbone of new political institutions to fight segregation and other limits on Shangaan aspiration. Many joined Mission or Ethiopianist churches. In 1934 a newspaper was founded with the expressed purpose of fostering Shangaan national pride. Yet, prior to this point, Shangaan ethnicity had been less tightly constructed, encompassing vast linguistic and cultural variation. One was labeled Shangaan primarily because of what one was not—namely, South African. One Lunda strategy was to move into that space. Upon arrival in South Africa they would live, work, or simply associate with a group of Shangaan long enough to pick up sufficient language skills to pass as Shangaan in a new location. The aim was not to live with Shangaan, but to wrap themselves in the Shangaan reputation for hard work and put it to use in a non-

Shangaan area. Isaac Nkemba and Jake Ndumba were two among many who left Matonchi Plateau armed with these fragments of knowledge. They succeeded in making it all the way to Cape Town and secured jobs as laborers working on port revitalization.

The Story of Ndumba, aka Mr. Jake

Jake Ndumba was a small, wiry, talkative man with an unparalleled fascination with and appreciation for languages. He also possessed an amazing facility and an insatiable appetite for learning them. Ndumba did not simply imitate speech patterns; he imitated the totality of a speaker's being: his vocal inflections, hand motions, body movements, facial expressions, clothing style, and social etiquette. At heart Ndumba was perhaps an actor, and South Africa for him was but one big improvisational theater, with roles limited only by one's imagination. Ndumba's narrations about the Cape hold little in common with standard historical treatments of that time and place. There is no mention of the angst and uncertainty created by the continual government effort to move Africans out of central Cape Town. Nor does he comment on the devastating impact of the abolishment of the African franchise in 1936 or the subsequent collapse of the national African protest movements into an increasingly smaller number of less effective groups. To Ndumba, these were heady days. Urban South Africa was a kaleidoscope of people and places, sights and sounds. Style upon unimaginable style jostled for a place in the sun. Ndumba not only learned Shangaan; he became Shangaan. Then he became Xhosa, then Zulu, then Sotho, then even an Afrikaner. He changed his identity as readily as he changed his clothes. He worked all day, and at night floated from shebeen to shebeen, from one African location to another, playing one character after another. He did a little amateur boxing, first under one name, then under another. Indeed, he was obsessed with boxing in general, with heavyweight champion Joe Louis in particular. Fifty years after the event, Ndumba could still give an impressive round-by-round, blow-by-blow account of the 1936 Joe Louis–Max Schmeling fight. He spoke vividly of the deep sense of despair that descended on him with Louis's defeat that night. He remained mostly drunk and depressed until Louis regained the title the following year.

During the Second World War, Jake Ndumba enlisted in the South African Army, the UDF (Union Defence Force). Later in life, he couldn't quite remember why or under what guise he managed to get accepted. He recalled that he might have been slightly inebriated at the time. But coming from rural Zambia where it was still being debated whether Africans ought to be allowed to possess muzzle-loaders, the thought of actually being issued a shiny new machine gun and being sent off to shoot Hitler was clearly a powerful inducement. But neither Ndumba nor any other African would be called upon to do much shooting in their military careers. The African National Congress had come out strongly in favor of the war with Germany. The South African government had urged Africans to volunteer in great numbers. But to maintain the morale of White South African recruits, this had to be a white man's war. Africans could be drivers, ditch diggers, stretcher bearers, or cooks. But for the most part, they would not be armed.

For no discernible reason after boot camp Jake Ndumba was assigned to a battalion as cook. Having absolutely no experience, and receiving no training before being shipped out to Madagascar, Ndumba resorted to simply dumping whatever food he was issued into huge vats of boiling water and calling it soup. What was not eaten one day would be served up again the next. No fresh soup until the old soup was finished. Perhaps the grueling experience the troops were undergoing in Madagascar sapped their energy for rebelling against Ndumba's monotonous fare. He remained the cook when his regiment shipped out to Burma to assist in the Kabaw Valley Campaign. There he became fluent in the Burmese language and added Burmese soup to his menu. In later life Ndumba would joke that his toughest task during the war was figuring out how much food to cook on a given day since he never knew how many men might not return from the front alive. In more quiet moments, alone with his most trusted cohort, he would confess to being absolutely terrified the entire time. He could not imagine that even hell itself was worse than war. But mostly Ndumba loved to speak of what the war taught him about humanity. All men are the same. Black, white, yellow, or brown, they are all capable of incredible acts of bravery, they are all prone to shit in their pants with fear, and they all bleed when they meet a bullet.

After Burma, and a long ocean voyage, Ndumba found himself in France. It took him a while to figure out where in the world he was, a bit less time to figure out how to speak the local language, and even less time to notice that these Muzungu women had few qualms about sex with Africans. The war seemed to have been winding down. That is to say, there were not bullets constantly flying over his head as there had been in Burma. He was able to spend his days perfecting his new French soup and his nights learning about French sexual practices. Back at Matonchi decades later, he would publicly hint at his expertise in this area. The specifics, however, were reserved for cohorts-only conversations.

At the conclusion of the war, Ndumba was decommissioned, given £2 cash and a khaki suit of clothes as severance pay, and returned to his job with the harbor authority in Cape Town. One monumental day, years later, he was present when an American battleship pulled into the harbor. As the troops came ashore in waves of small boats he noticed the playful camaraderie between black and white American troops. His own military experience, except for the encounters in France, had been a thoroughly segregated one. Overwhelmed with the desire to be part of, to learn from, and to immerse himself in the integrated American military experience he shouted out to one boat, in his best imitation of American movie-speak, "Hey Jack, where da hell ya think ya goin'?" "Hey Jack," one of the African Americans shouted back, "where da hell ya think we should be goin'?" Surprised that real Americans had deemed him worthy of a response, he nervously rattled off the names of the most prestigious clubs in town before his senses returned; he remembered and felt compelled to explain that they were "Whites only" clubs. The Americans not only seemed undaunted by Ndumba's rejoinder but indeed seemed gleeful at the prospects of direct confrontation with South African racial politics. "Hey Jack," someone shouted, "show us the way, and the night is on us." It was a night that Ndumba would still be reliving nearly fifty years later. It was the night that he first adopted the name Mr. Jake (a Lunda-Anglo-American pronunciation of Mr. Jack). It was also the night he perfected his American accent. With his American entourage, Mr. Jake saw the inside of places and aspects of life in South Africa never before imagined. The Americans were a rough bunch that took great delight in manhandling any white South African who even hinted at the impropriety of mixed-race fraternization. American soldiers had been given a sort of immunity in South Africa. Everyone knew that Americans were loud and aggressive, and they were clearly now an unrivaled superpower. The population had been encourage to simply grin and bear the brief American presence for the sake of potential postwar development assistance.

Late in life Jake married a South African woman and had two daughters. But he remained something of a gadabout. Around 1980, beginning to feel his age, Jake made plans to return to Matonchi Plateau with his South African family. They accompanied him as far as the Zambian Copperbelt but wanted no part of rural Zambia. Some sort of split occurred, the details of which Jake avoids discussing. The wife and daughters returned to South Africa. Jake proceeded onward to the plateau, laden with consumer goods of all sorts, which rapidly disappeared as he distributed them as gifts to relatives he had not seen in decades. Jake got a job as the cook at the Franciscan Catholic mission on the Lwawu River that had been established in his absence.

Upon her husband's death in 1950, Mrs. Patterson had asked the Brethren at Kalene Hill to establish a mission on Matonchi. As they were unable to do so in a timely manner, she approached a Catholic priest with the same request. In 1951 two American Franciscans, Fr. Rupert Hillerich and Fr. Adrian Peck, both trained in Indiana and Ohio, arrived on Matonchi ready for duty.[18] They first made camp in a tent at a spot given them by Mrs. Patterson and then built a Lunda-style "pole and dagga" church. It is said that Mrs. Patterson almost immediately took offense at the style of these American Catholics. They casually smoked cigarettes, drank alcohol, and shared meals with the natives. They were curious rather than condemning of African ritual life. In general, she found them too slovenly to serve as the needed examples of European superiority. In 1954, Mrs. Patterson kicked the Catholics off the plateau. Undeterred by this act, and indeed buoyed by the enthusiastic African response to their initial efforts, the Catholics moved two miles to the Lwawu River and began constructing what would become one of the most impressive mission stations in the Northwest, second only to Kalene Hill.

The Americans manning the mission station in the 1980s were immediately enchanted with the returning Mr. Jake, the wiry little man with an endless supply of stories, told in a great Texas accent. He could also tell those same stories in any of two dozen other accents. The job as cook, however, only lasted a year or so as the Franciscans became quite tired of soup every day. But they found Jake a series of increasingly menial jobs around the mission, mostly to keep an eye on him and to hear his stories. He died in 1990.

Between the time of his return and his death Jake was engaged in nearly perpetual conversation with Bug, Cricket, Table, Towel and others of his generation who had remained at Matonchi. Decades of experiences were unraveled and shared, as bit by bit the world here was juxtaposed to the world out there. Whenever and wherever the *ataata* were spotted swapping stories, an audience would invariably assemble.[19] That even the young would gravitate toward such gatherings and listen intently attests to the power of well-told stories—particularly so in an environment that produces few other diversions. A junior big man might contribute a bottle or two of the local brew to enliven the proceedings. Another big man might have a plate of food sent over to encourage the storytellers to linger a bit longer. In the autumn of their lives the *ataata* became virtual performance artists, shuttling leisurely across the landscape, being wined, dined, enticed, and cajoled into performing the bits and pieces of their lives for the benefit of those who follow. On the one hand, individuals are inseparable from the stories they weave. One essentially becomes one's stories. Individuals wear their separate tales as markers of identity just as those in the West may drape themselves in their professional accomplishments. On the other hand, collections of stories can overlap, complement, and reinforce one another in ways that present a distinctive reality. The collective stories of the *ataata* cohort are such an entity, presented as a gift to the larger group. Invariably they are told over and over until they become deeply etched on the consciousness of all. Such stories inform and educate broadly about the world. They offer specific tools and techniques for engaging the world. They provide psychological comfort and, above all else, confirm Lunda humanity by making manifest their capacity to take on the world and survive. They instill confidence while perhaps also issuing a challenge to younger generations to go forth and aspire to even greater heights than the *ataata* reached. By the time Mr. Jake Ndumba died, his stories had been well absorbed by those who remained. His flair and style of self-presentation extended the meaning of being Lunda. His unrestrained affection for Americans, black and white, resonated well with local experiences juxtaposing the behavior of the British Pattersons with that of the American Catholics. The image of Americans as a friendlier people, more open to things African, more worldly, more technologically savvy, and ultimately more worthy of emulation than the British would be continually reinforced in subsequent generations. Eulogizing Mr. Jake most moanfully and elegantly at his funeral was his life-long buddy from the plateau and Cape Town, Isaac Nkemba.

Nkemba's Story

Isaac was as quiet and reserved as Jake was effusive and outgoing. In many ways the two might be considered opposites. Yet they might be more aptly viewed as simply occupying different points on the *ataata* continuum—points that were, in fact, not too widely separated. Isaac and Jake were equally driven, ambitious, and clear about the objectives of their respective South African experiences. Whereas Jake wanted to become the ultimate chameleon, able to blend in perfectly in any social setting, Isaac's aim was to stand out in any crowd because of his dignity and elegance. Whereas Jake desired to master as many social personae as humanly possible, Isaac focused all his energies on mastering just one role. Isaac was captivated by the style and mannerisms of those Africans in the townships some called *ooscuse-me*. They were generally regarded as decent people, more educated, more refined in speech and behavior than the *amagoduka* (semi-urban types still tied to the countryside), the *tsotsis* (young urban thugs), or the *amatopi* (trader and tradespersons without much formal schooling). Many a negative term, however, was hurled at the *ooscuse-me* class by other Africans: Euro-imitators, assimilationists, sellouts, collaborationists, and so forth. But none of this deterred Isaac. To him it seemed that all the vital institutions of African town life—churches, social clubs, welfare societies, trade unions, and political parties—were dependent for their operation upon *ooscuse-me* money, knowledge, political contacts, and organizational skill. They were, in essence, the backbone of African social life. And Isaac aspired to join their ranks, recognizing that Cape Town was a place where social class often overshadowed ethnicity and language. Thus, while Jake immersed himself in the boozy atmosphere of South African nightlife, Isaac enrolled in literacy classes, joined clubs, and attended community functions. While Jake became proficient in the ways of shebeen queens and jazz musicians, Isaac gained similar fluency in middle-class comportment.

The more educated a man was, and the longer he had been in town, the more likely his associations depended upon like interests and personal friendships rather than ethnic-based "homeboys'" networks. *Ooexcuse-me*, in general, formed one of the closest-knit African communities in Cape Town, primarily because there were relatively so few of them. The elements of their identity were fourfold, according to Isaac's indoctrination. Attire, for one, was extremely important, with a strong preference for suits, vests, ties, and top hats. They eschewed the flashier styles of dress favored by lesser-educated blacks, who were heavily influenced by American gangster movies: zoot suits, two-tone shoes, and pencil mustaches. The *ooexcuse-me* class had a penchant for conservatism. Much time was expended conferring on which type of shirt collar, or tie pattern, or cuff width, purchased at which stores, best represented the aesthetic ideals of the group. Even minor variations were cause for concern.

A global perspective was a second feature of class affiliation. The lives of the lower classes may be consumed by the struggles of the moment, but *ooexcuse-me* cultivated the capacity to transcend time and space. They incessantly read newspapers, listened to radio news broadcasts, and attended lectures by other elites. They discussed the latest proclamations of world leaders, cricket scores from the West Indies, aviation records from America, and theatrical production from the Royal Albert in London; all with equal fluency and urgency, all as if it actually mattered in the progression of their own lives.

The nature of one's abode was, likewise, critical to membership in the *ooexcuse-me* class. For men such as Jake Ndumba, home was simply an efficient pad from which to launch one's assault on the world each morning, the dark den to which female prey might be lured in the evening, and the place to recuperate in between. For the *ooexcuse-me* class, however, home was a monument to middle-class sensibilities. It had to reflect erudition and urbanity. It had to be stuffed with stylish furniture, real china, fine photographs, books, and the largest radio one could afford. The home had to reflect a concern for emerging notions of beauty, an appreciation for neatly trimmed yards with flowers, splashes of color, carefully draped cloth, and collections of bric-a-brac carefully displayed to catch the eyes of guests and to move a conversation along. Tea, elegantly served, was the preferred liquid stimulant of *ooexcuse-me,* rather than the *skokiaan* and *isiqataviku* ("kill me quick") of those attached to shebeen life.

Fourth, *ooexcuse-me* domestic relations stood in sharp contrast to those of other classes. Neither polygyny nor out-of-wedlock relations were acceptable. Notions of social and economic equality between husbands and wives were more widely adopted. Frequently both worked, and both contributed to childcare and maintenance of the household. They made joint financial plans and supported one another's intellectual pursuits and business initiatives. The spatial separation of the sexes in public that characterized rural life was moderated by the *ooexcuse-me*. Husbands and wives might walk side by side to church and other social events, and they might even be seen dining together in public restaurants.

The two friends from Matonchi Plateau—Jake, the exuberant one, and Isaac, the quiet one—worked together on the docks in South Africa. Yet, each night they disappeared into separate worlds or, again more aptly, different corners of the same world. They coordinated their efforts at remaining in touch with those back home, sending a steady stream of text, written and oral, northward via chains of returning migrant workers. They, in turn, shared and savored each juicy morsel of information about Matonchi that found its way south. Jake and Isaac managed to stay reasonably well apprised of births and deaths, new laws, and changing political fortunes on the plateau. Likewise, Jake and Isaac's stories were widely circulated, critically examined, and deeply mined for useful details, particularly by those intent upon venturing forth from the plateau. The words, the themes, and the lessons embedded in the stories of Jake and Isaac were constant companions of those raised on the plateau. To witness the actual performance of those stories by the lead characters, however, would require decades of patience.

Isaac's tales sent to the plateau from South Africa in many ways paralleled those of Jake. There is virtually no mention of the tension and turmoil that must have plagued the lives of blacks in South Africa. Rather he focused solely on the opportunities available. For Isaac, life in South Africa was a picnic; more specifically, a Sunday picnic on Table Mountain. The routes to the top via winding paths or cable cars, the proliferation of wild king protea flowers, the scurrying rock dassies (curious mammals eager for handouts), the blue mountain range to the east, and the bay below are elements of the South African landscape emblazoned on the consciousness of all at Matonchi. The details of past picnics dominated Isaac's letters while he was away and his oral presentations upon return to the plateau. Interestingly, Isaac's near obsession with picnics would stimulate the thinking of younger Lunda and provide them the rudimentary framework of a new social institution.

Wubwambu (friendship) differs in fundamental ways from other relations, most notably in its paucity of ritual embellishment. The broad arrays of ascribed and achieved relations that make up the Lunda world of connections are, for the most part, inseparable from well-established sets of rituals for periodically marking, manifesting, and intensifying those relationships. Weddings, funerals, coming-of-age ceremonies, curing rites, induction into hunter societies, even contemporary church baptisms and ordinations all contain elements that publicly point out the relations between individuals, make explicit the rights and duties embedded in those relations, and envelop the connection in an aura of timelessness, sanctioned by God, the ancestors, or the vital force of the group. Collections of friends endeavor to use style as a marker of their relationship, developing distinctive jargon, manner of greeting, modes of dress, and so forth. But these stylistic features lack the animating power of more deeply entrenched rituals. Thus, *mapikiniki* (the picnic) has been emerging for some time as a term, a set of activities, and, indeed, a ritual of cohesion and intensification of friendship. It contains the standard features of all rituals: a symbolic separation from mundane life, a reincorporation at the end, and a liminal phase of peculiar conduct in the middle. As yet, however, its symbols remain unsaturated, its format actively under construction.

Adopting and transforming the picnic into a Lunda ritual of intensification requires the creation of new aesthetics: new notions about pleasant arrangements of people, places, purposes, and, of course, food. Should the picnic be single or dual sex? What is the ideal number of individuals to invite? Who to include, who to exclude? Where should it be held? Certainly at a pretty place, but what, precisely, constitutes a "pretty" place? The Lunda may have held widely shared notions about a good place for planting, or an ideal site for a homestead, or even a majestic spot to hold court, but they had a rather underdeveloped notion of a landscape that is simply beautiful to sit in, stare at, or peer from. Surely decades of interaction with Europeans had hinted at a different aesthetic. The Fishers, the Pattersons, and others had invariably chosen to build on the highest spot in their respective territories. However, for the Lunda, hewers of wood and drawers of water, these places were excessively cold and windy, and ridiculously far from the river. But Europeans could hire water carriers and were perhaps ill suited to life in the steamy river valleys. The selection of hilltops, some thought, was simply a matter of pragmatism. But those such as Bug and Towel must have witnessed Mr. and Mrs. Patterson gazing at the sunset, night after night, with rapt attention. Surely they would have led the speculation about which particular arrangements of land and sky, rocks and rivers, were deemed "pretty" according to European sensibilities. Those who had perhaps seen a few American or European movies in town could also contribute to the discussion. But Isaac was acknowledged by all to have mastered the topic.

The proper food for a picnic is still an area open for experimentation. The alimentary fare at most Lunda rituals varies from that of everyday meals solely by quantity. Huge mounds of *nshima*, boiled cassava flour, accompanied by assorted stewed meat and vegetable dishes were the invariable offering. Such a meal requires two weeks of preparation time. One had to dig up cassava roots, soak them in the river a week, peel and pound them to a pulp, dry and sun-bleach them for a week, pound them to a flour, sift and boil them while stirring vigorously. Vegetables and meats would require their own tedious rounds of preparation to move them from vine and hoof, respectively, to the cooking pot. Feast days were characterized by labor-intensive, time-consuming activities that separated men and women for most of the day into different cooperative spheres. Songs, storytelling, and other forms of amusement would no doubt add a festive air to the preparatory work. It was also an opportunity to share news, knowledge, technical tips, and perhaps feelings about recent events, all within strictly gendered spaces. Meals tend to be served toward the end of a ceremonial day, with diners divided into clusters by age and sex.

To those raised with Lunda notions of a feast, a picnic presents a series of challenges. Food, as a central element of a picnic, must be "good" food. But it must also be portable and easily prepared. It cannot send men to one corner and women to another. Unfortunately, Lunda cuisine is wholly unsuited to the task. Local fast food consists mostly of roasted roots, chewed on solely to keep hunger pangs at bay until *nshima,* "real" food, arrives. Fruits offer some possibilities, but they could not provide the basis of an acceptable meal. Isaac would add to the local alimentary options the results of South African experimentation: sandwiches and canned sausages, barbecues and bean dishes, casseroles and cakes, cheeses and chocolates. These items, being difficult and expensive to obtain in Zambia and requiring a cultivation of the palate to fully appreciate, make excellent symbolic objects for cementing friendships. They lend the picnic an ambiance of august modernity, the investment elevating Amabwambu to a status of the highest order. Few members of the senior genealogical generation understood this urgent desire of the young to assemble at "pretty" places for the purpose of consuming rare and costly foods. But Isaac did. Having lived the majority of his life among friends rather than kin, dependent upon relationships chosen rather than those assigned, he was cognizant of the power of newly constructed rituals to solidify a newly constructed social world. His awareness of and contribution to this emerging reality on the plateau would endear him greatly to the younger generation.

In Cape Town Isaac met and married his soul mate, Nellie, a woman whose yearning for education and gentility rivaled his own. She was a Xhosa speaker, sufficiently light brown to "pass" as a Cape Coloured. Until 1953, members of this ethnic category retained the right to vote in Cape elections. Even after the franchise was revoked, they retained certain freedoms of movement, residence, and employment that those deemed pure African were denied. Isaac and Nellie took full advantage of this ambiguity to enrich their lives, to place their seven children in better schools, to shop in more stylish stores, and, of course, to picnic in prettier spots. Isaac returned to Mwinilunga with the quiet dignity of an elderly patrician: well fed, impeccably dressed, and with a graciously mannered family. He exuded success. Unlike Jake, he did not quickly dissipate his wealth on the plateau, but rather built a fine house in the Boma, forty miles away, started a little tea shop and tailoring business, hiring family and friends to do most of the work. He cultivated contacts among district government officials, merchants, and church leaders, and became a well-respected member of Boma society. He visited the plateau regularly but managed to avoid being drawn into local intrigue, feuds, and disputes, behaving nobly toward all and receiving similar treatment in return. When Senior Headman Kankinza, the last Chifunga of the *ankaka* generation died in 1984, it was time for the *ataata* generation to step forward and claim leadership on Matonchi Plateau. Isaac Nkemba was by far the popular choice, even though he was not actually residing on the plateau at the time. Initially he rejected the idea of acceding to the Chifungaship, acutely aware of the temporal, emotional, and economic demands of the job. As senior headman he would no longer be able to avoid the problems of others, but would be expected to insert himself forthwith in search of a solution. After months of pressure from his classificatory brothers and age mates, continual flattery for his accomplishments, and appeals to his sense of duty, a plan emerged that would allow Isaac to become Chifunga while not totally abandoning the life he had so carefully pieced together in the Boma. He would construct a new house and divide his time equally between the plateau and the Boma.[20] Isaac's presence on Matonchi would infuse the area with a sense of style and grace and a feeling of connectedness to the larger world. His widely acknowledged erudition would lend an air of refinement to local problem solving. His urbane demeanor would be a source of pride for all who could claim association.

Isaac intended to benefit from the arrangement as well. The services of a senior headman are generally rewarded with gifts of labor and local produce. Isaac would use those resources in establishing a large farm at Matonchi, sending commodities to be sold at his shop in the Boma. There was always a ready market for cassava and fresh vegetables. Additionally, the plateau was well situated to do business in game meat, *chituba* (cane rat), honey, and other forest products, not all of which were strictly legal and thereby were extremely profitable. Isaac's ability to imagine a life that connected Plateau and Boma was accentuated by his personal concept of distance, cultivated by years of life in South Africa. The Boma was only forty miles away, a distance he and many South Africans had commuted daily. Although no mode of motorized transportation connected plateau and Boma yet, Isaac dreamed of possessing an automobile someday. In the meanwhile, he would travel by bicycle.

Isaac was enthroned as Chifunga with a full week of pomp and pageantry. Things went well for the first few years, but then he was plagued by a series of tragic events. One son committed suicide, another died of AIDS, and a third was constantly involved in petty theft around the villages. Isaac himself suffered long bouts of illness. Witchcraft, resulting from jealousy, was suspected of being at the heart of his adversity. By the mid-1990s, with advancing years and failing health, Isaac could no longer travel back and forth regularly on his bicycle. He chose to live virtually full-time on the plateau, primarily because he increasingly lacked the resources to stock his business in the Boma, and hence the headmanhip became his principle source of security.

In the late 1990s a shadowy collection of white South Africans was moving about in northwestern Zambia, ostensibly looking to invest in a series of small village shops. Upon hearing of Isaac's time in South Africa, meeting him, and speaking with him in Afrikaans, they advanced him nearly five thousand kwacha worth of goods to set up a store on Matonchi Plateau.[21] Many locals suspected that the South Africans' involvement with village shops was simply a cover for their true business: smuggling diamonds out of neighboring Angola. Some were disappointed by Isaac's association with such unsavory characters. Others were simply disappointed that he did not offer credit on commodities more generously. In any event, headmanship and shopkeeping do not make a good match. Fewer and fewer people took their problems to Isaac, slowing the flow of tribute and thereby deepening his dependence on the shop. Increasingly Isaac's reputation became tarnished, his utility diminished, his clothes threadbare, and his stories repetitive. Isaac had mastered the ways of the world and brought them back to Matonchi. The plateau had now nearly consumed Isaac, leaving him wizened and forlorn. But much of what he was and what he realized has been absorbed and transcended by the succeeding generation.

Those Who Went Back and Forth: Waylesi the Piece Worker

Chifunga village, as noted earlier, is actually a cluster of separate villages abutting one another on Matonchi Plateau. The spatial integrity and political autonomy of each is respected by the others. It is only the historically portentous position of Chifunga that makes of the cluster something greater than the sum of its parts. This senior headmanship is well known throughout Lundaland, has attracted able leaders over the years, and has served to forge pan-village cooperation on an impressive scale. Yet, individual villages remain important for setting limits, opening up opportunities, and generally establishing the tone of one's daily life. Some villages are big and sprawling, others tight and cluttered. Some can be characterized as harmonious, energetic, and prosperous. Others may appear contentious, indolent, and impoverished. Waylesi was born into a village more like the former. With a large cooperating female work force, there was never a shortage of freshly pounded cassava flour or fresh greens and beans to serve as relish. A large complement of males amply supplied the village with meat and other forest products, kept the houses in fine repair, and periodically entered the world of cash employment to supply the village with cloth, soap, salt, sugar, cooking oil, and other commodities increasingly deemed necessities. By all accounts the village was a bustling place with a critical mass of skilled individuals, functioning almost as a world unto itself. Among its members were talented musicians, singers, dancers, beer brewers, and storytellers, making it a fun place to which even nonmembers gravitated to pass their leisure time.[22] At the risk of conjuring up overly romantic images of a "merrie olde Africa," Waylesi's memories of his childhood were indeed full of warm and cozy imagery, never experiencing hunger, fear, or loneliness, surrounded and protected on all sides by doting relatives. Surely, the historical record reminds us that this was a time of great uncertainty—the consolidation of colonial overrule, constraints on physical movement, labor conscription, the burden of taxation, an influx of European settlers, and overall colonial meddling in African affairs. Yet, within the embrace of Waylesi's village one could forget, for long stretches of time, the imperatives of the outside world or imagine them less onerous and intrusive than they actually were.

It would seem that Waylesi's life strategies were guided by a desire to keep his childhood dreams alive and to create for his own offspring a social space similar to the one that nurtured him. He showed little interest in conquering the larger world and transforming himself as Jake and Isaac did. Nor did he demonstrate much interest in nestling up close to the Pattersons, recasting himself in accordance with their notions of African propriety in exchange for steady remuneration as Bug, Table, and Towel did. Perhaps he lacked the intellectual facility and the social flexibility of the former group. Perhaps be lacked the innate curiosity and the acquired foresight of the latter. But perhaps he was simply more contented with his present circumstances, more comfortable with his current persona, and more assured of his capacity to construct a gratifying future than members of the other groups. Waylesi, certainly in later life, exuded a quiet confidence and an air of serenity that rivaled the comportment of any of his peers within the *ataata* cohort. Likewise, between the barefoot days of his youth and his accession to the headmanship of a large and stable village lies a life as rich and full as any on the Matonchi Plateau.

The necessity of cash was an inescapable reality for the *ataata* generation. A large cooperative village could easily achieve self-sufficiency in food and shelter, diversion and stimulation. But twentieth-century life required much that could be acquired only with European currency. For the males of Waylesi's village, periodically venturing forth in search of cash was a rite of passage, a self-sacrificial act undertaken for the betterment of the larger community. With the help of Bug and others, Waylesi would secure the occasional "piecework" with the Pattersons—a clearly delineated task in exchange for a specified amount of money, no matter how long the task took to complete and with no continuing obligation implied between worker and employer after completion. Once, he was hired to build fences for cattle paddocks. In another instance he was contracted to plant hundreds of mango tree saplings on a terraced hillside. On still another occasion he was paid to hollow out a fifteen-foot-high termite mound to be used as a smoke house. In each case Waylesi barely understood the task at hand and thus had no way of knowing if he was doing a competent job. Erecting fence posts, cultivating orchards, and curing meat in enclosed spaces had not been part of his upbringing. He was forced to simply mimic every motion observed in the few examples presented before he was left to work alone. In later life he would joke about the time he stopped to scratch his balls every 30 seconds because his trainer had done so, with Waylesi thinking perhaps this was a white man's ritual to ensure the fertility of the fruit being planted. Ultimately it would not be the quality of his work but rather an ill-understood hostile response by the Pattersons to perhaps a look deemed insolent, a stride too haughty, or a demeanor of ingratitude that would send Waylesi searching elsewhere for piecework.

Waylesi's next foray for cash would lead him to Mutshatsha, a small town three days' walk north into southern Congo. The Benguela railway from the Angolan coast into Central Africa had only reached Chinguar on the Bihe Plateau when the Pattersons arrived in 1921. Many had speculated and hoped that the eastward extension of the railroad would run through Mwinilunga on its way to the Katangan and Northern Rhodesian copper mines. But engineering and political concerns pushed it northward into the Belgian Congo. When the new line was inaugurated in 1931, Mutshatsha had been selected as a major railroad maintenance center. As this was Lunda-speaking territory, it presented none of the linguistic and cultural challenges encountered by those traveling east and south. Indeed, over time, many young men from the Matonchi Plateau would find their way to Mutshatsha. Some would remain for extended periods, marry, raise families, and serve as host to kin coming up from the south. Work, for the most part, was plentiful. Although Luba was the preferred ethnic group for hard work and higher-paying mine jobs, Lunda had many job options as well. Managing and moving railroad supplies absorbed laborers by the hundreds. Track maintenance and ditch digging absorbed hundreds more. Some from Matonchi would draw upon their involvement with the Pattersons to present themselves as experienced cowboys, thereby moving to the front of the hiring line at local cattle ranches. Others would accept employment in the commercial agriculture sector as pickers and processors of crops destined to feed mineworkers. As the population of Mutshatsha expanded, opportunities opened in the wholesale and retail trades, food and lodging establishments, light manufacturing, and, of course, the various branches of the entertainment industry, legal and illegal. Mutshatsha was a hard-edged town, a crude and vulgar place where outbreaks of infectious disease were common, crime was high, and the pay was generally low. Those who survived Mutshatsha returned to the plateau with an aura of toughness, rather than with a veneer of worldliness. But for some, Mutshatsha remained the preferred destination. It offered flexible opportunities. One could virtually change jobs at will. And it did not require one to suffer angst over identity or hide one's origins. Quite the contrary, Mutshatsha was a Lunda place. Periodically Congo authorities would try to portray the Northern Rhodesian Lunda as the source of all that ailed Mutshatsha. Yet, most attempts to curtail their movement across the border were unsuccessful.

Waylesi would make nearly two dozen trips to Mutshatsha over the course of his life, trying his hand at as many different jobs, none of which he particularly enjoyed. Most trips were of a few months' duration in the dry season when agricultural duties on the plateau were at a minimum. However, the dry season happens to be the best time of the year for hunting, fishing, and honey gathering. Likewise, weddings, rites of passage, curing rituals, the visitation of distant kin, and the brewing of local alcohol are concentrated in the dry season, giving that time a distinctively festive atmosphere. These were activities Waylesi greatly enjoyed. Hence only rarely and with great reluctance would he spend an entire dry season away from the plateau. On nearly a dozen occasions Waylesi ventured further abroad to the Copperbelt and the capital city of Lusaka. These were long and torturous excursions where he experienced the full brunt of the abuse, castigation, and denigration that often characterized Lunda life in town. Occasionally he succeeded in sampling some of urban life's more seductive elements. Mostly he just survived. Nevertheless, he always managed to find piecework that paid significantly more than those jobs in Mutshatsha, and he returned safely to tell the tale to all on the plateau. The stories of town life by short-term residents such as Waylesi may not be as intense, as deeply felt, or even as deeply insightful as those of men such as Jake and Isaac. But their stories are always more timely, providing new gossip to stimulate fireside discussions, data on current market prices for those considering transporting goods to town, and insights on hiring trends for the potential job seeker. Recent returnees were also expected to provide entertainment through commentary on the latest music, films, and fashions. Indeed, it was their job to mediate the experiential gap between rural and urban dwellers. On one memorable occasion, circa 1950, Waylesi returned with the first wireless radio most on the plateau had ever seen. When he turned the dials on his battery-powered, saucepan shaped radio, and first voices and then music poured out, things changed forever. The first change was his name. That was the day, in fact, he became forever known as Waylesi (pronounced "y-less"), named after the miracle he had brought from town. Similarly his village was renamed "wireless" village, as it became a place of pilgrimage for the thousands desirous of hearing the magical box. Other changes would be slower in coming; changes in notions of time, space, connectedness, political identity, musical preferences, social propensities, and so forth. Bug, Table, and Towel had explored the outside world by penetrating deeply the inner space of the Patterson's private domain. Jake and Isaac had gone out, embraced the world, and brought it back embodied in their own personage. Waylesi had brought the outside world back in a box and played it nightly for all to hear. At least, that is, when batteries were available.

All three groups of the *ataata* generation led rich and fascinating lives. Their days may have been remarkably different in tone and style, pacing and productivity. Yet, in their later years, representatives of all three groups would find themselves back together on the plateau, having arrived at remarkably similar conclusions about the changing nature of the world and the enduring meanings of human existence. In many ways they tell one story, not three, for their lives were never fully disconnected. Those who led the more peripatetic existence, such as Waylesi, may have been in the statistical majority. They were the elastic connections that kept the *ataata* world one. They were the human transmitters, receivers, and amplifiers of stories meandering back and forth between the Cape and the Copperbelt, the plantations of Southern Rhodesia and the cattle ranches of Mutshatsha. It is noteworthy that a generation born into a world that predated the presence of telephones and postal systems and for the most part illiterate, nevertheless developed the capacity to remain in touch across the numerous decades and vast distances that physically separated them. In some respects the struggle to maintain this capacity is a reflection of a particular consciousness, of value placed on human connections. In other ways it is constitutive of that consciousness. All the *ataata* would come to recognize that the world is filled with weird and wonderful things, much that should be avoided but also much that is worthy of pursuit. All concurred that the future belongs to the educated. They thus collectively lobbied government officials for an increase in classrooms built and teachers assigned to the plateau. The *ataata* contributed substantially to raising school fees for the best and brightest youth, even at times by selling off livestock and other assets. Yet the *ataata* also knew that the world could be a hard place, and that traditional forms of social connections, cemented by rites of passage and acts of respect for the ancestors, could smooth the rough edges and ease the moments of despair. The *ataata* had withstood the continual condemnation of their identity and the vilification of their character. They had had to psychologically reconcile their pride of place and cultural accomplishments with the objective reality of the often far greater accomplishments of others. They had managed the disorientation that came with the realization, for example, that their most elaborate architecture was not very elaborate by world standards, that their most sophisticated cooking was not after all especially sophisticated, that their most renown heroes are not particularly well known globally, and that even their sex lives, according to Mr. Jake at least, were not among the world's sexiest.

Lunda sacrifices performed to communicate with the spirit world are of three varieties in a rigidly prescribed order: a chicken is always the first offering; then, if necessary, a goat; and, if further needed, a cow. It is said that a chicken, as a small irresistible morsel, is ideal for opening a crack to the spirit world. The goat pushes the crack open farther, and then the cow completely opens the doorway to the other world. We might meaningfully compare the Lunda generations to the chicken, goat, and cow vis-à-vis their respective roles in opening the door to the European world rather than spiritual world. The *ankaka* generation peeked through the crack and saw enough of Muzungu to make out the fuzzy outline of a new world. They put together some rather interesting composites of who the Muzungu were and what they wanted from Africans. The *ataata* generation, like the proverbial goat, pushed the door open farther. By working in Muzungu houses, farms, and factories, and even fighting in their wars, this generation was more fully capable of plotting the dimensions of the new world and assessing the skills needed to survive therein. In the next chapter we begin exploring the world of the cows, the Chifunga clique—those born on the steps of a door already slightly ajar.

Headman Chifunga in ceremonial attire with his classificatory brothers on Matonchi Plateau.

One of a dozen structures built by the Franciscan Friars that constitute Lwawu Catholic Mission.

(*Right to left*) Gabriel Katoka, Greenford Kataloshi, Noah Kataloshi (with daughter) and Kabanda. Leisure time on a Sunday afternoon by the waterfalls on the Lwawu River.

Stone Mafulo (*center*) contemplating a piece of music that will ultimately be added to the repertoire of the Catholic Church choir.

Elias Kangasa and son during one of the frequent quiet moments they spent together.

Noah Waylesi in rakish straw hat toasting the camera.

Recent arrivals from Angola in village of grass houses, bustling with productive activities.

Friends joking around over a bottle of hard liquor after work.

Ambitious young Godfrey Mukandenge showing off his radio, cigarette, new tie, and expanding crew of supporters.

Young Angolan aspiring to be a local big man.

Part Two

*A*MABWAMBU, OFFSPRING OF THE *ATAATA* GROUP AND the main focus of this text, are the Lunda's postwar generation. They hold much in common with their similarly labeled counterparts in Europe and the United States. Yet, they are products of and subsequent producers of a profoundly different social world. Their parents were no doubt affected by the war. Some had been impressed into service as supply carriers or generators of essential commodities. Yet few of the *ataata* had seen frontline action, Mr. Jake being a notable exception. Fewer still had probably experienced World War II as an apocalyptic struggle between good and evil, with group survival hanging in the balance. Nor are Amabwambu a "baby boom" generation, the inevitable outgrowth of pent-up biological urges to create life after the experience of so much life-taking, or the psychological need to repeople landscapes denuded by the unleashing of obscene destructive forces. The war did not radically change Lunda reproductive strategies, demographic patterns, or domestic relations. Nor did it reposition Mwinilunga within the global economy. Northwestern Zambia was as marginal a place after the war as it had been before the war.

Yet, some of the emergent social and technological phenomena that transformed postwar Europe and the United States also reached deep into the heart of Central Africa. The telecommunications revolution, shrinker of the space-time continuum, made its local impact through the efforts of the Central African Broadcasting Service (CABS). The proletarianization of education through the rapid expansion of public schooling manifested itself locally in the competitive construction of classrooms by expatriate Catholic and Protestant missionaries. Even the development of the Amabwambu group can be seen as the local corollary of the rise of youth subcultures in the West that challenged prevailing paradigms, questioned authority in general, and demanded greater social acceptance of individual style. Indeed, the cry for freedom in all its various guises, from personal liberty to ethnic autonomy to national independence, provides the unrelenting soundtrack framing the lives of Amabwambu.

The pages that follow are not biographical sketches of individual Amabwambu members. The focus is not on personal predilections or idiosyncratic inclinations. The aim, rather, is the search for shared consciousness that is forged out of shared experiences and the collectively constructed meanings assigned to those experiences. As often noted, consciousness is a slippery thing, no more easily grasped by the possessor than by the outside observer. Consciousness is essentially an interpretation of reality. It is the embodiment of experiences, the persistence of inborn propensities, and the basis of strategic and tactical engagement with the world. It can be observed in spontaneous reactions, conditioned reflexes, and well-thought-out responses to the contingencies of life. The Amabwambu, like groups of humans everywhere, must navigate their way through a world of preexisting structures. From parents and grandparents, affines and lineage elders, they were taught the proper relationships between humans and the environment, the individual and the group, men and women, the young and the old, the rich and the poor, "us" and the "other," the physical world and the metaphysical world. The notion of structure as webs of relations and their specific manifestations among the Lunda has been examined in detail elsewhere. Here we acknowledge that even as a generation of youth actively seeks to imbibe or embrace the grand traditions of the elders, it is also continually confronted with the contingent, the novel, and the socially unresolved. The pages that follow (1) sketch out the broad dimensions of the Lunda world of structure into which all the Amabwambu were born and through which they had to pass on their way toward developing their own unique consciousness; (2) present the historical array of new sociological phenomena that pressed in on the Lunda world, for which there was no preexisting collective interpretation, and hence tended to provoke uncertainly in all generations; and (3) provide snapshots of the quotidian, vignettes of daily life, and fragments of news-making events, some of which may ultimately mean very little, but that nevertheless at the moment of occurrence captivated local attention, stimulated local thought, informed local strategies, or at the time merely stood in ironic juxtaposition to life on the plateau. I eschew the temptation to overprocess and oversystematize the interaction between daily events and inherited traditions in the creation of consciousness. Certainly I propose no simple dyadic linkage of cause and effect, or experience and outcome. The complex interplay of facts, suppositions, extrapolations, imaginings, and feelings involved in the formation of consciousness is beyond the competency of this author to definitively sort out. I instead invite readers to join me in visiting the times, places, people, and processes that shaped the Amabwambu world and, to the degree that confidence permits, add their own interpretive spin to those suggested herein.

The Amabwambu are a group of roughly a dozen males, the core of which has remained remarkably stable for nearly four decades. Most were raised on or near Matonchi Plateau and acknowledge the Chifunga as their senior headman. Although core members may have a younger brother or cousin strongly affiliated with the group, membership for the most part is not based on kinship. These are males who shared significant early life experiences and developed similar or complementary tastes, values, habits, aims, and aspirations. They have long confided in one another, jointly experiencing life's most intimate joys and sorrows. They are mutual witnesses to each other's progressions through the cycles of life. They have grown up and are now growing old in each other's presence. And they do so primarily because they like one another. They are friends.

The Amabwambu are a unique local clique. First, they are a uniquely well-educated group, having been among the first classes trained by American Catholics, the Franciscan Friars at Lwawu Mission. Second, they possess uniquely strong entrepreneurial impulses. Honed and supported, again, by American Catholics, they have been at the forefront of experiments with cultivating new crops, processing old crops in novel ways, pioneering a range of new productive activities, and developing the networks for marketing nontraditional commodities and services. Third, as a result of these successes, many among the Amabwambu have become widely recognized as *mukulumpi*, elders or big men, at a far earlier stage of life than any in the previous generation. Some are well-known headmen in their own right, having founded large villages. Most have attracted a substantial personal following of junior males. Many in the older *ataata* generation now quietly defer to younger Amabwambu in the sponsorship of traditional rituals, in amassing bridewealth to assist junior males, and in legal dealings with government departments and international agencies.

The stalwarts of the Amabwambu clique include Kataloshi (whose name literally means "little long pants" because his grandfather supposedly defied Patterson by adopting this element of European style, and who is the shopkeeper near Lwawu Mission), Kapala (whose name means "the little impala," and who is the tractor driver for the mission), Katoka (sociable, well liked, ever ready with an amusing story but not as ambitious or as successful as the others), Mafulo (solid, hardworking, most dependable employee at the mission health clinic), and Kanasa (savvy straddler of tradition and modernity). The tales of this clique will, at times, be juxtaposed with the tales of others in their cohort group who trod a different path. Most notably, Benson and his clique stand as the archrivals of Amabwambu, although not necessarily in an overtly competitive or malicious manner. Indeed, there is much friendly intercourse between the two groups and demonstrable generational and territorial unity in the face of those from other times and places. But Benson represents an alternative set of perspectives on life, a differing approach to achieving big-manship. He has sought to position himself as a paragon of tradition, a champion of Lunda ways of knowing and doing. Benson prides himself on never having set foot in a Muzungu classroom, never having begged the missionaries for "piecework" to tide him over during lean times, and never having spent the day standing in line for medicines from the Catholic clinic to cure his ails. In a country where English is the official language, where even the most remote and illiterate villager makes a determined effort to master at least a few phrases, Benson refuses to utter a single syllable in English. Those who persist in speaking English in his presence are variously treated with condescension, suspicion, and outright contempt. Benson eschewed newfangled occupations and productive activities in favor of seeking his fortune the old-fashioned way, that is, by acquiring as many wives as possible, who with the help of numerous daughters generate a mountain of surplus food and brew beer for sale in their spare time; by siring many sons who hunt, trap, fish, and gather honey and other wild foods from the forest; and by converting any surplus cash immediately into trade goods, especially making strategic purchases of essential commodities, such as matches, soap, cigarettes, cooking oil, kerosene, candles, salt, seeds, and so forth. Benson is particularly well known for maneuvering to buy up all of a particular commodity and thereby inducing artificial shortages. Thus, if Benson has it, then probably no one else does. And the price is double the usual. Benson has cultivated a no-nonsense persona, rarely smiling or joking. His dreadful mien intimidates customers and kinsmen alike out of seeking better terms of trade or goods on credit. The size and obsequiousness of Benson's retinue camouflages his rather modest physical stature and has elevated him to the rank of big man far in advance of most of his contemporaries.

The heuristic framework selected to add order to the stories that follow consists of six historical moments. Although arranged somewhat in chronological sequence, it should be clear that they are not temporally discrete events. They overlap in their unfolding, draw meaning from one another, and collectively influence the outcome of subsequent events. Yet despite having fuzzy conceptual borders, each social phenomenon has a distinct analytical center, one that challenges or reaffirms the utility of preexisting presumptions and practices. As such, these six moments provide as good a perch as any from which to view the Amabwambu consciousness being shaped over time. The moments to be examined, in brief, are (1) the establishment and expansion of St. Kizito School at Lwawu Mission, (2) the introduction and spread of the saucepan radio, (3) the merger of Northern and Southern Rhodesia with Nyasaland to create the federation, (4) the Katanga succession in southern Congo, (5) the struggle for independence and the emergence of the new nation-state of Zambia, and (6) from one-party rule to neosubjugation by international financial institutions.

3

Coming of Age at St. Kizito

As toddlers, Amabwambu witnessed the decline of the Patterson Place and the rise of Lwawu Mission as the local portal to the Muzungu world. Mr. Patterson died in 1950, after having dominated events on Matonchi Plateau for nearly twenty-eight years. Mrs. Patterson continued on for a while, but without the energy and drive of earlier times. The Franciscan Order of Catholics, on the other hand, was brimming with vitality. It would expand its presence in western Zambia, directly engaging the previously unchallenged Plymouth Brethren in a not always friendly competition for Lunda hearts and souls. Lwawu Mission was selected as the vanguard of that thrust. As noted earlier, Fathers Rupert Hillerich and Adrian Peck, originally from the American Midwest but with four years of urban Copperbelt experience, arrived on Matonchi Plateau in 1951. At the invitation of Mrs. Patterson they completed the construction of a church on her property before year-end. When the relationship soured, and Fathers Rupert and Adrian were ejected three years later, they moved to a new site outside the limits of Patterson landholdings, near the Lwawu River.[1] The new area was sparsely populated with plenty of room for future expansion. The river would provide an ample supply of fresh water, and its rapids and waterfalls would provide the scenic beauty, the sine qua non of European habitats in Africa. In 1955 Brother Louis Fouquette and Father Gerard Scioscia were added to the crew at Lwawu. Brother Louis became the building specialist, overseeing the construction of a new church, house,

and kitchen. Father Gerard joined Father Adrian in translating Catholic cate-
chisms and hymns into the Lunda language. This group also brought into being
an ever-expanding number of out-stations, that is, village congregations under
local African leadership, with an itinerant expatriate Catholic priest periodically
hosting mass and communion. Scores of out-stations would be operational within
the first decade of Catholic proselytizing.

By 1958 Brother Louis had constructed a magnificent church of brick, cement,
and plaster, with a high cathedral ceiling, stained-glass windows, massive wooden
doors, elaborate altar, and religious relics, and capable of seating perhaps four
hundred parishioners. A five-bedroom friary with separate living room, kitchen,
and dining room, plus a detached dormitory capable of sleeping dozens more,
was completed in 1961.[2] A small clinic and a garage and workshop were built in
1962. Toward the end of the year, the era of Coleman lanterns and candles came to
a close at Lwawu with the installation of a three-thousand-volt generator. In years
to come the largest medical facility in southern Mwinilunga would be constructed
at Lwawu, along with a convent to host a group of Baptistine Sisters who would
staff the new clinic.[3] Buildings of various types would continue to sprout up on
the landscape. The rumble of cars, trucks, and tractors and the screech of mills
and motorized tools would increasingly dominate the local soundscape. The
Lwawu River was dammed in the 1970s, and a hydroelectric plant generating fifty
thousand volts was installed in the 1980s.

The Plymouth Brethrens' justification for establishing economic enterprises
in Africa had been to compensate for the absence of a home organization capable
of financing mission activities. Each of their stations, thus, became a successful island of entrepreneurship, or it withered away over time. Clearly the Catholics
could make no such claim. Being part of the most centrally organized and best-
financed missionary moment in history, they could have funded all local activities with foreign resources. Yet, in Mwinilunga they followed many of the practices pioneered by the Brethren. For the Catholics, involvement in local economic
life was simply one more strategic tool for capturing the attention of potential
converts and for bestowing benefits on the already converted. There was a barely
submerged assumption that concrete demonstrations of Catholic mastery over
the material world would convince Africans to take more seriously Catholic
teachings about the spiritual domain. Additionally, expatriate Catholics desired
as their legacy a network of African Catholic communities, capable of building
and maintaining their own church premises, recruiting and educating their own
clergy and lay leaders, and ultimately sending out their own missionaries to lands
not yet touched by the word of God. It was clear that the economically depressed
conditions in Mwinilunga would have to be ameliorated substantially before any
of this could come to fruition. The place to start, it was generally agreed, was

with the creation of a vanguard group of young Africans whose educational and economic attainments would validate the possibilities of developing indigenous Christian leadership, demonstrate the methods by which this could be accomplished, and thereby fire the imagination and secure the continued support of far-flung Catholic communities extending from Rome to Midwest America. Amabwambu would be part of that vanguard. A meeting of the minds and spirits took place between a group of energetic and idealistic young Americans, and an even younger but equally enthusiastic group of African males. A covenant was sealed, not in writing, but no less fervently embraced for the lack of paper and ink.

Fathers Rupert and Adrian had laid the groundwork while residing at the Patterson Place with the establishment of Matonchi Lower Primary School in 1952. Rather than bring the students to them, however, they built the small clay and straw thatch classroom a mile away, amid the cluster of villages that then constituted Senior Chief Kanongesha's *nganda* (capital village). This act perhaps contributed to Mrs. Patterson's rescission of sponsorship of Catholic activities. As additional context it should be noted that Mwinilunga has for nearly half a century been an arena of contestation between a double dichotomy: things American and Catholic versus things British and Protestant. As in most struggles, the need for clear lines of engagement at times supersede the need for accuracy. For in truth, some of the Catholics who contributed to the development of Lwawu Mission and its out-stations were British, as well as Irish, Italian, German, Swiss, and Dutch. Likewise, some of the Brethren were Canadian and Australian. But Lwawu received much of its financial and material support, as well as personnel, from a diocese that straddled the Ohio-Indiana border. Hence, its buildings, environs, and all who dwelt therein were saturated with a mid-American ambiance and ethos. Concomitantly, the Commonwealth connections of the various Brethren missionaries provided them with a unifying set of symbols that contrasted significantly with American ways of being. One substantive distinction between the two camps, again greatly oversimplified, was their respective convictions about the role of education. The Brethren, for the most part, cultivated anti-intellectualist sentiments. They eschewed studies in literature, art, philosophy, and the humanities in general. "Book learning" was only necessary as far as it enabled one to read and to interpret for oneself God's word as presented in the Bible. Any other educational pursuit that did not focus on the acquisition of concrete and useful skills was an exercise in vanity. The network of schools set up by the Brethren in Mwinilunga was informed by this principle. Three or four years of classroom work was deemed more than sufficient for Africans, after which they were channeled into the building, farming, or healing trades.

Logic alone might suggest that a religious community based on producing individual exegetes (the Brethren) would place greater emphasis on developing a lively mind than would a religion based on obedience to ecclesiastical authority and rigid adherence to ritual practices (the Catholics). Yet this was not the case in Mwinilunga. Perhaps this outcome had more to do with individual eccentricities than with denominational differences. Father Adrian, in particular, established a direction, a tone, and a style of engagement on Matonchi Plateau that would characterize and guide the Catholic educational thrust for decades to come. Father Adrian admitted that prior to his arrival in Northern Rhodesia he had but limited expectations for the learning capacity of Africans. His early interactions with African students, however, convinced him otherwise. He soon realized that African youth were every bit as apt, ingenious, and intellectually well endowed as the students he had taught in Ohio for seven years. Additionally, Africans were far more enthusiastic and appreciative when provided with opportunities, far more attentive and obedient in the classroom, and far more respectful and gracious when addressing those who instruct them. Father Adrian also thought he saw in Africans an innate spirituality, an inherent appreciation for a world beyond the physical, and a deeply embedded urge to seek out life's moral path and to contest evil in all its forms. Africans would not only make good Christian converts; indeed, they would make good Christian warriors battling on behalf of and thereby adding to the strength of the global Christian community. He aimed to educate his new charges as broadly and profoundly as his resources would allow. Father Adrian would spend thirty-six years in Northern Rhodesia/Zambia and would come to be regarded by many in his order as the finest missionary ever sent to that region.[4] To the people of Mwinilunga he would become Kanzayanga, the faithful guide to a new world and way of thinking—one who would assuredly act on behalf of the people, even if it brought him into conflict with other Muzungu. Perhaps Father Adrian's most significant contribution was his sustained efforts to improve local education. The lower primary school was a fine introduction to the world of formal education, but much more was needed.

After a decade of thought and planning, St. Kizito School came into being in 1963 as an upper primary boarding school for boys, principally for those leaving the Matonchi lower primary school and for Catholic boys from other missions who might be interested in joining the Franciscan Order. Brother Joseph Weissling from Ohio, who had taught on the Copperbelt for five years, was tapped as first headmaster. Out of the first intake of twenty-four students to enter grade five, six became teachers (one a primary school headmaster and another a deputy headmaster), one went to college in the United States and then joined the Psychological Testing Services at the University of Zambia, three joined the Zambian Army, reaching the rank of major at last contact, one went on to study in the USSR, several became successful businessmen in town, and so forth.[5] Throughout the school's existence students at St. Kizito routinely exceeded the pass ratio on national standardized exams by over 100 percent.[6] Their performance was so spectacular that the school was formally investigated on several occasions, being suspected of impropriety, such as somehow gaining access to exam questions prior to official testing dates. Yet the fame of St. Kizito spread throughout the nation. By the mid-1970s the president of an independent Zambia enrolled his youngest son at St. Kizito. Immediately thereafter, the new Zambian elite descended en masse upon Lwawu Mission with their children in tow, attempting to buy, bribe, or bully their way into St. Kizito. Brother Joe chose to phase out the school altogether rather than allow its original mission to be subverted.

The Amabwambu were one class removed from the first intake. By all accounts they were a bright group, but they neither scored well enough on exams to garner a college scholarship nor were interested in joining the Franciscan Order. All have spent stretches of time on the Copperbelt but have a clear preference for life around the mission. They were fortunate to pass through St. Kizito at an amazing point in its history. The glitches of the first class had been worked out, and the young, mostly American staff was brimming with energy, charged with enthusiasm for a noble experiment. St. Kizito was not simply a boarding school, but was a total immersion experience. In theory, English was the national language of instruction and testing throughout Zambia. Yet in many day schools teachers spent the overwhelming majority of the time addressing students in their indigenous tongue, throwing in the occasional English phrase. Government-run boarding schools offered students more time away from the distractions of village life, linguistic and otherwise, but for the most part they were staffed with nonnative speakers of English. Exposure rather than fluency was the best they could offer. Thus, students tended to flounder on English-based exams, with less than one in four being selected to continue schooling after each level of national testing. St. Kizito was different, however. English was the only language permitted, and students were monitored at all times to ensure that the reality conformed to the rule. Young staff members such as Brothers Joe, Bryan, and Tony remained with their charges around the clock. Whether the boys were sleeping, eating, studying, or playing, there was always a Franciscan brother in the mix. Even in later life one can identify a St. Kizito boy by his mastery of English with the fluency, cadence, and lexicon of a native Midwest American. Yet, they were immersed not only in the sounds of Americana but in its cultural accouterments as well. They learned the intricacies of baseball, football, and basketball, rather than the cricket, rugby, and soccer that were standard recreational fare at other Zambian schools. They were fed, if not outright fattened, on American cuisine, regularly finding pancakes and syrup, hotdogs and hamburgers, and steak and potatoes on the dining hall table. The mission's support network back in Ohio and Indiana provided a steady stream of used clothing and donations of factory irregulars. St. Kizito boys, thus, even dressed as their American counterparts. At worst they may have been a season or two out of fashion by U.S. standards, but that still qualified them as trendsetters nonpareil on the local stage. Someone in the mission support group had a connection with a T-shirt factory in Texas. Lwawu was thus flooded with clothes emblazoned with "Aggies" and "Longhorns" logos, as well as others that sported commercial catch phrases intelligible only to consummate consumers of American television. With electricity and a thirty-foot radio antenna St. Kizito could provide its students daily access to the world beyond. Boys back in the village might sit around the campfire after dark being entertained by tales of the elders, constructing impromptu plays, or, if batteries were available, listening to a scratchy broadcast from the capital on a saucepan radio. St. Kizito boys, conversely, could simply flip a switch, turn night into day, finish up their homework, play cards or board games (Monopoly being a favorite), and read the most recent newspapers and magazines from America, all while the shortwave radio brought them the latest music and news from around the world. Alternatively, they could sample new country western records on the phonograph, practice some guitar cords with Brother Bryan, work on their typing with Brother Joe, learn more about photography from Brother Tony, or rerun the latest film acquisition on the house movie projector. Those must have been intoxicating times for young boys from the village. But all of the above are but elements of style, the veneer of consciousness. The real impact of the St. Kizito experience on the consciousness of Kataloshi, Kapala, Katoka, Mafulo, Kanasa, and others emerged from its interaction with other agents of upbringing. The core messages emanating from St. Kizito variously contested and complemented those that characterized the traditional village worldview.

Too Many New Mouths to Feed

C.A.P. REPORTER

Tomorrow morning there will be another 80 or 90 thousand new mouths to feed in the world adding to the present overpopulation, and in particular in Africa this is the psychological time to discuss family planning.

This was said at Lusaka Rotary Club's weekly luncheon yesterday by the guest speaker, Miss Edith Gates, who has for years worked on family planning programmes in many parts of the world.

(*Central African Post,* April 13, 1959, p. 3)

The Franciscans brought with them to Mwinilunga a distinctly Midwestern sensibility about the relationship between people and land. They had grown to maturity observing a landscape, flat and fertile, extending to the horizon with immaculately maintained rows of corn, soybeans, wheat, or barley. It was land that through careful management could reward its owners with hundreds of bushels of a saleable commodity per acre, land that could sustain extended families for generations, providing each with a better life than the previous. The intense greens of the Mwinilunga rainy season led the Franciscans to overestimate the fertility of local soils. The bleak arid browns of the dry season, they reasoned, could be easily overcome with irrigation. Management was the key in any event. Yet, many of the Franciscan's early forays into agriculture, like those of other expatriates, failed miserably. Their attention was at times diverted toward other projects. Brother Tony, for example, began to experiment with fishponds in the late 1960s. In the early 1970s experiments with game ranching began with the donation of fifteen impalas from the government Game Department. Nevertheless, confidence remained high that with hard work, common sense, and the judicious application of science, agriculture would ultimately triumph.

Since the 1950s, much has been learned about the fragility of tropical and subtropical soils. Mwinilunga, additionally, is part of a geological region that suffered a cataclysmic upheaval, convoluting the substrata and bringing to the surface oscillating bands of clay, loam, and sandy soils that switch places every few yards. The land is rugged and rocky with heavy metallic content. The humus layer is generally thin with overall soil fertility varying from poor to extremely poor. It rains everyday for nearly half the year, and virtually not at all the other half. Little about Midwest American farming is applicable to local conditions. The Franciscans thus increasingly placed their faith in the agricultural science being generated in Central Africa. They listened and recorded CABS radio broadcasts by the Ministry of Agriculture and collected brochures from the agricultural extension services. They lobbied continually and ultimately successfully for the placement of an agricultural extension officer at Lwawu Mission, for whom the Franciscans built a house and provided transportation and communication services. With generous support from home, the Franciscans were able to buy two tractors and hire labor gangs to remove rocks and tree stumps and to level an expanse of ground making it suitable for machine plowing. They experimented with the latest hybrid seeds and newly developed chemical fertilizers, pesticides, and herbicides. It was a determined effort to demonstrate the human capacity to master nature, to establish the viability of modern farming practices, and, indeed, to give impetus to an agricultural revolution in Mwinilunga that presumably their students would lead. The Mission's agricultural thrust received such a continual infusion of overseas cash and materials that it is difficult to ascertain if it ever actually achieved a state of self-sufficiency or sustainability. Regardless, it managed to create a wonderful impression, particularly on the impressionable minds of young students. The mission grounds were increasingly covered with a neatly trimmed Kentucky bluegrass hybrid, stands of swaying pine and eucalyptus trees, and sprays of red poinsettias and purple bougainvillea. Fruit orchards and irrigated vegetable gardens generated the produce to counterbalance the heavy meat-laden mission diet. And just beyond view, rows of maize saturated with chemicals managed to overcome all the obstacles and sprout their golden ears.

The students at St. Kizito were simultaneously bombarded with idyllic images of modern farms in American magazines and movies, receiving regular encouragement from national radio broadcasts to pursue modern methods while also being daily witnesses to the outcome of Catholic agricultural experimentation. From huge midwestern silos to Copperbelt storehouses to local Catholic granaries, maize and modernity provided visible evidence of surplus accumulation that appeared to greatly exceed that possible via the Lunda's traditional cultivation methods.

As the classes of St. Kizito students who did not head off to college or pursue town careers returned to the village in search of economic opportunity, the mission convinced the National Agricultural Marketing Board (NAMBOARD), a parastatal organization with the exclusive mandate to provide agricultural inputs and to purchase crops nationwide, to establish a collection depot at Lwawu. The mission constructed and maintained the physical facilities for NAMBOARD, primarily because it gave a boost to local agriculture by allowing young farmers to buy improved seeds, tools, fertilizer, and other inputs, as well as to sell their surplus locally, circumventing the need to transport commodities to the Boma or beyond. In time the mission took to renting out one of its two tractors to local farmers, as well as purchasing an electric mill to grind maize into flour and a press to extract oil from sunflower seeds to encourage the production of those crops. The mission had a vested interest in the economic success of its young protégés. Any amount of personal and organizational investment was deemed justifiable as long as it moved that group one step further along the road toward modernity.

World Acclaim for Russians

The moon is "Red"

MOSCOW, SAPA-REUTER

Russia's hammer-and-sickle was firmly planted on the moon today after a 233,600-mile journey through space.

The Soviet emblem, rocketed to the moon in a "flying laboratory," is believed to be lying between the Sea of Serenity, the Sea of Vapours and the Sea of Tranquility—a triangular area to the upper right of the centre.

Russia's Lunik II hit the moon two minutes 24 seconds after 11 p.m. South African time after being separated from the last stage of its carrier rocket.

(*Central African Post,* September 14, 1959, p. 5)

On the surface one could identify a seamless logical thread linking national radio and mission messages about land. Both argued strongly in favor of stability of land tenure and the application of scientific management. The mission was, in fact, unique among local social groups in having pursued and secured formal title to its property. But over time, the mission would come to realize what the Lunda had long known, that movement and segmented landholdings were the most effective tools for dealing with highly variable levels of soil fertility. The mission found itself planting maize on one spot for two or three years and then, after declining yields, forced to seek out fresh soils. Likewise, mission personnel began to pay closer attention to the specific attributes of the red, black, and brown soils that invariably commingled in every garden plot. Over time, the borders of the mission became increasingly Africanized as specific crops followed ribbons of fertility and soil types across the landscape. Hence, in many ways the gap between mission and tradition was not so great after all.

With regard to the relationship between the individual and the group, the St. Kizito experience reaffirmed rather than contradicted prevailing beliefs. The Lunda social world provides wide latitude for individual expression while producing dense matrices of nested and overlapping social groupings. On the one hand, people are given much control over the timing and pacing of their own lives. Babies are fed whenever hungry, allowed to sleep whenever tired. A child is sent to school whenever he or she begins to demonstrate an interest in learning. Boys are sent through maturation rites when they begin to behave as men, be that twelve or twenty years old. One can assume responsibilities early in life, marry, have children, begin to take care of one's parents, and join the ranks of community leaders while still quite young. Or, one can delay the assumption of such responsibility until late in life. Additionally the Lunda individual is given much freedom of choice in deciding which social groupings are most meaningful at each particular stage of life and which will hence absorb proportionately more of that individual's time and attention. Society provides a rich array of options. The household, the village, the lineage, the in-laws, the hunting cult, the curing society, and the cohort are all groups within which individuals can choose to comfortably ensconce themselves.[7] But if these groupings are to exist in useable form, to be viable systems of support and security when needed, then one's relationship with that group must be kept active, carefully cultivated and nurtured through demonstrable social acts. The precise mix of relationships in which an individual chooses to invest his or her time, emotions, and physical energy may vary over the life cycle, as new opportunities emerge, and old opportunities take on new meaning. These groupings are, in a sense, the raw material out of which the individual sculpts a life of connections. Groups vary in the demands they make on members and in the rights and privileges they confer in return. This plethora of opportunities for developing connections mediates against the need for conformity to one particular pattern of behavior, thought, or action. The individual is free to develop his or her own unique personal style while simultaneously pursuing productive and comfortable connections. The social system as a whole can be characterized as one that promotes the passionate drive to protect individual autonomy while endeavoring to build up widespread linkages.

The St. Kizito experience added new layers of possibilities to an old conceptual matrix. Classmates, "old boys," and fellow alumni make potentially useful allies. In the case of Amabwambu they became good friends and partners for life. Beyond the local context, however, a larger world of connective possibilities radiated outward from St. Kizito. The mastery of English and the mantle of Catholicism placed the boys within elite networks extending throughout the country.

Indeed, the Franciscans regularly took their young charges on outings to other mission stations, Catholic youth retreats, and choir competitions, including some held in major cities and towns. Contacts made and experiences shared would often set the stage for return visits.

The impact of the mission message on the relationship between young and old is varied and complex. Amabwambu, for example, spent many of their formative years encased in a world where foreign knowledge outshone and outperformed the local assemblage of facts and beliefs in positioning individuals to capitalize on extant economic opportunities. The words of elderly Muzungu might be heeded. Yet, far greater emphasis would be placed on listening to lectures, perusing texts, and scrutinizing educational broadcasts than seeking out the wisdom amassed by elderly people. In the final analysis, however, missionaries could provide the methods, means, and materials for joining the newly emerging social and economic stream, but they would not be emulated as models of comportment once success was achieved. The missionaries clearly had many admirable qualities, collectively and individually. A deep and abiding emotional bond developed between them and their students that would only become stronger and more richly textured with time. Yet, the Franciscan vow of celibacy would never be interpreted as anything but strange, if not outright dangerous. The image of a dozen white men in robes living together in one house and a dozen women in robes living in a separate dwelling a few yards away, with no intimate contact between the two, did not fit neatly into any local cognitive framework. Nor would the series of justifications put forward by the Franciscans be widely accepted as convincing. Models of and models for contemporary living would have to be sought out elsewhere.

"Negro in Cabinet" Storm

WASHINGTON, SAPA-REUTER

Controversy was mounting here today over Republican hints that they will appoint a Negro to the Cabinet if they are returned to power in next month's election.

Some Republican leaders fear the storm may damage the prospects of Vice-President Richard Nixon, the party's Presidential candidate, winning over voters from the traditionally Democratic and race-conscious South.

(*Central African Post*, October 19, 1960, p. 1)

Those who managed to establish lives in the city no doubt found models among the successful new urban elite who lived in apartment complexes or walled compounds with maids, houseboys, and gardeners, drove cars, and worked in offices. For the Amabwambu, however, who collectively chose to pursue rural lifestyles, the *ankaka* and *ataata* would continue to provide much of the symbolic substance of success. As noted earlier, in the traditional scheme of things, age, wealth, and prestige were a linked triad. Yet, age was singled out as the dominant idiom for an individual's social ranking. Age was, in a sense, a condensation for a bundle of socially significant achieved conditions. It might include the size of one's household, productivity of fields, number of children, hunting skills, business acumen, cash holdings, oratory skills, and so forth. The composition of the bundle changes over time. The significance ascribed to individual components within the bundle likewise changes over time. But the logic of significance remains firmly rooted in plans for both life and the afterlife. The essence of life is to become both *mukwakuheta* (one who possesses many things) and *mukwakwashi* (one who helps many people). Such individuals are adorned with praise and surrounded by followers anxious to do their bidding. They invariably receive the loudest greeting, the most comfortable chair, the largest plate of food, the juiciest piece of meat, and the largest cup of wine. Their personal names become topographical references, used to identify the rivers, plains, hills, and forests of the areas they occupied. The Lunda landscape is an ever-evolving map of power relations, literally saturated with the names of famous big men, old and new. Furthermore, the Lunda tend to believe that relations developed in life persist into the afterlife. Thus achieving the statuses of *mukwakuheta* and *mukwakwashi* assures one of contentment and respect not only in this world but in the next one as well.

The Lunda system glorifies hard work and individual initiative in the creation of surplus and yet also encourages the widest distribution of that surplus by providing physical and metaphysical rewards to those who do so. If young men are fortunate enough and clever enough to make comparably large social contributions, then they come to be regarded in the same fashion as would an elderly *mukwakwashi*. Indeed, as their wealth and prestige rises, so too does local reckoning of their age.

Most Amabwambu, as is explored in greater detail in chapter 9, have combined the skills acquired at St. Kizito and their continued privileged access to mission tools, tractors, transport, and other advantages with their superior understanding of the world beyond Mwinilunga to found villages reliant upon a mix of traditional and nontraditional economic activities. The cultivation of the basic staple, cassava, is always part of the mix. Other components variously include the commercial farming of maize and sunflowers, irrigated vegetable gardening, the construction of fishponds, maintenance of pineapple plantations, tending livestock, small-scale merchandising, and the sponsorship of alcohol brewers, carpenters, bricklayers, basket weavers, and other artisans. Amabwambu have tended to selectively invite young relatives to join their villages and to share and contribute to its diverse resource pool, thereby setting the stage for future expansion in new areas. With increasing profitability, Amabwambu begin to selectively invite elderly relatives to their villages as well. Not only can elders provide many useful services such as childcare, tending the sick, processing food, and looking after the village while others are away in the field, but more importantly, only the presence of elders can transform a collection of households into a real village. The ideal village must contain representatives of all the generations. Elders attract other elders, bringing with them knowledge of history, proverbs, and judicial precedence, lending an air of stability to the village. The presence of the elderly serve as proof that life's many obstacles can be overcome, lending confidence and inspiring courage in the young. Additionally, the presence of the elderly is needed if Amabwambu are to make successful claims not just to the status of big men but to that of village headmen as well.

On one level, the new Amabwambu villages contrasted mightily with villages of old, where individuals took pride in their association with long-standing villages, and eligible men waited patiently, sometimes for decades, for their turn at headmanship to arrive. Yet, on closer inspection, today's pattern of headmanship based on achievement rather than ascription holds much in common with its traditional counterpart. Succession among the Lunda tended to be adelphic, passing through a line of classificatory brothers by age before dropping down to their classificatory sons and nephews in the descending generation. Because the reckoning of age was not strictly chronological but highly influenced by a malleable mix of social characteristics, achievement tended to dominate even in the traditional context. Those deemed most competent would usually emerge as headman. Those deemed less so would be continually overlooked until they either left the village or quietly withdrew from the struggle for leadership. Secondly, Amabwambu tend to recruit followers primarily from among their matrilineal kin. Thus, the actual social composition of Amabwambu villages today—the range and ratio of relationships between headman and residents—varies in no significant way from those of villages a half-century ago.[8]

The Amabwambu's relationship with the elderly has thus been a project continually under construction. As toddlers, the Amabwambu's grandparents had perhaps been the center of their world. Grandparents offered information and entertainment, comfort and encouragement as needed. By the time Amabwambu reached upper primary school at St. Kizito, the grandparents probably appeared as relics from another era, variously a source of embarrassment and pity. When Amabwambu returned from their brief experiments with urban living, ready to settle down locally, they began to reconnect with grandparents. Now the Amabwambu are fully immersed in lives of responsibility, with duties to kin and clients, and with competing claims on their time, money, and emotional energy, expected to manage the rough edges of daily life and to resolve the major conflicts and minor squabbles that gnaw at the social fabric of village life. The elderly have reassumed their place on the pedestal, the very model of substance and style, compassion and resolve, dispensing advice that encapsulates yet transcends the moment, draped in an elegance that only time can weave. Amabwambu will no doubt increasingly add their own layer of style to the condition of elderhood. But it is unlikely they will devise any serious challenge to the existential linkage of *mukwakuheta* and *mukwakwashi* or profoundly modify that special bond between the young and the old.

One might expect that the Catholic Church, as a religious organization with the expressed aim of spreading the word of God, would have a most pronounced impact on Lunda notions about the relationship between the physical and metaphysical worlds. Yet it is not unambiguously clear that this has been the case. As noted earlier, the Catholics followed the Brethren's lead in accepting the Lunda term *Nzambi* as an appropriate appellation for the Christian High God. That simple choice no doubt implied to local minds that Muzungu were not attempting to introduce a new deity but rather were bringing novel information about an old High God. Furthermore, conversion to Christianity appeared to require relatively few modifications in prevailing beliefs, with the Catholics requiring fewer still than their Protestant competitors, the Brethren. From the beginning, Fathers Adrian and Rupert had set a tolerant tone, regularly smoking and drinking alcoholic beverages with the local folks, studying rather than condemning local customs. Subsequent priests at Lwawu would continue the trend by seeking points of overlap and complementarity between Catholicism and Lunda traditions. Over time priests began participating in the closing ceremonies of boys' circumcision camps and even girls' puberty rites, offering prayers blessing the newly initiated and welcoming them into the Christian fold. For additional flair, an abbreviated Catholic Mass might be appended to traditional ceremonies, complete with Holy Communion. The Catholics were absolutely against witchcraft, but so was every right-minded Lunda. Catholics spoke out against polygyny but were quick to make accommodations or to turn a blind eye should a polygynist or his wives wish to join the church. Indeed, many Lunda concluded after reading the Bible that it was the Franciscans themselves, rather than God, who found polygyny to be a problem. Yet for the Catholics, reading and interpreting the Bible was not the supreme or even an expected act of faith. Exegesis was the province of specially trained religious leaders, with ultimate authority residing in the pope. What was required most of the individual was participation in a limited set of rituals.

Amabwambu perhaps received more training in Catholic doctrine than all but a few who formally entered the order. Yet, the long-term impact seems to have been the inculcation of a strong dose of liberalism, a religious tolerance bordering on cultural

African Demand for Cars Reaches New Heights in Lusaka

C.A.P. REPORTER

More Africans bought cars in Lusaka last year than ever before and paid higher prices than they have in the past. A Lusaka licensing officer said that 2,000 new car licences were issued in Lusaka last year and "the majority of these were to Africans." Before last year they mostly bought vans or trucks and thought it madness to buy a car just to sit in. But this attitude has changed drastically now, especially among the Government Africans.

(*Central African Post*, January 11, 1963, p. 3)

relativism. Amabwambu say and believe all matter of different things about religion. They regularly debate among themselves the relevance of particular religious expressions, the relationship between God, angels, and ancestors, the location of heaven, the meaning of eternal life, and so forth. Convictions change over time, and the intensity of concern with religious matters ebbs and flows. Kapala, for example, the well-paid and highly regarded tractor driver for the mission, had three wives until recently. He never attended Sunday Mass, joking that being forced to spend eight hours a day, five days a week, working at the mission was religion enough for him. In truth, Kapala is complex beyond any encapsulation. He was raised in a polygynous village. His own father had been a headman with three wives, a dozen children, and a village full of kin and clients. Kapala apparently thrived in that environment, growing up, by all appearances, happy and well adjusted, with a keen sense of humor and an equally strong sense of responsibility. He may have been ready to party at the end of the day, but during daylight hours he was among the hardest working individuals on the plateau. He built up a large, well-maintained village, kept his wives and children dressed in the most recently available fashions, dug and stocked fishponds, borrowed the tractor frequently to cultivate his own cash crops, and took care of many elderly relatives, including his father. Kapala publicly expresses nothing but appreciation for the opportunities that had come his way via his long association with the Franciscans. Yet, in quiet, less-guarded moments Kapala might reveal his long harbored and unresolved feelings about his ardent pursuit of Muzungu knowledge in his formative years at the expense of familiarity with and appreciation for Lunda things. It would appear that much of Kapala's early adulthood was dedicated to overcoming a nettlesome sense of incompleteness. He was determined to master the esoteric knowledge of his own culture. Over a several-year period Kapala scaled back on his socializing with Amabwambu in favor of spending more time with his elderly father and listening to the stories of senior generation males. He particularly sought out the least-well-known aspects of history, the nearly forgotten elements of etiquette, and the deepest mysteries of Lunda philosophy. He developed an intense interest in herbalism, experimenting with his own concoctions whenever ill. During the time spent with Amabwambu Kapala would increasingly divert the conversation away from usual topics about pop culture or promising new areas of profitable pursuit and toward questions of Lunda culture. Some suspected that Kapala's newfound interest was a strategic move, the adoption of a style designed to enhance his reputation among the elderly and boost his ranking among the assembly of local big men. A few speculated about more sinister intentions. Occasionally, Kapala would disappear for a day or so. Some suspected he was off with a diviner or some other instructor of the dark arts, that is, learning sorcery. But one day, without any forewarning, Kapala announced that he was converting to

Christianity. To highlight the seriousness of his convictions, he also announced that he would cease being a polygynist. He would honor Franciscan teachings that portrayed the monogamous Christian family as an expression of faith by entering the doors of the church with just one wife. Some of Kapala's peers thought he was joking, others thought he had taken one home-brewed concoction too many, and still others thought it was a ruse to get rid of a couple of wives. After months of speculation, all were shocked when Kapala revealed his marital plans. He noted that he had always loved his three wives equally and had treated and provided for them equally. It would be unfair to single one out for special treatment at this point. Hence, he would divorce all three. As the mothers of his children, however, they could remain in his village. He would support them all. But he intended to marry a nursing assistant at the mission and begin living a Christian life.

By all appearances, Mafulo was the most devout Christian among the Amabwambu. He would arrive at the mission early each morning, labor in the clinic all day, and then cross the greens to the church building in late afternoon to conduct rehearsal as the master of the Lwawu Mission choir. Perhaps only the Franciscan Friars spent more time in the church building than Mafulo. It is difficult to disentangle Mafulo's love of music from his love of the church. In some respects he is engaged in conducting his own musical ministry, only nominally under the auspices of the Catholic Church. Mafulo has been obsessed with music as far back as anyone can remember. He has learned to play every instrument that appeared on the Mwinilunga scene. Beyond his mastery of traditional drums and percussion, various Franciscans over the years have taught him to play the guitar, harmonica, and even accordion. Mafulo is virtually never silent, always humming, whistling, singing, or tapping out some possible new arrangement, toying with musical scores in his head. He is quite popular with local youth, attracting many of them to the Catholic Church as a spiritual home, but also as the site with the largest collection of musical instruments in the area, a framework that allows for the steady improvement of musical skills and the largest local stage for carrying out performance impulses. Mafulo is also at the forefront of organizing choir competitions, often compelling the Franciscans on short notice to load up the lorry, pack a picnic lunch, and transport the choir great distances to share music, food, and fellowship with other youth within the far-flung Catholic network.

America's Colour Bar Is Slowly Crumbling

NEW YORK, N.A.N.A.

The colour barrier is slowly crumbling in America's south. More Negro pupils now attend schools with white children than ever before. When schools and colleges opened this month, nearly 500,000 Negro boys and girls were in "integrated situations" in southern public schools. An estimated 2,500 Negro students have enrolled in the previous all-white public colleges and universities.

Integration is gaining ground in the Deep South and with less violence than at any time since the famous Supreme Court decision of May 17, 1954, outlawed "Separate but equal" schools. (*Central African Post*, October 14, 1965, p. 5)

Fiercely scolded by the head priest on one occasion for making such unauthorized arrangements, Mafulo left the Catholic Church and took up the position of choir-master at a local Protestant church, taking a noticeable number of Catholic youth with him. He was quietly enticed back within a couple of weeks.

Despite machination on behalf of music, Mafulo's Christian faith appears deeply embedded in his character. He was a voracious reader of the Bible, able to spout off long passages, chapter and verse, in a way more indicative of Protestant rather than Catholic upbringing. As an aspiring big man he has sponsored a boys' circumcision camp and performed musically in many others. He was frequently at the center of festivities at girls' maturation rites and local weddings. But he would not participate in curing cults, exorcisms, or any other rituals that aimed at conjuring up and making appeals exclusively to the ancestors. Mafulo had indeed been profoundly changed by his association with Christianity. For traditional Lunda, there was no heaven above or hell below. The metaphysical world shared space with the physical world. The spirits of the dead wandered around the same places they had frequented when alive, seeking only to be remembered by kin and hurling illness and misfortune on those who forgot. Whereas Mafulo held open the possibilities that ancestors did roam the landscape, he was adamant that good ancestors went up to heaven, and the power of God exceeded that of all the ancestors combined. Thus prayer to God was all the ritual cure anyone needed.

Kataloshi was perhaps the most circumspective of the Amabwambu. Like the others, he grew up to have a large and productive farm and many dependents, and he played a significant role in sponsoring local events. He was also the owner of a small retail shop adjacent to the mission, specializing in basic commodities such as soap, salt, sugar, cooking oil, kerosene, matches, and the odd bit of clothing, as well as seeds and tools in season. Perhaps his quiet and cautious nature had been shaped or accentuated by the contrasting needs of maintaining his customer base, protecting the profitability of his establishment, while managing the daily on-slaught of credit seekers. In any event, Kataloshi was far more likely to be found listening than talking, rarely feeling compelled to elaborate on his own beliefs and feelings. He went to Catholic Mass every Sunday without fail, even when ill. But then again, the hundreds who attended Mass would congregate at Kataloshi's shop afterward to inspect his goods, make needed purchases, down a cup or two of lo-cal brew, catch up on the previous week's news, make plans for the coming week, gossip with old friends, or seek out new ones. Sundays belonged to the priest and Kataloshi. They both had to perform; the show had to go on regardless of how they individually felt. However, their partnership ran deeper. Kataloshi lacked any form of transportation and was, hence, totally dependent on the Catholics to keep his shelves stocked. Without regular and predictable mission trips to the Boma or town, the area would suffer shortages, and people would be at the mercy of itin-erant bicycle merchants or commodity speculators such as Benson, who reaped the windfall profits of their own artificially induced shortages. The Franciscans, as the largest employer of wage labor in the area and as Christians concerned with the quality of life of their parishioners, have ample reason to combat inflation, natural or otherwise. Both compassion and economic expediency dictate the wisdom of a stable local consumer price index. The Franciscans work with Kataloshi to achieve that end. They might make bulk purchases in town with their own funds, advancing the goods to Kataloshi with the stipulation that he sell at a specified price. At times they might use Kataloshi's shop as the distribution outlet for goods received from aboard. Concomitantly, this arrangement allowed Kataloshi to offer his family and friends privileged access to scarce, exotic, or simply interesting commodities. In the final analysis, interpretations of the finer points of religious theory were of little interest to Kataloshi. He was a devout Catholic. He performed the rituals of faith. The Franciscans were his friends. End of story.

Katoka and Kanasa were difficult personalities to read—outgoing and effusive some days, seemingly shy and reticent the next. Not only did their opinions about spiritual life seem to swing widely from one position to another over the years, but they also varied greatly from one context to another. At times it appeared that Katoka and Kanasa followed the path of least resistance, simply nodding their heads in agreement and acquiescing to the opinions of their host. Theirs seemed to be a search for advantage or utility. Around the mission they were pious Catholics. Drinking home brew with Benson they were ardent traditionalists. But at times, a radically different demeanor was on display. Katoka and Kanasa would debate one another with a nearly frightening ferocity, staking out diametrically opposed positions with a passion that suggested much pent-up animosity. But during calmer moments they assured others that they were best of friends who simply enjoyed a good argument.

Perhaps the essential lesson to be drawn here is that ultimately religion does not matter. Membership in the Amabwambu clique is based not on sharing one particular set of religious beliefs but rather on sharing the experience of collectively confronting the same range of beliefs. Arriving at different conclusions about existential matters may animate debates, but it cannot call into question long-term loyalties or be allowed to impede long-term economic strategies. Perhaps such an approach to philosophical matters extends naturally from Amabwambu exposure to Catholic tolerance and the Catholic search for accommodation. Indeed, several new Christian religions in Mwinilunga are socially insular, demanding exclusivity of interaction among its membership. Adherents to the New Apostolic Church or the New Jerusalem group are ordered to limit their contact with those of opposing sects. But Amabwambu liberalism also extends naturally from traditional Lunda beliefs. Lunda discussions about the metaphysical world are invariably bracketed by qualifying phrases indicating lack of absolute certainty, such as "It is said," "I have heard," or "The elders believed." Only those who have actually visited the metaphysical domain, seen its denizens, and observed their relations can speak authoritatively about that world. And to the traditional imagination, only prophets, diviners, witches, and sorcerers could make such a trip and return to tell about it. Thus, to speak with too great of an assurance about metaphysical matters is to risk having one's humanity examined. Yet the fact that many people have strayed away from these beliefs but Amabwambu have not would suggest that Catholic teachings, in ways perhaps not readily known to the Franciscans, buttressed, reinforced, and preserved many traditional approaches to matters of doctrine. To the degree that a traditional Lunda canon existed, it was probably less about determining the outcome of debates and more about determining what was worthy of debate in the first place.

Finally, the St. Kizito experience profoundly affected Amabwambu notions of "Us" and "Them." Lwawu was firmly situated in the center of Lunda territory. Father Adrian and subsequent priests had labored to translate the Bible and Catholic catechism into the Lunda language. Sunday Mass was always given in Lunda. But in every way possible, St. Kizito students were immersed in nationalist thought, encouraged to embrace their national identity, and prepared to take their place on the national stage. Here again, the Americanness of Lwawu Mission came into play. Americans found the continued existence of colonies in the mid-twentieth century unimaginably anachronistic and bristled at the periodic need to secure permission from British officials to travel, make purchases, or carry out religious activities. Catholic tolerance was not extended to things British, with the Franciscans rarely passing up an opportunity to ridicule British suzerainty, trivialize British culture, or circumvent British oversight. Lwawu was saturated with an aura of defiance, a place confident of impending independence long before most people were convinced of its inevitability. Indeed the Franciscans took all the St. Kizito students into Mwinilunga Boma to ensure their presence at one second after midnight, October 24, 1964, when the Union Jack was lowered for the last time and the flag of Independent Zambia was raised in its stead.

Lwawu Mission donated considerable support to the newly independent government. As noted earlier, it served as a quasi-government agent for the Department of Agriculture, building and maintaining a collection depot for local marketable crops and using its own transport and financial resources to cover the periodic shortfall in agricultural inputs. The mission also housed, fed, and provided transportation for agricultural and veterinary extension officers, hosted government officials on constituency tours, and supported a host of government development initiatives over the years. Amabwambu may endeavor to demonstrate their mastery over the local, but they also think of themselves as Zambians, make claims on government resources as Zambians, and generate expectations for the future as Zambians.

4

Harry Franklin's Saucepan Special

Nearly half a century ago, sociologist David Riesman, in contrasting the diverging impact of orality versus literacy on the construction of consciousness, noted that preliterate peoples are "led by folk tales and songs to identify with the tribe as it has been and will be, or possibly with a legendary golden age but they are not incited to imagine themselves outside its comforts and coherence" (*Selected Essays*, 34). Literacy, on the other hand, particularly after the eighteenth-century flowering of the novel and the newspaper, allows for the construction of a secondary reality, one utterly disconnected from the day-to-day world of the reader, one organized and sustained perhaps by principles previously unknown or presently unacceptable. Literacy, thus, is not simply a matter of learning to read, of comprehending the connection between symbols and sounds, but is a process of retooling the mind to perceive and accept a form of reality beyond immediate experience. Print can cognitively liberate individuals from the social constraints of prevailing beliefs, from the physical confines of time and space, and even from the limits of their own imagination. Initially in the West only a literate minority had access to this secondary reality. However, the rapid diffusion of literacy and the expansion of the publishing industry allowed the masses to progressively participate in experiencing and constructing secondary realities. In the early twentieth century the mass media of radio and film would join print as windows to other worlds.

In Africa, by contrast, all three media were introduced in less than half a century, and for most people within one generation. Furthermore, the lack of attention given to African education under colonial rule amplified the power of radio and film for reaching the multitude who could not read. In rural Mwinilunga, in particular, radio was by far the preeminent vehicle bringing the larger world to the local scene.

Kennel Club Annual Show

C.A.P. REPORTER

This year the Northern Rhodesia Kennel Club will hold its annual championships in conjunction with the Lusaka Agricultural Society Show.

The championships will be held on Sunday August 2, and entries, which are already coming in, will include animals from Salisbury, Bulawayo and the Copperbelt.

Entries close on July 11. This year the judge will be Mrs. Eileen McQueen, of Cape Town, who is a judge of all breeds.

(*Central African Post,* July 3, 1959, p. 5)

Broadcasting to Africans in Northern Rhodesia began in 1941 with the establishment of the Central African Broadcasting Service (CABS). The colonial government set up a small shortwave station in the new capital, Lusaka, and a series of community receivers to keep Africans informed of the progress of the war, to stimulate support for the war efforts, and to convey orders in the event of serious emergencies.[1] Harry Franklin, chief information officer of the Northern Rhodesian Department of Information, initially ran the station in his spare time. His department's goals were "to interpret government policy and actions to the territory's people, to advise the government on public opinion and public relations, to develop and exploit the media in aid of the administration and its technical departments, and to publicize the territory beyond its borders" (Grotpeter, Siegel, and Pletcher, *Historical Dictionary of Zambia,* 104). Franklin was an English liberal who devoted unusually high levels of passion and energy to bettering the African condition. After the war he expanded CABS, personally lobbying the British government and public for financial assistance to buy more powerful transmitters and to set up a modern production studio. Franklin, after several disappointments, found a British company that was willing to manufacture a dry-battery receiving set cheap enough for Africans to buy and durable enough to withstand the rigors of the African environment. Thus, a metal encased radio, nicknamed the "saucepan special," was introduced in Northern Rhodesia in October 1949 that sold for little more than the equivalent of ten U.S. dollars. An estimated 1,200 sets were bought by Africans in the first four months of sale, rising to over 30,000 by 1954.[2]

With the aim of expanding the focus on African education and entertainment, Franklin assembled an exceptional staff for CABS, one that offended many colonial European sensibilities by its brazen disregard for the Colour Bar, both in the station and in their private lives.[3] Michael Kittermaster as broadcasting officer was the chief of staff who was noted for not only being comfortable working with Africans but also for frequently socializing with them in public and even inviting them into his home in suburban Lusaka. Such intimacy between black and white was an uncommon occurrence and a frowned-upon sight in the 1940s and 1950s. Kittermaster was, thus, under constant attack throughout his tenure. But Harry Franklin, who was quite the iconoclast himself and who in 1951 established the first interracial society in Lusaka, the Kabulonga Club, shielded Kittermaster from European demands for his dismissal.

Another popular member of staff was Alick Nkhata—announcer, guitarist, singer, and one of the earliest recorders and champions of African traditional music. Yet Nkhata was also at the forefront of the creation of a uniquely African genre of pop music. Nkhata, significantly, was born of mixed parentage, a Bemba mother and a Tonga father, in 1922. Trained as a teacher, he would go on to serve in Burma during World War II as a sergeant in the East African Division. Afterward, he traveled extensively throughout East, Central, and Southern Africa recording traditional music under the direction of ethnomusicologist Hugh Tracey, then director of the International Library of African Music. As one of the original on-the-air personalities for CABS, Alick is best remembered for his repertoire of songs, simultaneously poignant and humorous, about contemporary town life. As described by anthropologist Hortense Powdermaker, who was present during those heady days of the early 1950s, "He sang of town 'wives' who painted their lips, of the awkwardness of wives from the rural areas, of the loneliness of men away from home, of the fear of dying away from relatives, of the joys of town life, of drinking, of 'jiving,' and of sex. Often he used traditional music, but his themes were new and so was his guitar" (*Copper Town*, 233–34). Nkhata also gave impetus to the CABS field-recording program. CABS staff traveled extensively throughout the countryside, recording traditional music wherever they found it. The best recordings were aired on Saturday mornings. This program provided many Africans with their first and certainly their best exposure to the myriad musical forms of their fellow countrymen.

Another popular member of staff, Edwin Mlongoti, adapted the African tradition of storytelling to the new medium. In addition to the recitation of tales, fables, and proverbs, he organized impromptu radio plays. With virtually no rehearsal, an

Negroes Rocked Moscow

C.A.P. CORRESPONDENT, MOSCOW

Moscow's staid old Tchaikovsky Conservatory will never be the same again. And if there is a single piano or bass fiddle left in one piece it is not the fault of the two American Negro jazz artists who this week rocked the hall with the hottest music ever heard there.

Dwight Mitchell and Willie Ruff, known to most young modern jazz enthusiasts in the United States and known also to television audiences and record collectors as one of the best duets in the business, staged an impromptu concert for the students.

Theirs was a major breakthrough in a field where the American State Department and the Soviet Ministry of Culture have long been hopelessly deadlocked.

(*Central African Post*, July 7, 1959, p. 9)

ensemble cast of four or five Africans would produce ten- to fifteen-minute plays. Mlongoti would sketch out a general plot, casually assign roles—for example, a chief new in town, his country kinsman, a shopkeeper, and a policeman. The cast would then step before the microphone and extemporaneously interact around the chosen theme. The result, like an Alick Nkhata song, was usually hilarious on one level, profoundly sad on another, yet always deeply insightful and thought provoking. Pop songs and improvised plays on the radio were arenas where tradition met modernity, the rural confronted the urban, and the predictable world of ascribed relations gave way to the confusing array of possible connections.

Radio staffer Sylvester Masiye harnessed the energies created in these musical and dramatic formats, bringing them into sharp focus in his discussion program on topical issues. Here the relationships between village wives and town prostitutes, witchcraft and Christian rituals, tribal customs and urban etiquette, chiefly prerogatives and colonial proclamations were endlessly examined from historical, ethnic, regional, gender, and class perspectives. CABS radio programming, perhaps reflecting the lives of some of its listeners, moved seamlessly from village life to town life without any sense of disparity or disjuncture. Indeed, CABS was simultaneously reflective and constitutive of a new culture emerging, first on the Copperbelt, then increasingly emulated in the most isolated rural reaches of the colony.

The radio station broadcasted in English one day a week, usually Sunday, and in one African language each of the other six days. Out of the roughly seventy-two languages spoken in Northern Rhodesia, Bemba, Nyanja, Tonga, Lozi, Ndebele, and Shona were the original chosen broadcast languages. Lunda was not added until 1960. Yet, despite the grumbling over this linguistic slight, most in Mwinilunga listened to the radio whenever they could, wherever they could. After all, several hours of programming each day were devoted to the playing of continuous music that highlighted yet transcended various regional forms. Next, *Zimene Mwatifunsa* (listener "requests") was an extremely popular program in which Africans sent messages to relatives and friends in different parts of the territory, accompanied by the playing of their favorite record. Such messages might include information about births, deaths, engagements, marriages, new addresses, job promotions, training programs completed, or new acquisitions. The songs selected each show spanned a diverse spectrum, including modern, African tradi-

Queen Liked Stampede

CALGARY (ALBERTA), SAPA-REUTER

The Queen and Prince Phillip enjoyed the thrills and spills of the cowboy chuck-wagon races at the famous wild west "Calgary Stampede" so much that they stayed an extra half hour last night.

During the races the Queen at times waved her hands excitedly, smiled, laughed and chatted. The Prince, who constantly waved a newly-acquired 10-gallon hat, seemed to enjoy the spectacle even more.

(*Central African Post,* July 10, 1959, p. 1)

tional, American cowboy, "jive" songs, and Christian hymns. "Modern" music in this context was most often tradition-based music but about contemporary issues, accompanied by new instruments such as the guitar. Many such songs mixed English and African vernacular, thereby contributing to the creation of a uniquely pan-Zambian patois. Most modern songs offered advice about experiences villager had not had and yet would certainly encounter should they venture forth into the urban milieu.

After music and "requests," news was the next most popular program.[4] Listening to the news gave one the feeling of participation in a larger world. Indeed, radio imposed a sense of order on that world by presenting it in measured bits at predictable intervals, thereby reducing imagined fear of the unknown. Hearing of newly enforced laws, recently proposed regulations, changing weather patterns, or emerging global trends contributed to a perception of security, of mastery over one's times. Radio news also created a novel sensation of movement. Every evening there was a plethora of new reports. In the village world things tended to move more slowly. A single case of theft or adultery might captivate local attention for days on end. But in the world of radio, events chased after events at a dizzying pace. One had to gear up one's perceptive capacities to stay abreast of this fast-moving world.

Finally, ministries of government seized upon the medium of radio to inform and educate the general public in ways that furthered their respective mandates. Among the programs developed were weekly series on new agricultural and veterinary practices, health and hygiene issues, household management, and financial planning. There seemed to have been a genuine effort to bridge the experiential gap between the colonial government's world of bureaus, budgets, revenue projections, and labor statistics, and the African world of farms and families, factories and marketplaces. Radio programs continually experimented with heuristic devices that could effectively translate the abstract features of governance into concrete examples comprehensible to the uneducated masses.

Until the 1960s, radio in Northern Rhodesia was a completely noncommercial, government-financed enterprise. Its programs for Africans were designed and implemented by a small, close-knit staff of dedicated and enthusiastic individuals. In some ways, the government-controlled environment worked to the advantage of these early radio pioneers, offering them time, flexibility, and creative possibilities that commercial radio can rarely support. Because commercial radio places programming decisions in the hands of businesses dependent on public patronage, it tends to water down its messages in an effort to appeal to the broadest possible audience. Commercial radio eschews risk taking, embracing instead the most universally accepted norms and values of society. Noncommercial radio, however, can be transformative. In the Northern Rhodesian case, radio repeatedly put forward themes initially unpopular or irresolute, giving them extended public airing and ultimately serving as a crucible for social change and the emergence of many trans-ethnic beliefs, values, styles, and social strategies.

"Colour-bar" Outcry

NEW YORK, SAPA-REUTER

A nationwide furore over whether America's "Wimbledon," the exclusive West Side tennis club, operates a colour bar has ended with the resignation of its president and a statement that no such barriers exist.

The club's board of governors in a statement last night said it had accepted the resignation of the president Mr. Wilfred Burgland "to avoid any embarrassment to the U.S. Lawn Tennis Association and the club."

There had been demands that national championships and Davis Cup matches be withdrawn from the club stadium after Dr. Ralph Bunche, Negro Under-Secretary at the United Nations, said Mr. Burgland told him his 15-year-old son could not be admitted.

(*Central African Post,* July 15, 1959, p. 12)

The compendium of broadcast themes presented below begins the process of introducing early radio social ideas and ideals that charmed some Lunda listeners, while challenging others. This exercise foreshadows the prolonged and dynamic interaction between prevailing local beliefs and new beliefs arriving via the airwaves. First, and foremost the radio called into question Lunda notions about the relationship between themselves and physical space. An unspoken agenda of CABS was to buttress and fortify people's identification with that distinct and sovereign political entity called Northern Rhodesia. The Lunda of Mwinilunga were represented as an inseparable part of that unitary state. Clearly, in the 1950s a good many Lunda still held out hope for the reconstitution of Lundaland, a territorial reuniting with their kinsfolk in Angola and Congo. The radio, in essence, denied any such possibility. The geographical reconfiguration imposed by Britain, Belgium, and Portugal was an unassailable reality that could never be undone. Furthermore, whereas Lunda were entitled to move freely within Northern Rhodesian spaces, even among those previously considered enemy territory, they could not move outside it without expressed government permission. Thus, spontaneous visits to cross-border kin became criminal acts.

Movement is a core metaphor among the Lunda. It is synonymous with knowledge, as in an old proverb: wisdom comes with miles, not years. Travel is the prerequisite for discovering new resources, uncovering new opportunities, and encountering new techniques and technologies. Those who have traveled the farthest from home are reckoned to have best seen and mastered the world and are hence the wisest. The untraveled cannot seriously compete for leadership among the Lunda. Movement is also a standard method for dealing with life's most troubling moments. Famine, fear of witchcraft, infertility, failure in a succession struggle, or a general lack of success in a particular location are all dealt with through movement. The view from the plateau is one of endless horizons extending in all directions. It is a landscape that invites exploration, examination, and colonization with meaningful activities. It is a world of people constantly in motion. Yet the radio championed a different aesthetic, one in which stability was the core characteristic of a much-coveted modernity, and the itinerant tribesman was the antithesis. The modernization project in its various guises sought to slow the movement of people across landscapes, across international borders, even across ecological niches. The colonial Department of Agriculture fought against *chitemene,* the local system of slash-and-burn agriculture that kept people in place for only a few years before they moved on in search of fresh land. The department labored to inculcate a new consciousness about land. Rather than conceiving of it as something to be conquered for its most valuable substances (game meat, wild foods, firewood, construction materials, and the fertility of its soil), land should be the subject of comprehensive long-term management strategies. Rather than being an abundantly available self-renewing resource, land is best viewed as a scarce commodity whose utility can be sustained only through the careful application of scientific knowledge. The sanctity of private property and the unquestioned primacy of machine agriculture are the ultimate conceptual markers of this consciousness. Neat rows of houses with cement walls and tin roofs, rather than scattered compounds of clay houses with straw-thatched roofs, are the equivalent visual markers. Thus, while much of CABS programming praised African traditions and contributed mightily to both popularizing and preserving its music and oral arts for posterity, other streams of radio messages led a clandestine assault on some of the fundamental pillars on which African traditions rested.

Radio was also the site of considerable commentary about the relationship between the individual and the group. Much of the humor of an Alick Nkhata song, for example, is the subtle mockery of individuals holding fast to the traditional customs and habits of their rural group even as they moved into the more diverse and particularistic environment of the urban world. Such songs, for example, speak of the newly arrived person from the countryside who cannot reach his urban destination because of the impulse to stop and greet each individual he passes and to bow down before every elder on the city street. One song jokes about the new wife from the countryside who when asked to fix tea for the first time cooks the leaves like vegetables and proudly serves them with groundnut gravy. The emerging genre of African pop music on the radio took urban

Space Man Has Good Chance

NEW YORK, N.A.N.A.

Chances that the first American space man returns to earth alive are as good as — or better than — those of any jet plane test pilot, according to rocket pioneer Dr. Willy Ley. He said that the U.S. astronauts, seven of whom are now being trained, are getting more thorough preparation than any test pilot in history.

Safety precautions in the vehicle which will carry one of the seven into space two years from now will be so great that even technical failures will not jeopardise the life of the passenger. (*Central African Post,* July 27, 1959, p. 5)

encounters as its primary source of inspiration. The serious message embedded in its humorous scenarios is that traditions developed to mediate relations among ethnically, linguistically, and occupationally homogeneous peoples provide a woefully inadequate foundation for decoding the perplexing array of urban conundrums. The songs speak of the city as a culturally inchoate arena where individual cleverness and creativity, rather than inherited wisdom, are the keys to survival.

Some pop lyrics did glorify a generalized African tradition, heaping value on the collective caring and sharing that typified rural existence, and even advocated remembrance of the ancestors as a spiritual necessity. But that traditional world of collective decision making and collective responsibility resided in a place far removed from the quotidian negotiations of urban life. The city, in essence, was a place of persons, not groups. One entered as an individual and rose or fell on individual merits. Additionally, city culture was increasingly portrayed as the new national culture. The social arrangements and aesthetic forms evolving out of the complex commingling of ethnic groups in urban spaces was being codified, repackaged and re-presented to Northern Rhodesian Africans to imbibe as their own regardless of where they lived.

Complementing the music programming and trumpeting the same themes were the Edwin Mlongoti plays and the Sylvester Masiye topical discussions. Government ministry–sponsored programs, however, tended to dispense with humor in favor of a steady flow of information heralding new products and practices. Larger yields and hardier herds were available to the individual willing to follow the advice of his local agricultural or veterinary officer. Healthier children and happier families could flow from the advice of public health and medical officers. Job promotions and economic security were the stock-in-trade of the training officer. In each case the subtext is clear. The knowledge that defines the modern world, and that determines one's position within that world, does not emanate from the minds of rural elders and is not encapsulated in the tribal wisdom of the ages. The modern world explodes the traditional relationship between the individual and the group, and between young and old. An industrious, well-educated youth can attain wealth and privilege far beyond the reach of his contemporary elders. And it was the radio that alerted the nation to this possibility.

Mining, the activity that dominated the national economy, is an overwhelmingly male profession. Much

Red Offer to Scrap A-bombs

MOSCOW

Mr. Nikita Khrushchev, the Soviet Prime Minister, has offered to destroy immediately Russia's stockpile of atomic rockets "which could wipe off the face of the earth all our potential enemies" if other powers follow his example. In a speech published here last night he said he had visited a Soviet factory where 240 rockets with hydrogen warheads were manufactured in a year and asserted "we are ready to sink all this in the sea in the interests of ensuring peace on earth."
(*Central African Post*, October 18, 1959, p. 1)

of the urban commentary was thus addressed to males, by males, for the benefit of males. Women could enter into song and plays as wives or "good-time girls." But the theme was usually their impact on men's prestige or paychecks. Colonial policymakers, however, were thoroughly convinced that the key to uplifting the nation was in the hands of women. As primary childcare givers, women were responsible for the bulk of early education, the key shapers of ideas and attitudes. The subject of girls' education thus figured prominently in government radio programming. Parents were encouraged to enroll daughters in local primary schools right alongside their sons. Much of the focus, however, was on hygiene and homecraft study. In some cases government funding was available to churches and other organizations that offered classes on these topics to women. There is an extensive literature on colonial concerns with African hygiene in general, with much of it converging on the bodies of African women in particular. They were portrayed as perpetually dirty, drenched in sweat, wrapped in layers of soiled cloth, harboring untold diseases, a urinating baby invariably strapped on their back, and ever-encased in a halo of flies. Outrageous claims were made about how African women dealt with their monthly menses, buttressed by reference to African traditions that isolated women and forbid them from handling food during that time of the month. Many European shopkeepers, in fact, placed an outright ban on African women entering their establishments and secured legal support for declaring them walking health hazards.[5]

The project of cleaning up the African woman, it was thought, would check the spread of disease and lower the infant mortality rate. But the ultimate aim for some was to prepare her for domestic service. Whereas it was believed that mining would invariably lead African men to modernity, the best hope for African women was closer association with European women. By working under Madam's supervision, African women could be drawn ever closer to European values, tastes, and norms and could pass these new sensibilities on to subsequent generations. But before European women could be expected to permit African women in their homes, the latter would first have to be sanitized, taught basic English, and exposed to the tools and standards of modern domestic science. They would have to become familiar with gas stoves, ovens, and refrigerators, learn to cook according to recipes, and be introduced to sewing, knitting, and needlepoint. Thus, little of the resources invested in girls' education was aimed at opening doors to the professions, but rather at making African women acceptable to enter European kitchens.[6]

In any event, more young girls found themselves in classrooms, many in basic primary schools alongside boys. Walking, at times, long distances to and from school together, jointly cramming for upcoming exams, indeed being cooped up in a small room all day with only brief recreational breaks, produces a camaraderie between boys and girls unlike that experienced by any previous generation. The

Officials "In Dark" on Trotters Visit

KITWE

Northern Rhodesian basketball officials are still in the dark on the proposed tour of the Harlem Globetrotters.

The United States' Information Service has not yet replied to the inquiry made by Mr. M. Higgins, chairman of the N. Rhodesian Basketball and Volleyball Association.

However, preparations are going ahead to provide the best possible facilities for them, should they come.
(*Central African Post,* December 16, 1959, p. 16)

heavily genderized world of the Lunda with segregated spaces for work and play, had kept males and females separate in the public domain. Beliefs about the differing existential status of males and females and the metaphysical dangers of unregulated interaction had erected additional barriers to cross-gender contact. But the emerging urban world that arrives via the airwaves mediated the distance between the sexes. As noted above, it attempted to liberate the individual from group constraints. It privileged acquired traits over ascribed statuses. It placed shared vision and values over shared ethnicity as the more powerful basis for marriage unions. As such, it challenged the fundamental Lunda notion of marriage as a lineage alliance and a vehicle for keeping clear the distinction between us and the other.

Increasingly, religious programming took to the airwaves in Northern Rhodesia. Catholics and Evangelical Christians, for the most part, peddling individual conversion and individual salvation, in their own ways reinforced the above messages of modernity. Life, as they present it, is about powerful individual choices rather than adherence to inherited beliefs. The consequences of those choices are eternal: eternal paradise or eternal damnation. Radio ministries thus seek to fortify individuals, enticing them to make the difficult decision of ecclesiastically forsaking their ascribed group and spiritually resituating themselves within Christian communities. If one does not exist locally, then the radio church becomes the surrogate community. Christians are exhorted to enter into matrimony only with other Christians, thus again challenging the traditional role of marriage in alliance building, in the creation of a supportive network of affines, and in the maintenance of ethnic identity. Christianity inserts itself within and reconfigures the relationships on which ethnic solidarity is based.

Back at Matonchi Plateau, the above messages resonated powerfully with some, irked and irritated others, and were probably ignored by still others. Clearly radio acting alone could not be declared a medium of change. Its power comes from augmenting and amplifying other agents of change. Working collectively, however, these agents can justify perspectives, validate strategies, and legitimize choices perhaps not fully appreciated or accepted locally. Amabwambu were perhaps more sensitive to CABS radio messages than others in their immediate area. To begin with, they were the first generation for whom the presence of radio was a taken-for-granted part of daily life, a constant companion throughout their upbringing, a source of entertainment, and a font of information, ever available, as they labored to construct individual styles and collective consciousness. Even so, the local milieu in which Amabwambu were enmeshed diverged in significant ways from that of their age mates. A life-long relationship with the Catholics at Lwawu Mission station mitigated the gap between the diurnal reality of Amabwambu and the secondary reality of the radio. Other members of the cohort may have experienced a profound sense of incongruity juxtaposing their world of village norms and duties with the urban-based events and values emanating from the radio. For Amabwambu, however, there was little disjuncture between the messages from afar and those percolating nearby. Amabwambu grew to maturity in a world that flowed seamlessly from Matonchi Plateau to the Copperbelt and beyond. Although they did not necessarily travel any more extensively than others of their generation, they were, indeed, privileged to have the world brought to them at Lwawu Mission.

Tarzan in Real Jungle

NAIROBI, SAPA-REUTER

Several hundred of Kenya's Masai and Kikuyu tribesmen are working as film extras for a new Tarzan adventure being filmed around Lake Naivasha, 50 miles from Nairobi, where a film company has built an entire village on the lake shore.
(*Central African Post,* February 29, 1960, p. 7)

5

The Federation

The St. Kizito thrust to inculcate a sense of identity among its students that would transcend ethnicity is inseparable from the corresponding influences of larger Central African processes. One of the most important phenomenon to which Amabwambu had to respond was the decade of intense political activity aimed at bringing to an end the Federation of the Rhodesias and Nyasaland. The idea of joining the separate British territories in Central Africa under a unified political structure had been periodically tabled, debated, and ultimately dismissed since the beginning of the twentieth century.[1] At mid-century, however, sufficient pockets of support emerged, both in Europe and Africa, to give new impetus to the idea. The conjuncture of features that made unity more tenable in the early 1950s has been rigorously debated elsewhere.[2] Variously they included (1) the 1948 coming to power of the National Party in South Africa and the concomitant British fear that Southern Rhodesian settlers, many of Afrikaner origin, might be drawn into closer relations with a regime that had harbored many Nazi sympathizers during World War II; (2) the 1949 achievement of formal recognition by the African Mineworkers Union of Northern Rhodesia, demonstrating emerging African industrial muscle and the continual insistence from the British Colonial Office that in Northern Rhodesia the interests of Africans should remain paramount, combined to greatly intensify the insecurity of European settlers; (3) rapidly rising copper prices generating abundant capital that could be best absorbed regionally through investments in Southern Rhodesia's burgeoning industrial sector; (4) the mutual benefits of a free trade zone guaranteeing no tariffs on copper ore moving south or manufactured goods moving north; (5) the greater ease of controlling and allocating labor as needed between mines and plantations; and (6) the 1951 rise of a Conservative government in Britain, shifting the balance of power as it was more willing than previous Labour governments to accept verbal assurances from settlers that power would be shared with Africans in due course if federation was allowed to proceed.

Seizing the moment, European settlers spoke boldly and openly of their aims, either as if Africans could not interpret their intentions or were powerless to act against those intentions. For example, one member of the first federation conference openly acknowledged: "The main reason why we need a Federal State in Central Africa is because this will enable us to loosen the grip of the Colonial Office on the Territory" (reported in Clegg, *Race and Politics*, 161). He further noted, "Europeans struggle to oust the Colonial Office, for the modern concept of Trusteeship, of helping technically backward peoples to bridge the gap between the past and present and fashion a new national synthesis, is equally incompatible with the sine qua non of the European community" (210). In the interest of settler development, the Colonial Office had to be moved aside.

Thus, in 1953, the power structure in British Central Africa changed radically when the protectorates of Northern Rhodesia and Nyasaland and the self-governing colony of Southern Rhodesia were linked in a federation. Under this alignment European settlers became more powerful in establishing policy, the Colonial Office proportionately less so. Africans in all three countries uniformly opposed federation. Most feared the northward spread and territorial intensification of Southern Rhodesian racial attitudes and ordinances.[3] It was a colony well known for its harsh restrictions on African landholding, participation in governance, and organization in the workplace. The Colour Bar and the pass laws tightly controlled where Africans could be and when and how they could get there. Many Northern Rhodesian Africans had been contract laborers in the south. Their tales of woe were constantly retold in even the most remote villages. Northern Rhodesian Africans forwarded a petition to the houses of Parliament in

CARLTON
(Europeans Only)
Nightly 8:15 p.m.

Saturdays 5:15 and 8:30 p.m.
Matinees Wed. and Sat. 2:30 p.m.
❖
TONIGHT AND THURS. 19th
The Great Comedian
FERNANDEL
And
ZSA ZSA GABOR
In the side-splitting Comedy
Public Enemy
No. 1
French Dialogue–
English Sub-titles
British Movietone News
Supporting Programme
❖
MATINEE TODAY 2:30 p.m.
A science horror thriller
Invasion of the
Body Snatchers
❖
(*Central African Post*,
March 18, 1959, p. 6)

London, forcefully manifesting their concerns against federation, signed by 120 chiefs.[4] Indeed, through nationwide fundraising efforts an African delegation was dispatched to London in May of 1952 to present objections to federation directly to the British government. One delegate, Senior Chief Chitimukulu of the Bemba, in an interview in the *Nottingham Journal*, stated: "I would like to hear what we have done to violate the agreement with Queen Victoria, that we should live under her and be given protection. We look upon federation as a proposal to bar Africans from advancing in the administration of their own government. My people will not, in any way, accept federation" (Makasa, *Zambia's March to Political Freedom*, 79).

The federation issue would dominate Central African political, social, and economic life for the next decade. Its dissolution became the supreme objective of African politicians. Anthropologist Hortense Powdermaker, who arrived in Northern Rhodesia the year federation was instituted, noted, "When I began my field work, the meaning of the new political union became quickly apparent to me because the fear of federation and the loss of land was dragged into almost every interview and conversation, regardless of context or relevancy. I never interviewed specifically on the subject of federation, but most Africans, with or without European education, young and old, appeared to have a compulsive need to talk about it" (*Copper Town*, 63).

Federation brought to the forefront longstanding African ambivalence about the status of Europeans in Africa, divergent notions that in some cases reached back to the eighteenth century. There is, on the one hand, the benevolent European coming to put down slavery, end tribal wars, and introduce Africans to the benefits of commerce, Christianity, and civilization. In certain contexts these incoming Europeans were embraced, particularly by Africans on the losing end of regional wars or in the less favored groups within despotic regimes.[5] Yet, there is also the counter image of Europeans as evil personified, cannibals and vampires that are as hungry for African flesh and blood as they are for African land. Both images often co-existed in the same time and place, and even within the same mind. It may take but one incident to move the perceiver from one extreme position to the other. Powdermaker perhaps summed it up best, noting that

> for most Africans, the ambivalence continues. In their imagery is the picture of the "good" or "proper" Europeans—the missionaries, the district officers, and an occasional employer or supervisor—all interested in helping them enter the modern world; on the other side are the bad Europeans, the settlers, with their alleged cannibalistic desires in the background and in the foreground their overt manipulations to keep Africans on the lowest economic and social level. One group is temporarily in

Africa to help the Africans. The other hopes to be there permanently and
to hold on to its political and economic power. (*Copper Town*, 62)

Land and blood, witchcraft, and predation are the themes that would dominate African discourse about the imposition of federation. There was, for example, a radical increase in rumors of Banyama,
vampire men who supposedly abducted Africans,
conveying them to evil Europeans, who either extracted their blood and brains or transformed them
into zombies who labored clandestinely on European farms or in factories without the need of food,
water, rest, or pay.[6] The notion of Banyama had been
present as early as the 1920s and had intensified with
wartime blood drives, but it became particularly
virulent just before and during federation. Not all
Banyama were believed to be Europeans, however. Quite the contrary. Any African who served or simply spoke favorably of the Federation government risked
being labeled Banyama. Even the cultural heroes of the Central African Broadcasting Service were branded Banyama at one point, their sin being their straightforward, matter-of-fact reporting of the coming of federation on the radio without commentary, expressions of horror, or statements of personal opposition. At
various times Copperbelt cities were awash with pamphlets accusing Europeans
of selling poisoned sugar to make African men impotent and African women
sterile, or claiming that certain canned meats contained processed African flesh.
Older notions about Europeans making wine out of African blood and cheese out
of African brains intersected with newer notions about the utility of African body
parts and bodily substances in medical research.

Contrary to rumours

WE HAVE A FULL AND
COMPLETE RANGE OF
FIREARMS AND
AMMUNITIONS
Stanley, Day & Co. Ltd.
TELEPHONE: 82191
P.O. Box 326
(*Central African Post*,
March 20, 1959, p. 12)

African fears that federation would lead to large-scale land alienation were
not without foundation. The European population in Northern Rhodesia would,
indeed, climb from 37,000 in 1951 to 72,000 in 1958. Few issues provoked stronger
emotions than the Federation's continual tampering with land policies, variously
redefining broad expanses as Crown Land, Game Reserves, Protected Forest Areas, Native Trusts, and European Settlement Areas. Concerns about rights in land
cut across all ethnic and occupational categories. Villagers and townsfolk alike
were united in their view that access to land was the only real safeguard against
unemployment and the only trusted source of security in old age.

African fears of being totally overwhelmed, devastated, and even devoured by
a European onslaught were perhaps no less rational than the fear of land alienation. There was a quasi-schizophrenic character to European federalist discourse,
striking a solicitous tone toward Africans at times, resonating with intimidation

at others; promising to cultivate a stable African labor force one moment, fearful and threatening to crush it another moment; speaking of partnership one day, warning of African annihilation the next. Sir Roy Welensky, founder of the Northern Rhodesia Labour Party, member of the Legislative Council, vigorous campaigner for the amalgamation of the two Rhodesias, and later the prime minister of the Federation, horrified Africans when he boldly stated in the Legislative Council on July 3, 1952: "I say this to the Africans. If they do not come with us on federation, and I do not mean it as a threat, if they do not come with us, they will meet with the same fate which came to the Red Indians in the United States of America, they disappeared" (Makasa, *Zambia's March to Political Freedom*, 78).

Welensky's vitriolic speeches appeared in mainstream newspapers and local African newsletters and were spread by word-of-mouth by the unremitting flow of people linking cities to townships to villages. His speeches were the subject of radio debates, political rallies, and village fireside chats. Welensky, for many Africans, was the personification of the federation movement, indeed, the very symbol of European domination.[7] A large, menacing-looking individual, he had been a successful professional boxer, holding the title of heavyweight champion of Rhodesia, 1926–28. Before entering political life he became an engine driver and was elected chairman of Rhodesia Railway Workers' Union branch at Broken Hill in 1933. Throughout his life he would retain the basic reflexes of a white trade unionist, who might on occasion speak of his support for the improvement of African material conditions, but who far more frequently saw Africans as competitors for "European" jobs. His distrust and impatience with the British Colonial Office was palpable, and he constantly accused it of limiting the opportunities of blacks and whites alike. Widely acknowledged as a white supremacist, Welensky was the son of a South African immigrant from Lithuania, but he himself had been born in Salisbury, Southern Rhodesia. Yet here he was leading the settlers of Northern Rhodesia into a union that would siphon off the region's wealth to the noticeable benefit of his hometown. Salisbury would be selected as federal capital and business headquarters and would become the recipient of a disproportional amount of federal investment. An explosion of new banks, manufacturing concerns, service establishments, and residential estates would sprout up in and around Salisbury. The road, railway, and communication network would likewise be greatly expanded. All taxes raised within the three territories were first forwarded to Sal-

Multi-racial Bar Licence Suggested

C.A.P. REPORTER

Legislation providing for multi-racial bar liquor licences would be a useful step in the right direction, said a Lusaka publican, Mr. Peter Spooner, at a meeting between representatives of cafe, hotel and bar proprietors and African National Congress here on Wednesday.

"If we could get someone to take one out—even if it were sponsored almost like a Government 'pub'—Europeans and Africans would grow accustomed to being together," he said.

(*Central African Post*, May 22, 1959, p. 5)

isbury for accounting before reallocation. Northern Rhodesian Africans took to calling the place Bamba Zonke (take all).

One of the most talked about "takings" was of the Zambezi River. In 1955 Welensky oversaw the decision to build a dam and hydroelectric power station on the Zambezi River at Kariba, nullifying a much earlier plan to build the station on the Kafue River. The latter site would have been cheaper by all estimates and more profitable for Northern Rhodesia. Building the dam at Kariba, however, meant flooding over two thousand square miles of territory and producing the largest artificial lake in the world. Concomitantly, over thirty thousand residents in Northern Rhodesia on the northern bank of the Zambezi River were forcibly resettled with no consultation and very little warning, while the power stations were constructed on the southern bank of the Zambezi, symbolizing the predominance of Southern Rhodesia.

It has frequently been said that the federation period made everyone in British Central Africa politically aware. Protests against federation gave rise to a new generation of African leaders, helped crystallize a new nationalist discourse, and brought into being new mechanisms for animating and orchestrating mass political action. Federation sparked the flames of African protest that would not be extinguished until the Federation collapsed in 1963, followed by Northern Rhodesian independence the following year.

During this period Mwinilunga's connections to the outside world strengthened. Explosive growth in mining and secondary service industries, combined with increased local access to mission-managed education, enabled proportionately more Lunda to secure employment on the Copperbelt. This increased movement of informed individuals along the rural and urban nexus was complemented by other information sources, such as the ever-expanding number of saucepan radios, the periodic availability of mission-sponsored film shows, and the ever-widening circulation of books, magazines, and newspapers from town. By the late 1950s the *African Newsletter* was being produced in Mwinilunga, a little cyclostyled journal whose pages were filled primarily with greetings from Lunda migrants to kin back home, interspersed with articles about the latest news, music, and fashions in town.[8] Political tracts and position papers regularly appeared on the landscape as urban-based groups made appeals for rural support.

Yet, in other ways Mwinilunga remained strangely apart, detached from the federation fervor and

U.K. Democracy Too Dangerous Here—Moffat

C.A.P. REPORTER

Sir John Moffat, newly elected to the Northern Rhodesian Legislative Council as leader of the Central African Party, thinks the British system of parliamentary democracy too dangerous for implicit adoption in the Federation.

He was speaking to the Lusaka Rotary Club yesterday on the dilemma facing Europeans living in view of the great differences in racial population the Europeans long-term chance of survival was hazardous.
(*Central African Post*, March 25, 1959, p. 3)

political agitation that dominated Central African urban life during the 1950s. The relationship between local Europeans and Africans was, for the most part, excellent. A new Kanongesha was inaugurated with two days of pomp and pageantry well attended by Europeans in the district in 1953. The Lunda emperor, Mwantiyamvwa from Congo, visited Mwinilunga for the first time ever in 1956, presiding over a unique and deeply emotional convocation of all the Lunda chiefs in Northern Rhodesia. The event was well supported by European members of local government. Chief Ikelenge was awarded the queen's medal for long-term service to the colony in an impressive local ceremony by the Northern Rhodesia government in 1958. One international mineral survey party after another wrote glowing reports about the mineral potential of the Mwinilunga District throughout the 1950s.[9] New roads and bridges were built to facilitate further exploration. All Lunda chiefs were given vanettes, or utility vehicles, to ameliorate the transportation shortage in their respective areas. Additionally, several chiefs and other enterprising Africans had become prosperous enough to purchase their own personal motor vehicles. In short, the 1950s were generally a socially and economically rewarding period in Mwinilunga. Much of this newfound wealth was based on the production of surplus commodities for the mines. Although European farmers had been given a virtual monopoly on supplying the food needs of mineworkers, they simply could not keep up with the demands of the boom period. Cassava meal was in particularly high demand. Mwinilunga was able to ship roughly four hundred tons of surplus cassava per year to the Copperbelt in the 1950s, indicating widespread involvement in cash cropping and a broad reaping of its attendant benefits.[10] Thus, local economic contingency rather than national political posturing seems to have established the local quotidian rhythm during most of the decade of federation.

Yet, Mwinilunga could not remain isolated from larger issues of state indefinitely. The politicizing moment would begin with a quiet request in the late 1950s from then District Commissioner (DC) P. O. Bourn for the African members of the local Native Authority (NA) government to append their signatures to a document approving the concept of establishing Protected Forest Areas in Mwinilunga.[11] Although at times the Native Authority had routinely rubber-stamped policies originating in the district commissioner's office, this particular request was greeted with a small measure of suspicion. The NA asked for clarification. "Game Reserves," "Native Trusts," and "Crown Lands" were designations with which they were already familiar, even if corresponding boundaries were not always clear. But what were "Protected Forest Areas" (PFAs)? The DC's rambling response about the need to manage nature responsibly for the sake of future generations and the nation as a whole only served to provoke greater suspicion among NA members. They began to ask more probing questions. The DC

switched tactics, demanding that the NA sign off immediately under threat of losing their jobs. Yet, they
held firm, declaring that they had no authority to sign
away their people's land. The matter could only be
resolved through direct discussion with the people.

Apparently caught between the demands of his
superiors at the provincial level to formally secure
local permission before proceeding with land reclas-
sification and the need to reassert his local authority
in the face of budding African opposition, DC Bourn

continued to vacillate, demanding compliance one moment, the next moment
pleading that all was well and that PFA was in everyone's best interest. A series of
meetings was held throughout the district to provide DC Bourn an opportunity
to explain the concept. He assured crowds of locals that protected forests would
still belong to them. The land was not being taken from the people by the government. Locals could still gather honey, graze their cows, and so forth. The only
change would be that trees could not be cut down. But what about access to bark
rope, poles, rafters, and thatching grass, the locals wanted to know. Could they
hunt, trap, and fish? And if the aim was merely to protect trees, why could not
houses be built and gardens tended in PFAs as long as no trees were harmed? Lack-
ing patience and short on diplomatic skills, Bourn frequently tried to divert attention away from complex issues by talking of the hydroelectric potential of
Mwinilunga, the possibilities for agricultural expansion to feed the mines, and
how these opportunities could be lost is PFA was not approved rapidly. Such
statements confused rather than clarified Bourn's objectives. Local concern, of
course, was that PFA was simply a prelude to a European takeover—ffolliot
Fisher, for one, was attempting to expand his holdings again. Additionally, other
strange Europeans, believed to be Southern Rhodesians, had been seen touring
the district.

For several months Bourn attempted to win over the support of local chiefs
through a crude display of government largess. Chiefs were wined and dined in
the Boma, presented with fancy new robes, promised raises and perhaps new vehicles once the matter of PFAs was resolved.[12] Meanwhile, at another level, contact was being established between locals and Harry Nkumbula's African National
Congress (ANC), the nationalist organization spearheading much of Northern
Rhodesia's anti-federation protest. Congress added a wider dimension to local deliberations. It was clear that this was not merely a local phenomenon; rather,
throughout Northern Rhodesia vast acreage was being reclassified as "Protected
Forest." One clear aim of the process was to curtail African movement across the
landscape. British rule had initially restricted African residence to registered vil-

lages. In Mwinilunga, that requirement had been lifted only in 1952. Locals then began to pour out of artificially large villages, dispersing themselves across the countryside in a fashion that more closely paralleled the natural distribution of water, flora, and fauna resources on which village life depended. Indeed, the local reliance on *chitemene* (slash-and-burn agriculture) might send whole villages moving every three to four years. This demographic pattern strained the capacity of government to conduct censuses, provide services, monitor movements, and mobilize labor as needed. Appeals by government officials and chiefs alike for people to settle in larger villages were little heeded. Thus, rather than reinstitute policies mandating where African must live, this time government rules would state where African could not live. The new policy would also address the serious concerns of European agricultural specialists about the long-term deleterious effect of clearing gardens by burning the underbrush.

Gangs of Europeans Are Becoming a Nuisance

BY LUCIFER

Lusaka, it seems, is developing is own brand of Teddy Boys. They roam the streets in large gangs, behave as rowdily as possible and seem to take great pleasure in beating Africans.

There is nothing wrong with good, honest fun and even teenage pranks—provided they do no damage and commit no nuisance—but behaviour which reflects on a whole community or race must not be tolerated. (*Central African Post*, July 20, 1959, p. 2)

From increasingly politicized local perspectives the above reasons were an attempt to cloak more sinister objectives. With a population density of only 6 persons per square mile, Mwinilunga was hardly in danger of being deforested by the few acres cleared annually by fire. Second, the level of services provided by government, whether in health, education, or agricultural development, was too pitifully low to warrant consideration in residential strategies. "Protected Forest" was simply land being set aside for future European development. Africans, concomitantly, were to be crammed onto Native Trusts land as labor-in-reserve for European enterprises. This realization, accurate or not, was the clarion call, summoning Mwinilunga to wake up and join the ongoing struggle against federation. Some conservative elements wrote letters to Queen Elizabeth, notifying her that their land was being stolen and their chief, Kanongesha, deposed by the district commissioner. The letters were either intercepted or forwarded back to Mwinilunga, where District Commissioner Bourn read them aloud at a public meeting, naming several individuals whom he accused of stirring up trouble at the behest of the African National Congress. He warned of grave consequences. Yet, the result of this attempt at intimidation was to further radicalize the local population. News from the front, including details of recent rallies and boycotts in town, the substance of political speeches, and the analysis of the emerging African leadership, permeated local discourse. Around nightly fires, talk of crops, cattle, and the good old days gave way to critical inquiry and political strategizing. The African National Congress seized the moment to formally recruit new members and to train local cadres in techniques of political activism. The timing was propitious. A focal point for pent-up political energy arose almost immediately: the Monckton Commission.

The Monckton Commission was jointly set up by the British Conservative Party and the Federation government in 1960. For nearly a decade European settlers had been telling the world, and themselves, that Central African unrest was fomented by a handful of half-educated African demagogues with a mystical hold on their even less-well-educated brethren. The purpose of the commission was supposedly to hear what the "real" Africans had to say in advance of a comprehensive Federal Review Conference. The twenty-five-member commission, headed by a British banker and dominated by British Conservative Party politicians, was shunned by the British Labour Party. Some African nationalist organizations chose to boycott the proceedings on political grounds as well.[13] First, the matter of self-government and independence, they asserted, was an inalienable right of Africans, not a matter for negotiation or justification by a commission. Second, the commission's mandate specifically forbade it from hearing evidence on or considering the possibility of secession by individual states. Thus, the whole operation was seen as a political charade contrived by British conservatives and federal supremacists to perpetuate European dominion over Africans. The Lunda, however, would ultimately choose not to heed the call to boycott the commission hearings. In a grassroots exercise unlike any in recorded or remembered history, local headmen presided over village discussions, senior headmen fired up debates among clusters of villages, and chiefs convened territory-wide deliberations until a consensus emerged, and a document was produced that reflected the broadest and most concise thinking among the Lunda on the issue of federation. Copies of the document were carefully transcribed by the literate, over and over, until virtually every village had its own replica. Some were scrawled on the pages of school exercise booklets. Others were crammed into the blank spaces inside mission-issued Bibles. Every copy was treasured for what it was: a representation of a unique historical moment in which the collective thoughts of the Lunda took on a heretofore unseen form.[14] In this discrete document, written in English, contents of the Lunda mind became transportable and capable

"The Wayward Girl" Not for Africans

C.A.P. REPORTER

"She fought for love in a city of violence and terror." That is how the posters describe the film "The Wayward Girl" which is to be shown at the Palace Cinema in Lusaka next Tuesday, Wednesday, and Thursday.

"Africans have been banned from attending," Mr. V.D. Mistry, the cinema manager said today.

He explained: "The film contains some beach scenes of women in bathing costumes and also a fight inside a women's prison. The Censorship Board decided it was not suitable for African . . ."

(*Central African Post*, August 11, 1959, p. 1)

of being comprehended far beyond the reaches of Mwinilunga. The Lunda were justly proud of its production and took steps to ensure its broad dissemination. Local leaders sought out commission representatives, requesting and receiving an opportunity to present their findings.

Evidence of the Lunda Ndembu Native Authority, Mwinilunga District, to the Monckton Commission, March 1st 1960

We are the Chiefs, Councilors and elected members of the Lunda Ndembu Native Authority, Mwinilunga, and we speak for the people of Mwinilunga District, who number 30,000.

1) The commission should remember that at the beginning of Federation, the chiefs and people did not agree to it. They still do not agree to it. We are refusing Federation because we do not wish the ruling to be changed from that of 1924. This rule came from the colonial office.

2) From 1953 when Federation was imposed the ruling of the Government of Sir Roy Welensky has troubled and disturbed our rule by the Northern Rhodesian Government.

3) The bad things we have seen are as follows: everywhere people meet there have been detectives, and this has not been good.

4) Federation has not advanced African education fast enough because so much of the money has gone to Southern Rhodesia, and the Federation Government dictates to our Government.

5) The Northern Rhodesian Government is in the hands of the Federation government; as ministers from the Federal Party are in the Northern Rhodesian Government.

6) Hospitals. It is difficult to get sufficient medicine for our hospitals and dispensaries, as the health services are controlled from Southern Rhodesia.

7) Since Federation very many Europeans have arrived in the Federation. We do not want so many; we fear that they will take our country; and they say that black people are dirty.

8) Post office. Many post offices have been built, but postal charges have gone up, and higher customs duties have been imposed.

9) Information. Wireless were free, but now they are taxed, and the Federation has taken our money.

10) The reason why we refuse Federation is because we fear that the rule from England may end, and as yet we are unready to stand on our own feet. If that is done we shall be treated as slaves. The Europeans who are born in Africa are not good to Africans.

11) We do not want the three countries put into one because in a democracy the majority should rule, and we are at present ruled by a minority.

12) A colony should not be combined with a protectorate because a colony like Southern Rhodesia is one thing, and a protectorate is another. We are afraid of a state of emergency and policemen with guns, when there is an outbreak. The guns are brought by Welensky. What are they for? To fight Africans or to fight the Queens power. The Africans have no arms.

13) We still believe in the Agreements we made that we should be protected until we are ready to stand on our own feet politically, socially, economically, so that we will take over ruling ourselves. In our ruling, if it comes, there will be no discrimination.

14) Federation. We do not want Federation to disturb our future, because that lies in our own hands. Federation should be taken away with its bad ideas. It has brought no good to us in the last 7 years. If the Federation is broken up we can see who is really fit to rule. We should have more African seats in Legislative Council, and also in posts of importance in Government, without any question of colour.

15) We think that our children should go to the same schools as Europeans. We know that many Europeans come here for work, but they are not the owners of the country.

16) We have seen the results of Federation where many people were killed with guns at Kariba.

17) Federation is dangerous because at the beginning of 1955 Sir Roy Welensky went to England to say that Africans have agreed. The Queen believed him that they had agreed, but he lied. If Federation endures they will go on saying things that trouble us. If there is one man in Northern Rhodesian who agrees with Federation then let him go and live where the Federation people come from.

18) The reason why we refuse Federation is because Federal Government makes us unhappy and we fear it and there are many things to complain about. Does the Queen not find us good leaders at present instead of putting us in the hands of the Federation Government. We need the Queen's Government to give us what we still need.

19) <u>Land</u> In the old days of the BSA company, we did not live well. However, in 1930 we began to have a good understanding with the authorities, and the chiefs were given power to rule. We had Native treasuries established; there was nothing wrong, and no troubles between Africans and Europeans.

20) But when Federation came we saw Europeans coming to apportion our lands. Therefore we fear. We do not want to be like Southern Rhodesia. Their African people are not happy. We are afraid that the Queen's Government has put us in the hands of Welensky and we shall be treated as slaves.

21) If the Queen's Government has put us in the hands of the Federation Government we are already slaves. If a person has lived with his father, and then his father hands him over to another, then he is a slave. That is why people are not happy: if many Europeans come, they will take the country. Today we are pleased that the Queen's Government has sent the Commission to hear our complaints, and we are happy.

22) We wish to live under the Queen's Government; if we are put under the Federation we shall come out from Government of the Queen, as we refuse Federation.

23) We have this example from Chief Ikelenge's country. Some Europeans from the Federation Government came to make a road, and began to cut down trees and demolish houses and latrines in the capital. People came running to Chief Ikelenge, saying "they are destroying our houses, they

have come from Salisbury, and tell us to take our goods outside at once, and they are cutting down all the trees." Chief Ikelenge went there quickly. He asked them what they were doing, destroying houses. They said "what are you." Chief Ikelenge told them he was the Chief. They said to him, "get off!" Chief Ikelenge said, "are you the King or Queen of England, that you are doing this." They replied "we do not ask the provincial commission or the district commission when we are working, we are from Salisbury and don't listen to anyone else." Chief Ikelenge said that that was his village, and to stop destroying it. They replied "Get away you black man." Chief Ikelenge then told the African labourers to stop destroying the houses; and they did. Others went on, but the people told them to listen to what the Chief had said. Then all the labourers stopped work; and when the man in charge said they would be dismissed, they agreed. Chief Ikelenge met the District Commissioner and the Police Officer on their way to Sakeji School, and told them about it. The District Commissioner was annoyed; but they found they had gone off to their camp. The Police officer told the people in charge to come to the Boma, and they were given a case. They were fined a total of £25, £5 to the Chief for disrespect, and £20 compensation for the houses. This was something we found out about the Federation Government.

24) Finally we stand by the preamble to the constitution which states that British protection should not be withdrawn until the majority of the inhabitants of the country so desire. This does not mean simply a majority in parliament or legislative council, as the franchise is at present such that the majority of the people in the territory are represented by too few members. In addition so far as this territory is concerned, we stand by the Moffat Resolution of July 1954.

25) We are the loyal Chiefs and people of Mwinilunga, who have lived well with Government for many years and we ask you to weigh our words well. We do not write to the newspapers or make speeches but we carry very great responsibilities; and without our work the Government could not go on.

The above document presents a wealth of hermeneutic opportunities, providing deep insights into Lunda perceptions of history, current political context, international relations, and their own evolving sense of identity. It forcefully states that chiefs and people were against federation from the beginning, have not wavered in that judgement, and remain united and passionate in their opposition to federation now. The most frequently stated reason, explicitly and implicitly, is a deep and abiding fear and suspicion of federalists, or Southern Rhodesian whites in general. There are eleven references to them as having "troubled and disturbed" the Northern Rhodesian government and having planted spies wherever people gather. Spies, as people with secret identities and hidden agendas, forcing others to fear openness of thought, speech, and movement, embody much that is locally associated with witchcraft. As such they rekindle images of Banyama. Concomitantly, Southern Rhodesians are accused of abusing black people, even chiefs, claiming they are "dirty." Locally the term "dirty," just as in English, means the opposite of "clean," which in Lunda can be glossed as either *kadi majilu* (to be without mud or dirt) or *tooka* (to be pure, open, public). In the latter sense, an accusation of "dirtiness" is primarily an accusation of witchcraft. Hence, the above document conforms to Lunda philosophical inclinations in its simultaneous concern with both physical and metaphysical conditions and actions. Southern Rhodesians are further charged with treating Africans as slaves, being well armed and willing to kill Africans with little provocation, and having actually done so in the Kariba basin.[15] Indeed, "white people from Salisbury" becomes shorthand for longstanding images of the "bad European." They are the ones who have not come temporarily to help Africans, but the ones who intend to stay permanently and devour Africans. There are four references to Southern Rhodesia figuratively sucking the lifeblood of Northern Rhodesia by its southward diversion of money, water, and health and educational resources. Roy Welensky, the huge man who would beat down Africans, who had hinted at their extermination, is the personification of this fear. His name appears four times as a pseudonym for the Federation as a whole.

Land, of course, emerges as a fundamental concern. There are four specific references to a fear of losing land under federation to a swarm of Europeans from the south. The document pleads for protection with five references to the 1924 agreement that rescinded British South Africa Company rule and converted Northern Rhodesia into a protectorate of the British Colonial Office. Again and again the Lunda express their need for the security provided by that agreement. The document mentions the queen nine times. On occasion it addresses her directly, assuring her that the Lunda remain loyal subjects, informing her of the misdeeds her subjects have suffered at the hands of federalists, and urging her to personally intervene on her subjects' behalf.

"Keep Your Children Busy" — Lusaka's Shops Plead

Pilfering increases with N.R. school holidays

C.A.P. REPORTER

There has been a spate of shoplifting in Lusaka since the school holidays began and European schoolboys who have nothing else to do than wander aimlessly round stores are largely to blame.

(*Central African Post,* August 26, 1959, p. 1)

In harking back to the 1924 ruling and appealing for the maintenance of protectorate status, Lunda discourse seemingly stands out as uniquely retrogressive for its time. By 1960, virtually every African political organization throughout the Federation was calling for absolute and unconditional independence, not a return to protectorate status. Indeed, statements such as "we are pleased that the Queen's Government has sent the Commission to hear our complaints" might suggest that the Lunda lacked a sophisticated understanding of the distinctions between Labour and Conservative parties in Britain and knew equally little of the convergence of interests between the latter and the federalists in Central Africa. The statement also indicates limited knowledge of the division of responsibilities between elected governments and the royal family. The expression of support for the 1954 Moffat Resolutions also placed the Lunda at odds with prevailing African nationalist sentiments.[16] White liberals in the colonies might have praised the resolutions for their multiracial tone, their support of a transitional period in which neither racial group would have an advantage, their advocacy for the protection of everyone's rights and interests, and the right for people to progress according to their own abilities without regard to race and color. Yet, African nationalists viewed the resolutions as simply one more attempt to delay granting full freedom to Africans immediately, by enacting yet one more interim agreement. However naive the Lunda may have been about the intricacies of British politics, they were most certainly intimately familiar with the strategic thrust of the Northern Rhodesian nationalist mainstream. Yet, they were equally aware of their own position on the political and economic margins. Most other regions of Northern Rhodesia were far more developed, had long had better educational and training opportunities, possessed a more developed infrastructure, and had greater access to urban markets and services. Thus, it was well known locally that other groups were better positioned to reap any benefits that full independence would bestow, and being far more numerous, they would certainly become politically dominant in the event a majority-rule election was held. For the Lunda, the more local the government, the better. National would be preferable to federal, but a district commissioner system dependent on local "Native Authorities," chiefs, and headmen would be better still than a powerful national government, controlled, for example, by Bemba, Lozi, or any other group that had not historically treated the Lunda well.

School of Modelling Re-opens in Lusaka Next Week

BY SARA ANNA

The Lusaka School of Modelling, which has been in recess for a short time since the last three-month course was completed, is to re-open next week. Vivacious, French-born Mrs. Aimee Anderson, a former co-principal of the school, is teaming up with petite, fair-haired Mrs. Linda Saunders from Scotland to help women in Lusaka, from teenagers to grandmothers, acquire poise, confidence and dress sense.
(*Central African Post,* January 13, 1960, p. 7)

The document presented to the Monckton Commission, however, is not a narrowly proscribed ethnic treatise. In addition to its mention of pan-territorial processes such as increasing tariffs on mail and communication, the rising cost of living, the perceived lack of separation between national and federal governments, and the inequitable distribution of mutually generated resources, the document also draws attention to the oscillating and shifting nature of Lunda identity at this point in history. The document does not speak with a single voice, but is rather an attempt to harness and contain a multiplicity of voices for a single purpose. All Lunda were against the Federation. The Monckton Commission provided the platform to loudly proclaim that point. Yet, the document is also formal evidence that the Lunda recognized a hierarchical array of nested identities. Although it is initially presented as the voice of the "people of Mwinilunga District," at times it speaks of Northern versus Southern Rhodesians, and at other times "Africans" or "Black people" are juxtaposed to "Europeans." As such, some of the references to "we" are unclear. Is it we the people of Mwinilunga, we the people of Northern Rhodesia, or we Africans in general? Likewise, the expression of fear that "bad whites" will take "our" country leaves open the possibility that country could variously mean Northern Rhodesia as a whole or Lunda lands more specifically. In the context of the Monckton Commission, such nuances held little importance. But such questions will certainly move to center stage in the next episode of history.

Amabwambu were in the carefree clutches of childhood at the time of the Monckton Commission. Yet, to a man they can remember the impact of those days on their inchoate assumptions about identity. Nothing was resolved; rather, the possibilities were expanded. All that talk of federation, of hearing about a forced union with Nyasaland and Southern Rhodesia, of endless debates about Bemba versus Lozi intent, and nightly assessments of competing nationalist organizations propelled the process of deciding where Lunda interests were situated at that particular historical moment. The Lunda were prodded from all sides, implored to join one historical stream or another, urged to choose between contrasting identities. The heat and passion of the moment and the potential enormity of the consequences made indecision untenable.

Northern Rhodesian settlers with federalist leanings opted for the uniform application of the label "African" to all dark-skinned Native peoples without regard for differences in geographical location, educational attainment, social comportment, or political persuasion. "Rhodesian" was an appellation they hoped to reserve solely for those of European origin. The Northern Rhodesian Mineworkers Union (NRMU), for example, only represented Europeans. The African Mineworkers Union (AMU) represented the dark-skinned workers in the same mines. Africans, as a category, were to be locked into well-ordered sets of duties and responsibilities that subsidized the statutory rights and privileges of Northern Rhodesians. Many European liberals, however, fought for the inclusion of Africans and the uniform application of the rule of law by expanding the usage of "Rhodesian" to cover all who resided within its borders, irrespective of color or class. Interestingly, a host of radical new leaders such as Kwame Nkrumah of Ghana and Patrice Lumumba of Congo argued against the intensification of local and regional identities, urging instead that all those native to the continent unite as "Africans." Thus, whereas, European federalists sought to construct a homogeneous African mass for ease of containment, Pan-Africanists saw the same process as a vital step in the accumulation of power. Meanwhile, some blacks in the Americas whose political tracts were circulating in Central Africa constructed Pan-African dreams that advocated an even broader application of the term "African."[17]

The position of most Northern Rhodesian African nationalists was to join with their counterparts in Southern Rhodesia and Nyasaland in a series of mass protests designed to make the Federation ungovernable and thereby contribute to its breakup. The local nationalists, in effect, argued for the sanctity of those borders constructed at the Conference of Berlin as well as for a cohesive identity for those who dwelled within. They rejected the label "Northern Rhodesia," however, variously proposing terms such as "Muchinga," "Zambesia," and, finally, "Zambia." Traditional chiefs everywhere were concerned, no doubt, about the impact of national identities on local sentiments and the outcome of shifting power arrangements. The Lunda were particularly uneasy. Their territory had been butchered at the Conference of Berlin, divided among three European powers. To now ignore their cross-border kin and fight for union with an aggregate of historically antagonistic groups was not wholly appealing. For those who resided on Matonchi Plateau, within eyesight of Angola, it was not simply a matter of ethnic sympathies and historic rivalries. The smooth functioning of the local subsistence economy and the maintenance of key social relations both necessitated continual cross-border contact. Grass for thatching was most abundant on the plains stretching into Angola. The largest supply of poles for rafters lay just beyond. Hunting, trapping, and fishing were more productive on the less densely populated Angolan side of the border, and medicinal plants grew more profusely.

"Shorten Your Skirts Women of Lusaka" Says Expert

BY SARAH ANNE

A plea has reached me to "make the women of Lusaka shorten their skirts." Even the dress bought locally last month is, by the fashion standards of Europe and England, too long. Miss K. Falwasser, buyer for a large group of stores in the Federation, tells me that your dress should just—but only just—cover your kneecap. That is the length decreed by the fashion houses of Italy, Germany and England, visited by Miss Falwasser in a recent three-month tour. She has come back full of delight at the prospect of a really colourful range of clothes for the next Rhodesian summer.
(*Central African Post*, March 27, 1960, p. 4)

Roughly one-third of the Lunda population in Northern Rhodesia had been born in Angola, and an equal ratio of locally born had spouses from across the border. Strong connections with Lunda populations in the Congo persisted as well. Nationalist rhetoric did not speak to these issues. As a result, the identity options were perhaps scrutinized more intensely. To be or not to be Lunda, Mwinilungan, Northern Rhodesian, Zambian, Central African, African, or Pan-African was not really the question, however. Which to be, when, and why was the more complex query. The nationalist forces had a full head of steam, amassing supporters, harnessing power, and orchestrating civil unrest in the name of Zambianess. Yet, other forces were powerfully influencing Lunda constructions of consciousness. The outcome, of course, cannot be reckoned through a numerical or quantitative comparison of the array of forces supporting one choice over another. Rather, they all contributed to an expanding repertoire of identity possibilities, increased opportunities for experimentation, and a heighten sense of urgency, ultimately demanding clear demonstration of identity adopted. Previous generations of Lunda may have been able to ponder issues of identity more quietly, arrive at decisions more individually, and implement them more surreptitiously away from the prying eyes of the plateau. But Amabwambu spent their formative years in a cauldron of identity politics. Theirs was a world perched on the precipice of change. The old world was too unstable to be sustained much longer; the new world had not yet come into view. For those more centrally located the nationalist voices may have resonated most loudly. On the margin, particularly on the plateau, a competing paradigm was heard with equal clarity from just across the border.

Barotse to Send Delegation to London

Paramount chief will put case for 1960 talks

C.A.P. CORRESPONDENT, MONGU

The paramount chief of Barotse-land, Sir Mwanawina III, plans to lead a delegation to London "When the time is ripe" to lay his peoples' case concerning the 1960 constitutional talks before the British Government.

"... we are quite confident that in spite of European settlers' clamour for dominion status and responsible government, Her Majesty's Government will continue to safeguard and preserve its treaty obligations to the Barotse nation, and will not be persuaded to hand us over to independent settler-Governments in the Federation."

(*Central African Post,* May 25, 1959, p. 1)

6

Voices from across the Border
Lunda in the Congo Crisis

The parceling out of Lundaland between Britain, Belgium, and Portugal had been but an incidental consequence of a much larger competition among those three nations. Little Portugal had been attempting to stake out a swath of African territory extending from the Atlantic to the Indian Ocean, linking its claims in Angola and Mozambique. Britain had been the somewhat hesitant accomplice to Cecil Rhodes's "Cape to Cairo" dream. King Leopold of Belgium had been angling for the rubber and ivory wealth of the Congo River basin. The competition for Central Africa had intensified when the extent of mineral resources in the Katanga region became better known. The compromise worked out over the conference table reflected European strategic alliances and relative military capacities, paying minimal attention to the political and cultural realities of Central African peoples. Stories of a "Lunda Empire" may have excited the European imagination, but they did not constrain the pen from rending it asunder, at least on paper. On the ground, the main thrust of the colonial enterprise—mineral exploration, mining, railroad building, urbanization, and attending to European settler communities—rendered a divided Lundaland even more marginal. Its three parts occupied the regions least central to the respective economic interests of Britain, Belgium, and Portugal.

Accordingly, accounts of Lundaland during the early twentieth century are virtually non-existent in the standard history text of all three countries. Yet, buried

145

in reports from the field and in the notes of district commissioners and provincial officers is evidence that the tripartite division of Lunda territory did not destroy the prestige, potency, or political relevance of the Lunda Empire. Although its leader, the Mwantiyamvwa, and his capital city, Musumba, were situated well off the beaten path, in a neglected corner of southwestern Congo, it remained one focal point of political reckoning for hundreds of thousands of Central Africans. Borders may have been a nuisance at times, but they were sufficiently permeable to allow the continued exchange of symbolic material that linked thousands of seemingly separate polities. Historically, the Lunda Empire had not been based primarily on linguistic and cultural affinity, but rather on economic and institutional connections. Expansion from the center had not been by conquest per se, but via the steady incorporation of peoples on the margins through the dispensation of prestigious titles to local rulers that linked them to the Mwantiyamvwa. The relationships among various titleholders were expressed in a kinship idiom.

A Boycott of Stores Begins in Lusaka

C.A.P. REPORTER

Lusaka's Indian traders were this morning feeling the brunt of a new African National Congress boycott of stores, which was ordered at an A.N.C. meeting in Chibolya township yesterday.

"Since Europeans will not implement partnership and the Indians are trying to take part in the government of the country to which they only came to trade, they will not see a penny of our money."
(*Central African Post*, July 6, 1959, p. 1)

A local successor would inherit each title, its authority and its preexisting relationships to other titles in accordance with a local tradition known as positional succession and perpetual kinship.[1] This process was replicated time and again, creating in Central Africa an array of similarly organized polities, bound by fictive kinship and shared relationship to the Mwantiyamvwa and his royal court at Musumba.

Among the Lunda of Zambia, the title of senior chief Kanongesha is unique to this upper Zambezi context and is said to place him in the relationship of "son" to the Mwantiyamvwa. Those on Matonchi Plateau say that the title of Chifunga is similarly unique and is reckoned as a senior in-law of the Kanongesha and, by extension, an in-law of the Mwantiyamvwa as well. But scattered throughout Mwinilunga to this present day are dozens of titles, identical in name and historical function to counterparts at the royal court in Congo. One finds, for example, *tubanji* (the war leaders), *kanampumba* (the council head), *nswana muropu* (the heir apparent), *mwadi* (the senior wife), and so forth, assisting the Kanongesha, in theory at least, in his round of royal duties. Titleholders with identical names can also be found among the Cokwe, Lwena, Mbundu, Luchazi, and other groups stretching over a thousand miles from the Luapula River in northern Zambia to the Bihe Plateau in western Angola.

The Lunda Empire expanded in spectacular bursts between the sixteenth and eighteenth centuries, in tandem with equally energetic upswings in economic engagement with the Atlantic trade world, particularly through the ivory and slave trades. Thus, it would be naive to ignore the role of violence, both applied and threatened, in the construction of the empire in favor of arguments about symbols of prestige. Nevertheless, the salient point is that many Central African traditional leaders, bound to the Mwantiyamvwa by relations of kinship, loyalty, and perhaps even tribute, rule over populations that are not essentially Lunda in speech or customs. In the Lunda Empire linguistic and cultural affinities are secondary to economic and institutional linkages. These linkages are embodied in the person of the Mwantiyamvwa, and hence, the legitimacy of chiefs throughout Central Africa rests on their relationship to Mwantiyamvwa. Ignoring colonial divisions, hundreds of Angolan and Northern Rhodesian chiefs, upon ascension to their local throne, continued to trek to Musumba and performed acts of obeisance in hope of receiving ritual items of confirmation from Mwantiyamvwa in return. The supreme symbol of chiefly authority was a *lukanu,* a bracelet supposedly made from human genitalia and soaked in sacrificial blood. In some cases, where local electors were divided and unable to reach a consensus, a message was sent to Musumba asking the Mwantiyamvwa to determine the most legitimate candidate. History, furthermore, is replete with examples of pretenders to various thrones scattered throughout the Congo, Angola, and Northern Rhodesia literally racing to reach Musumba ahead of other claimants, laden with tribute for Mwantiyamvwa through which they hoped to preempt the competition.

To this day, Musumba lives on, in local imagination, as a quasi-sacred city, the epicenter of a unifying tradition, and the font of political legitimacy. Our earliest written description of the place comes from explorers Capello and Ivens in 1882. Although Musumba was long past its zenith, they nevertheless commented on the capital's commercial vibrancy by noting "vast markets, true bazaars containing straight lanes or streets where flour of various kinds, ginguba, palm oil, fresh and dried meat, massambala, salt, tobacco, maluvo (palm wine), mabellas, and other articles are displayed, and are bartered for merchandise, such as blue and red baize, cottons, printed calico, large white and small red beads, powder, arms and bracelets."[2] Two years hence the city would be sacked and burned to the ground by well-armed Cokwe groups. Yet, a decade later in 1896, when an agent of the Congo Free State, Captain Michaux, made first contact with Musumba, he was astonished by the size and appearance of this capital. It was surrounded by

Congo Cauldron Bubbles Over in Bloodbath

C.A.P. AFRICA NEWS SERVICE

After a year of riots and arson the Belgian Congo cauldron has bubbled over in Stanleyville, 1,000 miles inland from Leopoldville, land of the Leopard Cult which has always been a source of nagging worry to authorities in the area.

With at least 70 deaths there it brings the tragic account of Congo 1959 to about 400 lives lost in outbursts from the Atlantic to the Nile.

(*Central African Post,* November 2, 1959, p. 1)

a moat and heavy fortification. There was a full kilometer from the entryway to the place he was received by Mwantiyamvwa. He estimated the population to be thirty thousand, making it the largest single assemblage of people in the interior of Central Africa.[3]

Records show that the Kanongesha inaugurated in 1927 made the two-week-long walk to Musumba and received a fresh *lukanu* in return.[4] The Ikelenge inaugurated in 1951 made the pilgrimage to Musumba the following year, presenting the Mwantiyamvwa with the gift of a "saucepan special" radio. He was particularly well received, returning to Mwinilunga as a hero, heavily laden with symbolic objects as testimony to his esteem in the eyes of the emperor. Indeed, this Ikelenge was chosen to organize the coronation of the Kanongesha who would ascend the throne in 1953. Mwantiyamvwa himself would cross the border to visit Mwinilunga in 1956, granting audience to all his subject chiefs in Northern Rhodesia. In that same year, by invitation, he nominated his daughter to fill the open chieftaincy among the Lunda at Chavuma, an area in Northern Rhodesia over 350 miles south of Mwantiyamvwa's capital. The daughter was enthusiastically received by the local people, but the decision was overruled by Northern Rhodesian colonial authorities fearful of where such a trend might lead.[5] The Mwantiyamvwa also toured Mwinilunga in 1960 and again in 1961.

The capital city, Musumba, was continually whittled down in scale throughout the early 1900s. The small Belgian force dispatched to rule Katanga repeatedly expressed profound trepidation over such a dense concentration of people under the direct control of one individual. By midcentury, residence at Musumba proper had been restricted to titled court officials, royal artisans, and close family members of the Mwantiyamvwa. Even so, it remained with a population of approximately three thousand people, living in neatly ordered and well-designed brick houses, with new-style sanitation facilities and ablution blocks (bathhouses).[6] Musumba no doubt appeared as a Shangri-la to Mwinilunga chiefs whose tumble-down capitals rarely exceeded a hundred individuals. Tales of Musumba were constantly on the lips of those residing in Mwinilunga. Thoughts on palace proceedings reverberated though local consciousness. But Musumba refused to exist solely as an emblem, an allegory, or a representation of a Lunda paradise lost. It was very much a flesh and blood part of Katanga. When Katanga convulsed, Musumba became agitated as well. When Katanga bled, Musumba also exuded its life force. Thus the Lunda of Mwinilunga did not peer

"Universal Suffrage Now Would Bring Chaos" — Van Eeden

C.A.P. REPORTER

Immediate universal suffrage in the Federation will bring chaos, said Mr. G. F. M. van Eeden, Dominion Party M.P. for Lusaka Rural, in Lusaka yesterday. Speaking at the United Northern Rhodesia Association Study Conference, he said: "If power is granted in such a rapid fashion to a largely primitive people we will probably die in the horrible convulsion which follows."
(*Central African Post,* November 2, 1959, p. 1)

across the border with blinders focused solely on Musumba. They observed, experienced, learned from, and contributed to the confusing and contradictory array of actions and reactions throughout Katanga during what came to be known as the Congo Crisis.

Katanga: Milk Cow of the Congo

By 1960 over thirty thousand Europeans lived in Katanga. At nearly 2.1 percent of the region's population, this was the densest concentration of Europeans in the Congo, comparable in size to European populations in Kenya and Rhodesia.[7] Although the area around Musumba was not the focus of much development effort, Katanga as a whole was relatively highly industrialized and urbanized, with over a third of the region's population living outside the traditional milieu as wage earners. With proceeds from the mining of copper, silver, germanium, platinum, palladium, radium, uranium, and zinc, Katanga alone provided roughly 50 percent of the Congo's total revenue. As early as 1910, European mining interests argued strongly for the unique status of Katanga, lobbying for autonomy from the colony's capital at Leopoldville. The right to report directly to Brussels was deemed preferable to subordination to Leopoldville, with its early reputation for lavish public spending and administrative megalomania.[8] Indeed, there was a violent European reaction to centralizing measures introduced in 1933 that would have strengthened the capital's hand in Katangan affairs.

Successive Belgian administrations maintained intense but ambivalent relationships with the Lunda and their leader, the Mwantiyamvwa. The combined impact of Musumba's distance from the mining towns, the Mwantiyamvwa's resistance to labor recruitment in general, and the mineowners' specific reticence about Lunda suitability for underground work meant that much of Katanga's growth was based on immigrant labor from non-Lunda groups, most especially Luba. Furthermore, the Lunda area itself was heavily interspersed with Cokwe-speaking people, many living in villages under Lunda chiefs. Cokwe began venturing into Lunda territory back in the mid-nineteenth century when the Portuguese royal monopoly on ivory was abolished.[9] The price of ivory immediately tripled, and exports jumped accordingly. In 1832 only 3,000 pounds of ivory were exported from the Portuguese port at Luanda. By the 1840s over 100,000 pounds were being exported annually. In subsequent years the wax and rubber trades would come into their own as well. The Cokwe were uniquely well situated, territorially and occupationally, to profit from these commodities. They had long been skilled hunters and blacksmiths who were masters of the forest domain and could better maintain and repair firearms than any of their neighbors. Their modus operandi, after hunting out their own area, was to slowly infiltrate the unoccupied woodlands around the villages of others, perhaps providing blacksmith services and offering shares in ivory, wax, and rubber revenue. But slowly Cokwe would come to numerically dominate the area and would change the rules of engagement in their own favor. The Cokwe were particularly famous for capitalizing on the misfortune of other ethnic groups by enticing them to pawn females during times of trouble. Yet, rather than hold these women for later redemption, Cokwe men would immediately marry them, awarding full group membership to the resulting offspring. They were thus capable of expanding at a phenomenal rate. By 1885 they were sufficiently numerous and well armed with guns to sack Musumba and put the Mwantiyamvwa to flight. Perhaps as many as ten thousand Lunda were sold into slavery by the Cokwe. The Lunda had only just reorganized and begun a counteroffensive when colonial wars of "pacification" put an end to the conflict. The Lunda, however, won the diplomatic war, convincing the Belgians of Lunda suzerainty over territory they had yet to reconquer from the Cokwe.

The intertwined nature of Lunda and Cokwe villages frustrated all efforts to draw up clear ethnically based administrative units, as was possible in most areas of the Congo. Cokwe loudly resisted placement under the overall authority of the Mwantiyamvwa, even as the latter remained adamant in his demand for Cokwe tribute for the use of Lunda land. Belgian administrators, torn between romantic notions of an ancient Lunda Empire and the contemporary reality of Cokwe intransigence, tried one scheme after another to finesse ethnic antagonism.[10] Experiments with Cokwe paying rent for land, without coming under formal Lunda authority, were strongly resisted by both parties. Efforts to disentangle and reposition Cokwe and Lunda into separate villages were met with even greater hostility. The relationship became ever more caustic in the lead-up to Congolese independence in the late 1950s and early 1960s.

"Respect Chiefs" Urges Chona

C.A.P. REPORTER

African self-government and independence in Northern Rhodesia will be near-impossible if chiefs do not identify themselves with "their own people" in the struggle against "foreign domination and settlerism," said United National Independence Party president, Mr. Mainza Chona, today.

While appealing to Africans to respect their chiefs, Mr. Chona at the same time said: "Chiefs are, generally speaking, completely ignorant of what we stand for."
(*Central African Post,* December 16, 1959, p. 6)

In the Congo, as in the Rhodesias to the south, the first generation of nationalist political parties was an amalgam of ethnically based mutual associations. Immigrant Luba in the mines organized the first mutual society in 1955 to protect themselves from the tribulations of doing dangerous yet profitable work in a foreign land and the concomitant jealousy and suspicion that it provoked among local residents. The Cokwe of Lundaland followed suit within months, mobilizing around their own sense of neglect and deprivation vis-à-vis their more prestigious neighbor, the Lunda, and petitioning colonial authorities for equal treatment. In 1956 the Association des Tshokwe (Cokwe) du Congo, de l'Angola et de la Rhodesie (Atcar) was formed with the much more ambitious aim of rallying all Cokwe in Central Africa. In short time virtually every group in Central Africa, large and small, formed its own ethnic association. Yet, it was the Cokwe awakening that was viewed as a particularly ominous threat by Lunda and colonial officials alike. The administrator of Dilolo noted:

> The Tshokwe (Cokwe), who are currently scattered over the Lunda lands, do not realize that they represent a large majority of the population in this territory. Led and advised by the founders of [Atcar], they will become aware of their strength and use it toward political ends to supplant the Lunda chiefs and to take back from them the lands they claim to have conquered before the Europeans' arrival. In fact, the (Lunda) chiefs understood at once the danger which the tshokwe associations represented to them.[11]

The Lunda, who as noted earlier were more adroit at bridging cultural and linguistic differences than mobilizing around them, attempted to counter the trend of ethnic intensification by forming an organization to promote territorial rather than ethnic unity, *associations de ressortissants,* open to all. Local Lunda chiefs, with mixed populations, observed the growing militancy of their Cokwe subjects with particular dread. Additionally, the new Lunda educated and urban elite who were profoundly aware of the role of organized strength in nationalist politics, along with members of the royal court whose privileges were under attack, urged a more vigorous response by the Mwantiyamvwa. When he failed to do so, the tide of popular support swung toward another popular Lunda leader, Moise Tshombe.

Educated by American Methodist missionaries, product of a wealthy merchant family, and son-in-law of the then-current Mwantiyamvwa, Tshombe was sufficiently well connected and politically savvy to take up the mantle of Lunda leadership. He quickly set about amalgamating the numerous and weak *associations de ressortissants* under the Groupement des

More than 20 Africans Wounded as Lulua and Baluba Clash in Congo

LULUABOURG

More than 20 Africans were wounded in clashes over the weekend between the Lulua and Baluba tribes, the Belgian News Agency reported.

Fighting between the two tribes broke out afresh on Friday night in one of Luluabourg's African communes. Police were rushed to the trouble spot and made several arrests.

A roadblock

On the same day a European schoolteacher driving towards Luluabourg was stopped by a makeshift roadblock set up by one of the roving bands of warriors. She escaped unharmed, but her car was damaged.
(*Central African Post,* January 4, 1960, p. 1)

Associations Mutuelles de l'Empire Lunda (Gassomel). He then worked to unite the various ethnic associations into a pan-Katanga political party under the one common complaint, the overwhelming representation of non-Katangan Africans in the labor market believed to be the result of an official policy of favoritism toward "outsiders." On October 4, 1958, the Confederation des Associations Ribales du Katanga (Conakat) was formed as an organization of "authentic Kantangans" to protect their interest from "strangers." Its membership initially included Lunda, Luba, Cokwe, Yeke, Sanga, Tabwa, and Bemba. But the perception of threat was not uniform. The Luba of Katanga living in the cities, for example, felt close links to the Luba of Kasai, who were declared "strangers" by Conakat leadership. By 1959, the Luba ethnic association had ceased to participate in Conakat, mainly because of the latter's increasingly violent anti-Kasai position. The Cokwe also refused to participate in Conakat because the agenda of the Tshombe-dominated organization overshadowed their specific grievances with the Lunda.

The Luba and Cokwe became allies as the "Cartel" calling for the independence of the Congo as a unitary state at the earliest possible moment. Conakat, however, came out in favor of an autonomous and federated state of Katanga in which the reins of power would be in the hands of authentic Katangese as represented by Conakat. A European settler party, also in favor of Katanga autonomy, joined Conakat and played an increasing role in financing the whole organization as well as lobbying for support in official and business circles in Belgium. Katangan politics of the late 1950s were a convoluted array of overlapping and competing concerns, a complex web of shifting alliances, and a Gordian knot of strategic thrusts and resultant consequences. Lunda actions and reactions are still best captured in Edouard Bustin's *Lunda under Belgian Rule* (1975). In summary, one strand of historical activity led to Katangan secession after Congo independence in 1960, fully backed by the settler community and international business interests. A separate but related cluster of events inflamed the passions of Lunda particularism. An industrial recession that began in 1957, the first since the Great Depression, sent thousands of angry workers back to the countryside. Nearly twenty thousand flooded into Lunda territory alone, a volatile and militant element that only served to increase tension between Cokwe and Lunda. There were major clashes between Lunda and Cokwe communities around the rural Congo town of Kolwezi that lasted two days, causing a conflicting number of deaths on both sides. Smaller clashes occurred throughout the district.

A third strand of activity led to a last-ditch colonial effort to prop up the Mwantiyamvwa and the Lunda Empire. One subset of Europeans recognized that Congo independence was inevitable and rapidly approaching. Yet they were still more comfortable with an Africa made up of tribes and chiefs than one ruled by *evolues,* or men of the new black bourgeoisie such as Patrice Lumumba and Joseph Kasavubu, the leading Congo politicians of the day. The Lunda Empire seemed a polity particularly amenable to revitalization. Attempts were made to organize royal constituency tours to show the extent and reach of Mwantiyamvwa's power and respect, not just within the Congo, but in Northern Rhodesia and Angola as well. Records show that in January and February of 1960 both Mwantiyamvwa Ditende and the governor of Katanga wrote separately to various authorities in the Congo, Angola, and Northern Rhodesia to inquire about the number of Africans who continue to recognize the Mwantiyamvwa's paramountcy.[12] The reply from the district commissioner of Mwinilunga estimated that 74,328 Lunda plus a further 12,351 Luchazi, Cokwe, Lamba, Mbundu, Kaonde, and BaLuba in his territory acknowledged the Mwantiyamvwa. As noted earlier, a visit was hastily organized.

It has been suggested that two anthropologists, Daniel Biebuyck and Fernand Crine, played a significant role in fanning the flames of Lunda nationalism. Biebuyck's book, with its most favorable account of a Lunda Empire, appeared in late 1957. Crine was actually present at Musumba in 1959–60, supposedly giving Mwantiyamvwa and his court theoretical ammunition on imperial concepts. A letter from the court in 1960 to Belgian authorities, justifying the empire's continued existence, smacked suspiciously of a scholarly dissertation on the historical, political, and customary law of the Lunda, complete with dense anthropological jargon.[13] In any event, the term "Lunda Empire" became a household word in Europe, among militant Lunda in the Congo, and even in Mwinilunga.

Indeed, all the clusters of activities noted above extended a tentacle or generated a parallel process within Mwinilunga. Many Kanongesha Lunda had been vanquished and sold into slavery by the Cokwe in the late 1880s. Thousands more had been forced to take cover in the forest, living in small bands as hunter-gatherers, ever ready to flee before the approach of better armed Cokwe. The continued presence of Cokwe in Mwinilunga District was an ongoing reminder of a humiliating historical episode, a visible stain on the glory of the Lunda Empire. The emergence of a pan-Cokwe movement in the 1950s, with strong support throughout Northern Rhodesia, and the outbreak of violent Lunda-Cokwe clashes in Kolwezi, a scant thirty miles from the border, reopened barely healed wounds. Furthermore, to ensure that younger Lunda fully adopted the correct political

Rebellion Denied

LUANDA, SAPA-A.P.

Portuguese authorities have denied reports abroad of an armed nationalist insurrection in Angola.

The Portuguese denial was made because of statements in the United States by two directors of the American Committee on Africa who said that an armed nationalist insurrection with arms smuggled from abroad had broken out.

Portuguese sources said reports from many points in Angola said that peace had not been disturbed. The Portuguese said that there were no indications of conspiracies or movements to disturb the present colony's status.

(*Central African Post,* March 9, 1960, p. 1)

stance vis-à-vis the Cokwe meant dredging up and constantly retelling painful stories from the past and thereby reliving them afresh. Such was the context that nurtured the local appeal for a pan-Lunda nationalism, bringing into sharp relief the opposing force of national borders versus historical affinity.

Dr. Banda Looks North for Another "Association"
But alliance with Southern Rhodesia — "Never, never"

C.A.P. CORRESPONDENT, LONDON

Dr. Hastings Banda is looking north. In a dramatic first Press conference since he was released from Gwelo Jail and watched by more than 8,000,000 British televiewers, he declared that he was thinking of an association of independent Nyasaland, Tanganyika and Northern Rhodesia. He said he had "not very detailed" discussion with Mr. Julius Nyerere on the alliance.

Asked if he would consider any association at all with Southern Rhodesia. Dr. Banda shouted: "Never, never, never." (*Central African Post,* April 8, 1960, p. 1)

As leader of the movement for Katangan self-determination, Moise Tshombe has been variously labeled a reactionary, an instrument of Belgian imperialism, a front for international mining interests, a tool of the European settler community, a self-absorbed elitist, or, conversely, the champion of a new African bourgeoisie. He consistently described himself, however, as an arch Katangan nationalist, fighting for the rights of all legitimate Katangans, be they African or European. Nowhere in any of Tshombe's writings or speeches is the slightest suggestion that his actions were framed by his Lunda identity or motivated by a desire to revitalize the Lunda Empire. Yet, across the border in Northern Rhodesia, this was, indeed, virtually the sole interpretation of Tshombe's actions. Many strongly believed that the excision of Katanga from the Congo was but the first step in the emancipation of contiguous Lunda territories in Angola and Northern Rhodesia. The Lunda of Mwinilunga cast Tshombe in the role of historical redeemer, one who would reunite what had been dismembered at the Conference of Berlin. Tshombe's filiation and personal achievements provided the symbolic material to elevate him above the status of profane politician toward something more akin to the dynastic heroes of old, venerated in oral traditions. First, Tshombe was a direct lineal descendent of the Mwantiyamvwa overthrown by King Leopold's agents in the late 1880s and a member of a lineage still revered as stalwarts of resistance. Second, Lunda tradition has long heaped praise on individual entrepreneurship, creativity, and the willingness to explore new productive options and to experiment with new social alignments. Tshombe's unique accomplishments in education and commerce and his obvious success at political organizing placed him in a peerless category. Third, initiating fundamental political change was never the natural province of a sitting Mwantiyamvwa but rather was the historical role of the uniquely positioned outsider. Many saw Tshombe as just such a portentous figure. Furthermore, in Lunda tradition, an outsider could be transformed into an insider, and a usurper of power could be transformed into a legitimate authority by virtue of marriage to the old leader's daughter. Tshombe, as noted earlier, was indeed the son-in-law of the then-reigning Mwantiyamvwa.

On July 17, 1960, Tshombe formally declared Katanga to be an independent state, severed of all connections with the Congo. This action was heartily endorsed by Mwantiyamvwa and met with widespread adulation in Mwinilunga. But a tremendous amount of money was at stake in the disposition of Katangan resources, hence Europeans and Africans alike were intensively scheming with their cross-border counterparts. Sir Roy Welensky, prime minister of the Federation of Rhodesia and Nyasaland, for example, was reported to have been seeking an association with an independent Katanga, based on the opportunities for more efficient management of labor and the joint marketing of complementary mineral resources.[14] Federation leaders, in fact, allowed Tshombe to use Northern Rhodesian soil in his attempts to outwit United Nations forces sent to stop Katanga secession. Meanwhile a Rhodesian newspaper incited European settler fears by reporting that Tshombe's ultimate project was to unify Katanga with Northern Rhodesia under the authority of a single black government.[15] Tshombe's main opposition in Katanga, the Luba and Cokwe organization called the Cartel, had also for years proclaimed its belief in Tshombe's intent to secede from the Congo and unite with Northern Rhodesia. Yet it was not clear whether they expected a black or white government to emerge from that union. There was also speculation in some quarters that the Bemba, who dominated the labor force in Northern Rhodesian mines, and many of whom had kin across the border in the Congo, were similarly fascinated with the idea of union. In actuality, Tshombe had met with two sets of African nationalist leaders from Northern Rhodesia. He denounced the group headed by future president Kenneth Kaunda as extremist, Lumumbist, and perhaps even Communist, and threw his support to the African National Congress (ANC) of Harry Nkumbula.[16] That support, as is explored in greater detail in the following chapter, included a monetary component. There is, however, no written evidence that it included any offers of post-independence unification. Nevertheless, that act would influence Mwinilunga's relation to the Northern Rhodesian nationalist movement for decades to come. Kenneth Kaunda's United

Guinea Leans on Russia, Arms Pour into Conakry

C.A.P. AFRICA NEWS SERVICE, CONAKRY

Western observers and officials in Guinea are dismayed as recent events show President Sekou Toure leaning more and more toward Russia.

Automatic weapons and even military aircraft have been off-loaded in Conakry in alarming numbers during the past six weeks and this is regarded as an attempt by the Guinean Government to beat a possible attempt by the Western powers to introduce a ban on the Summit talks agenda on the supply of weapons to Africa's new independencies.

(*Central African Post,* May 6, 1960, p. 3)

National Independence Party (UNIP) would make few early inroads in Mwinilunga, while those political activists associated with Harry Nkumbula's ANC would be enthusiastically received.

Social movements need not be propelled by actual shared "imaginings." A dovetailing of disparate actions that creates the impression of shared imaginings will work just as well. Despite denials by all parties involved, which perhaps the Lunda of Mwinilunga never heard, the belief that Katanga succession was about the reunification of the Lunda Empire remained unshakable. Rumors of machination by Welensky, the Federation, the Belgians, and the Bemba were dismissed as irrelevant or proffered as evidence of Tshombe's supreme skill at manipulating the shifting array of extant political forces. When Tshombe used Angolan territory as a staging area for several military operations during the secession and during two subsequent periods of exile, it was assumed that he was doing so with clandestine support of Angolan Lunda rather than with the full knowledge of Portuguese colonial authorities. When Tshombe made his final military attempt to subvert the Congo from Angola in November 1967, hundreds if not thousands of armed Kanongesha Lunda were among his ranks. With defeat, they dispersed broadly. To this day, in virtually every major village cluster in Mwinilunga, including those on Matonchi Plateau, one finds elderly "Simba warriors" reminiscing about their role in almost reunifying the Lunda Empire.

Particularly strange was the Lunda response to the organization known as the Congolese National Liberation Front (FLNC).[17] Created in 1968 and based in Angola for roughly a decade, this armed group of "Congolese" fought alongside African nationalists of the Popular Movement for the Liberation of Angola (MPLA) to liberate Angola from Portuguese rule. In return the group received arms, material support, and a base of operation just west of Mwinilunga from which it launched two unsuccessful attempts to overthrow the Congo government by way of Katanga in 1977 and 1978. The FLNC proclaimed itself a Marxist-Leninist organization and heir to the Patrice Lumumba political tradition. All its literature speaks of a global struggle against imperialist powers, of which the United States is the leading force, that sabotaged Congo independence, assassinated Lumumba, and installed Mobutu to protect their interests. The FLNC repeatedly made it clear that, despite the choice of Katanga as a point of initial attack, it had no secessionist aims and, in fact, denounced Moise Tshombe and his movement as Belgian puppets. None of this rhetoric, however, prevented many Lunda from recasting this group as Lunda nationalists at heart. They were using Tshombe's old military base in Angola. They launched their attacks via the same route that Tshombe's forces had used. The first city they liberated was Kolwezi, the most Lunda of all urban centers in Katanga. They had a leader named Nathaniel Mbumba, obviously Lunda in origins.

Thus, while the clamor for Northern Rhodesian independence grew ever stronger, many in Mwinilunga were tuned in to different voices, voices that were nearer and dearer, more urgent, and more relevant, voices that resonated more profoundly with local notions of historical connections and causality. Tshombe had arisen on the scene almost as a dream from the collective Lunda consciousness, convincing them that lines drawn on maps by Europeans were not immutable, that the pen merely records history—it is the sword that actually makes history. Tshombe dared the Lunda to think boldly. A paradise lost could be regained if all would only seize the moment. Or, at least, the Lunda thought that was Tshombe's message.

The Congo Crisis had begun when the Amabwambu were still preteens. But they had recently completed their month-long Mukanda initiation rites, so they were men by local reckoning. But what kind of men were they: Lunda or Northern Rhodesian, Zambian, Central African, African, or Pan-African? Answers would be provisional for some, shifting with notions of momentary utility, yet for others they would remain constant regardless of context, simply growing ever deeper and denser with time.

Ike Says "No U.S. Troops"

NEWPORT (RHODE ISLAND), SAPA-REUTER

President Eisenhower feels that countries other than the United States should provide troops needed to restore order in the Congo, the White House said yesterday.

The United States Navy Department announced that the aircraft carrier Wasp is steaming towards the South Atlantic, and "will be available to assist in the evacuation of American nationals from the Congo if the situation requires."

(*Central African Post*, July 13, 1960, p. 1)

7

The Emergence of a New Nation-State

The elements composing the standard history of Zambian independence include (1) the development of ethnic-based welfare societies in urban centers to accommodate the needs of workers displaced from village support networks; (2) the amalgamation of these societies by a new African political elite in the post–World War II era to address issues of broader concern; (3) a split among that leadership leading to the development of two major African political parties in the run-up to independence; (4) the eventual triumph of the United National Independence Party (UNIP) under the leadership of Kenneth Kaunda; (5) independence from Britain in 1964, which was followed by (6) the declaration of a one-party state under UNIP in 1972 and the virtual collapse of opposition politics in Zambia.[1] Indeed, viewed from the center of political action, this particular outline is perhaps as effective as any other at constructing a linear narrative from the myriad social acts that ultimately transformed the British colony of Northern Rhodesia into the independent Republic of Zambia.

African reaction to colonial rule and the concomitant imposition of taxation had been immediate, widespread, and complex.[2] It ranged from armed resistance and attacks on colonial officials to spiritual responses through prophetic and anti-witchcraft movements. Some groups, including the Lunda, attempted to migrate en masse out of the reach of colonial forces. By the late 1920s, however, collective action was primarily focused on obtaining the best accommodation to the new political dispensation. Taxation had become a reality, wage employment a necessary pursuit. Copper mining provided the bulk of jobs in the colony, absorbing as many as thirty thousand men by 1930.[3] Mining compounds and the towns to which they gave birth were vibrant and rambunctious settlements, kaleidoscopic collections of ethnic groups and practices, constantly shifting residential arrangements and patterns of conflict management. European mine owners, for the most part, provided many of their workers' basic needs (food, clothing, shelter, medical care), as well as rudimentary entertainment. But it would remain for the Africans themselves to give organizational form to their need to maintain connections with their rural communities and to re-create in town the cycles of ritual performances and cultural practices that underpinned and animated ethnic identities. An array of welfare societies rapidly emerged to address both the utilitarian and esoteric needs of specific groups.[4] Ethnic-based welfare societies developed the transportation and communications links needed to routinize the flow of news, commodities, and cash between town and country. These societies enabled members to stay abreast of events back home, to safely remit funds in a timely manner to family members in need, and to receive in return packages of the most-yearned-for local delicacies. Welfare societies provided the space and the occasions for members to jointly partake of the foods, drinks, music, language, and social etiquette that evoked a sense of communitas amidst the otherwise depersonalizing and atomizing environment of mine compounds.

Life in town, however, was not merely a challenge to one's emotional and psychological well-being. Mining, in particular, was an exceedingly dangerous activity. Mishaps were frequent, tempers erupted constantly, and grievances accumulated daily. Only collective action with the potential for disrupting production would be taken seriously by mine officials. Individuals, or even small collections of individuals, could be summarily dismissed and replaced rather quickly. Welfare societies were useful networks for mobilizing support for one's case against the mines, for accessing information on litigation procedures and industrial precedence, and as a source of temporary support should one's case fail. Welfare societies could assist in one's repatriation to the countryside in the event of job loss or ship one's body home for burial in the event of death. Through welfare societies a set of Africans gained expertise in organizational finance, recruitment, mobilization, and management. In rural areas leadership continued to be located within traditional status-based gerontocracies. But in town and in the mines youthful leadership was emerging based on personal achievement, organizational skills, and the mastery of urban contingencies.

Given the central role of mining in the Northern Rhodesian economy, one might expect organized labor to have presented the biggest challenge to the status quo. Indeed, continual efforts were made to establish a broad-based organization to represent the interests of African mineworkers. The first collective action, however, did not occur until 1935.[5] In that year African miners, to protest low pay, deplorable housing conditions, and rising tax rates, staged a strike, closing mines throughout the Copperbelt. Police killed six workers at one site while elsewhere the strike was peaceful, with workers quickly returning to the job. Although brief and ineffective, the strike served as the first evidence of an emerging consciousness based on shared economic interests rather than narrowly proscribed ethnic concerns. A more serious round of mineworker strikes occurred in 1940, ending with seventeen strikers killed and at least sixty-five injured.[6] The response of both government and mine management to the strikes was to strengthen the "tribal" character of urban administration.[7] So-called tribal elders had been inserted in some compounds as early as 1931. The system now became more widespread in an attempt to manage grievances by directing Africans to vent their frustrations through ethnic channels. In 1938 "tribal councillors" were similarly set up to hear cases and mediate disputes in municipal townships. Appointed tribal representatives, however, were widely ignored. In the absence of political organizations, Africans continued to rely on cultural associations and welfare societies to assess public opinion, generate strategies, and mobilize for action. In 1947 the British Labour government sent out a Scottish trade unionist, William Comrie, to assist African efforts at forming a union.[8] Despite British efforts the African Mineworkers Union of Northern Rhodesia would not achieve formal recognition until 1949.

By way of contrast, African welfare societies throughout the colony had met as early as 1933 to form a national union of concerned Africans. Despite formal opposition from the colonial state, in 1946 the Federation of African Societies of Northern Rhodesia was brought into being. At a July 1948 meeting this group made explicit its political aims and by unanimous vote renamed itself the Northern Rhodesia African Congress (NRAC).[9] Subsequently, in 1951 Harry Nkumbula, son of an Ila subchief, London School of Economics–trained teacher, charismatic nationalist, and fervent opponent of the Central African Federation, was elected the new president of NRAC and promptly changed its name to the African National Congress (ANC). This group held as its sole objective the defeat of the initiative to merge Northern Rhodesia, Southern Rhodesia, and Nyasaland into a single political unit dominated by European settlers. Although the ANC would fail to stop the imposition of the Federation, it set the stage for the subsequent nationalist movement. For the first time Africans had joined together as Northern Rhodesians, forged a political agenda, and honed new leaders. Among those leaders were Simon Kapwepwe and Kenneth Kaunda, who would both grow increasingly disenchanted with what they saw as Nkumbula's lackluster leadership. Unable to unseat him in the ANC, they formed their own nationalist organization that would ultimately lead the nation to independence as the United National Independence Party.[10] Kenneth Kaunda would become president, Kapwepwe would become vice president, and Nkumbula would be the leader of the opposition party in Parliament.

Time and events surrounding the birth of the nation moved at a dizzying pace. In the five years between 1959 and 1964 three general elections were held, each under a different constitution, each accompanied by much racial and regional posturing, threats and counterthreats, shifting alliances, acts of intimidation, outright violence, wholesale destruction of property, and the shattering of lives and livelihoods. As late as 1958 only eleven Africans had been allowed to register to vote in Northern Rhodesia. Within five years that number would exceed a million. In 1958 Northern Rhodesia was governed exclusively by white men. Seventy thousand whites dominated the economy, controlled the flow of imports and exports, and owned and managed all mining operations and most of the commercial farms. Yet in 1964 Africans grabbed the reigns of government and initiated the process of Zambianizing industry, business, the civil service, the military, the judiciary, and the professions. History books tend to portray the end of British rule in Central Africa as a rather benign affair. British prime minister Harold Macmillan realized that the "winds of change" were sweeping across Africa and thus set the colonial office on track to identify the genuine representatives of the people, hand over power, and make a graceful exit.[11] Certainly in comparison to developments in Algeria and Kenya, Zambia's independence was a relatively bloodless event. Yet, as noted earlier, the European settler community in Central Africa was deeply entrenched and violently opposed to the idea of African majority rule. Their political leadership mobilized manpower, public opinion, and a substantial war chest, vowing to thwart African independence at all cost and instead to move the amalgamated territories of Northern Rhodesia, Southern Rhodesia, and Nyasaland to full dominion status under white rule in 1960.

African leadership countered with its own rallying cry of full independence in the year 1960. Black and white political movements, like two freight trains bearing down on one another, were set on course for

After the Fulani
N. Nigeria is now on its own

BY P.J. MONKHOUSE

The Northern region of Nigeria has become self-governing in regional affairs—roughly 18 months after the Eastern and Western regions, and 18 months before the Nigerian Federation as a whole.
(*Central African Post,* April 8, 1959, p. 6)

an inevitable collision. African leaders organized mass meetings to prepare and fortify the population for a showdown. Violence was seen as inescapable, and the mechanisms for its unleashing needed to be created. Youth groups and "action groups" were rapidly trained to carry out acts of sabotage or to confront colonial security forces when the time made it necessary. The level of militancy escalated as African leaders sparred rhetorically, competing with one another to demonstrate their boundless passion, fearless resolve, and willingness to sacrifice their own lives in the coming struggle. They called upon the masses to prepare to do likewise. The year 1960 as the "year of dying" became the African political mantra of the era. "To win the battle against 'foreign government' and Federation, Africans would exhume their dead and call on their unborn children."[12]

Most African leaders were jailed for a time or "rusticated"—that is, exiled to sparsely populated rural areas for a defined period. Yet, new leaders immediately rose up to take their place. One after another African political party was banned. Yet, again, new or retitled political groupings were quickly constructed to keep up the pace of mass politicization and mobilization. During one particularly tense three-month period the African defiance campaign resulted in 38 school burnings, 60 roadblocks, 24 bridges destroyed, 27 deaths, over 3,000 arrests, and 2,691 convictions. Kenneth Kaunda promised colonial officials that the next stage of protest would make the Mau Mau crisis in Kenya look like a child's picnic.[13] The settlers' united front began to show signs of strain and uncertainty over the appropriate way forward. The colonial office took the initiative, stiffened its resolve. and placed Northern Rhodesia on the fast track to independence.

Passion unleashed is not necessarily passion dissipated. Once African men and women had become sufficiently emboldened to stare in the dreadful face of colonialism without blinking, they could not easily be cowed back into political passivity. The small taste of power that lingered on the palate from the successful campaign for independence left many individuals hungry for more. Indeed, British acquiescence accentuated rather than curtailed conflict in the territory. Previously all Africans had been united in agreement that federation was a bad thing. The daily indignities of the Colour Bar, job discrimination, and consumer mistreatment served as prima facie evidence that white minority rule was the number one enemy of all Africans. But the imminent arrival of independence required a shift in focus from destructive impulses to generative ones. Regional groupings and social strata long united in mutual hatred of one system now needed a shared vision on which to model a new system. Yet, when confronted with the reality of conflicting political paradigms, competing economic strategies, and contrasting personal styles of leadership, the African monolith gave way to myriad splinter groups. The time, however, was not yet ripe for African political pluralism. The agreed-upon electoral process preceding independence would be a multitiered affair, with an upper and a lower roll. It was designed to ensure Europeans ample representation in parliament in hopes of allaying their fears of an African monopoly on political power. However, should Europeans vote as a unified bloc, as they were widely expected to do, and Africans split their vote among several parties, Europeans might yet end up controlling the reigns of government. With that possibility as a backdrop, African electoral politics took on a new sense of urgency. Alliances were formed and broken almost weekly. Unity conferences were proposed and repeatedly undermined. Leaders alternately praised and vilified one another in rapid succession. The cry for African unity was the constant refrain at every political rally. But at what cost, was the unspoken reply. A virtually incomprehensible event was about to take place. A set of Africans could soon be ushered into the state house, into Parliament, into provincial governors' mansions and mayors' offices across the country. Yet there were far more political activists who had risked life and limb for the struggle than there were political positions to be doled out as spoils. Unfortunately, the historical tide that produced individuals willing to give up their lives during times of conflict was not also able to produce sufficient individuals willing to give up claims to jobs in the name of peace.

UNIP under Kenneth Kaunda and the ANC under Harry Nkumbula were particularly successful at absorbing small groups, while beating and otherwise intimidating other African parties out of existence. Youth wing thugs on both sides are believed to have tortured and killed opponents in the name of national unity. A complete accounting may never be done. Instead, sanitized treatises have been written by nearly all the major players on both sides extolling their own patriotic virtues and vision for the country, while pointing out the moral or intellectual shortcomings of their opponents. Meanwhile, Europeans continued to utilize the security forces to sow discontent wherever possible and to use their considerable resources to attract African candidates and sway African votes toward European political parties. A single linear narrative could never encapsulate or encompass the myriad intersecting stories, events, plots, conspiracies, shady maneuvers, and backroom machinations that produced the first independent Zambian government in 1964. Traditional histories have tended to dwell on the ever-evolving relationships among one-time allies Kaunda, Nkumbula, and Kapwepwe and

> **"Remove the Stigma" Plea**
> *N.R. Eurafricans bid for British citizenship*
>
> C.A.P. REPORTER
>
> A resolution saying that Northern Rhodesian Eurafricans should be granted British citizenship by the British Government was passed by the Eurafrican Association at their conference in Lusaka this week. (*Central African Post*, July 15, 1959, p. 1)

their European counterparts John Roberts and John Moffat. Those histories also tended to have an urban bias. Cities were presented as the principle sites generating novel political thoughts and practices. Rural politics was characterized as a simple contest for the loyalties of chiefs, with the assumption that subjects would naturally follow. Sincere-sounding promises about the continuing recognition of the traditional role of chiefs after independence was the usual ploy. Yet, from a rural perspective the struggle for independence takes on different tones and shadings. Other players come into sharper relief. Other concerns emerge as more pointedly vital. The gaze of Matonchi Plateau, in particular, was more intensely focused on the actions of three local characters: a politician, a chief, and a bandit. Each is both loved and hated by differing segments of the local population. Each is the stuff of legend whose exploits are still being dissected for meaning to this present day. The life of each transcended the corporal and became an allegory for the broad array of Lunda relations with the new nation-state.

Njapau: The Politician

Ronald John Njapau was for some in Mwinilunga the very personification of Harry Nkumbula's African National Congress. In the early 1950s when anti-Federalist feelings set the stage for African political mobilization, Nkumbula had been a tireless campaigner, perpetually in motion organizing spirited informational and recruitment rallies even in the most remote reaches of Northern Rhodesia. Njapau attended such an event, was inspired by the message, and became one of the first in Mwinilunga to devote himself wholeheartedly to political activism. A generation of men senior to Njapau, such as S. Tepa, R. Mangangu, and B. Mashata, would formally occupy the top leadership positions in the local ANC branch.[14] Yet, young Njapau is remembered by many as the ANC's most forceful and dedicated local voice. Long after the others had switched loyalties or dropped out of politics altogether, Njapau would remain the pillar of the ANC in the area. By 1958 the ANC's headquarters for Northwestern Province was in Mwinilunga, and Njapau was its provincial secretary.

After several arrests and periods of rustication Nkumbula became noticeably less energetic, less militant in his rhetoric, and less devoted to direct participation in rural political affairs. He concentrated more on maintaining his power base and popularity within the central party organization and among urban-based constituents. Nkumbula became increasingly lax in handling party affairs, often arriving late at public meetings, sometimes skipping long-scheduled events altogether.[15] Despite continual advice to the contrary, he refused to delegate responsibility, frequently made arbitrary decisions, declared those who disagreed with him enemies of the struggle, and orchestrated their removal from party leadership positions.[16] His closest allies were burdened with the task of hiding his moodiness and intemperance from public view.

Correspondingly, rural chapters of the ANC became semi-autonomous operations, struggling for their own survival with little assistance from national head-quarters. Local cadres sold party membership cards and solicited donations, with little of the money actually being forwarded to town. Instead it was used to cover local expenses and compensate local organizers. Thus, while the image of a dedi-cated, vigorous, and fiery Nkumbula lived on in the minds of many rural resi-dents, Njapau was, for all intents and purposes, the manifestation of that vision in Mwinilunga.

The local branch of the ANC, as noted earlier, had made its presence felt first in opposition to District Commissioner Bourn's 1957 proposal to establish Pro-tected Forest Areas in Mwinilunga. On the one hand, that campaign had not been particularly successful. Despite vociferous opposition at village meetings through-out the territory, Bourn had managed to coerce those Africans in the Native Au-thority (NA) system into signing the proposal. Since the NA was the colonially recognized voice of the people, the establishment of Protected Forest Areas be-came a fait accompli as Bourn was able to pass the plan up to his superiors as hav-ing been formally approved in Mwinilunga. On the other hand, the presence of the ANC in the area challenged the Native Authority members to become a gen-uinely representative body. The district commissioner could threaten their liveli-hood by withholding salaries. The ANC, as a counterweight, could threaten their reputations, or perhaps even their lives.

In July 1959 the district commissioner banned the ANC branch in Mwinilunga, forcing members of the Native Authority to approve an order to that effect.[17] The ban not only accentuated the militant appeal of the ANC locally, but also drove a wedge between the people and NA members that the latter would be compelled to reconcile. Accordingly, a year later when the ANC mobilized local opinion and led the effort to testify negatively before the Monckton Commission on the future of federation, the document constructed was formally presented as that of the Lunda Ndembu Native Authority of Mwinilunga.

When Kaunda, Kapwepwe, and others became thoroughly disillusioned with the ANC under Nkum-bula and organized the rival United National Inde-pendence Party (UNIP), Mwinilunga did not ini-tially present itself as fertile political ground. Some chiefs opposed the new group, believing that its leaders thought chiefs were too unsophisticated to participate in governance. Some senior residents simply found UNIP leadership too young to merit the re-spect already accorded the venerable "old lion," Harry Nkumbula. For others, the

Gun Shops in Lusaka Sell Out Stocks

C.A.P. REPORTER

There is not a pistol or revolver to be bought in Lusaka. The three firms in town selling firearms reported today a com-plete sell-out of these types of weapons. The spokesman of one shop selling firearms told me: "If I had 100 revolvers and pistols I could sell them all today."

(*Central African Post*, July 29, 1960, p. 1)

ethnic affiliation of politicians was a matter of concern. Animosities still lingered in Mwinilunga toward the Luvale to the south and west, who along with the Cokwe had enslaved thousands of Lunda-Ndembu between 1850 and 1900. Kaunda's last place of rustication had been in Luvale District, and his presence had stirred quite a following among that group. Additionally, Nalumino Mundia, the deputy treasurer of UNIP sent to head up the recruitment campaign in Northwestern Province, was a Lozi. The Lozi king during early talks with the British South Africa Company had claimed suzerainty over all of Lunda lands. Indeed, he had very nearly convinced the company to include the Lunda within his demarcated protectorate. Thus, suspicion of Lozi intentions lingered among the Lunda. For still others, the ANC was too deeply entrenched in their political consciousness. UNIP was a needless threat to African unity.

Kenneth Kaunda's first campaign attempt in Mwinilunga on behalf of UNIP thus met with misfortune. After holding a meeting in Solwezi, the capital of the district to the east, Kaunda and his entourage proceeded westward to Mwinilunga. Subsequently, one of his followers wrote: "Before crossing Lunga River [the gateway to Lunda territory], we were informed by our UNIP officials that trouble awaited us. For the ANC supporters of Harry Nkumbula were ready, with bows and arrows, spears and other weapons, to kill us. Having known the turbulent nature of that district, they, on their advice, decided to make a U-turn."[18] Kaunda and his entourage turned south and campaigned instead in Lozi and Luvale territories.

Njapau was not simply a local boy holding down the fort in the outer reaches of the African National Congress's urban-based political empire. Indeed, he occupied a unique and at times critical position within the broader ANC movement. It was through Njapau that Nkumbula first established political contacts with Moise Tshombe of the Congo. Speaking the same language, members of the same ethnic group, Njapau and Tshombe would establish a relationship that influenced the shape of political events in both Northern Rhodesia and the Congo. Tshombe's declaration of Katangan independence from the Congo on July 17, 1960, was fully backed by the European settler community and international business interests. Clearly, Tshombe was desperate for recognition among regional African leaders as well. More pragmatically, he most assuredly needed support on Katanga's southern border as he was surrounded on the north by Congo and international forces intent on ending Katanga's secession. He needed an alliance with Northern Rhodesia.

From the party's inception, Kenneth Kaunda and UNIP had been actively involved in the Pan-African Freedom Movement for East, Central and Southern Africa (PAFMECSA). With the independence of Tanganyika in 1961, that group chose to redirect its energies to Northern Rhodesia. At its February 1962 meeting in Addis Ababa the group elected Kaunda its new president and began raising funds for UNIP. Kaunda used his new platform to speak out ever more vigorously for pan-African unity, condemning those who placed barriers in its path. Accordingly he was forced to condemn Katangan secession as factionalism harmful to Africa's long-term development. As noted earlier, Tshombe countered, accusing Kaunda and UNIP of being extremists, Lumumbists, and perhaps even Communists. In any event, evidence suggests that Njapau secured for the ANC a contribution of £24,000 from Tshombe in the lead-up to the 1962 election for internal self-rule, a considerable sum in an era when a new car could be purchased for £500. Indeed, much of the money was spent on a fleet of campaign vehicles.[19]

The results of the 1962 election were disastrous for the ANC, both nationally and locally. The ANC only won 5 seats in the newly constructed national legislative body. UNIP won 14 seats, and, frighteningly, the European group called the United Federal Party (UFP) won 15 seats. An ANC coalition with UNIP would bring an African government to power. Yet Nkumbula basked in the limelight for weeks as the "reluctant bride," flirting with both UNIP and the European UFP.[20] He solicited and rejected a string of offers, personal and political, changing his mind in the press virtually daily. Ultimately he would join UNIP, driving a hard bargain that gave his ANC party half the cabinet positions in the new government and reserving the position of minister of education for himself. However, at every perceived slight he threatened to pull out of the coalition and join the Europeans. Indeed, in the lead-up to the 1964 election for total Zambian independence, Nkumbula would lead the ANC into a union with the Europeans of the UFP. Such mercurial behavior led to the virtual dissipation of what little remained of Nkumbula's national reputation.

"King of Jazz" Arrives in City Today

C.A.P. REPORTER, F.B.C.

S-Day is here — S for Satch, Louis Armstrong, the world's most famous jazzman. He and his group are due at Lusaka airport at 12:30 and will play at the Showgrounds for two and a half hours tonight.

(*Central African Post,* November 18, 1960, p. 1)

Meanwhile in Mwinilunga, ANC candidate Silas Chizawu apparently ran a spirited campaign in 1962. As the education councillor of the Lunda Native Authority, he was widely acknowledged for his role in bringing new credibility to the NA. He had duly pledged to work for greater unity between the province's chiefs and had advocated an increase in their pay and extension of their powers. He warned the chiefs that UNIP would join hands with Nkrumah of Ghana and Banda of Malawi, new breed African leaders who upon gaining power immediately abolished traditional chieftaincies. Though there was some speculation that the Lunda element would clearly support the ANC because of the party's friendship with Tshombe, only 264 voters supported Chizawu. He was defeated by UNIP candidate Samuel Mbilishi, who received 1,419 votes.[21] A complex web of local features no doubt informs this outcome. Mbilishi was a member of the Native Authority, a senior councillor who outranked Chizawu. Mbilishi was also the son of a senior chief in the region. Furthermore, Mbilishi was the more experienced and better connected politician, who had actually run for office in 1959 as an ANC candidate. Some local people privately contend that the 1962 election in Mwinilunga was less than fair and representative.

The qualifications for voters nationally as set out in *The Northern Rhodesia (Electoral Provisions) Order in Council, 1962* was a complicated system mandating two separate classes of voters, the upper roll and the lower roll. Four general qualifications applied to all voters:

1. Citizenship of the Federation or of the United Kingdom and Colonies or the status of a British Protected Person by virtue of his connection with Northern Rhodesia;
2. Twenty-one years of age;
3. Two years' continuous residence in the Federation;
4. Literacy in English (with some exemptions)

Additionally, to qualify for the upper roll one needed to further demonstrate an annual income of £720 or immovable property worth £1,500. Advanced education could partially substitute for income and property requirements. Individual holders of certain professions were also exempt. Those pertaining to Africans included chiefs, members of the Native Authority, and holders of certificates of honor or any other award from the queen. To qualify to vote on the lower roll one only needed to demonstrate an annual income of £120 or immovable property worth £250. Otherwise one could qualify by demonstrating literacy in the vernacular and being a member of a category that included the Native Authority, tribal councillors, headmen, pensioners, registered farmers, and members of prescribed religious bodies. Wives qualified for the same roll as their husbands, but only the senior wife of a polygamous marriage could rely on her husband's status.

A separate slate of candidates was put forward on each roll. Voters could select only from among those candidates on the roll for which they qualified. Fourteen of the 34 seats being contested were reserved for the upper roll. The framers of this two-tiered franchise knew all too well that few Africans would qualify to vote in the upper tier. Indeed, only one of UNIP's ten candidates on the upper roll managed to win a seat. And that was in the one district in which the UFP did not actually field a candidate. Nkumbula's ANC managed to place five candidates on the upper roll, but none managed to win. The upper roll was mostly a European affair. Yet even lower-roll qualification was open to abuse. Only 1,953 Africans managed to meet the lower-roll requirement and registered to vote in the entire Northwest Province, an area whose total population probably exceeded 70,000. This miniscule proportion, furthermore, contains virtually no representation from Chief Kanongesha's territory, long an area of staunch support for the ANC.

Much of the apparatus of voter registration was still in the hands of colonial officials. One can only guess how their long running battle with the ANC might have influenced their interpretation of individual eligibility. Few Africans locally held permanent jobs, title to land, or school diplomas. Village homesteads were regarded as being of little value, and literacy was a very subjective quality. Furthermore, distances were vast. Registration and polling stations were few. Those managing elections in rural areas had immense latitude in determining the size and characteristics of the electorate. Had they for some reason found UNIP's Mbilishi more to their liking than the ANC's Chizawu, they probably had the means to influence the results according. The area was rife with rumors that this had indeed been the case.

European machinations aside, the election results revived for some, initiated for others, regional tension among distinctive Lunda populations. First, there is a longstanding east-west divide. The Lunda east of the Lunga River, locally known as Akosa, have historically recognized Chief Musokantanda as their paramount. The vagaries of colonial borders, however, placed that chief's capital on one side of a line in Belgian territory even while many of his subjects were placed on the other side under British rule. Chief Sailunga ruled over the area as Musokantanda's highest-ranking subordinate in Northern Rhodesia. Yet, he fought continually, without success, to be recognized by colonial authorities as a senior chief on par with the Kanongesha. For many in the center of senior chief Kanongesha's territory, including those at Matonchi, it was those Akosa Lunda who had voted en masse against the "Kanongesha candidate" Chizawu out of sheer jealousy and contempt.

Space Man Attempt Shortly

WASHINGTON, SAPA-A.P.

America's top space administrator said yesterday that the first American attempt at rocketing a man into space may come "very shortly after the first of the year."

(*Central African Post*, November 21, 1960, p. 1)

Still others viewed the election as a manifestation of a north-south split. Chief Kanongesha's subordinate to the north was Chief Ikelenge. His territory encompassed the Plymouth Brethren's huge mission station, hospital, school, and farming complex. It was a Lunda area uniquely dense with wage earners and vibrant with commercial activity. Moreover, it held the largest concentration of Europeans west of the Copperbelt. The mission-run Sakeji boarding school was itself home to over two hundred European children by the early 1950s. Ikelenge was a highly educated Christian, having been schooled alongside the European children. He was witty, urbane, and quite wealthy in comparison to the other Lunda chiefs. His parents had perhaps primed his far-reaching vision by curiously naming him after the most exotic place they had heard of, London. When he was a young man, London had served as a court clerk to his father, the previous chief Ikelenge, and as a treasury clerk to the previous senior chief Kanongesha. London had apparently always been ambitious. As noted earlier, after assuming the title of Chief Ikelenge in 1951, he traveled to the palace of the Lunda emperor Mwantiyamvwa, in the Congo, presenting him with a radio and receiving prestigious royal regalia as gifts in return. Such gestures of fealty are more generally characteristic of senior chiefs rather than subordinate ones. Furthermore, Ikelenge's personal management of the new Kanongesha's two-day grand coronation in 1953 stood more as a testimony to his own superb organizational skills and ebullient sense of style, in many ways overshadowing the Kanongesha altogether. Such things are not quickly forgotten.

With irrigated farms, marketing of nontraditional crops, and a string of small businesses, Ikelenge had sufficient resources by 1954 to purchase his own automobile.[22] Government officials had long considered him the most progressive chief in the district, a model they wished others would emulate. The people of Ikelenge area had welcomed the initial influx of European missionaries and embraced Christianity, while Kanongesha area was still somewhat skeptical of the missionaries' motives. When taxation was introduced in 1913, Ikelenge people calmly complied, while the people of Kanongesha area fled to Angola in fear. Accordingly, the first native courthouse with a cement floor was built in Ikelenge's territory.[23] And his administration was the first to be trusted with the establishment of and direct control over a Native Authority treasury. In 1958 the governor of Northern Rhodesia Sir Evelyn Hone presented Ikelenge with the Queen's Medal of Honour. It should be noted that, unlike many other Europeans, the governor had an excellent relationship with UNIP's Kenneth Kaunda, believing him to be a man of high moral character who would work diligently to maintain interracial peace in post-independent Zambia. Whether or not the governor attempted to sway Ikelenge in UNIP's direction is not known. Certainly it is known that the European Liberal Party attempted to recruit Ikelenge as a candidate for its slate.

Those around Matonchi and Kanongesha's core area more generally were deeply suspicious of Ikelenge's long-term intentions and angered by the preferential treatment given his territory and the wholesale neglect of their own. Some speculated that he might be positioning himself to succeed the current Kanongesha. Others feared he might side with those wishing to abolish traditional chieftaincy altogether in exchange for an appointment as the district's new post-independence political leader. His area surely contained an abundance of individuals with the economic wherewithal to have qualified for the 1962 franchise. Perhaps it was the people of Ikelenge who had done in the "Kanongesha candidate."

Njapau's response to the ANC's electoral defeat was twofold. First, under circumstances that remain unclear, in 1962 he put pen to paper, laying out a master plan for reconstituting a pan-Lunda empire in central Africa.[24] He crafted a document addressed to all Lunda people of Zambia, Katanga, and Angola, as well as the Kaonde and Lamba, asking them to reject the new Zambian government. He accused the new prime minister, Kenneth Kaunda, of being a foreigner and a Communist and the new government of being as bad as the old colonial one. He advocated that setting up such a Lunda empire would be in keeping with treaties between the queen and Lunda chiefs. He further asserted that the new empire could peacefully come into being with the assistance of President Tshombe of Katanga, the government of Angola, missionaries, and the European political party of Zambia. Some have suggested Njapau concocted the plan of his own accord and forwarded it to Tshombe in a plea for political assistance. Others have suggested that the document was created after Tshombe had already pledged such support and was simply meant to demonstrate that Njapau personally or the ANC more generally supported Tshombe's dream of an empire. In either event, a string of concomitant occurrences would keep the idea of empire floating through public consciousness for years to come. And in Kanongesha territory such ideas always resonated particularly loudly.

Evidence suggests that in 1963 Tshombe promised to donate an additional £100,000 to the ANC if it reorganized along more efficient lines and curtailed the role of Nkumbula, who had become an embarrassment.[25] Although it was not clear how the transfer was to take place, or who was to verify the reorganization, the suspicion in many quarters was that the money was forwarded to Southern Rhodesia to be managed by Roy Welensky, prime minister of the Federation and arch enemy of African independence. Concomitantly in that same year, the European party UFP, desperate to stave off a UNIP victory in the upcoming 1964 election that would usher in full independence, struck a deal with Nkumbula, who was desperate to remain a political player on the national stage. The result was an ANC-UFP alliance. Shortly thereafter campaign literature from one of the ANC's Copperbelt offices boldly spoke of a grandiose scheme for a powerful Northern Rhodesia–Katanga Federation under the leadership of Nkumbula and Tshombe, with the whites of both territories playing a supporting role. Subsequently there was evidence of ANC-UFP assistance to ex-Katangese gendarmes for obtaining Northern Rhodesia passports to facilitate their movement to Spain to see Tshombe.[26]

> ### Russians Send a Man on Space Flight
> *Major Yuri Gagarin is still orbiting*
>
> Radio communication being maintained
>
> MOSCOW
>
> Russia launched a spaceship with a man on board on a round-the-earth orbit today. He is still orbiting.
> (*Central African Post*, April 12, 1961, p. 1)

Tshombe's pragmatic approach to politics, his willingness to work with any and all who could strengthen his grip on power, suggests that a pan-Lunda union was not his prime objective. Yet his rhetoric was sufficiently vague and his political maneuverings sufficiently cryptic to allow for creative interpretation. Men such as Njapau would move into that interpretive space and create visions that would propel their careers forward. The timing was propitious. Emperor Mwantiyamvwa's visits to Mwinilunga in 1956, 1960, and 1961 had evoked intense images of a Lunda golden age. The Lunda around Chief Ikelenge may have found present circumstances quite to their liking. But for those in the more underdeveloped areas around Kanongesha, images of past glory and future possibilities were quite comforting. Thus, after having watched his candidate go down in defeat in 1962, Njapau wrapped himself in a cloak of Lunda particularism and declared himself a candidate for the 1964 election.

Njapau is remembered as having been a masterful campaigner. His style rekindled memories of the passion and scholarly erudition of the early Nkumbula. Yet his campaign agenda remained distinctly local in focus: the need for more roads, schools, jobs, and clinics. In addition to being an engaging speaker, Njapau was a savvy tactician. The ANC had had plenty of support in the last election, but most of that support had not yet secured the franchise. Things would be different this time around. The local ANC set about training Njapau supporters in the skills they would need to secure the right to vote. The biggest threshold for many would be overcoming the requirement for literacy, the test for which was the correct filling out of a voting application in the presence of electoral officials, without assistance. The ANC had copies of the application printed and widely distributed in loyal villages around Kanongesha, teaching supporters to memorize the precise combination of letters to be placed on each line. On the day of reckoning some had their applications rejected when they became confused and began writing on the wrong line. But many more were successful. In a shock that reached the capital city, Njapau defeated the UNIP candidate Peter Matoka, 9,379 votes to 6,953. UNIP officials, having thought that Mwinilunga was safely within the fold, became irate. Ikelenge and Sailunga, both now openly UNIP members, came out publicly against Njapau, hinting at voter irregularities. Njapau was actually assaulted by egg-throwing protesters in Lusaka when he went to claim his seat in Parliament.[27] Nevertheless, he would serve until 1968, becoming nationally well known for two things: his uniquely outspoken nature in support of Lunda causes in Parliament and his treason trial. The trial is described later in the chapter.

Kanongesha: The Chief

Kanongesha's well-known support for the ANC was not without its consequences. The ANC-UNIP coalition government that pioneered African internal self-rule in 1962 paid its debt of support to rural traditional authorities by sanctioning the creation of a House of Chiefs as an adjunct to Parliament in the capital. The main function of this body was to review and comment on proposed legislation, particularly as it might impact upon "the common man" in rural areas.[28] Its decisions would not be legally binding, but as the last governor of Northern Rhodesia, Sir Evelyn Hone, noted at the inaugural meeting under the new internal self-government constitution, "The resolutions of the House will always be given serious consideration and in this way it can influence the decision of Government."[29] Or as Kenneth Kaunda would later say to the chiefs, "It is our intention that the status and standing of this House should be maintained within the framework of the constitution, and that Ministers should obtain the advice and opinions of this House on all matters which are the direct concern of the chiefs and their people."[30] Twenty-six chiefs, 3 or 4 from each province, were selected to represent the 230 formally recognized traditional chiefs throughout the country. A UNIP-commissioned panel selected Chiefs Ikelenge and Mumera and Senior Chief Ishinde to represent the Northwestern Province, a move designed to both humiliate and intimidate Senior Chief Kanongesha.

Despite grand rhetoric to the contrary, UNIP rapidly reduced the House of Chiefs to a perk awarded to pliant and supportive traditional leaders, never allowing the body to become a full partner in governance. A perusal of the House of Chief's transcripts reveals that in the early days the chiefs did, in fact, deliberate over a range of pertinent issues, including proposed modifications in the nation's judicial system, land reform, rural education, and development strategies. Proposals from chiefs may have been entertained by other branches of government but never implemented. As chiefs became increasingly vociferous about their obvious marginalization, government leaders became increasingly blunt and high-handed in their dealings with the House. Kaunda is recorded as having told the chiefs, "You, together with the UNIP and government of which you are a member, can influence change."[31] But he then went on to note,

> Some chiefs spend all their time drinking, doing nothing but waiting for checks from Government. If the House wishes to be taken seriously, it needs to discipline such Chiefs. . . . Chiefs are part and parcel of the Zambian Government.

Pens and Watches

Blue serge suit is becoming African status symbol

LIBREVILLE

One of the most precious status symbols in the new Africa is the blue serge suit. The makeshift government offices in the young capitals and the diplomatic cocktail parties abound with eager officials (mostly in their 30s) wearing the serge as though it were a uniform.

Quite obviously the grey flannel suit of the legendary Madison Avenue status-seeker is unsuited to the tropics. So lightweight blue in these latitudes serves for what might be termed importance in the third degree. The first and second degrees of importance in Africa are represented by the pen and the watch.

(*Central African Post,* May 8, 1961, p. 5)

They are paid by Government from public funds for the work they are expected to do. The party and Government expect and demand them:

—to implement Government policy, not to oppose it

—to disseminate government principles and ideas, not to oppose them

—to lead and guide the people, not to mislead and misguide them

—to promote unity, not to destroy the spirit of unity

—to eliminate divisive and destructive forces

Any chief who opposes Government policy, frustrates Government's efforts, flirts with or supports divisive or opposition elements, must not expect recognition or payment by this Government.[32]

This was no idle threat. Kaunda would frequently demonstrate that as the new supreme chief of Zambia, he would tolerate no dissent from subordinates. Yet, apparently keeping Kanongesha out of the House of Chiefs had in no way curtailed his political fervor or local influence. When elections to local councils were held throughout the country in 1965, four ANC candidates won in Kanongesha territory. The chief had campaigned actively on their behalf. The reaction from the capital was swift and merciless. The Kanongesha became perhaps the first chief in the nation to be summarily deposed by the UNIP government on the grounds that his behavior was creating divisions that adversely affected the nation's development.

The Kanongesha was dismissed from office on December 16, 1965.[33] Four days later his subordinate to the south, Chief Chibwika, was named the new Kanongesha. The old Kanongesha is said to have gone immediately into self-imposed exile in Angola. A month later a few lines in a Zambian newspaper reported that ex-chief Kanongesha had died in an auto accident in Angola. Others in the vehicle, including his senior wife, escaped injury.[34] UNIP may have initially assumed that that was the end of the story. In truth, it was the beginning of a new chapter of intense anti-UNIP sentiments that would characterize central Mwinilunga for decades to come. Even some who had remained neutral in the ANC-UNIP dispute, or who had actually been swayed by the pragmatic benefits of supporting the UNIP, were nevertheless incensed that government would interfere with the most sacred right of a people—to select their own traditional leader. Chibwika no doubt had his supporters, particularly among extended family and friends. But many Lunda vowed never to accept him as senior chief and to remain devoted to the old chief.

Even words of his death in Angola did not abate that loyalty. Indeed, many did not trust the report. For years to come, Njapau, the local representative in Parliament, would still be urged to argue unceasingly for the reinstatement of the old chief.

The old Kanongesha, with an extensive entourage, left Mwinilunga and resettled in a military camp in Angola along the Mazezi stream. The camp, code-named Mawaya, was run by a Portuguese national called Geoffrey or Sefulle. It was one of a string of facilities being set up to support the overlapping geopolitical interests of the remaining white-ruled countries in Southern Africa.[35] There was a collective desire to check the southward march of African nationalism, and a clandestine campaign of destabilization was being concocted. From 1964 onward, Kenneth Kaunda, long a strong voice for pan-Africanist cooperation in the region, combined his rhetorical support for African nationalist movements with concrete offers of military training bases and logistical support. As would become common knowledge later, Zambia indeed became a place of exile and military training for dozens of groups fighting against the white minority governments of Angola, Mozambique, Namibia, Southern Rhodesia, and South Africa. This made Zambia a primary target. Mawaya camp had been set up specifically to train disgruntled Zambians to invade and overthrow the UNIP government.

The best evidence suggests that the old Kanongesha was indeed killed when his vehicle accidentally ran over a landmine. A new Kanongesha, by the name of Kazimini, was elected by the exiled Lunda contingent in Angola. Supposedly, females and elderly males built houses, planted gardens, and carried out the mundane functions of daily subsistence. Young males mostly trained in the ways of guerrilla warfare, occasionally joined by other disgruntled young males from the Zambian side of the border. Over the years a number of attacks on Zambian soil would be attributed to this group. On December 15, 1966, for example, a small, armed group attacked a Luvale village just inside the Zambian border in an area long claimed by the Kanongesha. On January 26, 1967, a bridge connecting Mwinilunga District to Kabompo District in the south was burned beyond use. Dozens of attacks took place against villages associated with the new Kanongesha. An extensive campaign was waged to stop the 1968 election in Mwinilunga by burning polling stations and sending messages of intimidation to villagers. In 1971 a

80 M.P.H. Death Cloud

Winds carrying radioactivity

World horror is mounting

WASHINGTON

As world reaction and horror mount today the initial fallout from Russia's 30-megaton nuclear test is moving in a cloud about 100 to 150 miles wide and at a speed of about 80 m.p.h. over the Soviet Union, the U.S. Weather Bureau estimates. If the present east–west atmospheric wind patterns continues the first fall-out should reach the North American Continent by tomorrow or Friday.
(*Central African Post*, October 25, 1961, p. 1)

public bus was severely damaged when it ran over a land mine on the main road to Mwinilunga Boma.

The true identity of those perpetrators may never be known. In a region of the world that is trisected by three barely discernable national borders, patrolled by three antagonistic national armies, periodically being contested by dozens of armed movements, few are in a position to authenticate the participants in such isolated events. But a tone had been set, and an ideology of protest given physical manifestations. Generations of Lunda youth would come of age in an environment steeped in suspicion of government intentions, saturated with the symbols of government neglect, and rife with debates about the legitimacy of claims to traditional authority. For some, the spiritual center of the Lunda-Ndembu nation had shifted westward to Angola. The real chief was there. Real men with the courage to stand up for truth and tradition were there. Furthermore, the national government seems disturbingly prone toward actions that reignited such sentiments, fueling discussions about the true nature of the relationship between the Kanongesha Lunda and the national government.

In 1967 the police in Mwinilunga, none of whom were Lunda, stopped a man perceived to be acting suspiciously. Upon rigorous interrogation it came to light that he was a close associate of the old Kanongesha and was one of the Lunda exiles now living in Angola. He claimed to have come across the border solely to visit family and to attend to his property in Mwinilunga. Yet on his person the police found a document entitled "New Plan for North-Western Rhodesia to Join Lunda with Angola," the pan-Lunda strategy from years earlier listing Njapau as author and acknowledging the Kanongesha as one of the movement's traditional leaders.[36] This document, which apparently had not previously circulated in government or UNIP circles, set off an uproar that immediately reached the capital. Njapau was arrested for treason forthwith, and by some accounts was repeatedly beaten and tortured. Any mention of the constitutional clause concerning parliamentary immunity from prosecution or even the expressed need for due process was met with sharp rebukes. Mwinilunga was portrayed in the press as a hotbed of treachery and sedition, a territory locked in conspiratorial embrace with the worst enemies of the Zambian state. Anyone in Mwinilunga linked to Njapau or the old Kanongesha, be it by kinship, friendship, or simply residential proximity, felt the heavy hand of the police. Mwinilunga became a territory under siege; its citizens were systematically brutalized, with many forced into flight across the border into Angola.

The rush to punish Njapau was slowed by a Zambian judiciary determined to assert its autonomy vis-à-vis the executive and legislative branches of government.[37] Indeed, in those early years of independence the judiciary had yet to be

"Zambianized." It still contained mostly European judges resolved to impress upon the young nation the concept of separation of powers. Government prosecutors formally charged Njapau with taking men to Angola to undergo military training with the intent of overthrowing the government. The High Court's presiding justice, Ifor Evans, in a courageous act that would bring down scorn on him for years to come, found Njapau not guilty. The justice expressed his belief that there was clearly something more to ex-chief Kanongesha's self-imposed exile in Angola than met the eye. In his closing statement he noted, "I am left with suspicion that Njapau and others have been engaged in activities prejudicial to the state and that this investigation had merely touched the fringe of such activities."[38] But the judge further noted that the document serving as primary evidence had been written prior to the creation of the independent Republic of Zambia in 1964, and nowhere in the document does Njapau advocate military training or the use of force. The court was thus compelled to find him not guilty. In short, from a legal prospective, the government's case was weak. Yet, from the prospective of commonsense, it was clear to all that something fishy was going on in Mwinilunga.

The ordeal had taken its toll on Njapau. He would not campaign for reelection the following year, virtually disappearing from the political scene altogether. Additionally, the activities of the Kanongesha group in exile would gradually wind down over time. But the Lunda would not remain long without a potent symbol of resistance to UNIP's quest for unassailable sovereignty. Nor would they quietly acquiesce to their status as a marginal province yielding to the power of a new nation-state, yet not receiving the benefits thereof. A couple of hundred miles to the southeast, in Kaonde country, a new bit of fishy business would emerge.

Asians' Haircut Campaign Sparks Talks by Barbers
Pickets threat is denied

C.A.P. REPORTER

Hairdressers in Lusaka are to hold a meeting tomorrow night to discuss the question of Asians who have been coming into their shops asking for haircuts. One city hairdresser said that the Asians had threatened to picket barbers' shops by sitting and waiting for a haircut. (*Central African Post*, November 1, 1961, p. 7)

Mushala: The Bandit

Adamson Bratson Mushala was one of seven sons of a Kaonde headman whose village was located twenty kilometers west of Chizela, just south of the West Lunga National Game Park that served as the divide between Lunda and Kaonde territories.[39] The historical relationship between the two groups has been exceedingly amicable. The Lunda acknowledged the Kaonde as people distantly related to their own emperor, Mwantiyamva of the Congo, and thus treated them as *wusensi* (joking cousins). In theory at least, Lunda and Kaonde could travel in one another's territory in complete safety, taking hospitality freely wherever they found it. Encounters between the two people were usually characterized by a good deal of light-hearted teasing and jovial wisecracking.

Mushala was born in 1935 and educated at the nearby mission school run by the South African General Movement (SAGM), a group closely allied with the Plymouth Brethren missionaries firmly established at Kalene Hill and throughout Mwinilunga. The SAGM shared with the Brethren a rather narrow view of mission work. Schooling was not essentially an intellectual enterprise. Africans should be taught just enough to read the Bible, to preach and teach others, and to make a living through simple trades. Any more education than that would lead to vanity, it was thought. Nevertheless, Mushala ultimately succeeded in completing standard six (grade eight), which would have been sufficient to place him among the educated elite Africans in Northern Rhodesia at that time. Yet unlike many of his classmates, Mushala did not head for town upon graduation to seek a white-collar job as a clerk in the mines or ministries. Rather, he joined the game guards. After training he was stationed nearby in the West Lunga National Game Park. He was later promoted to game scout and then game cropper. However, he would never be promoted to the more technical and lucrative position of game ranger, a job classification generally reserved for Europeans.

The few snippets of information available about Mushala's life up to this point do not reveal him to be a particularly congenial individual. Some, in fact, might see early evidence of antisocial behavior bordering on the psychotic. For example, it is said that as a young student he refused to use the same pathway others used to reach the schoolhouse. He insisted on walking on ground untouched by others. Whenever he discovered someone had walked in his special path, he would change it immediately. Later, as an adult, Mushala was described as crude, self-centered, even egotistical, but always political. He hated the European rangers under whom he was forced to work, denouncing them as foreigners in his country. Yet, he was also rude to Africans, frequently bullying those he thought did not show proper respect for his authority. On more than one occasion he beat and threatened to shoot hunters found within the park, not out of concern for the animals, but because they had not sought out his personal permission to hunt.

Sometime in the late 1950s Mushala began to support Kenneth Kaunda's UNIP in the area around Chizela, supposedly raising funds by selling party membership cards. He had to be very careful about his involvement because civil servants were not allowed to participate in party politics. That UNIP was a banned party at the time would have made his infraction all the worse. For reasons utterly unknown, Mushala apparently quit his job with the Department of Game and Fisheries and in 1960 became a fulltime political activist for UNIP. Being more highly educated, more passionate, and more ruthless than those around him, Mushala quickly rose up the ranks of the local party hierarchy. From the chairmanship of a small branch, within a year Mushala had moved on to become the constituency chairman of Chizela District and then on to provincial headquarters. He was a hard worker, no doubt, but was again described as arrogant, ambitious, a one man show, abrasive, and not one to accept his superiors' orders without question. Those were difficult times, however, and men of action ruled the day. In 1961, when, according to some, UNIP unleashed its master plan of civil disobedience and sabotage, Mushala acted. He was associated with the burning down of Mutanda Mission School, the very place he had received his standard six certificate. He was further suspected of assaulting two policemen near the district headquarters, participating in acts of arson in Kabompo and Chavuma areas southwest of his home turf, cutting the only telephone lines that linked Northwest Province to the Copperbelt, and unsuccessfully attempting to burn the Mutanda bridge, the sole road link between the district capital and Mushala's home area to the south.

Anticipating that the next stage of the struggle for Northern Rhodesia's independence would require even more horrifying acts of violence, UNIP sent Mushala to China along with a few others to study guerrilla warfare from June to October 1962. But during Mushala's absence the political climate changed tremendously. Europeans seemed to have finally acknowledged the evitability of African majority rule. The antagonism between African and European parties was accordingly toned down, the apocalyptic rhetoric curtailed. Thus, when Mushala returned, primed for action, there was little need for his specialized Chinese training. His contemporaries, who had remained behind rather than preparing for battle, were instead intensively jockeying for political spoils.

Mushala's experience in China had apparently not been a pleasant one. In the future he would speak out often and angrily about the evils of the Chinese system. Yet he had endured that experience, expecting to be treated as a hero upon his return home. Instead, he found himself marginalized as a late entrant in the battle for political patronage. It is said he had wanted the position of director the Department of Game and Fisheries but was instead appointed deputy secretary to the Education Committee at party headquarters in Lusaka. Mushala accepted the position, for lack of any better option, but attempted to elevate his status in

Coloured Community "Up in Arms" over Criticism
Lusaka call for statistics

C.A.P. REPORTER

The coloured community in Lusaka is up in arms about a "sweeping statement" made by Mrs. P. Buchanan, a welfare officer, at a Lusaka Rotary lunch recently.

"I challenge her to produce statistics to back up her sweeping statement," said a Coloured technician who lives at Thorn Park, Lusaka. Mrs. Buchanan said that ignorance, poverty, disease and immorality are rife among the Eurafrican community. "We feel very strongly that unless they learn to help themselves and take part in our activities they will get absolutely nowhere."

(*Central African Post*, November 18, 1961, p. 7)

life through developing a business enterprise in his home area as well. UNIP had used some of its international financial contributions to create the Credit Organisation of Zambia (COZ), a unit designed specifically to loan money to former freedom fighters.[40] Unfortunately, by the time Mushala submitted his proposal for funds to establish a fishing cooperative in the Chizela region, the money had run out. Mushala refused to believe that explanation, convinced instead that he was personally being discriminated against by the new director of Game and Fisheries, the unit that he coveted and the unit that had been required to review the proposal in question. In truth, the money had indeed run out. But after much public ranting and writing angry letters to top UNIP officials, Mushala ultimately received sufficient funds from party coffers to begin his new project.

Mushala's temperament perhaps doomed the enterprise from its inception. The new fishing co-op quickly ran into debt as Mushala bought vehicles and office equipment, rented space, and mobilized participants. He ran the co-op as if it were his personal property. Fishing equipment was dispersed to co-op members, and fish were later collected and sold in various towns, with all the money going directly to Mushala. There were few records generated to document, explain, or quantify any of these transactions. Mismanagement lead to unaccounted-for losses of over £8,000 within two years. Finally fed up with Mushala's autocratic and erratic behavior, in addition to concerns about the propriety of his managing a fishing co-op in Chizela while simultaneously being on the party payroll for a job in Lusaka, government officials moved in, seized vehicles and equipment, and closed the co-op. Mushala was now set on a self-destructive course.

In 1966 Mushala definitively broke with UNIP and joined a newly formed opposition group, the United Party (UP). This party, claiming that UNIP was rife with nepotism and also opposing UNIP's emerging philosophy of "Humanism" and its inexorable march toward establishing a one-party state, initially drew membership from both major parties, UNIP and the ANC.[41] The party was particularly strong in the western region of the country where the perception of neglect by government ran high. UNIP dealt brutally with the new party, arresting its officials on the flimsiest charges and urging gangs of UNIP youth to beat up United Party supporters. After particularly violent clashes in August 1968 in which two UNIP officials were killed, the United Party was banned and its leaders restricted.[42] Mushala himself was rusticated to Chinsali, detained in a rural area nearly six hundred miles from his home base. Upon release, Mushala and a host of others simply joined the still legal ANC party and continued in opposition to UNIP. Within two years Mushala had become president of the northwestern provincial branch of the ANC-UP pact. He would withstand another round of detention, a few beatings, and the constant threats of being charged with treason. Yet he held fast to his opposition to UNIP.

In 1974 Mushala gave up hope on the utility of peaceful protest and participation in opposition politics. The law changing Zambia into a one-party state had been enacted the previous year. The Chinese, whom he so deeply detested, were building a major new rail line in the eastern region of Zambia, again accentuating the isolation and neglect of the west. A new system of registration began issuing some Lunda, Luvale, Cokwe, and Kaonde in Mushala's area with alien national registration cards, throwing into question their Zambian citizenship and hence their right to vote. There was talk in some quarters of the need to overthrow UNIP by force. Mushala, as he had done once before, left the country to be trained for this task. This time, however, the destination was Angola.

By some accounts Mushala and a group of followers left Zambia with the support and encouragement of the South African Department of National Security (DONS) and the Portuguese organization Policia Internacional de Defesa do Estado (PIDE). Eyewitness accounts from Mwinilunga claim that Mushala and several senior ANC officials had visited the exiled Kanongesha group on several occasions at their camp near Kalunda Boma in Angola. On another occasion Mushala was seen deep in Angola traveling with a military convoy to Cazombo, where he met with Portuguese officials and learned something about the international support that could be made available to those willing to militarily oppose the so-called Communist UNIP government of Zambia. He received a Land Rover on that occasion, returned to Zambia, and began ferrying family members and supporters to the Kanongesha camp in Angola. There he and his men were armed and trained in guerrilla warfare and the handling of small arms and explosives.

There are numerous versions of the next stage of the tale. Some have Mushala and Kanongesha collectively terrorizing the border region for years to come. Some have Mushala disappointed at the low level of Portuguese assistance and ultimately stealing weapons from a local armory before fleeing back to Zambia. And still another version places Mushala and his men in a military training camp in Namibia, under the sponsorship of South Africa. Indeed, Pieter Botha, then minister of defense for South Africa, acknowledged knowing of Mushala. In response to a Zambian protest before the United Nations Security Council about South Africa's destabilization campaign, Botha responded that Mushala and sixty-seven of his followers, including wives and children, had indeed arrived in the north of South-West Africa (Namibia) on

African Witchdoctor Signs for a Major Film Role

BY RITA RIXON

An African witchdoctor has been signed for an important role in 20th Century-Fox's "The Lion," now before the cameras in Kenya. M.K. Rhamadhani, a descendent of eight generations of witchdoctors, will play the role of Bogo, the African houseboy in the gamekeeper's lodge occupied by William Holden, Capucine, Trevor Howard and Pamela Franklin.

(*Central African Post*, December 22, 1961, p. 4)

Sunday, November 17, 1974. They had been flown in from the north, on a plane that had given no prior notification of its arrival.

He presented his group as refugees and asked for asylum. The authorities were thus confronted with a difficult situation. After consideration of the alternative, it was made clear to them that asylum was conditional—the condition being that in no circumstances would they undertake, nor would they be allowed to undertake, any subversive activities against Zambia. Subsequently it became doubtful whether Mushala would abide by his undertakings. That is true: we doubted his sincerity and consequently he was separated from his followers. Both he and they were then restricted to two camps at different locations. Attempts were made to keep them occupied by offering them work. For example, a number of Mushala's followers agreed to assist with guard duties at a local road construction project. However, they proved to be so inefficient that we had to return them to the main group within a short space of time. . . . During the night of 7th and 8th December 1975 Mushala and a number of his followers absconded, after raiding a store-room in the vicinity. Efforts to track them down failed, as rain had obliterated their tracks. I wish to state very clearly here that Mushala is no friend of the South African government and neither is the South African government a friend of Mushala's. Mushala was granted asylum for humanitarian reasons. He is a disreputable character who became a nuisance and an embarrassment to us.[43]

However incomplete our knowledge of Mushala's venture into Angola and Namibia may be, the next stage of the story is exceedingly well known. Mushala and a group of men returned to Zambian soil in January of 1976. For the next six years they orchestrated a reign of terror throughout the west and northwest that left scores dead, hundreds injured, thousands paralyzed with fear, and the Zambian police and military establishments utterly perplexed by their inability to bring Mushala to justice. Time and again Mushala defeated increasingly larger forces, escaped increasingly more elaborate ambushes, and thwarted increasingly more sophisticated intelligence gathering. In short time Mushala became a legend with an ever-expanding array of metaphysical attributes: the power of invisibility, the capacity to transform himself into an animal, the knowledge of incantations and "medicines" that turned bullets into water.

In truth, a more likely explanation for Mushala's success was simply good training in the basic techniques of guerrilla warfare: superior knowledge of the theater of operation, flexibility and mobility of aim and execution, and local logistical support. Mushala set up camp in the West Lunga National Game Park. It was the place he had worked as a young game guard, the landscape he perhaps knew better than any other person, and one he certainly knew better than the succession of troops sent to apprehend him, most of whom were not even from the northwest. Mushala and his small band of men moved rapidly across the terrain, ranging widely, attacking where least expected, disappearing into the bush only to re-emerge hundreds of miles away. He robbed government payrolls when he needed cash, bought or took food from isolated villages, and kidnapped young men to replenish his fighting force and young women to serve as bush wives to his soldiers.

Yet, far from pursuing a life of simple banditry, Mushala attempted to project an image of himself as a freedom fighter, waging war on behalf of the peoples of the Northwest against the one-party state, communism, and government neglect. He tried to politicize local villages through a constant barrage of literature detailing his grievances, his intended targets, and his ultimate plan of action. His frequently stated objective was to bring into being the United States of Zambia with paramount chiefs as the heads of individual states. Mushala composed documents that delineated with great precision the names of administrative units in his new government, the division of responsibilities between departments, the function of the civil service, the proposed educational system, the economic development agenda, welfare programs, and foreign policy initiatives. He described an eight-year transition period during which he alone would serve as president and commander-in-chief, before handing over power to an elected leader.

As a rebel hiding in the bush, constantly on the run from government troops, Mushala managed to keep up a remarkable letter-writing campaign. He wrote to Paramount Chiefs throughout Zambia urging them, as future leaders of his state governments, to stop their subjects from voting in the currently illegitimate elections. He wrote to church leaders throughout the northwest informing them that his targets included any vehicles, polling stations, bridges, schools, local courts, and bars. All were objects directly or indirectly associated with government presence. Bars were probably added to the list in recognition of the fact that they tended to serve food as well as bottled beer. Hence, their clientele would most likely be employed outsiders, such as soldiers, teachers, and government officials. Genuinely local people tended to eat at home with kinfolk and drink home-brewed alcohol. Mushala wrote Jonas Savimbi, leader of the Angolan rebel movement UNITA (National Union for the Total Independence of Angola), proposing a united anti-Communist

Liz Wants Eddie Back

C.A.P. CORRESPONDENT, NEW YORK

Liz Taylor's high-flying romance with Richard Burton is on the wane. Now Liz wants Eddie back.

According to reports here she has been telephoning Eddie Fisher in Los Angeles every day for the past week from Rome. She sent him a mass of flowers for his opening at a night club there.

(*Central African Post*, June 1, 1962, p. 1)

front against the governments of their respective countries.[44] Mushala also requested Savimbi's assistance in securing ammunition. Mushala wrote the United
Nations accusing Zambia of using torture, detainment and murder against those
who oppose one-party state. He indeed accused Zambia of being even less democratic than South Africa. Mushala is furthermore known to have written radio
commentators of the Zambia Broadcasting Service telling them to stop referring
to him as a criminal on the radio, or they would soon be shot. In one strange
incident the government intercepted a letter from Mushala to an officer at the
American embassy in Lusaka requesting a new radio, a pair of binoculars and
scholarships for his men to study medicine in the USA.[45] It was not clear how
Mushala came to know this person. But the fact that the letter was sent to the personal rather than embassy address, and that the American in question had recently visited the Northwest created such suspicion that he was declared persona
non grata, and asked to leave Zambia immediately.

Despite all else, fear was no doubt Mushala's greatest ally during his six-year
rebellion. He managed to exploit local mythopoeic motifs, to associate himself
with unspeakable powers, and to conjure up the most profound metaphysical
angst. His daily regime of baths, dietary restrictions, medicinal concoctions, and
mysterious unaccompanied walkabouts in lands dense with dangerous animals
terrified even his own men. Many who had been abducted and forced to join
Mushala's band were too frightened to flee even though he might be absent for
days on end. Villagers were frightened to report on his whereabouts because he always escaped capture and returned to exact retribution from those who plotted
against him. He was President Mushala, owner of the land, the lion of the Lunga
National Park, the one with nine lives, he who is everywhere at once, the wind, and
the liberator. In some instances the fear of Mushala was so great that separate units
of the security forces panicked and exchanged gunfire, each believing that the other
was Mushala's gang. Fear of Mushala, however, was not limited to those residing
in the northwest. Indeed, he made periodic and well-documented trips to urban
areas both to recruit new followers and to intimidate old foes. When twenty-nine
girls were killed in town between 1980 and 1981 by the so-called Lusaka Strangler,
many believed it to be the work of Mushala. Any large-scale crime anywhere that
left the police befuddled was potentially the work of Mushala.

The Zambian government increasingly blamed the delay in capturing Mushala
on support by local people. Accordingly, those in the northwest were subjected to
a campaign of intense interrogation, intimidation, and torture in the name of extracting information about Mushala. Few were spared the pain and humiliation,
as even senior chiefs, accused of allowing Mushala to operate in their area, were
beaten in front of their subjects. The government offensive against Mushala increasingly looked like an undeclared war on the northwest as a whole. For those

in Mwinilunga, it reopened the still festering wounds of a deposed senior chief, the Kanongesha, and a debarred popular politician, Ronald John Njapau.

Mushala was finally killed on Friday, November 26, 1982, in an appropriately mythic gun battle in the game park, supposedly betrayed by an old lover who led soldiers to his hideout in a fit of jealousy over his new and younger lover. Legend has it that she had stolen the secret of his invisibility and invincibility, rendering him weak and vulnerable to the soldiers' bullets. Yet, the story does not end at this point. The detention of suspected Mushala sympathizers continued unabated after his death. In fact, by some accounts there was an increase in detainees. Many of Mushala's men, including some who were initially abductees, were afraid to come out of hiding for fear of government retribution. For eight more years, under the leadership of Alexander Saimbwende, they would roam the backcountry of Northwestern Province, eking out an existence with the help of local villagers. This remnant of the Mushala gang made a point of seeking an audience with Lunda chiefs, assuring them of the group's nonviolent intent. They were reportedly well received. Indeed, young men frustrated by the lot of the Lunda under UNIP government rule would continue to replenish the ranks of the gang. It would not be until September 14, 1990, after an utterly exasperated federal government issued a full pardon, that Saimbwende and the few remaining members of the Mushala gang came out of hiding.

Mushala had been a Kaonde by birth, but his rhetoric was always regional in focus. He had fought on behalf of the neglected peoples of Northwestern Province, be they Kaonde, Lunda, Luvale, or Lozi. The historical animosities that divided these groups paled in comparison to the contemporary treatment they shared at the hands of the UNIP government. Mushala was strongly embraced by some Lunda because of his group's confluence with that of the exiled Kanongesha. Additionally, his number two man was a Lunda. James Kaimana, born in 1932 in Nyakulen'a area in

Clay's Chances—Nil!
Liston to win on quick knockout

MIAMI BEACH

The experts almost unanimously expect Sonny Liston to keep his world heavyweight boxing title tomorrow night by knocking out Cassius Clay in short order. (*Central African Post*, February 24, 1964, p. 6)

Zambezi District, educated up to standard six, was widely regarded as the most dangerous of all the members of the Mushala group. He was the best marksman, the most physically adroit, and the most brutal of the bunch. Tales of his swimming across crocodile-infested rivers and making daring escapes often rivaled those of Mushala himself.

The lasting impact of the Mushala episode for some was a deepening sense that the policies of the UNIP government, just as those of the colonial government that preceded it, were antithetical to local interests. In some circles UNIP was deemed even worse than the colonial regime. It was controlled by a godless group of foreign Africans with imported ideas, Communists who knew little of conditions in the northwest, who had no interests in ameliorating local concerns, and who had fewer of the accoutrements of modernity to offer than their European predecessors.[46] In the minds of some, Mushala would join and thereby bring into sharper relief a pantheon of local heroes who had violently resisted the incursion of outsiders throughout the twentieth century. This group included the following:

1. Headman Kasanza, who shot C. H. S. Bellis, the first British South Africa Company official sent to stake a claim on Mwinilunga in 1907.
2. Shakutenuka, a Kaonde tax resister who killed a BSAC official in 1912.
3. Chilomba, a Lunda who stabbed to death two colonial officials in Kabompo District in 1963.
4. Chief Kanongesha, whose incursions into Mwinilunga in 1966 and 1968 led to the Njapau treason trial.

Even those who may have rejoiced at Mushala's demise would doubtfully deny the significance of his movement. His presence defined an era, his policies shaped a generation, and his rhetoric became the Lunda theme song, reverberating subliminally in the background of every conversation. Between the beginning of Mushala's campaign in 1976 and the general amnesty granted his gang in 1990, Amabwambu and their cohort came of age, savored the fruits of youthful experimentation, devised more mature plans, and in their late thirties and early forties emerged as leaders of their own large and successful villages. Educated in the unique Americo-Lunda environment of St. Kizito Catholic Boarding School, steeped in the emotional maelstrom of the Congo crisis, politicized by the opposition to the Central African Federation, Amabwambu's mature operational consciousness was honed on nightly fireside debates about the meaning of Mushala.

Congressman's Expenses' Trips
Beauty queen scandal
WASHINGTON, REUTER

Congressman Adam Clayton Powell of Harlem, New York, was accused yesterday of taking taxpayer-financed trips with a former beauty queen under assumed names and was ordered to stop paying his estranged wife out of Congressional funds. (*Times of Zambia*, January 5, 1967, p. 3)

At the most basic level, the decade-long presence of the Mushala gang in the West Lunga National Game Park changed the fundamental distribution of people across the landscape. For example, although Mushala and his men shot game for sustenance and, according to some, operated a thriving business in ivory in exchange for weapons, fear of the gang deterred others from venturing near the park. Consequently, exploding populations of animals, particularly elephants, bush pigs, and antelopes, flowed uncontrolled out of the park, threatening the safety of human settlements and the sustainability of human cultivation. Lunda populations shifted northward away from the dangers of the park, toward the areas of Kanongesha, Matonchi Plateau, and the Boma. Roving quadrupeds and well-armed bipeds accentuated the advantage of large villages as a defensive arrangement, curtailing the impulse of many to settle in virgin territory.

Mushala's political platform evoked constant debates about social identity. He added "Northwestern" as an operative category rivaling more narrow ethnic-based considerations of identity such as Lunda, Kaonde, Luvale, or Lozi. His movement provoked debates about spiritual beliefs, juxtaposing both traditional and Christian beliefs against the so-called atheist and Communist beliefs of the ruling party. The extended success of Mushala enlivened and invigorated questions about traditional metaphysical powers. Do Lunda magic and sorcery really work? Can the knowledgeable individual survive the total onslaught of the national police and army? Equally important was the widespread realization of the weakness of government in controlling the borders and in policing its own territory. The Amabwambu could now add their own layer of experience to the intergenerational dialogue about the power and political possibilities of porous borders.

One might suggest, with just a modicum of exaggeration, that the Lunda are bound less by what they do and more by what they think, and less by things agreed upon and more by things deemed worthy of spirited disagreement. Indeed, one might best map out a Lunda consciousness by the distinctive array of powerful debates:

1. Legitimate Kanongesha: the Angolan or the Zambian one?
2. Reconstitution of the Lunda Empire: possible or not?
3. National government's relationship to Mwinilunga: benign neglect or active policy of underdevelopment?
4. Local Europeans: good or bad?
5. Combatants in the Angola civil war: pro- or anti-Lunda interest?
6. Mushala: bandit or liberator?

8

Living on the Edge (of the IMF Leash)

The Mission Elite in the Making of an Elite Mission

To the degree that Lwawu Mission possesses a cohesive philosophy of economic development, it appears to be rather conventional in its basic assumptions. The Franciscan Friars utilize the "model project approach" that entails assembling the best components in one place to ensure the best possible outcome, in hopes that through diffusion the wider population will come to learn about and emulate successful project practices. Rather than assisting those most in need of help, the model project approach places the most fertile land, the most improved seeds, the most effective fertilizers and pesticides, the most advanced technology available directly in the hands of the most highly educated and motivated members of the local community. Yet, because the best, by definition, is always in limited supply, the numbers of individuals who can replicate the success of the well-supported model project is likewise limited. Furthermore, because the primary focus of the model project approach is on efficacy rather than equity, it often, with little fore-thought, disrupts preexisting socioeconomic balances, renders local leveling mechanisms ineffective, and exaggerates local inequalities. Amabwambu were cultivated by the mission to be a longitudinal model project. Time and again they were the first to experiment with novel crops, the first to receive new technologies, the first to use new productive networks, and the first to try out new forms of economic organization. Concomitantly, Amabwambu emerged as an undeniable local elite, a mission-created brotherhood whose status was inextricably linked to its access to mission knowledge, mission tools, mission finance, and mission contacts with governmental, nongovernmental, and international organizations.

The creation of the Lwawu Mission elite may have begun as an altruistic act by a set of young idealistic American Catholics in the 1950s and 1960s, but over time the relationship between producer and social product became one of interlocking dependence. In order for Lwawu Mission to survive, it had to continually supply its American supporters with stories of transformed African individuals, successfully torn away from primitive practices and perspectives, embracing Catholic beliefs and American cultural values. And in order for the mission elite, Amabwambu, to survive, it needed to make Lwawu the kind of elite mission establishment capable of demonstrating such profound transformations and thereby continue to attract the wide range of resources on which Amabwambu status was based. Mission staff and young African males each needed the legitimizing force of the other. Each group publicly supported the other, embellishing admirable traits and achievements while camouflaging flaws and failures.

Several features encouraged the development of intense long-term relationships between certain mission staff and a core group of African individuals. The size of the expatriate mission staff fluctuated greatly over the years, expanding to dozens when St. Kizito School was in full operation or when a fresh batch of apostolates was being trained, yet contracting significantly during periods of lesser activity. There were, nevertheless, a half-dozen Americans who spent the better part of their mission careers at Lwawu. Three in particular, Father Adrian and Brothers Joe and Louis, would spend decades working at the mission, punctuated only by brief sabbatical visits to the United States once every three years or so.[1] Father Adrian, Brother Joe, and Brother Louis, in fact, had a well-known dislike of town life, venturing there only when mission work required it. Indeed, so great was their love of life at Lwawu that they were known to have occasionally returned early from sabbatical leave. Longevity in a rather isolated rural area, in and of itself, is an ideal crucible for the production of intense affective bonds. Yet, those bonds did not necessarily expand in number over time. Brother Joe and Brother Louis in particular, perhaps because of the nature of their work at Lwawu, gained limited fluency in the Lunda language. Brother Joe was the original headmaster of St. Kizito School, the designer of its total immersion format, the ever-present taskmaster ensuring that his young charges spoke only English around the clock, insisting even that they learn to dream in English. Brother Louis, on the other hand, was constantly engaged in building up and maintaining the mission's physical plant. He was a quiet man who through trial and error and pragmatic reasoning managed to erect stone churches, a friary, a convent, a clinic, a gristmill, and a hydroelectric dam. He was not one for much small talk. And by selecting his laborers almost exclusively from among Brother Joe–trained boys, Louis was able to focus all his attention on the project at hand, unimpeded by the need to learn another language. Indeed, access to the education that Brother Joe offered and access to the cash-paying jobs that Brother Louis offered were two of the more tangible and immediate local incentives for learning English well. But in 1978 St. Kizito would close its doors for good and the quality of local education would drop precipitously. Few in the younger generation would achieve even modest competency, let alone mastery of English. And because Brother Joe and Brother Louis's skill in Lunda did not correspondingly improve, the walls of their social world would close ever more tightly around that first generation of African associates.

Demographic trends also contributed to the narrowing of social relations. Located less than an hour's walk from the Angola border, Lwawu Mission and environs has long been the destination of choice for a steady trickle of individuals seeking to escape the (un)civil war being waged on that turf. Outbreaks of especially intense fighting, however, have periodically sent tens of thousands of refugees fleeing toward Lwawu in energetic bursts. Most are Lunda with kin, real or fictive, on the Zambian side of the border and will ultimately be folded into the rhythms of daily village life. Nevertheless, mounting numbers of strangers drastically change the cozy and insular feel of social life around Lwawu. The pathways become increasingly crowded with alien faces, many with tortured gazes reflecting the unspeakable horrors witnessed in Angola. Others scurry about furtively, ever-fearful of spies supposedly planted among the refugees. In such a social context, a higher premium is placed on the familiar face. Particularly after a spate of thefts and break-ins around Lwawu in the 1980s, mission leeriness of strangers intensified.

The explosion of strangers on the landscape was also a concern for Amabwambu. Anything that made mission staff uncomfortable or that might provoke among them debates about the wisdom of their continued tenure at Lwawu threatened Amabwambu's security. Amabwambu, thus, took the initiative in protecting their benefactors from the physical and emotional onslaught of strangers. In one famous case a frantic Brother Joe reported a cow missing. Amabwambu immediately mobilized a host of young clients and kin to scour the area for clues. A swarm of flies around a pool of blood in the bush signaled the spot where the animal had been slaughtered. With finely honed tracking skills the Amabwambu's group was able to follow a faint set of footprints to the village of the perpetrator and recover the still fresh meat. In this particular case the criminal was not a stranger from Angola but rather one of the cowboys hired by Brother Joe, whose well-known mantra had long been "If I don't see you in church on Sunday, don't come by the mission asking for favors on Monday." The local Catholic congregation was thus disproportionately made up of young men seeking jobs and elderly women hoping to make a bit of profit by selling the mission food or other commodities. The cowboy in question had cleverly made his presence in church known to Brother Joe long enough to be rewarded with a mission job. Subsequent to this event, however, church attendance alone would not be sufficient to gain mission trust. All potential employees would be vetted through Amabwambu. Commodity sellers would be screened, and refugees seeking relief would be registered by Amabwambu. Time and again this group would prove its worth by ferreting out and exposing those who would overcharge, deceive, plot against, steal from, or in any other way seek to harm mission personnel or property. Accordingly, an increasing number of mission services began to be dispensed solely through Amabwambu. They would become the eyes through which the mission saw the local world, and the arms through which the mission reached out. Amabwambu would also become the lens through which the world viewed the mission. In their intercalary role Amabwambu were feared by some yet were highly sought out by others for the benefits they could bestow.

Peace Corps Not Spying

Alleged U.S. document a forgery says State Department

WASHINGTON, REUTER

The State Department yesterday put a "forgery" label on a document published by an African newspaper which alleges that American Peace Corps volunteers engaged in espionage.

Calling it an attempt to discredit the Peace Corps and embarrass U.S. relations with friendly African nations, the State Department said it was drawing attention promptly to the forgery because of possible ramifications throughout Africa. (*Times of Zambia*, January 5, 1967, p. 2)

Running for Their Lives: The Impact of Refugees

The notion of refugees as a distinct and easily definable sociological category is a difficult concept to sustain when applied to the Mwinilunga context. The Lunda have historically been a highly mobile population. Many of life's contingencies are dealt with through movement. The cultivation of cassava on weak soils, for example, necessitates a nearly annual shift to fresh lands. Death, disease, and intolerable neighbors are things that can be left behind through relocation. The losers in political struggles, those accused of witchcraft, and those simply not faring well may be expected to move on, starting life anew elsewhere. Wisdom and worldliness can be achieved only through travel. The discovery of raw materials and new economic opportunities are likewise the result of travel. In a 1985 survey, roughly two-thirds of adults in Kanonesha claimed to maintain contacts with family members in Angola and the Congo through intermittent visits.[2] And many had resided in those countries for extended periods. Hence, given the fluid relationship between people and land, debates about who is, and who is not a refugee are problematic.

Refugees signify, in a sense, a process more so than an assemblage of persons.

They represent a quantitative phenomenon that triggers distinctive qualitative responses. The needs of individuals may remain constant whether they cross a border in small family groupings or in a throng of thousands. They need orientation, a settlement site, farming land, sustenance until crops mature, access to building materials, and protection from exploitation. Yet size does matter; it is the basis for differing responses. When small groups of displaced persons leave Angola and relocate in Mwinilunga, most will be quickly and quietly absorbed into villages of kin or kindly local individuals. Their presence will hardly cause a ripple on the social or physical landscape. If arriving in slightly larger numbers, a group would most likely approach a chief or a senior headman and seek his protection, patronage, and permission to build a rudimentary village so as not to be separated. But large numbers of displaced persons trigger different and more wide-ranging responses. They must, under penalty of law, be reported to the federal government.

Large groups evoke multiple administrative concerns and set in motion local, national, and international chains of activities. Public health officials endeavor to stay apprised of potential pathogenic vectors. The vision of massive numbers of poorly nourished people living in hastily established and unsanitary conditions evokes fears of unchecked cholera and hepatitis outbreaks. Veterinary officials are concerned that incoming refugees with domestic animals may have breached protective livestock corridors. Security forces may have reasons to fear that still-armed deserters or even active combatants may have ensconced themselves among the refugees. Emotionally disturbed fighters regularly flee the war zone. Others arrive seeking to extend the war onto Zambian soil, doing reconnaissance of material goods available or assessing the location and strength of Zambian military forces in the region. Either group can pose a lethal threat to those that they perceive as foes.

Large numbers of displaced persons also trigger obligations under international law, the primary one being the notification of the United Nations High Commissioner for Refugees (UNHCR). This group dispatches or hires local teams of experts to rapidly assess the scale of the emergency, determine the general and specific needs of the population in question, command international attention, mobilize donations of cash, food, medicine, clothing, and other needed commodities, and, finally, construct a distribution network. In the case of Zambia this network invariably begins at the airport in the capital city, Lusaka. Rumors are rife that many of the better items are diverted into a separate distribution stream at this point. Highly prized canned meats, milk, high-quality blankets, utensils, sugar, soap, and cooking oil find their way into the more exclusive suburban shops patronized by the country's political and economic elite. Owners of such establishments are sometimes too smug to even hide the boxes labeled "Not for sale. Product of ——" or "Donated by ——" or "Gift from the people of —— to the people of Zambia." As goods destined for the refugees are transported over the nearly five hundred miles of bad road that separates Mwinilunga from the capital city, additional pilfering, some say, takes place at the provincial and district levels. Yet, despite these supposed indiscretions, hundreds or even thousands of tons of donated commodities have on occasion reached the end of the pipeline.

Needless to say, estimates of refugee numbers have a strong political component. There are pressures in numerous quarters to exaggerate the scale of emergencies in order to push commodity flows to the highest level possible. Whether corrupt officials seeking to generate opportunities for personal gain or dedicated aid workers genuinely moved by the wretched conditions of refugees, all act in accordance with the belief that more is better. For Amabwambu, the mid-1980s were defining moments. The UNHCR estimated roughly 7,000 refugees entered Mwinilunga District from Angola in the early months of 1986, joining the 4,000 who had been registered a few years earlier and the nearly 10,000 who had poured into the area after the failed 1977–78 invasions of Shaba Province, Congo.[3] The number of fresh arrivals would nearly double again by midyear.

Heart Man "Home in Three Weeks"

CAPE TOWN

Mr. Philip Blaiberg, who has had a young Coloured man's heart beating inside him for three days, is at present a little euphoric, Professor Chris Barnard, who led the operation, said here today.

The Professor told a Press conference the 58-year old dentist was in this state because he knew the operation was over and was successful. Also because the high dose of drugs he was receiving induced this feeling.

(*Times of Zambia*, January 7, 1967, p. 1)

Invariably Lwawu Mission would be selected as a UNHCR distribution site. Brother Joe would have preferred otherwise but refrained from protesting too loudly, fully aware that such selections were the sine qua non of a successful mission station. But he would try to minimize the impact on his routine by allowing Amabwambu to take the lead in the refugee registration exercise and the subsequent distribution of UNHCR commodities. Unfortunately, Brother Joe would be called upon periodically to "liberate" goods meant for the refugees from the Mwinilunga Boma government warehouse. Although the UNHCR earmarked funds to cover all labor and transportation costs associated with getting goods to Lwawu Mission proper, Boma officials frequently held things up claiming the lack of trucks, fuel, and laborers to do the off-loading. The Franciscans would have to use their own vehicles and workers to move the commodities the final forty miles to Lwawu. Attempts to gain access to or even an accounting of UNHCR transport funds were met with evasive government responses, sometimes tinged with threats.

The major question remains, however. If there is a constant trickle of refugees from Angola, how does one decide who is eligible to receive commodities at any particular UNHCR distribution? Brother Joe's thinking was clear and straight-forward: commodities should be reserved for the most recent arrivals. UNHCR mobilization was clearly in response to specific events, an intensification in war-fare that sent people fleeing into a neighboring country. He thus unproblemati-cally assumed that those who had come over within the last few months as a result of the most recent upturn in fighting would be the target group. But Amabwambu had their own slightly more complex notions. Experiencing war and fleeing one's village were not the operative conditions that separated residents from refugees. Productive capacity was the primary distinguishing feature. Refu-gees lack mature agricultural fields that not only provide sustenance but also serve as evidence of applied labor in the landscape, the locally acknowledged guarantor of rights in land and associated bundles of political rights. Hence, Amabwambu reckoned that anyone whose fields were not yet producing should be eligible to re-ceive UNHCR assistance. And because the local subsistence crop is cassava, which takes eighteen months to mature, the number of individuals defined as refugees by Amabwambu greatly exceeded the UNHCR's and Brother Joe's expectations. Yet Amabwambu constructed a criterion deemed fair by local standards, thus avoiding the prolonged acrimony that would surely have engulfed Lwawu had Brother Joe's more limited interpretation been applied. The productive status of cassava fields is empirically verifiable, a condition unambiguously clear to local observers. Thus during the 1986 exercise, Amabwambu managed, with little diffi-culty, to certify 3,600 refugees eligible for UNHCR assistance at Lwawu.

A typical UNHCR relief package might consist of a tub of dried, shelled maize, a blanket, a pot, a plate, a plastic cup and eating utensils, a pint of cooking oil, a bag of beans, and a tin of powdered milk per person. Hoes, knives, and axes might be allocated on the basis of family size. Foodstuffs would be distributed monthly until supplies were exhausted. The mission had the only mill in the area geared to grind maize into the grade of flour suitable for making *nshima*, the starchy con-coction at the heart of every Lunda meal. The charge would generally be one *kwacha* per tub load of maize, but since refugees generally have no money, the mis-sion would take one small bucket of flour as a service charge. Yet refugees had little appreciation for maize *nshima*, having been raised exclusively on cassava *nshima*. For the most part local consumption of maize *nshima* was limited to the small con-tingent of government workers assigned from other areas of Zambia or the few Lunda who had become accustomed to maize during extended stays in town. Thus, nearly all the UNHCR maize ended up on the tables of local schoolteachers, agri-cultural and veterinary officers, and clinic staff or was transported to town markets after mission milling. Most refugees quickly disposed of their allotment of maize in exchange for cassava, perhaps only vaguely aware of its actual resale value.

Lunda dining etiquette has tight circles of people taking food from communal dishes directly to mouth exclusively with the right hand. Water is taken only at the end of meals, again from one shared cup. Thus the amount of dishes issued the refugees was excessive by local standards. Most were quickly traded for more desirable goods. And few refugees had fled Angola so quickly as to have left behind their basic tools of production. Hence, the hoes, knives, and axes distributed by the UNHCR were readily converted into more immediately usable goods. Indeed, most of the UNHCR goods would ultimately end up in the hands of local citizens, who had in effect been caring for the refugees since their arrival in Zambia.

As noted earlier, the Lunda plant cassava continually throughout the eight-month annual rainy season, digging up mature roots as needed. Cassava left in the ground remains fully edible for up to a year and a half after reaching maturity. Rough estimates, however, suggest that at least one-third of the available cassava is never dug up. People tend to prefer the younger, more tender, and more easily processed plants, relying on older ones only in times of shortage. The Lunda, thus, possess the reserve capacity to absorb a fair number of new people quickly. The surplus cassava of the nearly eight thousand longer-term residents within walking distance of Lwawu Mission plus the vast array of wild foods present in the environment would have gone a long way toward feeding the refugees in the absence of any UNHCR assistance. Indeed, had there been no relief effort enticing refugees to amass at central locations, most would have ultimately distributed themselves across the landscape in accordance with the availability of wild resources: fruits and vegetables, game and fish.

But the initial covenant between residents and new arrivals was based on the provision of labor in exchange for daily rations. Refugees—men, women, and children—were adopted in small groups, plied with cassava from underutilized fields and set to work planting new cassava, making beds for streamside vegetable gardens, digging fishponds, or perhaps building corrals for goats or pigs. Newcomers can also stimulate a boom in local village expansion as they can be used to make adobe bricks and collect bamboo for framing, poles for roofing, and grass for thatching. They might also be put to work clearing intervillage pathways, strengthening local bridges, or cleaning communal wells.

The myriad and valuable uses for refugee labor and the general reluctance of refugees to refuse any requests from their sponsors in exchange for a commodity that otherwise had little value invariably led to

Smugglers of Congo Beer Net Thousands

BY TIMES REPORTER

Smugglers of Simba, Congolese beer, are taking advantage of the tall green grass to sneak through a stretch of the Congo-Zambia border about ten miles north of Ndola—and net thousands of pounds a year.

Truck-loads of Simba beer find their way to shebeen queens in Copperbelt towns. Bags of beer are transported across the border on bicycles and hidden in grass near the Ndola-Mufulira road for trucks to collect. Some smugglers who transport charcoal disguise the beer as bags of charcoal.

(*Times of Zambia*, March 7, 1967, p. 7)

fireside discussions of slavery "in the old days." The official history of Zambia presumes that the last slave traders were chased out of the country in 1912.[4] Yet observers in Mwinilunga have noted that slavery remained a very visible social institution in the 1920s. Anthropologist Victor Turner further noted that it was a barely concealed secret well into the 1950s.[5] Masters and slaves, alike, generally conspired to keep the details of the system from reaching the ear of colonial authorities. At times each might threaten to expose the other, but merely as a ploy for renegotiating the terms of engagement in the web of rights, duties, privileges, and expectations that blind masters and slaves over time. If a master married a slave, the offspring would be free persons. But a master also had the right to arrange marriages for his slaves, in which case all offspring became slaves. Over time, entire slave lineages might emerge, attached in subordinate fashion to a free lineage, the details perhaps hidden from the outside world by the seemingly egalitarian intercourse of daily village life. According to local oral tradition, some individuals became slaves as a result of debts or death payments, but most were reduced to slavery as a result of crop failure, hunger, or landlessness—conditions much like those experienced by contemporary refugees from Angola. Senior Chief Kanongesha and Senior Headman Chifunga frequently traveled about, holding village meetings and warning people not to prey on the refugees. Locals were urged to give refugees food in exchange for "piecework" (clearly defined tasks of limited duration), but not to enslave them. Yet, there is always much whispering about this or that contemporary big man who is amassing slaves. Such rumors join the existing stock of tales about well-known local lineages that have continued to remain secretly enslaved to other lineages in Mwinilunga since ancient times. The presence of new refugees simply provides fresh reasons to revisit such stories.

Hastily arranged sexual unions, however, are an undeniable social phenomenon that accompanies each influx of refugees. In some cases unattached female newcomers represent an opportunity for local males to marry with little, if any, investment in bridewealth. In the context of hunger and homelessness, marriage into a stable village may be preferable to the insecurity of refugee camp life. Such an attachment endows women with an immediate set of rights in land as well as social and material resources that can be channeled to family members. Needless to say, refugee families have been known to pressure their unattached females to respond favorably to marriage proposals. Mature women, in particular, may be quickly absorbed as second, third, or fourth wives of more established local big men. But many young women become concubines or outright prostitutes trading sexual favors for meat, tools, clothing, or any other commodity they or their families need at the moment. Refugee settlements are noted for the swarms of men circling them like vultures, gifts in hand, seeking short- or long-term sexual liaisons.

Newcomers from Angola are also viewed as potential providers of biomedical and metaphysical services. The Portuguese historically invested far less in the social infrastructure of their colonies than did their European counterparts elsewhere. Educational and medical facilities were terribly inadequate in urban areas and virtually non-existent in many rural ones. Lunda raised across the border in Angola, thus, had long remained dependent on traditional medical knowledge and spiritual practices to maintain individual and collective health. Accordingly, refugee populations tend to be comparatively dense in diviners, herbalists, and spiritualist practitioners of diverse genre. They are eagerly sought out by locals with lingering ailments that the Lwawu clinic had been unable to cure, by families experiencing a troubling number of deaths over a short period of time, or by those for whom the vicissitudes of life have not led to the desired level of fame or fortune. Invariably some individuals among the refugees gain widespread renown and make a comfortable living dispensing medicinal preparations and uncovering the spiritual sources of bad luck or the more earthly causes of abiding misfortune. At least they may for a while. Reputation is a fickle commodity. Those presumed to be endowed with extraordinary powers also provoke feelings of envy, suspicion, fear, and even loathing. One misstep, one miscalculation, or one impolitic witchcraft accusation can cause their client base to evaporate and can even place their lives in jeopardy. Furthermore, it is widely believed that those who can heal can also harm. The popular traditional doctor and the feared sorcerer differ only in intent, not in relative capacity. Thus even those who do good remain forever under a cloud of suspicion. As one member of Amabwambu was fond of saying: "We Zambians believe in medicines and hospitals. Those Angolans only have their witchcraft. They foment troubles, start rumors so they can ply their wares as diviners and doctors. They are desperate."[6]

UNHCR commodities allow refugees to branch out from their locally assigned roles as cheap labor, easy sex, dispensers of herbal cures, and clairvoyant links with the metaphysical world and become purchasers and consumers of local production. Although many of the goods distributed by the UNHCR represent a poor fit with immediate refugee needs, they are nevertheless excellent trade goods that generate interest among locals with disposable cash and sought-after commodities. With goods in hand, refugees become less reliant on lending themselves out as casual labor and can spend proportionately more time establishing their own villages and securing their claims to cassava fields and garden plots. It is, after all, through such activities that refugees gain the bundle of rights that accelerate and manifest their integration into the local social milieu. Survival strategies involving sex and seances, which generally take place after dark during normally nonproductive hours, can continue unabated. But the amount of casual labor available to the local population declines in proportions to the scale of UNHCR handouts.

Amabwambu are winners regardless of external contingencies. From the out-set refugees learn that making contact with this group rivals in importance the task of seeking that initial audience with senior headmen and the traditional chief of the area. As coordinators of the UNHCR registration exercise, Amabwambu possessed an immense amount of power in the eyes of the refugees. Although, as noted earlier, the qualifications for formal designation were rather straightfor-ward, there would invariably emerge the ambiguous case that called for a judg-ment. What about those individuals born and raised locally, with well-established kinship networks in Mwinilunga, who moved to reside with spouses in Angola only to be forced out by the war? Are they to be considered refugees or merely re-turnees? And what about the Angolans who, as a matter of course, spent extended periods with family in Mwinilunga? Are they to be considered refugees at the point where mounting trepidation constrains their return to Angola?

The real power of Amabwambu, however, resided not in their role as arbiters of ambiguity but in their function as brokers of knowledge. They took the lead in orienting refugees to the nuances of daily life around Lwawu far more so than did any traditional authority figure. The job of completing personal interviews, col-lecting basic demographic data, and developing statistical profiles brought Ama-bwambu into intimate and extended contact with refugees. A comfort level would emerge that would lead the refugees to rely heavily on Amabwambu information, instincts, and interpretation of the local reality. Amabwambu's association with Lwawu mission, with its gleaming white buildings looming on the landscape like Shangri-la, must have solidified in the minds of newly arrived refugees that these were men of substance, worthy of respect, admiration, and even obeisance.

Concomitantly, the nature of Amabwambu's engagement with the refugees generated information of the utmost importance to the local community. In the course of routine investigation Amabwambu would no doubt become aware of the composition of family groupings, the marital status of individuals, the extent of vocational training, and any special talents avail-able for hire. Amabwambu would broker the inter-action between residents and refugees, augmenting their own status as big men in the process. Those seek-ing employment and those seeking to employ would meet at Amabwambu's favorite hangout spot, Ka-toloshi's shop. Even when the shelves were practically bare, the shop was overflowing with useful informa-tion. It was the place to go to hear who was doing what, when, and at what cost. One could, for example, find out who had departed for the bush recently, what they intended to hunt, trap, or gather, when they might

Boxer Jailed for Murder

PATERSON (NEW JERSEY), REUTER

Former world middleweight contender Rubin "Hurricane" Carter was sentenced to two consecutive life jail sentences yesterday for his part in the mur-der of three people during an at-tempted bar hold-up here. (*Times of Zambia*, July 1, 1967, p. 2)

return, and how much the meat, honey, or other forest products might sell for should the individual be successful. Importantly for the refugees, at Katoloshi's shop they could receive advanced notice about the UNHCR goods to be distributed and solicit bids for their transference. In a sense, Amabwambu collectively served as a local commodities brokerage firm, daily quoting prices and projecting availability of goods and services accessible in rural Mwinilunga.

Diversity Pays: Managing the Portfolio of Physical and Financial Investments

Amabwambu lifestyle is dominated by the near feverish pursuit of new economic opportunities, producing frenzied bouts of activity engaging, employing, contacting, and contracting vast numbers of people. Amabwambu thus build up allies and possible supporters for future projects among people for whom even the potential for small sums of money is greatly appreciated, and who reciprocate with loyalty and gifts of affection for those who make such opportunities possible. Beginning in the mid-1980s maize farming became a major thrust. Amabwambu organized themselves into a cooperative, a unit formally constituted and registered in accordance with government policy at that time. As a consequence they became eligible to receive timely access to seeds, fertilizer, and other agricultural inputs, hands-on assistance from agricultural extension officers, as well as price guarantees and marketing facilities from the National Agricultural Marketing Board (NAMBOARD). The production of maize requires the mobilization of resources unavailable to most in Mwinilunga and a level of commitment of time and energy that few can sustain. Unlike cassava, which was planted in mounds dug up with handheld hoes, maize seeds needed to be planted in furrows. Plowing, thus, presented a major hurdle that few locals could clear. The Franciscans, however, generally had two functioning tractors, at least one of which could be made available for hire on any given day. Amabwambu had privileged access as one of their own members, Kapala, was the only African fully trained and trusted to drive mission tractors. Additionally, Amabwambu were among the very few to whom Brother Joe would extend credit for the use of mission equipment. Indeed, it was Brother Joe who had initially gathered the information on cooperatives, secured the application forms during one of his infrequent visits to town, and urged Amabwambu toward maize production with the personal promise of assistance. It should be noted that Brother Joe's interest in maize was given added impetus by his belief that the leftover husks and stalks would make excellent fodder for his burgeoning herd of cattle. Thus even if Amabwambu did not turn a profit and failed to repay the loans altogether, the mission would still benefit from the supply of high-quality feed.

Plowing, however, was not simply a matter of access to machinery and rental fees. Virtually all land in Mwinilunga sufficiently fertile for maize production is covered with trees, large or small, that must be cut down, and the stumps must be dug up so as not to damage the plow blade. Cutting and stumping are jobs for young males, usually those too young to be actively engaged in building up their own farms, too old to be totally dependent on family for support, and yet for whom there may be little alternative use for their time and energy. They tend to be a bit desperate and willing to work cheaply. Most will work for clothing, as they may have reached that age where personal appearance and the impression they make on the opposite sex are all-consuming concerns. Fortunately for Amabwambu, Lwawu Mission receives regular shipments of donated American clothing that, after being distributed by Brother Joe in exchange for his labor needs, may then find its way into Amabwambu hands. In exchange for complete outfits, including shoes, teams of young males negotiate to stump a specific plot, varying in dimensions according to the size and density of trees. They can proceed at their own pace, fast or slow, viewing the promised attire whenever they wish for added incentive, but the garments will not change hands until the entire task is completed.

Midway through the growing season, maize must be thoroughly weeded. This again is a task that need be completed by hand, but one that is appropriate for men, women, and even children. And unlike the task of stumping, which may be spread out over months, weeding needs to be accomplished over the shortest period of time possible. Toward that end, Amabwambu organized weeding parties modeled on *chenda*, traditional work parties. Alcoholic beverages, cooked meats, and sweet treats for the children would be assembled and ostentatiously and delectably displayed the morning of the well-announced weeding party. All willing to participate in the work share in the subsequent feast. Peer pressure, wisecracks, and running commentary on individual performance tend to exert sufficient guidance to bring levels of effort and levels of compensation into acceptable alignment. Amabwambu are uniquely well placed to organize such events. Their knowledge of hunting and brewing activities over a wide area, their disposable income, and their control over credit, commodities, and sought-after services enable them to make the timely transactions necessary for a weeding party to succeed.

Harvest presents yet another set of challenges. The ripe maize ears must be collected as rapidly as possible. Fortunately the harvest period corresponds to the early dry season, a time when competing demands for agricultural labor are relatively low. Workers, male and female alike, are paid per basket load. Yet individuals may be working for different media of exchange. Some seek cash, others might prefer cloth, salt, sugar, cooking oil, or soap. Some may prefer a bundle of commodities. Each harvester is free to shape his or her own best deal. Again, Amabwambu's privileged access to a wide array of goods underpins their capacity to

mobilize sufficient and timely labor where others might find it exceedingly difficult to do so.

Maize fields are under constant assault throughout the growing season from
birds seeking seeds, browsers seeking tender green shoots, and finally rodents
seeking the dried kernels. Brother Joe taught Amabwambu the midwestern American art of scarecrow building, but to no avail. Mwinilunga creatures seem little
fazed by constructions of wood and cloth. Gangs of real live children, however,
running, jumping, laughing, and screaming through the fields were the most
effective deterrent. For the gift of a soccer ball, new shorts, T-shirts, or sandals, or
the promise of sweets, young children not attending school could be easily induced to make the maize fields their regular playground. The number of plants
lost through rough play is quite small in comparison to the many more saved from
the unchecked onslaught of voracious pests.

Over time, it became apparent that maize drained
the soil of its nutrients far more rapidly than any
traditional crop. Yields could decline by as much as
one-third from one year to the next. Amabwambu,
for example, reaped roughly forty 90-kilogram bags
per hectare on freshly planted soil in 1984. Profit is
nearly impossible to estimate quantitatively given the
differing types and rates of remuneration for labor inputs. But qualitatively speaking, Amabwambu (1) paid
all laborers the full contracted amount, (2) bought
their wives two new panels of cloth each, although
tradition specifies only that a man must provide his
wife with one new cloth a year, (3) hosted a commu-
nitywide harvest party providing copious amounts of
alcohol and food to all who attended, (4) bought a
few personal items, (5) stashed a carefully guarded
amount of cash away, and (6) made a significant payment on the debt to Brother
Joe. A few weeks later, however, Amabwambu needed to negotiate another loan in
order to proceed toward next year's maize production. It was anticipated that the
second year would be much more profitable, principally because the tasks of tree
felling and stumping would not be a recurring cost. But in 1985 Amabwambu
barely averaged twenty-eight bags per hectare in their second year on the same
plots. The 1986 results were worse yet.

This experience only increased Amabwambu's belief in the necessity of a di-
versified economic agenda. One simply could not trust that a single economic activity would generate a guaranteed livelihood over the long term. The maize experience may also have tempered Amabwambu's notions about the meaning and

Death of the Dean

SPECIAL CORRESPONDENT

Langston Hughes, often called
dean of Negro American writers,
has died at the age of 65. His
voice is stilled, but the words he
wrote as poet, novelist, play-
wright, biographer, librettist,
journalist, editor and translator
are still in the hearts of countless
people whom he charmed with
his freshness and vitality.

As a chronicler of Negro life
in the United States, he caught
the sadness and wry humour of
his people with delicacy and
compassion.

(*Times of Zambia*, July 4, 1967,
p. 5)

relevance of profit. Maize production gave rise to an interesting set of social activities. Tractor plowing, weeding parties, commissioned child's play, a harvest
frenzy, and a post-harvest fete added a bit of color to the social landscape. Maize
production created rounds of unique interaction saturated with social, political,
and economic possibilities. Even in the absence of any after-expense benefits,
maize farming offered new opportunities for fun and profit and elevated Amabwambu's status even further, making them an even more attractive and interesting group with whom to be associated.

The unpredictability of maize production and the limited local desire for the
crop meant that cassava remained king in Mwinilunga. Amabwambu never overlooked this fact. Although cassava is dug up and processed exclusively by women,
men are expected to plant sufficient quantities for their own subsistence and to
feed the inevitable rounds of guests. Amabwambu estimated that a typical family
of six needed to plant two to three hectares, or roughly four thousand mounds of
cassava per year, for both personal consumption and for feeding visitors. To place
these numbers in context, if two members of a six-member family set about constructing an average of twenty cassava mounds per day, working five days a week,
in a little less than seven months they could plant six thousand mounds, 50 percent more than the amount needed. This estimate leaves a month free to attend
funerals, nurse illnesses, sit in on local palavers, and participate in the ceremonial
life. In short, meeting a family's need for cassava is not a particularly daunting task
given that production can be spread out over the entirety of the eight-month
rainy season. Yet Amabwambu spent no more than a token amount of their own
time in cassava fields, preferring instead to contract out the task. They might, for
example, offer one kilogram of dried meat for each twenty cassava mounds completed. Standard meat consumption is so low in Mwinilunga that a one-kilogram
piece would easily serve the needs of a typical family for a couple of days. At that
rate of exchange Amabwambu would need 200 kilograms of meat to satisfy their
minimum annual need, a figure equal to roughly six or seven large duikers or wild
pigs, or four or five bushbucks.

Amabwambu might secure some of the meat through their own efforts, organizing two- to three-day hunting parties both for the sheer joy and camaraderie of
the experience, as well as to maintain their locally important reputations as *ayibinda*,
hunters. Yet the bulk of the meat would usually come from other hunters, particularly those willing to split their catch fifty-fifty in exchange for the use of Amabwambu's modern rifles and a few bullets. Amabwambu would, no doubt, dispatch a
young relative or trusted client in the company of the hunting party to ensure that all
meat is, in fact, equitably divided and all bullets accounted for. The more successful
hunting groups may subsequently be called upon to secure meat as Amabwambu's
contribution to local cultural events, or simply for sale in Katoloshi's shop.

Securing meat for the household, however, is strictly a male province. Female labor is more easily attracted by the offer of small bags of salt or sugar, cups of cooking oil, or bars of soap. With the exception of Katoloshi's little shop, the store nearest Lwawu is forty miles away in the Boma. Itinerant bicycle traders who ply their wares up and down many rural pathways of Zambia only infrequently appear in Mwinilunga and then almost never during the rainy season. The area, hence, is extremely commodities-poor. Virtually any manufactured item will attract the attention of someone willing to dig a few cassava mounds in order to obtain it. Yet, whether male or female, all hired labor requires some measure of supervision or oversight. In the effort to quickly meet the quantity of mounds contracted, quality may suffer. Thus, again, making the rounds of their segmented holdings is one of the defining features of the Amabwambu lifestyle.

The convoluted nature of Mwinilunga's geology results in distinct bands of red clay, gray sand, and brown loamy soils, with more fertile black alluvial mixtures along rivers and streams. Amabwambu, like others in Mwinilunga, recognize the differential affinity of specific plants for each of these soil types and have thus accordingly gained usufruct rights to plots scattered across the landscape. Each Amabwambu member has a set of carefully tended streamside gardens where tomatoes, onions, cabbages, rape, spinach, and other vegetables are intensively cultivated with bucket irrigation. Gardens are left fallow during the rainy season and are cultivated when cassava planting ceases during the dry season. Annually Amabwambu plant small patches of millet on freshly cleared and burned ground. The resultant harvest is sold to local women who specialize in brewing *kachayi*, millet beer, which is the preferred alcoholic beverage for many ritual occasions. In the second year, sunflowers may be grown on the plots where millet was raised the previous year. The mission has a seed press that enables Amabwambu to produce what is frequently the only cooking oil in the territory. The sandier soils of Mwinilunga are excellent for pineapples, and Amabwambu maintain fields with thousands of the hardy plants. Indeed, for many Zambian urbanites, Mwinilunga is simply known as the pineapple province.

In an area where land is abundant, agriculture is a natural pursuit. Yet Mwinilunga is also well endowed with water resources. It is an environment highly suited for fish farming. As noted earlier, the Franciscans began experimenting with fishponds in the 1960s. By the late 1970s the mission was petitioning international organizations to provide local assistance.[7] During the 1980s the United Nations Development Program (UNDP) in conjunction with the Norwegian Agency for International Development

Beatle Paul Confesses to LSD Dabbling

Beatle Paul McCartney, who found himself the centre of a drugs row after he "confessed" in a magazine he had taken the hallucination drug LSD said recently "I will certainly take it again—if I feel like it."
(*Times of Zambia*, July 8, 1967, p. 5)

(NORAID) and later Africare provided training, tools, fingerlings for stocking, nets, and extension services to young males throughout Mwinilunga interested in pursuing aquaculture. Needless to say, Amabwambu were well represented in the first intake of students sent to the provincial capital to be formally trained in the construction and maintenance of fishponds. Upon completion of the month-long program, each received a grant of 750 *kwacha* to hire laborers. Although worth less than US$200 at the then prevailing exchange rate, within the local economy it was a sum sufficient to pay for nearly 200 man-days of labor. If converted into scarce commodities, however, it could generate twice that amount of labor.

The relationship between Amabwambu and their fishpond laborers was generally far less casual than their engagement with stumpers, weeders, or harvesters. Digging fishponds entailed acquiring new skills, responding to the hydrology of the landscape, paying careful attention to slope and gradient, and becoming acutely aware of soil composition and its water absorption characteristics. Fishpond laborers were selected with long-term potential in mind, including learning capacity, loyalty, and lineage affiliation. Indeed, many were younger kinsmen, consanguineal or affinal, willing to undertake hard and muddy tasks for little pay now in exchange for a share of the eventual product, as well as for the opportunity to acquire knowledge useful for the construction of their own ponds in the future. Within a couple of years some members of Amabwambu would have over a dozen ponds each, cropping several times annually and contributing significantly to local protein needs. Fish production, however, would oscillate over the years as they grappled with the impact of various feeding regimes, cropping schedules, silt and pollution build-up, and outbreaks of clandestine poaching. Yet fish production, no matter how large or small, added one more element to Amabwambu's stock of holdings that could be sold, bartered, exchanged, leveraged, pledged, or simply displayed to social and economic advantage.

Whatever profit Amabwambu managed to generate was neither banked nor hoarded but rapidly recycled into other enterprises. They would buy bolts of cloth for local tailors to sew into children's school uniforms throughout the year, recouping some of their investment at the beginning of each new school year. They would buy and distribute wooden planks to those with carpentry skills, sharing in the profit from subsequent sales of finished furniture. They warehoused thatching grass, bark rope, bamboo poles, adobe bricks, and other construction materials, buying from all comers for later resale during the building boom that accompanied each dry season. They bought up any animal hides that became available for resale to traditional tanners and cobblers making sandals, bags, and jackets. They financed basket and mat weavers, potters, charcoal burners, and trappers. They rented mission power tools by the day for use by others engaged in repairing local bicycles, farming implements, and household furnishings. They provided an outlet for the production of young girl-specific activities, such as fishing with baskets, digging up termites, and collecting caterpillars, mushrooms, wild fruits and vegetables, water, and firewood.

Ultimately the most prestigious investment was in cattle. By the late 1980s individual members of Amabwambu had begun to buy a cow or two annually from Brother Joe, whose herd, at nearly two hundred head, had then reached its desired limit. Brother Joe was now focused on quality, upgrading the herd at every turn. The least desirable stock was quickly disposed of, sold to Amabwambu at reasonable rates. Increasingly the style of each Amabwambu member became to maintain a distant farm to which cows could be dispatched without drawing the attention and envy of friends and neighbors. Each talked of some day cashing in all his investments in one grand moment and retiring forever to that particular farm. Semantically, however, *mafwami* (farm) came to mean something more than a place of agricultural activity. "Farm" came to equal "firm," a collection of economic thrusts and associated personnel. The ultimate desire of Amabwambu was perhaps most candidly expressed by Elias Kangasa one evening when he said, "I want to build a farm so exceptional that the elders must kill me out of sheer jealousy. I will die and leave them guessing how such a young man managed to do it."

In summary, Amabwambu's economic behavior created a multiplier effect that greatly extended the value of the limited amount of currency circulating around Lwawu Mission. In what was supposedly a subsistence economy, Amabwambu's actions sustained a diverse array of specialized production, while inviting others to develop unique skills and pursue nontraditional activities. Amabwambu's actions served as models and beacons of hope to local folks that they too could aspire to overcome and indeed decimate negative images of the Lunda that held current in urban areas. Yet, the boom periods of the 1970s were followed by the economic slowdown of the early 1980s and then the utter economic collapse of the late 1980s. A national period of economic recession and rapidly rising debt load ensued. The World Bank and the International Monetary Fund rode to the rescue, pumping cash into the Zambian economy in exchange for "adjustments" in government expenditures and fiscal policies. Those adjustments would dramatically change economic calculations and conditions nationwide.[8]

The Era of the IMF: The Economy Is SAP(ped)

Zambia's first national development plan, 1964–71, was largely guided by a set of policy recommendations by a panel of international economists: *The Economic Survey Mission on the Economic Development of Zambia: Report of the UN/ECA/FAO Mission* (1964). Locally known as the Seers Report, in reference to the mission's leader, Dudley Seers, it advocated rapid industrialization through targeted programs of import substitution. It urged the newly independent government to concentrate its efforts on successively nurturing the development of industries that could manufacture items locally to replace those currently being imported. The foreign exchange saved could be redirected to further accelerate the pace of industrialization. The report additionally suggested that foreign capital and expertise might be enticed to assist in the process, attracted by Zambia's abundance of cheap labor.

Government coffers were relatively flush throughout the 1960s, a consequence of prevailing high prices for Zambian copper.[9] Yet government prices paid to farmers remained artificially low in a concerted effort to contain forces that might raise the cost of living in Zambia, place upward pressure on wages paid to labor, and correspondingly frighten off foreign investors. In short, farmers' contribution to the development of the nation was expected to be the provision of cheap food for urban wage earners. Concomitantly the Zambian government embarked on campaigns to bring free public education and medical care to all its citizens. A massive building program saw the construction of roads, schools, and clinics across the landscape. But, in truth, almost 82 percent of total investments during the Seers Plan period went to the line of rail, the north-south corridor linking the major Zambian cities.[10] Thus, many rural farmers were not appeased. It seemed clear that government focus was on ameliorating the conditions of the urban citizenry. Rural dwellers by the tens of thousands gave up farming and flocked to the cities in search of jobs, subsidized food, and government housing. The second national development plan, 1972–76, acknowledged the quality-of-life differences between rural and urban areas, promising to make qualitative and quantitative improvements in rural schools and clinics, as well as to establish special development zones where the government would invest heavily in agricultural production.[11] Producer prices, however, were not raised sufficiently to reinvigorate rural life, and ultimately the slide in the world market price for copper would render the promised expansion in social programming meaningless.

Racial Violence near White House

FROM DAVID LAWDAY, WASHINGTON, REUTER

America's summer upsurge of racial violence exploded here early today but was quickly contained. Stoning, window-smashing and arson spread to within a mile of the White House.

(*Times of Zambia*, August 2, 1967, p. 1)

The global oil crisis of the mid-1970s would start Zambia on a downward slide from which it has yet to recover. Dependence on imported oil to fuel its energy-intensive copper industry rendered Zambia unable to effectively adjust and moderate the impact of rising oil prices that accompanied the emergence of a more united and aggressive OPEC. As the costs of producing copper soared above the selling price, foreign exchange reserves evaporated and government debt skyrocketed. President Kenneth Kaunda entered into negotiations with the International Monetary Fund (IMF) for relief in the form of debt restructuring and foreign currency supports. In exchange for aid, however, the IMF demanded that the Zambian government enact a structural adjustment program (SAP): a series of austerity measures that included removing subsidies on staple foods, reducing the size of the federal payroll, curtailing expenditures on social programs, as well as devaluating the *kwacha* against foreign currencies.[12] The IMF believed that the heavy hand of government distorted the operation of market forces, prevented commodities from finding their true value, and discouraged the development of a local entrepreneurial class. Curtailing government involvement in the economy and devaluing the Zambian currency would supposedly open the door to private investment in the production of goods and services, reduce inflationary pressures, and make Zambian products more attractive to foreign markets. Kaunda would vacillate greatly over the next decade or so, accepting foreign aid and the attached austerity agenda one moment, but in the next moment delaying full implementation, realizing the hardships that it would visit upon his most ardent supporters, the urban and rural poor. By the mid-1980s foreign governments and the IMF were taking an increasingly hard line with Zambia, demanding substantive change before the release of any more funds. Kaunda conceded. Yet when the partial removal of subsidies and price controls in 1986 led to strikes and bloody food riots on the Copperbelt, Kaunda reversed positions again, breaking with the IMF altogether. Humanitarian appeals, especially to former colonial ruler Britain, the European Community, and the more liberal Scandinavian nations kept a small measure of fresh funds flowing into Zambia, much of which was applied toward the extensive system of consumer price supports. Zambia's debt, concomitantly, mushroomed from US$623 million in 1970 to $7.2 billion in 1990. As the 1991 presidential election approached, Zambia found itself essentially bankrupt and isolated, unable to secure donor funds from any quarter, having exhausted nearly twenty-five years of global goodwill. In a campaign that garnered much international attention and no doubt attracted much foreign funding as well, Frederick Chiluba defeated Kenneth Kaunda with over 80 percent of the popular vote to become the second president of the Republic of Zambia.[13]

As a union leader, Chiluba had spoken out vehemently against austerity plans. Yet, upon assuming the presidency, Chiluba acceded to all IMF demands immediately. Government price supports were removed from food, health care, and transportation. The cost of education at all levels rose in proportion. Many government enterprises, including mines, mills, marketing boards, utilities, railroads, and the national airlines, were privatized by being sold to the highest bidder, often at a loss. Over a hundred thousand jobs were eliminated during Chiluba's first four years in office, a figure that represented one-quarter of all jobs in Zambia's formal employment sector.[14] Such massive unemployment in a time of rampant inflation reduced many formerly middle-class families to hand-to-mouth existence in the informal sector of petty trade, and many formerly poor turned to outright criminality to survive.

But what of Mwinilunga? What was the quotidian impact of the IMF's structural adjustment program on the world of Amabwambu? One of the first visible signs of the change in government policy was the closing of the NAMBOARD collection depot at Lwawu Mission. The provision of agricultural inputs, as well as the collection and marketing of crops nationwide, was declared "privatized." Any individual, private agency, or business syndicate wishing to speculate in these areas was now free to do so. The unfettered, invisible hand of the marketplace would determine the outcome. In truth, however, those farmers in the least accessible regions of the nation, those located the greatest distance from population centers, and those producing in relatively small quantities would suffer. The following harvest season was an unmitigated national disaster. Small farmers across the nation who had been lured into cash-cropping by NAMBOARD guarantees found themselves saddled with crops that no one showed up to purchase. Unprotected grain rotted in the fields, was attacked by rodents, or was otherwise rendered useless when soaked by the returning rains. Unable to sell their crops, many farmers were correspondingly unable to service their debts. Thus Zambia experienced not only a grain shortfall measured in millions of kilograms but also experienced urban migration on a scale previously unimaginable. The few private dealers who stepped into the NAMBOARD void were often merciless in their exploitation of prevailing conditions, purchasing crops from cash-starved farmers for pennies a pound and hoarding supplies in urban areas to drive up prices.

By contrast, Amabwambu fared relatively well. Brother Joe reclaimed the former NAMBOARD depot building, bought up produce sacks by the thousands on the spot market, and hired a couple of laborers to assist local farmers in storing their annual harvest safely at the mission. He cranked up the milling operation of both maize and sunflower seeds, satisfying the local need for mealie meal and cooking oil, and periodically sent a truck to town to sell any surplus, returning with seeds and fertilizers for the next year's effort. With the end of government subsidies and the precipitous decline in agricultural production, the price of food in urban areas rose abruptly. Ample profits could be made by those able to reach urban markets in a timely fashion. Brother Joe, to a large degree, was able to effectively replace NAMBOARD, shielding Amabwambu from the vicissitudes of open market forces. Yet on the other hand, the Franciscans had a network of major mission stations scattered throughout Zambia linked by ham radios that permitted daily communications. This, in essence, rendered the mission well equipped to play the new national game of buy low, sell high. Brother Joe could regularly confer with his colleagues elsewhere about the price and presence of agricultural inputs and current market conditions in order to accentuate the timeliness of his transactions. Brother Joe had few reservations about using this network for the benefit of Amabwambu. Yet he was largely unwilling to assume the level of risk that would come with substantially expanding assistance beyond that group. And the IMF-mandated end-to-government agricultural loan programs meant that few locally could garner the wherewithal to join this select group.

The national impact of the IMF-mandated structural adjustment program in the domains of wholesale and retail marketing, education, healthcare, veterinary medicine, energy, telecommunications, and transportation reverberated in ways that paralleled the experience in agriculture. Long-provided services disappeared virtually overnight. Those that remained were suddenly expensive beyond the reach of the average citizen. Yet, as one of the more neglected regions of Zambia, Mwinilunga perhaps experienced relatively less shock than those areas where government services had generally been more accessible in the pre-SAP era. Additionally, as in the case of agriculture, the mission was able to moderate some of the overall local impact. For example, while government clinics were closing in many rural areas, and even urban teaching hospitals were increasingly plagued with staff and drug shortages, Lwawu Clinic remained unaffected for the most part. Medicines continued to flow through the pipeline from overseas supporters. The nuns of the Baptistine Order continued to provide high-quality care, shielded by their semi-cloistered convent lifestyle from concerns about consumer prices, wage rates, and inflationary spirals. The mission assisted nearly neglected government functionaries—such as school teachers and veterinary, agricultural, and public health extension officers—to keep up their rounds of duties by providing them with cheap housing, food, transportation, and communication services. And Lwawu vehicles regularly plying the routes between Catholic mission stations, the Boma, and town continued unabated as the major arm of local transportation for people and produce.

As the physical body of government contracted ever smaller and its face receded ever farther away from local view, the power and impact of Lwawu Mission's social and economic development initiatives rose proportionately. But beginning slowly in the 1980s and accelerating in the 1990s, the mission was joined by an expanding array of nongovernmental organizations (NGOs):

Masai (and Mini Skirts) Get a Dressing Down

ARUSHA (TANZANIA), REUTER

The traditional dress of the Masai tribe—a skimpy bit of skin and some ochre paint—has vanished from this city in the past fortnight and been replaced by shirts and trousers or skirts.

After campaigning for months to persuade the nomadic, cattle-raising Masai to dress like other people, Regional Commissioner Aaron Weston Mwakang'ata issued an ultimatum last month. He announced that after New Year's Day anyone found in the streets inadequately clad would be locked up until relatives brought him trousers.
(*Times of Zambia*, January 13, 1968, p. 2)

the Swedish International Development Agency (SIDA), the Norwegian Agency for International Development (NORAID), German Technical Assistance International (GTZ), the British Volunteer Service Organization (VSO), the Belgian and French group Medecins Sans Frontieres (MSF), the United Nations Development Program (UNDP), the World Health Organization (WHO), Oxfam, Cultural Survival Inc., Africare, and international Catholic and Protestant relief agencies. Several organizations, as noted earlier, had been specifically invited by the mission, whereas others chose the area because the peripheral services that Lwawu Mission could provide accentuated the possibilities of success. Again, in the logic of the model project approach, Lwawu stood out as a uniquely attractive locale for experimentation with all manner of novel social and economic activity. Projects as diverse as beekeeping, furniture building, public health, and community-based resource management initiatives joined commercial maize and fish farming as local enterprises underwritten by overseas donors.

The emergence of the international NGO sector as a major provider of social and economic assistance in Africa during the 1980s and 1990s corresponded to the declining confidence of Western governments in the fiscal management skills of African governments. African leaders, falsely or not, were labeled as part of the problem, best circumvented by channeling foreign assistance directly to the most needy through the grass-roots thrust of NGOs. As noted earlier, however, assistance rarely goes to the most needy. Rather, it is those such as Amabwambu who are fluent in the language of foreigners, conversant with prevailing paradigms of development, and familiar with expected norms of keeping records and filing reports that actually attract the attention, the confidence, and the cash of aid organizations. I have written extensively elsewhere about local social networks constructed for the purpose of engaging NGO-funded projects, assessing the qualitative and quantitative dimensions of their resource endowment, and directing as much of that endowment as possible toward local social and economic ends.[15] Amabwambu members carefully cultivate relationships with NGO personnel, strategically position family or followers on the NGO payroll or within its client base, and otherwise gain as much control over the distribution of NGO benefits as possible. In the local contexts, benefits extend far beyond the stated objectives of development projects. The presence of NGOs in Mwinilunga, busily pursuing their own aims, expands the number of transportation options available to others, as well as the amount of cash potentially circulating around the landscape. NGOs can be utilized as avenues of communications, providers of technical advice, distributors of scarce commodities, consumers of local goods and services, sources of entertainment to moderate the monotony of daily life, and unwitting allies in a host of local ventures. Project equipment and cash not infrequently find their way into Amabwambu's personal portfolios of entrepreneurial activities.

Indeed, formal NGO aims may be of little local interest. Yet, projects may receive sufficiently high levels of support to achieve some measure of success for as long as the project also undergirds local initiatives.

Amabwambu stand out for their smooth and easy rapport with aid workers new to the contingencies of life in Mwinilunga. Their years of dealing with successive waves of expatriate Franciscan Friars from diverse social backgrounds, with varying temperaments and idiosyncratic work habits, has cultivated a comfortable curiosity about foreigners. Rather than the disconcerting and off-putting stares that tend to characterize most Lunda individuals' response to new and unusual people, Amabwambu emerge from the crowd offering orientation and hospitality to newcomers with a grace and confidence that marks them as the natural leaders of the area. They have elevated to a fine art the skill of quickly establishing conjunctures of interest with previously unknown individuals. Most useful, however, is Amabwambu's ingenuity at identifying the points of overlap between their own agenda and those of others; where labor invested in externally sponsored projects also contributes to strengthening personal projects. That is to say, Amabwambu's association with or participation in NGO schemes has not redirected energies away from prior economic activities. Rather, Amabwambu used their privileged access to NGO resources, just as they had used their privileged access to mission resources, to further expand their own list of economic activity and their own base of grateful clients.

IMF policy, in effect, eviscerated the Zambian government. Much of its duty in the areas of education, healthcare, agriculture, and community development has been parceled out among a mélange of international agencies. Yet whereas a government draws its mandate from and is accountable to the totality of its citizens, NGOs are allowed to pick and choose their subjects. Notions of efficacy tend to supercede those of equity. In Mwinilunga, Amabwambu were the big winners. The hopes and dreams of the younger generation were perhaps the biggest victims of Zambia's changing economic fortune. Education and the expanding welfare state no longer offer much promise of a better tomorrow. Government, the great equalizer, has virtually disappeared from the scene. The crumbling state infrastructure of roads, railways, and bridges has rendered Mwinilunga a territory increasingly isolated from the rest of the country. The way forward for many of today's youth is backward, back to the time when life was centered on the search for *mukwakwashi* (patron or big man). Amabwambu enterprises require an almost inexhaustible supply of youthful labor. As they move into their fifties, digging ponds, stumping fields, hauling 90-kilogram bags of maize around, and chasing down game in the forest become increasingly onerous tasks. Yet, not all youth are content to fight with one another for Amabwambu's favor and patronage. Pathways to fame and fortune via education and agriculture may have been closed by government acquiescence to IMF policies, but the age-old Lunda entrepreneurial spirit exerts itself in other arenas.

In the late 1980s, young Waylesi was doing what few others his age dared do. He regularly crossed the border and went hunting in Angola, alone. On one fateful occasion he was intercepted by a reconnaissance party of UNITA rebels curious about his condition and intention. Waylesi, seemingly unperturbed by the encounter, opened a bottle of *lituku*, a high-proof distilled liquor made from cassava, and offered to share it around while he and the soldiers talked. Impressed by the young man and his gift, the soldiers made an offer. If Waylesi would return to the same spot the following week with more liquor, they would reciprocate with bundles of fresh and dried game meat. The identity of those soldiers was never entirely clear. Nor was it known if those further up the UNITA chain of command were aware of the deal. But in short time Waylesi's little enterprise expanded beyond the provision of alcohol to include bags of cassava flour, radios, batteries, boots, clothing, and a range of manufactured goods available in Zambia, but not so in rural Angola. Concomitantly, Waylesi quickly became the biggest purveyor of game meat in Central Mwinilunga, turning his village into a bustling meat market attracting customers from across the plateau, day and night. Other young men would attempt to emulate Waylesi's enterprise, entering Angola seeking out soldiers with whom to do business. Some achieved a modicum of success. Some were captured and put to work building camp houses and clearing fields for the rebels. Others were forcibly inducted into the rebel army. And still others simply disappeared, leaving behind little evidence of their eventual fate.

The lucrative potential of cross-border trade with UNITA was not lost on Amabwambu. Nor were the dangers. Yet, as was the case in most other areas of economic life, Amabwambu had assets that few local youth could match. First and foremost, Amabwambu's special relationship with the refugee community allowed them to assemble a more detailed picture of people, places, and political relations on the Angolan side of the border. Second, Amabwambu were better placed to actually recruit recently arrived refugees to guide and oversee commercial convoys heading back into Angola. Third, Amabwambu were able to markedly increase the scale of cross-border trade. Rather than the lone individual lugging a sack of flour and a few bottles of liquor, Amabwambu organized actual caravans with a dozen or more porters

Riots Can Be Avoided This Year: Brooke

Senator Edward Brooke of Massachusetts said in Lusaka at the weekend he was optimistic the United States could avoid a long hot summer of race riots this year.

Mr. Brooke, the lone Negro in the Senate and a member of President Johnson's advisory commission on civil disorders, told a Press conference: "I am optimistic. I think that even though we have been plagued with these riots some of the conditions that caused them will be given priority so that we can prevent them in 1968."

(*Times of Zambia*, January 29, 1968, p. 7)

laden with a dazzling array of commodities. They were also willing to accept a broader range of items in exchange for their goods, including ivory, animal hides, and gems. The scope of their operation quickly attracted the attention of UNITA's regional leadership, who intervened to ensure that commodities flowed directly to their encampment without interference from lower-ranking troops. Soon, Amabwambu caravans were pushing sixty miles into Angola, visiting rebel head-quarters on an almost weekly basis. Such regular contact allowed Amabwambu to more precisely tailor the flow of goods to match evolving needs in Angola. It also facilitated the development of well-defined terms of trade and trust necessary to routinize relations of economic exchange. Brave young men continued to explore clandestine trade opportunities with semi-autonomous collections of soldiers nearest the border. But Amabwambu monopolized the more profitable portions of the trade with Angola.

The upturn in Mwinilunga cross-border trade corresponded to the period when UNITA and the Angolan government seemed on the threshold of imple-menting an agreement that would end the decades-old civil war. While guerrilla leaders and government officials met under lavish conditions in foreign capitals, rebel soldiers in the field were increasingly neglected and left to fend for them-selves as their supply networks withered. With a cease-fire in effect and few actual military operations to occupy their time, UNITA soldiers could pursue more profitable ends. Whatever their intellectual or economic shortcomings, they were without question the most well-armed individuals in an area of abundant natu-ral resources. Varying collections of troops and commanders arrived at differing conclusions about the best use of time and armaments. Some were content to hunt, dry, and smoke game meat in exchange for manufactured goods. Others specialized in the acquisition of and trade in ivory. Some pursued more complex extractive enterprises in timber, minerals, and gemstones. Thus, an army that in the 1970s and 1980s appeared unified in its effort to overthrow the so-called Com-munist government of Angola increasingly in the 1990s appeared to disintegrate into so many local warlords seeking their own best economic dispensation.

Diamond production would ultimately emerge as a particularly profitable sphere of operations. Initially extracted in northeastern Angola by soldiers or con-scripted village labor, diamonds flowed north, merging with the Congo stream of gems, controlled by Mobutu Sese Seko and marketed internationally by De Beers. Subsequently, however, pressure would mount on the global diamond industry, condemning its role in sustaining local wars, undermining human rights, and fostering the recruitment of child soldiers in Africa.[16] As Congo diamonds came under greater scrutiny, UNITA leaders sought out alternative marketing arrange-ments. Some looked east to Zambia. A shadowy network of South African expa-triates was hovering near the Zambian-Angolan border, talking of establishing farms and retail shops in the region but locally believed to be sneaking across the border to negotiate diamond deals at night. Amabwambu were also talking of diamond dealing as well but clearly recognized the dangers of talking too loudly. As the Zambian government contracted due to IMF-induced policies, the territorial integrity of the nation was brought into question. Fewer and fewer soldiers were available to patrol the border region, making it all the easier for well-armed or ruthlessly ambitious individuals to carve out commercial enterprises that thrived by mediating the differential mineral, manufacturing, and marketing capacities that intersected in Mwinilunga.

Living a Life (Making Living Meaningful)

The information above could lead one to envision the life of Amabwambu as the wearisome struggle to maintain status as a mission elite, frantically holding together a patchwork of productive enterprises, fending off the daily onslaught of requests from the desperately needy, ever engaged in recruiting useful clients, scheming to avoid the deleterious effects of IMF policies, and working day and night to stay one step ahead of a hard-pressing younger generation. Yet nothing could be further from the truth. Amabwambu's daily round of activities provide much in the way of amusement, gaiety, laughter, companionship, surprise, comfort, intrigue, and fulfillment.

The typical Lunda workday extends from 6 AM to 2 PM. The most arduous tasks are performed in the cool morning air; lighter tasks are done in the early afternoon. The hours after 2 PM are reserved for duties around the village or for socializing. Until the imposition of colonialism and European forms of time reckoning, the Lunda had a five-day week (*mulungu*), with the days simply designated as *lelu, haloshi, ifuku dina, kumadiki, ifuku dikwawu* (literally: today, yesterday, the day before yesterday, tomorrow, the day after tomorrow). Longer periods were expressed by modifying days with a number of weeks, for example *ha nyilungu yisatu haloshi* (on three weeks from yesterday). No one particular day was set aside for general rest or ritual. Individuals or villages worked and relaxed in accordance with their own productive schedule. Marketing was sporadic and decentralized, precluding the need for a designated market day. The time of day was indicated by pointing to a particular angle of the sun in the sky. Today, even middle-aged and elderly Lunda with watches still nevertheless confirm the time of planned meetings or events by extending an arm skyward in reference to the position the sun will occupy at the agreed upon time. Months denoted lunar cycles, with a period called *nkumbu* inserted to account for the extra days at the end of the year. The solar cycle was divided into three distinct periods: *nvula* (rainy season), *chishika* (cold dry season), and *non'a* (hot dry season). The intersection of lunar and solar cycles produced vastly different arrangements of activities throughout the year, giving each period its distinctive tone and tenor.

As noted earlier, the physical center of Amabwambu's social world is Katoloshi's little shop near Lwawu Mission. It is geographically situated at the juncture of the most heavily used pathways in the area and virtually equidistant from Senior Chief Kanongesha's capital village, Senior Headman Chifunga's village cluster on Matonchi Plateau, and the prime Lunda hunting and fishing grounds, the plains along the Luisaba River. As Amabwambu members make their individual daily rounds, checking on gardens, fishponds, the condition of livestock, the progress of sponsored craftsmen, the whereabouts of refugee allies, the status of fish and game traps, and the availability of desired goods, they invariably meet at Katoloshi's shop. Indeed, in the process of coming and going they commonly pass by Katoloshi's shop several times a day. There they discuss recent developments and future plans, talk about newly gained insights, and, of course, share a few cups of home brew and a joke or two.

Sharing alcoholic beverages is at the heart of most Amabwambu encounters. *Kasolu* (honey beer), *kachayi* (millet beer), and *lituku* (distilled cassava spirits) are the three principal types of beverages. Although there is much overlap in their periods of availability, each type dominates a particular portion of the year, adding its own literal and figurative flavor to the season. *Kasolu* is most abundant during the early rainy season, November to March, when local bees are their most productive. The sweet smell of fermenting honey wafting across a nearly iridescent green landscape is the most ubiquitous and sensuous indicator of that time of year. The rainy season is a time for planting the cassava that will not be ripe for 18 months. But the rains provide more immediate rewards as well—an explosion of succulent vegetables, wild fruits, berries, and mushroom. Fresh air, exercise, and a wholesome diet make the early rainy season a uniquely salutary period. People, plants, and animals all take on a healthy glow. It is a "sweet" time. *Kasolu* is the champagne of Lunda beverages, a celebratory libation meant to be shared with all. And because it is generally superabundant and cheap, men of Amabwambu's status have little reservation about offering a cup or two to any passing man, woman, or child who desires it. *Kasolu*, the mild golden nectar, is the perfect reward for a day of hard labor, an ideal representation of well-deserved leisure, a saturated symbol of nature's benevolence and the benefits of orderly human production.

Sophia Is Acquitted of Bigamy—At Last

ROME

A penal court today acquitted Italian film star Sophia Loren and her producer husband Carlo Ponti of bigamy after a complex five-year trial. A civil court ruling last year annulling their proxy marriage in Mexico in 1957 paved the way for their acquittal.

The voluptuous 33-year old actress and Signor Ponti—whose romance has been one of the most enduring features of the Italian film world—were not present in court.
(*Times of Zambia*, July 25, 1968, p. 1)

The conversations that accompany *kasolu* tend to be as mild and sweet as the drink itself. The early rains are a happy and optimistic time. There is little to bicker about. Flowing water and wine reawaken the fertility of the soil and rejuvenate the spirit of people respectively, bathing all of Lundaland in a powerful aura of amity. Few formal ritual gatherings are scheduled during the rainy season. Sharing bottles of *kasolu*, thus, represents the height of sociability.

Kachayi (millet beer) makes its presence felt from March through June, the end of the rainy season and the early dry season. This is often a troublesome period. The long months of toiling in the cassava fields in an atmosphere increasingly dense with malaria-carrying mosquitoes will have produced a sharp upturn in the number of debilitated individuals. This is also the time of *dikwilu* (meat hunger, craving for meat). As the rainy season progresses, animals disperse more widely across the landscape in accordance with the greater availability of food and water. They are also more difficult to spot in the dense vegetation. The return on energy devoted to hunting is so poor that even the best hunters refrain from the activity this time of year. Beans and groundnuts that could serve as alternative sources of protein tend to be slow growing and have, thus, yet to ripen. Hard work, dietary deficiencies, and malaria combine to hobble much of the population. Even those not actually bedridden may nevertheless find themselves weak, achy, and irritable. A general grumpiness settles on the territory. Arguments flare up frequently over matters that would be of little importance during other periods of the year. Seemingly minor affronts can lead to conspiratorial conclaves that threaten to reconfigure power relations and village unity. Social fragmentation is the order of the day.

Kachayi, correspondingly, is a drink that accentuates social fragmentation. Unlike *kasolu*, *kachayi* is always in short supply. Although millet was the Lunda staple crop several centuries ago, today it is grown only in small quantities and only for the purpose of making beer. Whereas *kasolu* is produced by both men and women, *kachayi* is brewed only by women. Making *kachayi* is also a more complicated and laborious process. Millet has to be sun-dried immediately after it is ripe, stone ground by hand to a precise consistency, mixed in the right proportions with a locally grown plant containing yeast-like qualities, and allowed to ferment in large carefully prepared calabashes under controlled temperature for nearly a week. The period of production corresponds to a time when women are indeed quite busy with other tasks and brewing thus represents a significant sacrifice of their time and energy. A calabash of *kachayi*, therefore, is a precious thing: rare, costly, and exceedingly delicate. The Lunda have no way of stabilizing the fermentation process of *kachayi*. A batch that is perfect one day will be vinegar-like and utterly undrinkable the next. Hence to acquire *kachayi* men must enter into a formal contract with a brewer by paying her the full amount in cash in advance and must be ready to receive the calabash on the day its content peaks.

"Organizing a calabash" of *kachayi* is a painstakingly tedious matter for men, saturated with social implications. Men need to first enter into extended discussions about the quality of past production by particular brewing women before formalizing an agreement with one. They need to inspect the various size calabashes available and settle on an acceptable price. They need to arrive at a fixed number of participants. More would lower the cost. But too many participants can reduce the per capita consumption below the level needed for the desired buzz. The alcohol content of *Kachayi* is rather low. The average man must drink a couple of liters or more before feeling any effect. Finally, men need to identify the time and location where the carefully defined group can secretly drink the calabash without being discovered by those who would surely crash the party if they knew its location. Often elaborate tales must be hatched to camouflage the group's whereabouts at the appointed time.

Amabwambu are well known for their capacity to have overlapping contracts with brewers in effect at one time, enabling them to have *kachayi* drinks among themselves two or three times per week. These events, with all their complex machinations and surreptitious ploys, reinforce the sanctity of the clique in opposition to lineal and affinal ties. The tone of conversation is less the frivolous gaiety that usually accompanies *kasolu* and more one of deep understanding, empathy, and commiseration. Outsiders may see Amabwambu as a group without problems, as individuals far more powerful than their years should permit. Only Amabwambu themselves are aware of the stresses and strains that each endures holding his fragile economic empire together, the pressures that come with sustaining so many clients, and the anxieties that accompany each new challenge. *Kachayi* drinks are group therapy, a time and a place where Amabwambu can relax, be comforted, and be consoled by understanding cohorts. A *kachayi* drink creates a space where Amabwambu can share deep concerns and apprehensions without appearing weak, revel in their accomplishments without appearing boastful, and proclaim future desires without appearing avaricious.

Kachayi is also the most spiritual of alcoholic beverages, supposedly the most ancient, and said to be the favorite of the ancestors. Wherever *kachayi* flows, the ancestral spirits gather. This evocative quality makes the presence of *kachayi* mandatory on all ritual occasions, even if only in token amounts. Correspondingly, the presence of *kachayi* elevates any occasion beyond the ordinary, making it a quasi-mystical affair. As such, one should refrain from talk of trivial matters, in favor of more weighty issues. While drinking *kachayi* Amabwambu tend to litter their speech with deep Lunda maxims, proverbs and witticisms. They juxtapose their conditions and accomplishments to those of their forebears. They sacralize their own suffering and exalt their responsibilities as divine obligations. They come away from this communion with the ancestors spiritually refreshed, more powerfully connected to one another and solidly affirmed in their sense of existential purpose.

Lituku (distilled cassava spirits) by contrast is nearly devoid of deep cultural symbolism. In fact, *lituku* is readily acknowledged as being non-Lunda in origin. Supposedly an Mbunda migrant from the west in the early 1900s introduced the current technique utilized for distilling high-proof alcohol. The raw material, cassava scraps, is, of course, abundant year round. Sufficient firewood to keep a distillery vessel boiling all day is the limiting factor. Hence, it is toward the end of the dry season that *lituku* takes its turn as the dominant drink. After several months of exceedingly arid weather, forest floors tend to be blanketed with dried fallen branches; no heavy chopping is necessary. Distillers, invariably mature women, rely on convoys of children carrying bundles of branches to fuel their enterprise.

Toward the end of the dry season wildfires burn off much of the local shrubbery and tall grass, leaving the plateau open and exposed and animals with few places to hide. As the animals congregate around the few permanent rivers, they become easy targets for hunters. Likewise, with falling water levels, fish are more easily trapped in the remaining pools. Thus while the late dry season is characterized by the increasing absence of fresh green vegetables, it is a time noted for the heavy consumption of meat, fish, and hard liquor. Additionally, because agricultural duties are generally at a minimum, weddings, boys' initiation rites, and other ceremonies are often scheduled for this period.

Lituku drinking provides neither light merriment nor spiritual communion with the ancestors. It is heavy stuff that loosens the tongue, clouds the senses, and numbs the brain from the very first sip. Its appearance unleashes an extended bacchanalian bash in the villages, a spree of hedonistic pleasure to pass the time until the appearance of rain signals the return to daily rounds of hard labor. *Lituku* is dangerous stuff. Obsessive amounts of drinking, often on borrowed money, invariably lead to fights over faded memories of who said and did what, to whom, when, and why. Cases of adultery skyrocket, the terms of their settlement as fuzzy as the consciousness that led to the act in the first place. *Lituku* releases the dark side of the persona, revealing dimensions of friends and foes never glimpsed on other occasions. For some, perhaps, drinking *lituku* provides a context

Coffin Ejected from Grave

SUVA (FIJI)

Mourners at a cemetery screamed in terror when a grave disgorged a coffin containing the body of a man they had just buried. Shortly after the burial of 45-year-old farmer Alo Mahoment at the cemetery of Fimi Island, the soil around the grave erupted and the coffin came to the surface.
(*Times of Zambia*, August 27, 1969, p. 2)

to shout out true feelings, to voice profound discontent, anger, or personal frustration. Then, if necessary later, one can take refuge behind the clouds of inebriation. Fortunately, Lunda tend to be exceptionally forgiving of words and deeds that flow from the influence of *lituku*.

Alcohol may help set the stage for the daily Lunda drama, but it is not the main act. Amabwambu, in particular, have a rich array of interactions, some centered as much on food as on drink. Sharing dinners, for example, is a routine affair, occurring several times weekly. Although cooking is exclusively a female task, husbands and wives rarely share meals together. Instead, a wife, in accordance with her own schedule of activities, prepares one large meal daily for her husband and places it in a designated spot. Typically it consists of *nshima*, a large mound of boiled cassava flour and two side dishes, generally one vegetable and one protein. The meal is stored in tightly covered dishes and is wrapped in towels to keep it warm and safe from pests. Husbands return to the village and eat their meal at their convenience, generally alone in their hut. For the sole purpose of adding a bit of variety to life, Amabwambu frequently assemble at Katoloshi's place at the end of their workday and collectively share the meal prepared by each man's wife. They walk en masse to the village of each man in turn, jointly sharing the meal prepared by each wife. It is the Lunda equivalent of a seven-course meal, with each course separated by perhaps a half-mile walk.

Music accompanies most Amabwambu activities. Some members, such as Mafulo, are particularly polished entertainers, capable of playing a wide range of string and percussion instruments and composing original songs. Others may be less talented individually but contribute nevertheless to the collective rhythmic output. There is, in fact, a popular repertoire of songs that all Amabwambu love to sing with great gusto, particularly after a few drinks. Additionally, nearly all Amabwambu maintain functioning shortwave radios, and most possess tape players of varying quality. Batteries, however, are a constant concern. They are frequently unavailable and are quite expensive when they are available. Thus as Amabwambu move about between villages, each member may carry a few batteries in his pocket, hoping to assemble sufficient energy to power the music machine at hand. Radio Zambia broadcasts quite a few hours of music each day. Radio South Africa has a powerful signal that fills in the gaps. Over the years Amabwambu have also managed to accumulate an impressive number of cassette tapes. Regional musical genres from throughout Central and Southern Africa can be heard nightly blasting from Amabwambu villages. Young folks and children will invariably gather within earshot to dance, jump around, and sing along. Congolese forms, such as rumba and soukous, appear to be the favorite African styles of music, especially by artists such as Franco and l'Orchestre O.K. Jazz, Tabu Ley Rochereau, Mbilia Bel, Papa Wemba, and Loketo. American country-and-western performers and Jamaican reggae musicians, particularly Dolly Parton and Bob Marley, stand out as international favorites.

Radios are also prized for their ability to bring daily news of the outside world. Amabwambu are fond of tuning into the global English service of the British Broadcasting Corporation (BBC) and the Voice of America (VOA). These programs spark loud debates among Amabwambu, in English, about the wider significance and potential local impact of faraway events. Although such behavior may contribute to Amabwambu's local aura of worldliness, many who are less fluent in English find it rude, impolite, and highly irritating. To speak a language that those present cannot fully understand is to provoke suspicion that one is speaking ill of those individuals. Indeed, Amabwambu sometimes boldly and deliberately use outbursts of English to drive away outsiders so as to enjoy a meal and perhaps some bottles of brew in peace.

Games are an often-utilized diversion. A widespread favorite is *kendu,* the marble game known elsewhere in Africa as *mancala, kpouebo,* or *nsolo.* The speed at which the game is played and the ease with which marbles can be hidden in the palms of the hand lead to endless but good-natured accusations of cheating. When the game switches to cards, however, accusations of cheating take on a more ominous tone. High-stakes gambling is common, with pots that can reach sums equal to several weeks' pay at standard mission wages. Yet usually Amabwambu gamble only among themselves, generously issuing credit as needed, holding one another's IOUs for extended periods, and probably coming pretty close to breaking even in the long run. The outcome of cards thus rarely places anyone's economic survival in jeopardy. It merely provides someone with the momentary thrill of victory.

Riddles and word games are perennial favorites. The latter most often consist of tongue-twister phrases that, when rapidly repeated over and over, result in a blending of words that tricks the speaker into saying something utterly vulgar. Such games are obviously more fun after a few bottles of *kasolu.* Additionally, literacy in two languages has done little to dampened Amabwambu's mastery of the oral arts. To a person they are eloquent and mesmerizing storytellers. The favorite topics are tales of metaphysical beings and supernatural happenings. Such stories are most effectively told late at night with the moon as the unwitting partner. The full moon casts eerie shadows upon the landscape, adding its own touch of the macabre to already terrifying tales. The new moon leaves the unelectrified countryside so dark that only the bravest dare venture away from the flickering embers of the village fireside.

The most luscious bit of intrigue, however, just as everywhere else in the world, perhaps, is illicit sex. On the one hand, Amabwambu can hardly be described as being any more lusty than the average Lunda male. Indeed, in many respects they are a remarkably restrained and conservative group, generally involved in stable long-term marriages, rarely participating in outside dalliances. Yet, because of their social and economic status, they are clearly better positioned to attract willing partners and, because of their constant movement, better positioned to act on impulses. Hence the occasional accusation of adultery does arise. A case is brought to public attention when an aggrieved husband goes to Senior Chief Kanongesha's capital village and "purchases" a summon for the nominal fee of 20 *ngwee* (cents). With this act the chief instructs one of his *kapasu* (messengers) to formally notify the accused that he has been duly charged and must therefore appear before the chief's court on a specified date. Husbands have been known to demand as much as 1,000 *kwacha* compensation from the opposing male in cases of adultery. The last Kanongesha, however, rarely awarded more then 200 *kwacha*. If the woman involved had been neglected by her husband, the fine might have been further reduced. Adultery, while rarely leading to outright violence, exposes one to the risk of profound humiliation by having one's private affairs publicly dissected in a well-attended forum, and by having to part with a significant amount of cash in the process. As noted earlier, women engaging in prostitution are prevalent throughout Mwinilunga. The price varies from 5 to 20 *kwacha*. Thus, risking a potential fine of 200 *kwacha* for one clandestine sexual encounter is a bold and foolhardy act, even for men of *Amabwambu's* means. Yet for some, more so than others, it is one of life's most irresistible challenges.

The Domestic Sphere as Arena of Articulating Tradition and Modernity

As explored in greater detail elsewhere, public interaction between married Lunda couples is quite minimal by Western standards. The strictly gendered division of labor sends each sex off in separate directions for most of the day. Even upon return to the village, men and women tend to assemble in separate circles, discuss distinctly different topics, and amuse themselves with contrasting modes of diversion. At first glance Amabwambu's relations with their wives might seem to fit a simple dyadic schema of male/modernity versus female/traditionalism. Amabwambu's immersion in a world of cash cropping, foreign NGOs, global politics, and international music contrasts mightily with their wives' entrapment in endless cycles of water and wood portage, ceaseless rounds of planting, pounding and preparing cassava, all accomplished with the ubiquitous baby strapped on the back. In truth, neither

James Brown Prices Upset Fans

BY TIMES REPORTER

Soul fans in Zambia welcome James Brown's arrival on December 10—but they're not so happy about the prices being charged to see him in action. Top prices at the Mulungushi show will be K10.

(*Times of Zambia*, November 18, 1970, p. 1)

ancient tradition nor contemporary government policies nor the current thrust of international aid agencies provide women with many opportunities for generating cash. Selling surplus food and alcohol and a modicum of craft production are the limited options. Yet, women are well aware of the value that their services contribute to their husbands' experiments with modern enterprises. And women's tastes for the rewards of modernity have developed and sharpened in tandem with those of their husbands. Amabwambu wives have come to expect store-bought dresses, imported jewelry, enameled dishes, and well-built furniture. They expect to appear in public with well-dressed babies in pastel sleepers with matching bonnets and booties. Tradition still dictates that each man buy his wife one new *chitengi* (colorful wrap cloth) each year, more if he is caught in some indiscretion. Amabwambu wives are content with nothing less than the highest-quality cloth imported from Congo factories. For them it is an embarrassment to be draped in inferior Zambian-made cloth.

Viewed from a more intimate perspective, during quiet moments away from the crowd, it becomes clear that the relationship between Amabwambu and their wives is no mere quid pro quo maneuvering for a fair share of the community estate. There appears to be a good deal more tenderness, more playfulness, and overall social equality in Amabwambu relationships than among the population in general. Away from prying eyes they do occasionally share a meal and confide in one another their hopes for the children's future. They might even do something their parents would never have considered: discuss future economic plans and actually coordinate some of their money-making activities. Traditionally, men and women keep separate accounts. There was little overlap in their respective obligations to the household, thus little need for fiscal coordination. Indeed, in the absence of gross neglect of responsibilities, it was considered impolite to inquire into a spouse's financial status. It is not unusual to observe among older Lunda couples the appearance of great disparity in the economic condition of husbands and wives. And not always to the husband's advantage. There are a number of women in Mwinilunga, well-known for their business acumen, who travel to town regularly to put away money in savings accounts, who are always well dressed in yards of the latest style of imported cloth, yet whose husbands walk around barefooted in tattered second-hand clothes.

Amabwambu and their wives are constantly mindful of one another's ventures and assist in significant ways. For example, in the course of their constant peregrination, Amabwambu seize upon fleeting opportunities to purchase honey or scarce millet in order to advance their wives' brewing activities. Subsequently they spread the word and steer clients and colleagues in the direction of their wives' brewing hut. Amabwambu also use their influence to position their wives to benefit from provisioning the mission with surplus food. Correspondingly, a wife might regularly prepare meals for her husband's clients in an effort to lower his cost of being a patron.

Interestingly Amabwambu's relationships with their principal wives began no differently than those of other men. Virtually none of them married childhood sweethearts or women they had courted for any length of time. For the most part, these otherwise very modern men allowed their parents to take the lead in selecting their spouses. In some cases Amabwambu members actually married a person they had seen once or twice. The wisdom of accepting such arrangements is widely acknowledged. Bridewealth is easier to assemble when one's relatives have agreed beforehand to the desirability of a linkage with the lineage in question. Marriage sanctions and legitimizes sexual activity, which is generally considered a good thing for both males and females. Marriage invariably raises one's social status, particularly if a child results from the union. Should the marriage prove disastrous, however, and divorce ensues, one can always shift the blame to the relatives. Concomitantly, in the event of divorce, the woman can legitimately seek support from her father, brothers, or uncles. There is little cultural stigma associated with divorce.

Bridewealth generally entails assembling massive amounts of food and drink for the wedding feast, along with perhaps a few lengths of cloth, some tools, pots and pan, and a few chickens or sheep to be handed over to the bride's kin. The amount of cash assessed is generally small but subjected to extended negotiations and machinations. When Katoloshi got married back around 1980, his in-laws insisted upon a 45-*kwacha* bridewealth payment. However, upon receipt of an initial down payment of 15 *kwacha*, they allowed the wedding to proceed. When the new bride, Miri, became pregnant with a daughter almost immediately, the in-laws quietly dropped their demand for the other 30 *kwacha*. In this matrilineal society it would have been considered in poor taste to continue asking for cash from the progenitor of a new lineage member, particularly so should it happen to be a female. Kataloshi's young brother, Greenford, took a similar tack five years later. Due to the increase in the family's social and economic status in the intervening years, and the declining value of the national currency, bridewealth in this case was assessed at 140 *kwacha*. Yet, Greenford managed to negotiate a down payment of 80 *kwacha*, ultimately avoiding the rest with a quick pregnancy.

Marriage, in a sense, is a process rather than an event. Its stages consist of parental release of the bride-to-be, full payment of bridewealth or its abatement, birth of the first child, and birth of the first girl. A couple becomes progressively more married with the passage of time. Emotional bonds, or the lack thereof, follow their own unique trajectory. In the case of Katoloshi and Miri, those bonds have grown noticeably stronger over the years. Although the shop is clearly Katoloshi's personal enterprise, Miri guides his choice of products aimed at the local female market. She quietly counsels him on the available styles, levels of quality, acceptable quantities, and price range consistent with local taste and resources. Merchandise stocked in the shop would have a decidedly male bias if Katoloshi had been left to his own sensibilities. Additionally, Miri masterfully handles potential customers who show up when her husband is away. If they have cash in hand and clear intent to purchase a specific item, she will fish out the key from its secret location, unlock the shop, and quickly complete the transaction. If, as is often the case, individuals are seeking to scrutinize the merchandise as a prelude to begging for credit, Miri will take on the docile demeanor of a wife who dares not disturb her husband's property. If the intent is not clear, Miri may delay the potential customer's departure until Katoloshi returns. A cup of brew and tantalizing talk are the usual tools to accomplish the deed. Katoloshi and Miri are, indeed, a team in ways that couples in the ascendant generation rarely were. Despite the nature of their public interaction, often characterized by formulaic greetings and the maintenance of spatial distance, Katoloshi and Miri are extremely close and sensitive to one another's social needs and emotional longings. They are clearly mapping out a life together. Neither suggestions of divorce nor whispers of infidelity have ever been associated with their relationship.

Katoka, however, seemed never entirely satisfied with his relationship with Ida. The two had been matched by their parents. But whereas Katoloshi and Miri had barely met before their wedding, Katoka and Ida were cross-cousins who had grown up in adjacent villages. It is always risky to speculate about the intricacies and nuances of interpersonal relations. Much is hidden from public view. But Katoka intimated on a number of occasions that he felt cheated by being asked to marry his cousin. He had grown up with fantasies of falling in love and seducing some exotic beauty in a faraway place. He imagined his peers dropping dead with envy when he brought his magnificent bride back to Matonchi Plateau. Instead, fate paired him with that dusty little cousin from next door.

The fantasy did not die with age. Indeed, as Katoka moved into his middle years, the pull of his whimsical childhood imaginings exerted ever-greater force on his consciousness. He began spending much of his leisure time up in the territory of Chief Nyakaseya, some fifty miles to the north. Staying in the village of a young male cousin, Katoka paraded himself about by day as the big man from Matonchi and spent his nights partying and boozing with all comers. Ultimately he would attract the attention of a very lovely, but very young and impressionable woman. A sexual relationship followed that quickly resulted in pregnancy. In the *mulonga* (formal council to address the matter) Katoka agreed with the woman's family that marriage was the only honorable outcome at this point. Yet, the family had deep reservations about allowing their lineage daughter to accompany this virtual stranger to an unknown village so far to the south. Some wanted him to live uxorilocally for a time, performing brideservice in lieu of bridewealth. But the fact that Katoka had a wife and family with prior claims on his time, labor, and resources rendered full-time residence in Nyakaseya an unfeasible option. Profound angst overwhelmed Katoka as he pondered the implications and possible responses. On the one hand, he wanted to live out his fantasy by marching into Matonchi with his beautiful young bride. On the other hand, he was terrified that Ida might not approve of the marriage. He was also terrified that his young love might bolt upon discovering that he was neither as rich nor as famous as he might have led her to believe. For months Katoka vacillated, surreptitiously dividing his time between Matonchi and Nyakaseya. Although family members and village mates grew increasingly suspicious of Katoka's periodic absences, only his Amabwambu peers were aware of the details. They, in turn, offered Katoka a plethora of conflicting advice and diverging opinions that only added to his quandary. One night, fortified with alcohol, he finally broke the news to Ida, laying out his intent to do the right thing by marrying the other woman. Ida's notion of the right thing, however, included bringing the other woman down to Matonchi to assume the role of junior wife rather than remaining in Nyakaseya bleeding off family resources for nothing in return. After a few tense weeks of indecision on Katoka's part, a major fight erupted between Ida and him. Witnesses to the actual event were few. Details concerning proximate causes were scarce. But the short- and long-term effects of the conflict were played out before the public gaze. Katoka required medical treatment at Lwawu Mission clinic for lacerations and bruises. He and Ida were soon divorced. He married his young lover in Nyakaseya, but she refused to come to Matonchi. At last contact, Katoka was visiting Nyakaseya regularly but still living at Matonchi, tending to his crops and other economic enterprises and dependent upon his mother and the wives of Amabwambu to prepare his daily meals.

Kangasa had no deep and abiding ambivalence about his sexual or married life. He would bed any willing woman simply for the love of physical pleasure and the thrill of conquest. And for the most part his indiscretions escaped detection. But his most enduring goal in life, as mentioned earlier, was to build up the kind of social and economic estate that would buttress his status in the afterlife. Kangasa was obsessed with notions of *mpuhu* (fame). He wanted to stand out, even from among his Amabwambu peers, as a uniquely enterprising individual who built up an enviable amount of wealth in both people and things. He dreamed of himself as someday the owner of a vast herd of cattle, the big man who provided the most meat at all ritual gatherings, the patron who commanded the loyalty of the most clients, and eventually the ancestor most talked about long after his death. Even if that talk was motivated by envy it mattered little to Kangasa. He perceived the Lunda as an inherently jealous people, for whom renown and notoriety were the same thing.

It had never been Kangasa's intent to remain monogamous. His relationship with Dorinne did parallel that of Katoloshi's with Miri in certain aspects. The two interacted as friends and partners in addition to their formal role of spouses. They cooperated in a range of economic activities and seemed quite comfortable teasing and joking with one another, sometimes even in public view. But all big men of epic proportion had left behind abundant progeny as ultimate testimony of their greatness. Hence Kangasa had been steadfast and honest in his intent to acquire additional wives when his economic circumstances permitted. Dorinne was thus not blindsided when Kangasa began to speak of his desire to marry a young woman from Sakapoti village. The negotiations proceeded smoothly with Dorinne's blessing. She subsequently took the lead in welcoming the new bride to Matonchi, showing her around with grace and style, easing her transition into a world of new faces, new places, and new responsibilities as a junior wife.

Kapala's marital transitions were detailed in chapter 3. An ardent traditionalist and a polygamist with three wives in his twenties, he purportedly converted to Catholicism in his late thirties and began married life anew with a single wife. Mafulo, likewise, pushes his strong Catholic beliefs to the fore to explain his preference for a monogamous existence. It is difficult to make powerful and comprehensive statements about Amabwambu and their relationships with women. The fact that they spend so little time with wives, not to mention mothers and sisters, leaves conclusions based on observation resting on a weak foundation. With caution and caveat I can only suggest the following observations: First, the long-held Lunda tradition of *chaambu*, the principle mandating physical and existential separation by gender, although evidently weakened, remains a powerful guide for interpreting the public comportment of Amabwambu.[17] Their periodic transgression of *chaambu* is a deliberate and self-consciousness act, a potent statement of the presumed uniqueness of their relationships with their spouses. But it is a statement that draws its power from acknowledging the continued existence of *chaambu* as the norm. Second, one increasingly explicit dimension of marriage, whether it be monogamous or polygynous, is as a component in long-term economic planning. The 60 percent divorce ratio that characterized the generation of Amabwambu's parents contrasts greatly with today's more stable unions in general and with those of Amabwambu in particular.[18] Third, incipient notions of romance regularly seep into Amabwambu's private conversations. Whether this was true of past generations is unclear. Neither the anthropological literature nor statements from older Lunda informants venture much into the realm of private emotion. Marriage was discussed solely in terms of its roles in the social and biological reproduction of society. Yet Amabwambu assign marriage expanded functions, including emotional health, psychological security, and even the fulfillment of fantasies. Fourth, the life course of Amabwambu demonstrates the continuing centrality of entrepreneurship, personal initiative, and individual style in the reckoning of social status. On the one hand, there remains broad agreement on certain goals. In particular, big-manship should be the highest aim of every Lunda male. Its attainment results in the leaving behind of one's name after death; it is impressed upon people and places. Mountains, river, plains, and forests are named after the big men who in life dwelled nearby. Children are given the name of a big man in hopes they will absorb and manifest some of his powerful essence. Personal names of big men become institutionalized as titles of headmanship and positions of ritual specialists. Yet, fame of this magnitude does not go to those who simply comport themselves well, follow traditional rules of etiquette, live long, and prosper. True eminence is reserved for the unique individual. Clearly he must build up an enviable estate and attract a multitude of followers. But he must also have a style all his own. We see this manifested in Amabwambu, a group whose cohesion is based less on shared agreements about the tactics and strategies of life and more so on the creation of a social space where men feel comfortable exploring different paths to the major objective. Those who would have the social and physical world renamed in their honor cannot do so by following anyone else's lead.

Remaking Ritual

In order to make the transition from big man of the moment to timeless legend, men must find favor not only among the living but among the dead as well. The ire of the ancestors can stop the upward rise of the most clever, competent, and hardworking of individuals. One simultaneously solicits and manifests favorable standing among members of the other world through the intensity of one's engagement with ritual life. Virtually all Lunda rituals, be they rites of passage or rites of affliction, attempt to conger up and call upon the power of the ancestors to either guide individuals through the metaphysically dangerous voyage from one social category to another or to heal those afflicted by spiritually induced ailments or misfortune. The success of any such ventures is a direct reflection of the ancestors' approval of the group at large and, of course, its choice of leaders. Ritual leadership, however, can be a dangerous business. It requires one to confront potentially incendiary issues that reside at the intersection of identity formation in youth, political struggles among adults, domestic tension between men and women, and the elemental forces that bind the physical world of the living to the metaphysical world of the ancestors. Those big men who would seek immortality must duel one another for prominence in bridging the gap between sacred and profane spheres of social life, transcending the interstice between the corporeal and the incorporeal.

The traditional Lunda lifestyle provides but a limited number of occasions for people to come together in large numbers. Small clusters of villages are often separated from one another by miles of vacant land. Production, for the most part, is accomplished individually or alternatively in small groups. There are no fixed market places or days where people exchange surplus commodities and insights on current affairs at predictable intervals. Rituals that mark social transitions (birth, maturation, marriage, and death) or those designed to address maladies or mishaps are thus the occasions richest in social possibilities. Such rituals provide the context for reconfirming or reconfiguring social relations, patterns of authority, and relative status among both the living and the dead.

Responsive and adaptive, the Lunda repertoire of rituals has grown immense over the centuries, providing a vast array of stylized enactments for addressing life's diverse contingencies. Each ritual has dozens of formally designated positions of authority, each demanding of its holder differing degrees of contact with spiritual elements, varying commitments of time to the study of ritual esoterica, and contrasting levels of material contribution to the success of the ritual.[19] Amabwambu have been able to take on levels of ritual responsibilities that in the past were reserved for men far older. The sheer size and layout of Amabwambu villages and their capacity to contribute meat and alcoholic beverages, as well as to recruit and guarantee the presence of the area's best singers, dancers, and musicians, have attracted the attention of all. Amabwambu have so raised the levels of expectations as to shame many seniors from asserting and assuming their natural right to host ritual performance. Men of the elder generation have also been overwhelmed by the speed and thoroughness with which Amabwambu have absorbed the complex volumes of arcane knowledge associated with rituals. Indeed, this ability to learn quickly and deeply is the very characteristic that brought Amabwambu into being in the first place. It was their dedication to scholarship, their openness to new ideas, and their personal discipline that had allowed them to succeed in the academically rigorous world of St. Kizito boarding school as youth. It was their continuing curiosity and willingness to learn new modes of economic behavior that had made them Brother Joe's favorites as young men. It was their intellectual alertness and fondness for experimentation that attracted the attention of international NGOs in their middle years. And these same characteristics seem destined to propel Amabwambu among the ranks of senior men well before their time.

Curing rites are performed less frequently today than in the past, and certainly less frequently than rites of passage.[20] Indeed, virtually all Lunda boys and girls still participate in their respective maturation rites. Girls are initiated individually, immediately after the onset of their first menstrual cycle, regardless of the time of year. Members of the extended family take the lead in orchestrating the rounds of public ceremonies and private events that culminate in social adulthood. Boys, however, are initiated in groups of a dozen or so individuals, once a year, during the cold dry season (July and August), in a month-long set of events known as *mukanda*. It is believed that it takes the collective action of the entire male community, living and dead, to turn boys into men. The boys are circumcised at the beginning of *mukanda*, but most of the month is given over to instruction and testing in the range of practical skills, social etiquette, historical insights, and judicial precedents whose mastery is expected of every competent adult male. *Chijika mukanda* (the inaugurator of the ritual), *kandanji* (the one in charge of the ritual), and *nfumu watubwiku* (the head teacher at the ritual) should all be elderly men of honor, selected on the basis on moral rectitude. The numerous men who will take turns instructing the boys should each be the most proficient and accomplished in the skills or topic being examined. The whole of *mukanda* is a hyper-formalized affair emphasizing social hierarchy and appropriate comportment among men of differing rank. As such, it embodies and reinforces extant social relations.

Throughout the year men jockey for leadership positions within the upcoming *mukanda*, indeed maneuvering to imprint their interpretation of the local male hierarchy upon the consciousness of the next generation of men. Amabwambu have been successful in appropriating ritual leadership for several reasons. First, they are able to vigorously and vociferously compete among themselves, asserting individual rights to formal roles within *mukanda* based on lineal or proximal links to the particular boys chosen to undergo the rites in a given year. Yet, such arguments take place far from the public ear. Once Amabwambu have reached an agreement among themselves, they close rank, throwing all their weight behind their chosen members. Indeed, to the outside world Amabwambu present themselves as a single-status entity. They collectively hold the same rank vis-à-vis any outside individual or group. To support the social rise of any member is, thus, to promote the upward movement of the clique as a whole. To guide public opinion toward their own private objectives, Amabwambu might quietly lobby support from relevant parents by impressing upon them the cultural authenticity and material niceties that would surely typify any Amabwambu-led event. Amabwambu might also directly negotiate with potential rivals, promising them some benefit in the economic arena in exchange for support in the ritual domain. Given the rich array of social, material, and intellectual resources at Amabwambu's disposal, it is not surprising therefore that much of ritual life unfolds with them at the helm. Elderly *ataata* (fathers) and *ankaka* (grandfathers) may be prominently displayed in honorific positions, but Amabwambu stand out distinctly as the most potent, dynamic, and captivating collection of individuals in the area, the ones who unquestionably embody the style and substance that animates the imagination of today's younger generation of males.

In conclusion, it should be noted that Christianity has had a profound impact on ritual life in Mwinilunga. At one level Christianity offers a perspective on the metaphysical world and notions of moral obligation that contrasts with traditional beliefs. The contrast, however, is not especially profound. Catholic priests and Protestant preachers have long spread their message of the scriptures to the most remote villages in Mwinilunga, believing themselves to be locked in a cosmic struggle with anachronistic forces of superstition and ignorance. Yet, in truth, the message promulgated has had minimal success at dislodging the underpinnings of traditional beliefs. Instead Christianity has, in essence, added its own layer of spirituality that buttresses the old and binds it with the new to produce a powerful and cohesive synthesis of beliefs.

The world of the ancestors continues to exist in the minds of most in Mwinilunga. It is a world not removed in time and space, but one that is superimposed on the here and now. The ancestors tread the same ground in death that they walked in life. They are present at every meal, listening in on every palaver, arriving at their own conclusions about guilt and innocence in every dispute. Their highest aim is simply to be remembered for their contributions to sustaining their kin group while alive and their current role of providing kin an umbrella of spiritual protection from potentially harmful denizens of the metaphysical world.

Those who have adopted Christianity acknowledge a high god as the almighty creator, the most powerful and compassionate of supernatural beings. But such beliefs do not invalidate the existence of the ancestors. God is the father of us all. Ancestors limit their concerns to a more finite set of individuals, their own kin exclusively. One should ask God's blessings on all undertakings. But just as surely one should invoke the presence of ancestors to participate in and watch over all family matters. Thus prayers to God and readings from the Holy Scriptures now regularly join age-old incantations and symbolic manipulations in hopes of bringing both God and the ancestors into the same ritual arena. Philosophical divergence among the population ranges from those who believe that God is all-powerful, but who nevertheless see no need to slight the ancestors, to those who believe that ancestors alone could probably accomplish the task at hand, but why ignore the possibility of a more potent power. Amabwambu's participation in local rituals has thus become all the more desirable. Even members who have vacillated over the years, ambivalent in their feelings about Christianity, are nevertheless sufficiently literate to pick up the Bible and read stirringly from its text. Members of the elder generation can perform this feat haltingly at best.

The Lunda's widespread and seamless incorporation of Christian symbolism, belief, and practice into their ritual repertoire is not historically unique. Indeed, many Lunda rites of affliction were borrowed from other African groups, near and far. Even the boys' rite of passage, *mukanda,* is so omnipresent in Central Africa as to make the identification of its place of origin an impossibility. The aim of Lunda rituals is efficacy, not cultural purity. And efficacy is a quality demonstrated rather than intellectually deduced. Amabwambu's long association with Lwawu Mission, their special relationship with successions of Franciscan Friars, and, in some cases, their weekly role in Catholic Mass is ample demonstration of their special link with the Christian god. Their personal success at such a young age demonstrates the power of that god and elevates Amabwambu personages to the level of Christian icons. Their presence and words at a traditional ritual lends the whole affair a special air of Christian authenticity and, hopefully, an efficacious outcome. In addition, Amabwambu's contact with Lwawu clinic, primarily through Mafulo's role as nursing assistant, means that if Amabwambu are involved in a boy's circumcision, for example, sterile surgical scalpels will no doubt be used and antibiotic ointment will be employed to speed the healing. If Amabwambu are involved in a curing rite, aspirins and other painkillers can be made available to alleviate the patient's discomfort until the actual spiritual cure is effected.

Amabwambu, the most seemingly modern men in Mwinilunga, have not condemned traditional rituals as archaic and out of step with current knowledge of human physiology, social psychology, and biological pathology. Instead, they have raised the importance and expected grandeur of rituals to the point that only they can effectively meet local ideals of excellence and efficacy. In doing such, Amabwambu have not only positioned themselves to meet the final earthly prerequisite of big-manship but have also begun the process of ingratiating themselves to the ancestors as well.

Conclusion

In Western scholarly tradition, reflections on the nature of friendship date back at least to the time of Aristotle. In *Nichomachean Ethics* he offers us a tripartite schema consisting of friends of virtue, friends of pleasure, and friends of utility. Friendships based on virtue (or morality) are accorded the highest honor, being presented as the truest form of friendship. In such relationships individuals desire the best for one another without ulterior motives or preconditions. In the other two forms there is a modus operandi, a reason behind the friendship. Individuals derive something pleasurable or useful from the relationship. Although they may like one another, the friendship itself can quickly dissolve if the motive for the relationship disappears.

Eric Wolf, in a similar vein, presents us with a twofold arrangement, contrasting emotional (or affective) friendships with instrumental friendships. In both his formulations, however, friendship fulfills deficits within people. Those deficits may vary from conceptual to concrete, from deep-seated psychological longings to public cravings for economic and political power. But even Wolf's emotional friendships contain elements of self-interest, although perhaps not directly obvious to the participants themselves. It is generally assumed that Wolf's instrumental friendships converge with Aristotle's friends of utility, and Wolf's emotional friendships correspond mostly with Aristotle's friends of pleasure. In both cases the latter category is accorded more value than the former, deemed to be more the model of true friendship, presumably because it is freer of overt acts of self-gratification.

Cora DuBois and Yehudi Cohen offer up frameworks that classify friendships primarily by the intensity of bonds shared rather than by the type of interests participants have in one another. For DuBois the relevant categories are exclusive, close, and casual friendships; and for Cohen, inalienable, close, casual, and expedient friendships. Yet despite a range of subtle and profound differences in their formulations, DuBois, Cohen, Aristotle, and Wolf all share certain basic assumptions about the nature of friendship. True friendships are dyadic. Whether they are classified as virtuous, affective, exclusive, or inalienable, real friendships are between two individuals. Polyadic relationships are invariably viewed as being of lesser intensity, of lower moral quality, and involving baser desires. This supposition permeates much of the sociological literature on the role of friendship in the life cycle of individuals, particularly in so-called modern societies. The polyadic adolescent peer group, for example, is commonly viewed as a necessary social bridge to facilitate the movement of individuals from the intimate world of family to the harsher world of adult responsibilities. Youth are excluded from full participation in the bureaucratic institutions of the adult world and are thus forced to rely on their own immediate resources for the development of a social group that can provide affective support, confirmation of personal identity, and a means for the furtherance of instrumental activity. Upon acceptance into the adult world, however, the adolescent peer group is, supposedly, no longer needed.

Our Lunda-Ndembu story certainly challenges the utility of the above formulations for explicating the enduring connections between Amabwambu. Those connections are not emblematic of one particular stage of psychological or sociological development. Indeed, the material contained herein might well contribute to emerging notions of identity as something that is continually constructed and transformed throughout life, rather than being a project that must be completed before the mantle of adulthood is bestowed upon an individual. Granted, early experiences and insights exert disproportionate influence on personality and behavior, as well as on perceptions of self and the larger world. Yet, life constantly presents the individual with new interpretive quandaries, the need to rethink and revise old strategies and even to concoct whole new approaches to effectively manage unforeseen circumstances. And even in the absence of monumental social change, individuals must still confront the abiding problems of life through the eyes of ever-shifting personas. Solutions devised at one stage of personal development may not be appropriate to another. As one's status changes from youth to middle-aged adult to elder, from single to married to widowed or divorced, from childless to parent to grandparent, from one relatively unknown to renowned pillar of the community, notions of acceptable behavior and suitable strategies must be continually rethought and revised. A group of intimate and longstanding friends provide an ideal vehicle for working out such arrangements over time. Indeed, in a world where social relations are both the means and the manifestation of success, such a group is an invaluable asset. Furthermore, although it is difficult to prove empirically, I firmly believe that the polyadic bonds of Amabwambu are not of lesser intensity or of lower moral quality or involve baser desires than dyadic relations. Certainly it has been demonstrated that those relationships have a useful and instrumental component. Yet, it is also evident that members of Amabwambu genuinely care about one another, are sincerely devoted to one another's success, and feel inextricably bound to one another for life and even beyond. The Lunda-Ndembu believe that relationships developed in life continue on into the afterlife. Thus among Amabwambu there is a collective identity and a collective consciousness without which individual identities would be greatly impoverished, and individual actions would be substantially devoid of force and meaning.

A second problem associated with affective approaches to friendship, of privileging type and degree of emotional attachment, is the tendency to ignore the organizational aspects of friendship. Much of the sociological and anthropological literature takes for granted that society itself provides all the meaningful institutional structures that govern interpersonal relations. Friendship is viewed as a mere option, an alternative, an emotional adjunct to or a momentary escape from social structure. At best the variability in the affective content of friendship is explained in terms of the diverse cultural frameworks in which it occurs. Interestingly, modern bureaucratic societies and societies where individuals are deeply embedded in closed corporate communities such as villages, lineages, and age-groups are both seen as ideal incubators of true friendships. In the case of the former, the selection of friends represents one of the few ways individuals can add a personal touch to an otherwise impersonal world of bureaucratic structures. In the latter case, friendship serves as the interstitial glue binding the distinct, separate, and non-overlapping corporate entities that make up an otherwise fragmented society.

The story of Amabwambu told here indicates the numerous ways in which friendship groupings are structures unto themselves. Certainly in a fashion consistent with Giddens's notions of structure, Amabwambu as a collectivity appears as both a medium and an outcome of purposive human effort. Amabwambu is an enduring concatenation of individual personalities and propensities, impulses and inhibitions, competencies and shortcomings, social links and spiritual associations, past histories and abiding hopes for the future. As such, Amabwambu spawn social acts, provide the raw material out of which social acts are crafted, and constitute the interpretive framework that gives social acts meaning. Rather than serving as a link between impervious social categories or as an escape from overly constraining social categories, friendship stands out in the Lunda-Ndembu case as a pleasurable, powerful, and self-constructed addition to the world of ascribed social units.

Sociocultural anthropology is perhaps unique among academic disciplines in the intensity and longevity of debates about the field's proper unit of analysis. Durkheim sent us in search of "social facts," defined as compelling and enduring sets of social and behavioral rules. Radcliffe-Brown insisted we focus instead on "social structure," orderly arrangements of statuses that persist through time. Malinowski offered up his own version of social structure as a vast conditioning system, partly sui generis, partly sustained by the purposive behavior of individuals. Yet Malinowski also warned us that our analysis of society is not complete until we have tackled what he called the *inponderabilia* of actual life: "the routine of a man's working day, the details of his care of the body, of the manner of taking food and preparing it; the tone of conversational and social life around the village fires, the existence of strong friendships or hostilities, and of passing sympathies and dislikes between people; the subtle yet unmistakable manner in which personal vanities and ambitions are reflected in the behaviour of the individual and in the emotional reactions of those who surround him" (Malinowski, *Argonauts*, 18). A detailed examination of these actions, supplemented with the subject's own thoughts on these actions, leads us, according to Malinowski, toward one of anthropology's highest objectives: deducing "the native's point of view."

Throughout the twentieth century debates raged over the most useful units of analysis, effective frameworks, appropriate paradigms, and suitable nomenclature. Yet, there was widespread agreement that anthropology's scholarly contribution needed to extend beyond the production of lists of rules, norms, and values, descriptions of social events, and models of organizational form and function. We needed heuristic approaches that somehow captured the essence of life elsewhere.

The unit chosen for this text was a clique, nested within a cohort group, moving through time and social space on the Central African plateau. The aim was to examine life not as deeply embedded regulations and immutable social categories, but as lived experiences. In many respects, it has been a search for styles rather than patterns, for perspectives rather than forms. Each member of the Amabwambu clique is also a member of a family, village, vicinage, cohort group, ritual association, and church congregation. The clique is both a solid assemblage in and of itself, as well as a site of overlap and interpenetration by other social groupings and their associated rules and values. The clique is a place of action and a place of interpretation. From our analytical perch within the clique we can see, as Evans-Pritchard noted long ago, that behavior does not extend unproblematically from forms of social organization. We must, indeed, creatively assess the possibilities inherent in the study of personal propensity and historical contingency. Feelings and reflections are every bit as important as forms and functions.

In a previous book (Pritchett, *Lunda-Ndembu*), I utilized a much more conventional approach in constructing the history and culture of the Lunda-Ndembu. I pieced together archaeological evidence on the sixteenth century, oral traditions about the seventeenth century, explorers' tales from the eighteenth century, missionary reports on the nineteenth century, colonial reports of the early twentieth century, ethnographic accounts from midcentury, and my own fieldwork of the late twentieth century. The story that emerged was a grand sweeping tale. Yet, no matter how well founded the tale may have been, no matter how solid the evidence on which it was based, no matter how clever the synthesis I constructed, the tale essentially remains my own. It is not a Lunda story. To the best of my knowledge, no Lunda has ever spent decades visiting the diverse archives in which the fragments of Lunda history are scattered. No Lunda has ever tracked down the dispersed accounts of early explorers or systematically sifted through the available archaeological data. No Lunda has ever extensively interviewed expatriate missionaries or consulted the collection of colonial reports. Thus Lunda social memory must necessarily differ from academically produced social history. Lunda sensibilities are necessarily infused with substances that differ greatly from those that frame anthropological accounts. And as such, Lunda consciousness remains hidden from view.

This present volume has thus veered away from the standard ethnographic format to explore alternative narrative contours. It is an attempt to grapple with the so-called *inponderabilia* of real life, to examine the actual flow of information and the precise unfolding of events on which the Lunda themselves reflected deeply, and out of which a unique consciousness emerged. In recognition of the vastly different interpretive possibilities residing within even the smallest cultural groups, this text has defined its unit of analysis rather narrowly—one small group of male friends. This exercise is underpinned by the belief that a deep and intensive look at consciousness construction among a limited number of individuals, juxtaposed with more traditionally wide-ranging ethnographic explorations, can lend itself to greater extrapolative opportunities than would more superficial treatments of larger social groupings.

Amabwambu were raised listening to the stories of *ankaka* and *ataata*, stories that were both reflective and constitutive of an enduring frontier consciousness. The Lunda may still dream of a past golden era when their empire was at the center of the universe, but for more than a century their survival has been contingent upon mastering life on the edge. They have cleverly colonized the interstitial region between competing polities, between contrasting islands of economic interests, and between diverse ecological niches. Such positioning accentuates the need for innovation and flexibility. Those at the center of production, extraction, or merchandising can perhaps throw themselves more wholeheartedly into a single specialized activity. But those who would thrive on the shifting margins of grand historical processes must be intellectually, organizationally, and productively nimble. Time and again, the Lunda have demonstrated their mastery of a unique domain of place and practice. They made their debut on the pages of European chronicles in the early 1700s as the principle provisioners of the caravan network that moved people and products between settlements, across the length and breadth of Central Africa. The Lunda were situated at the geographical point of overlap, where the Atlantic and the Indian Ocean trade worlds met and dueled with one another deep in the interior of Africa. The Kanongesha Lunda, in particular, moved up to the sparsely populated plateau around the source of the Zambezi River in the mid-1700s to specialize in the production of the newly introduced but highly productive crop, cassava. It is doubtful that the eighteenth- and nineteenth-century Central African trade system could have been sustained at the levels ultimately achieved without this single agricultural innovation.

During the early 1900s we find the Lunda probing the edges of the newly imposed Muzungu spheres of influence—British, Belgian, and Portuguese—spending the better part of two decades moving back and forth across fuzzy borders seeking the best political and economic arrangement of any given moment. Lunda of the mid-1900s possessed an acute awareness of the need to reassess identity with movement toward economic and political centers, with the adoption of Shangaan identity in South Africa being the most dramatic example. Yet everyone in Mwinilunga knows of this or that Lunda person who pretended to be Bemba in the Zambian Copperbelt, or Luba in the Lubumbashi mines in the Congo, or who took on a "deep Lunda" persona when moving about in Angola. Concomitantly, the protagonists of this story, Amabwambu, have a personal history of collectively mediating the social distance between the mission and the villages, between locals and refugees, between the Zambian government and international organizations.

The ability of Mushala the bandit to terrorize the center by controlling the margins made him the archetype Lunda hero. As had been Kasanza, who with one bullet to the chest of the British South Africa Company's first representative to Mwinilunga, C. S. Bellis, destroyed the myth of Muzungu invincibility, sending shockwaves that reached the center of the colonizing thrust. The myth of Moise Tshombe of the Congo as one who would remake the world, reuniting fragmented polities on the margins to produce a new center with the Lunda at its core, was the perfect psychological salve for aching frontier consciousness.

Likewise, we have seen that the radio is the perfect instrument for those who reside on the margins. From the moment Waylesi returned to Matonchi with his saucepan special tucked under his arm, the Lunda world changed forever. Contemporary urban discourse, Copperbelt pop culture, government ministry missives about the benefits of modern living, and news reports from global capitals were now available on a daily basis. No longer were the Lunda simply on the edge of British, Portuguese, and Belgian territories. They were now on the edge of everywhere. Today's shortwave radios reach to the ends of the earth, spewing forth an unbroken string of narrative and musical vignettes of exciting lives elsewhere, serving as continual reminder to the Lunda that they are, indeed, in the middle of nowhere.

From the periphery, the Lunda protested Northern Rhodesia's incorporation into the Central African Federation, while never participating fully in the confederation of ethnic societies that gave birth to the nationalistic thrust for Zambian independence. Their most famous elected representative to the central government, Ronald Njapau, spent his time in the capital city fighting against overwhelming odds to channel some small measure of national resources back to his neglected corner of the world. Yet the untimely discovery of an earlier indiscretion led to his trial for treason and an unleashing of retaliatory force on the Lunda population that would purge an entire generation of any hope that the central government would embrace them as genuine partners in the construction of a new nation. Subsequently, the contraction of the Zambian government under IMF mandates in the 1980s saw social services and economic opportunities retreat even further from the region. The Lunda would be left alone, forced to blaze their own economic trail, to forge their own identity—indeed, their own destiny.

For Amabwambu and their cohort, shaping that destiny would reinforce and even intensify the prevailing frontier consciousness and the drive to construct enduring social groupings based on friendship. Living on the margins requires fearlessness in the face of the unknown, flexibility in confronting conceptual and interpretive conundrums, a propensity to embrace novelty, and the willingness to move quickly toward opportunities and to move away from the lack thereof. The courage needed to meet the challenges of life on the margins is the principle product of Amabwambu and similarly constituted cliques. Nothing is more useful or more comforting in an environment of uncertainty than a stable social world of friends, going through life's biological stages jointly, witnessing one another's social unfolding, reinforcing one another's identities, expanding the capacity of the whole through the selective development of individual competencies. In Kapala Amabwambu has a mechanical genius, trusted even to drive mission tractors and to operate its gristmills. Katoloshi the shopkeeper is the master of merchandising, finance, and credit. Mafulo is the moral and musical center of the group, always the first to raise issues of fairness and the first to break into song, deep reflection, or momentary distraction as needed. Kangasa, boiling over with passion to succeed, drives Amabwambu forward when signs of complacency set in. Katoka, the romantic, starry-eyed dreamer, adds the much-needed touch of whimsy when the group is weighed down by the heavy details of daily life. He is also the flexible buffer between the more rigid personalities within the group. Jointly, Amabwambu is far stronger than the sum of its individual parts. It is a group valued not as an escape from structure or as an entity that bridges the space between highly separated, overly exclusive structures. Amabwambu is instead the material, the means, and the manifestation of a unique structure in its own right. It is a place where practical knowledge, shared dreams, and emotional longings meet in a psychologically supportive atmosphere. It is a place where individual aesthetic frameworks, individual notions of style, and individual senses of humor take on a collective form. It is a process by which autonomous beings commit themselves to one existential destiny, molding a set of relationships that will endure throughout life and continue into the afterlife as well.

Notes

Introduction

1. "Lunda" is the widest term of reference applied to groups of people in Zambia, Congo, and Angola that were associated in some fashion with a far-flung sixteenth- to nineteenth-century Central African empire. Myriad local terms of reference exist. The Lunda of northwestern Zambia, who are the focus of this study, are variously known as the Lunda-Ndembu, the Ndembu, the Kanongesha Lunda, the Zambian Lunda, or just simply the Lunda.

2. The value of Zambia's total mineral export more than tripled in the first few years after independence, rising from $334.6 million (U.S.) in 1963 to over one billion dollars by 1969.

3. It should be noted that the income disparities between Africans and European expatriates in Zambia was so great that GDP per capita numbers are deceptive. The average African in Zambia was certainly not two times better off than the average Egyptian or three times better off than the average Kenyan. But the average Zambian African enjoyed a significantly higher standard of living in the 1960s than at the turn of the millennium. However, the euphoria of the former period has been replaced by utter despair and the hopelessness of contemporary times.

4. A clear overview of research on youth gangs within American sociology can be found in Cummings and Monti (eds.), *Gangs*.

5. Paine's "Anthropological Approaches to Friendship" is frequently cited in sociological literature as the definitive statement giving unique status to friendship in Western societies.

6. Linton's remarks here are culled from a manuscript by Cora DuBois that grew out of a seminar on friendship held during 1955 and 1956 at Harvard University. In condensed form it appears as "The Gratuitous Act" in Leyton (ed.), *Compact*.

1. Tales of the *Ankaka*

1. For a fuller treatment of Lunda philosophical notions concerning "age" and its wider sociological function, see Pritchett, *Lunda-Ndembu*, chap. 4.

2. V. W. Turner, *Drums of Affliction*, remains the most comprehensive study of Lunda rites of possession. For a look at recent changes in the Lunda ritual system, see Pritchett, *Lunda-Ndembu*, chap. 8.

3. Senior Headman Kankinza, clearly the longest reigning Chifunga in history, died three months after my arrival in Mwinilunga in 1984. Stories of his life dominated nightly fireside conversations for months after his funeral. He had supposedly been a high-ranking chief in Angola who chose to move his people up on Matonchi Plateau, situated in British territory, at the beginning of the twentieth century. The British, however, would never recognize him as anything more than the highest-ranking headman in his area.

4. Bloch, in *Ritual, History and Power*, particularly chap. 3, most succinctly writes about this

sort of process as a "ritualization of power," where the unpredictable is made palatable by draping it with the aura of timelessness and therefore is more sacred and meritorious of respect.

5. The most comprehensive collection of Lunda-Ndembu oral traditions remains Schecter, "History and Historiography."

6. *Muntu* literally denotes a person. *Sa* and *Nya* respectively mean Mr., or father of, and Mrs., or mother of. Hence *Samuntu* and *Nyamuntu* can be glossed as either Mr. and Mrs. Person, or Father and Mother of People. The general terms for man and woman, however, are *iyala* and *mumbanda*.

7. Scholarly treatments of Central Africa's engagement with global trade networks can be found in J. C. Miller, *Way of Death,* and von Oppen, *Terms of Trade.*

8. See, Pritchett, *Lunda-Ndembu,* chap. 7, for a more detailed account of Ipepa the magician.

9. During the eighteenth century, in fact, only two European expeditions are known to have reached Lunda country: those of Alexandre da Silva Teixeira in 1794 and Elias Vieira de Andrade in 1799. The first British-led group, that of David Livingstone, did not reach the southern Lunda area until 1854.

10. Translations of the Pombeiros accounts can be found in Burton, *Lacerda's Journey to Cazembe.*

11. J. C. Miller, *Way of Death.*

12. Such accounts could be heard across the entirety of Central Africa. See, for example, Burton, *Lake Regions of Central Africa.*

13. Vellut, "Notes sur le Lunda."

14. See von Oppen, *Terms of Trade,* 438–40, for a synopsis of travelers' reports on the Upper Zambezi and Kasai Rivers, 1794–1907.

15. Literary sources that complement and confirm the accuracy of Lunda oral traditions include Harding, *In Remotest Barotseland;* Coillard, *On the Threshold;* Arnot, *Missionary Travels;* W. S. Fisher and Hoyte, *Africa Looks Ahead;* and M. Fisher, *Nswana the Heir.*

16. See Scapera (ed.), *David Livingstone; Livingstone's Private Journals; Livingstone's Missionary Correspondence;* and *Livingstone's African Journal.*

17. Arnot, *Garenganze.*

18. Scholarly studies of the Brethren include Rowdon, *Origins of the Brethren;* Embley, "Early Development of the Plymouth Brethren"; and Coad, *History of the Brethren Movement.*

19. Hammond, *Portugal and Africa;* Clarence-Smith, *Slaves, Peasants, and Capitalists* and "Myth of Uneconomic Imperialism"; Henderson, *Angola.*

20. M. Fisher, *Nswana the Heir,* chap 11.

21. Ibid., chap 6.

22. M. K. Fisher, *Lunda-Ndembu Handbook.*

23. The Boma Class in the narrowest sense refers to those Africans who worked for the Boma, or the Colonial Administration. Some acquired their position by virtue of their rank within the precolonial political system, e.g., traditional chiefs and headmen. Increasingly, however, the system came to be dominated by a new European-educated African elite, operating as court officials and development specialists. Wonderful accounts of the development of the Northern Rhodesian "Boma Class" in particular and the Native Authority system in general are contained in Chipungu (ed.), *Guardians in Their Time.*

24. NAZ (National Archives of Zambia) Mwinilunga District Notebook KSE 4/1, 150–200.

25. M. Fisher, *Nswana the Heir,* 67.

26. The most comprehensive treatment of beliefs underpinning Lunda divinatory practices remains V. W. Turner, *Revelation and Divination,* part two.

27. The most extensive examination of the dynamic clash between Western and African religions in Zambia, both at the level of theory and praxis, remains Van Binsbergen, *Religious Change in Zambia*, and Van Binsbergen and Schoffeleers, *Theoretical Explorations in African Religion*.

28. Scholarly treatment of the impact of changing terms of trade on Central African production for export can be found in J. C. Miller, *Way of Death*, and von Oppen, *Terms of Trade*.

29. The best history of the British South Africa Company is perhaps contained in Galbraith, *Crown and Charter*. For a more specific look at BSAC policy in Zambia, see Meebelo, *Reaction to Colonialism*, and Macpherson, *Anatomy of a Conquest*.

30. NAZ (National Archives of Zambia) Mwinilunga District Notebook KSE 4/1, 1–50.

31. See, for example, Vansina, *Kingdoms of the Savanna;* Thornton, "Chronology and Causes of Lunda Expansion"; and Reefe, *Rainbow and the Kings*.

32. NAZ Mwinilunga District Notebook KSE 4/1.

33. Ibid., P1, insert 4, details BSAC officer F. H. Melland's near obsession with attracting Musokantanda, a high-ranking Lunda chief in the Congo, to relocate to Solwezi district in Northern Rhodesia. Musokantanda seemed to prolong the courtship, extracting unnamed concessions before accepting Melland's offer. But his stay was brief. He returned to his old home in Congo, leaving a large area in Northern Rhodesia with no recognized senior chief.

34. Chipungu, *Guardians in Their Time,* chap. 2.

35. NAZ Mwinilunga District Notebook KSE 4/1, 28.

36. Ibid., 28–30.

37. Ibid., 30.

38. M. Fisher, *Nswana the Heir,* 63.

39. According to local memories, most of the major prides of lions had been wiped out by the 1930s. But copies of the *Solwezi District Newsletter,* a monthly publication of official pronouncements, news, and current events throughout the Northwest Region indicates that lion attacks in Lunda territory still occurred monthly through the mid-1960s.

40. For examples, see Schecter, *History and Historiography;* Thornton, "Chronology and Causes of Lunda Expansion"; J. C. Miller, *Way of Death;* and von Oppen, *Terms of Trade*.

41. Macpherson, *Anatomy of a Conquest,* 115.

42. NAZ Mwinilunga District Notebook KSE 4/1. p361.

43. Ibid.

44. Ibid., 97.

45. Ibid., 360–65.

46. Ibid., 109–15.

2. THE WORLD OF *ATAATA*

1. Abadian, *From Wasteland to Homeland.*

2. For a detailed look at the events leading up to this transition see Macpherson, *Anatomy of a Conquest.*

3. Snelson, *Educational Development in Northern Rhodesia,* 258.

4. The best current historical and analytical treatment of the degenerationist paradigm can be found in Dubow, *Scientific Racism in Modern South Africa,* especially chapter 5.

5. Galbraith, *Crown and Charter;* Gann, *History of Northern Rhodesia;* Stabler, "British South Africa Company Proposal," 499–528.

6. NAZ Mwinilunga District Notebook KSE 4/1, 28, 26–31.

7. Roberts, *History of Zambia,* chap. 10.

8. Vickery, "Saving Settlers."

9. Parpart, *Labor and Capital on the African Copperbelt.*

10. Chipungu, *Guardians in Their Time.*

11. *British News,* which invariable led off with a segment about the British royal family, was a standard part of the commercial movie package shown daily on the Copperbelt starting in the late 1920s.

12. On March 1, 1960, for example, the Lunda Ndembu Native Authority, including all the chiefs, gave evidence before the Monckton Commission, a body with a mandate to assess "Native" response to a merger of Northern Rhodesia, Southern Rhodesia, and Nyasaland. The twenty-five-point statement presented that day expressing strong Lunda objections contained ten specific references to the British queen.

13. In 1984, eighty-five-year-old Mrs. Patterson gave this account of her journey to Northern Rhodesia in a letter sent to a Franciscan friar, Brother Joseph Weissling at Lwawu Mission. The author was present when the letter arrived and was read aloud.

14. In South Africa the term "Cape Coloured" generally refers to people of mixed ancestry, usually of European and Cape Province African descent. Most are in fact of European-Xhoisan descent and speak Afrikaans as their native tongue. This group was afforded special legal rights of employment, residency, and movement not granted to "Black Africans," including the right to vote in Cape elections up to 1953. It was not uncommon to find individuals throughout the Southern African region of varying backgrounds appropriating this identity.

15. Some Lunda speak of the production of progeny almost as a sum-zero game. To have lots of children is to spread out one's blood, to weaken oneself, or to dissipate one's energy in this world in exchange for descendants, whose acts of remembrance will keep one alive in the next world. Infertile people/witches or sorcerers, by contrast, keep all their blood and all their accumulated energies to themselves, becoming very powerful in this world, but they leave behind no one to mourn or remember them and hence have no life in the next world. Additionally, witches and sorcerers are portrayed in Lunda legends as perpetually hungry for human flesh and blood.

16. See Berger, *Labour, Race and Colonial Rule.*

17. Perhaps the best account of the development of the so-called Shangaan can be found in Harries, "Exclusion, Classification and Internal Colonialism."

18. Personal communication from Fr. Adrian Peck and Bro. Joseph Weissling at Lwawu Mission.

19. During 1985 and 1986 rarely a day passed without my spending some time with Mr. Jake. The bits and pieces of his life in South Africa invariably encroached on every conversation.

20. Isaac Nkemba built his new house on a plot of land immediately adjacent to my own house, thus shifting the center of activity on Matonchi Plateau virtually to my doorstep. Isaac and I interacted daily as I assisted him in the garden, accompanied him on hunting trips, and sat in on his efforts at resolving local disputes.

21. At the time of the incident in 1994 the exchange rate was roughly 600 Zambian kwacha to one U.S. dollar.

22. Even in the 1980s and 1990s the Waylesi village remained a large, well-integrated unit on Matonchi Plateau, relatively autonomous and prosperous by local standards. Situated only a couple of hundred yards from my own house, it was a place that I spent some time nearly every day, socializing and listening to the stories of its elders.

3. Coming of Age at St. Kizito

1. Personal communication from Father Adrian Peck, 1982.

2. Lwawu Mission was frequently chosen to host regional and national Catholic convocations,

retreats, and training programs. It also served as one of the preferred stopover points for government officials on tour of Northwestern Province.

3. The Baptistine Sisters were a diverse and ever-changing assemblage of principally American, Italian, and Zambian nuns. None of the latter, however, was Lunda.

4. At the dozens of major Catholic gatherings in Zambia that I attended throughout the 1980s and 1990s, I noted that the name of Fr. Adrian was invariably invoked, his experiences recounted, and the continuing relevance of his insights examined.

5. Personal communication with Brother Joe Weissling, 1984.

6. A detailed analysis of St. Kizito student performance in comparison with those attending other schools in Mwinilunga is contained in Hoppers, *Education in a Rural Society*.

7. For a fuller treatment of this topic, see Pritchett, *Lunda-Ndembu*, chap. 3.

8. For data on the social composition of contemporary villages compared with those of the 1950s, see Pritchett, *Lunda-Ndembu*, 343–47.

4. HARRY FRANKLIN'S SAUCEPAN SPECIAL

1. The development of the Central African Broadcasting Services (CABS) is recounted in Franklin, *Report on the Development of Broadcasting;* Fraenkel, *Wayleshi;* Powdermaker, *Copper Town;* Hobson, *Tales of Zambia;* and Grotpeter, Siegel, and Pletcher, *Historical Dictionary of Zambia.*

2. The initial version of the saucepan special was produced by the Eveready Company in hopes of making a good profit through the sale of batteries rather than on the radios themselves. Within a few years, however, numerous other companies had introduced their own battery-powered shortwave radios to the Africa market.

3. The Colour Bar was an extensive system of formal regulations and social norms in Central and Southern Africa that kept African and European separate in occupational, recreational, and residential settings.

4. Hortense Powdermaker's survey of radio listening habits and preferences among urban Africans in the 1960s revealed a pattern that remained remarkably stable, varying little from the results of my informal survey among the rural residents of Mwinilunga in the 1980s and 1990s (*Copper Town*, 231–53).

5. Numerous firsthand accounts of European attitudes toward African women's hygiene are contained in the *Report of the Committee Appointed to Investigate the Extent to Which Racial Discrimination Is Practiced.*

6. This strategy was formally outlined in the report on discrimination cited in note 5 (13) and subsequently funded by the colonial administration.

5. THE FEDERATION

1. Much of the history of the idea of a Central African federation is contained in Gann and Gelfand, *Huggins of Rhodesia;* Mulford, *Zambia;* and Macpherson, *Anatomy of a Conquest.*

2. See Birmingham and Martin, *History of Central Africa*, 362–69.

3. One of the earliest African responses firmly opposing the idea of federation in writing is Banda and Nkumbula, *Federation in Central Africa.*

4. A copy of the petition can be found in Makasa, *Zambia's March to Political Freedom*, 176–78.

5. Meebelo, *Reaction to Colonialism*, details the varied responses to the European incursion in Northern Zambia by African peoples with regard to preexisting power relations.

6. The topic of Banyama and the role of rumors in Central African history is the subject of White, *Speaking with Vampires.*

7. There are two notable biographies of Welensky—Taylor, *Rhodesian;* and Allighan, *Welensky Story*—as well as Welensky's own autobiography, *Welensky's 4000 Days.*

8. Reference to and a few partial copies of this local newspaper can be found in the Zambian National Archives (ZNA), DC Conference Box no. 66.

9. Deposits of gold, diamonds, emeralds, copper, chromium, cobalt, lead, and uranium have been located throughout Mwinilunga by a host of mineral survey companies over the years. After the initial euphoria, these companies came to realize that the deposits are too thinly dispersed and thoroughly intermingled to make commercial scale extraction economically viable. Nevertheless, each new report sends the local imagination soaring.

10. Victor Turner's field research was carried out during this period of local economic boom, and the best quantitative evidence of its dimensions is contained in E. L. B. Turner and V. W. Turner, "Money Economy Among the Mwinilunga Ndembu."

11. Notes contained in NAZ (Mwinilunga District Notebook KSE 4/1, 423–24) confirm local accounts of events collected by author.

12. Notes contained in NAZ (Mwinilunga District Notebook KSE 4/1, 427) confirm local accounts of events collected by author.

13. The African nationalist interpretation of the Monckton Commission can be found in Makasa, *Zambia's March to Political Freedom,* 176–78.

14. The author located a few crumbling but still highly treasured copies of the Lunda's Monckton report while in the field. A clean and complete copy can be found in NAZ (Mwinilunga District Notebook KSE 4/1, 126–36).

15. Police shot a number of African protesters in the land-clearing exercise that led up to the construction of the Kariba Dam. The exact number of deaths has not been agreed upon.

16. The four Resolutions of 1954, proposed by Sir John Moffat and passed by the Northern Rhodesia Legislative Council, essentially sought to establish a multiracial transitional government as an interim step toward full African independence.

17. From Marcus Garvey and his Universal Negro Improvement Association in the 1920s to the Black Power Movements of the 1960s and beyond, a steady stream of Pan-Africanist literature has found its way from the United States to Central and Southern Africa.

6. Voices from across the Border

1. For a fuller description of the process see Schecter, "History and Historiography."

2. This description taken from Capello and Ivens, *From Benguella to the Territory of Yacca,* is supported by a host of subsequent European travelers in Central Africa.

3. See Bustin, *Lunda under Belgian Rule,* 45, for notes on Captain Michaux's 1896 expedition to the Lunda capital.

4. Mwinilunga district commissioner Bruce Miller noted in his report of August 29, 1927, that the new Kanongesha, having received a Lukanu from the Lunda emperor, would now be fully recognized as the overlord of the area. NAZ (Mwinilunga District Notebook KSE 4/1, 339).

5. Territoire de Kapanga, Rapport AIMO (1957), 21, cited in Bustin, *Lunda under Belgian Rule,* 167.

6. See Bustin, *Lunda under Belgian Rule,* 165.

7. Gerard-Libois, *Katanga Secession,* 51.

8. Ibid., 10.

9. See J. C. Miller, "Chokwe Expansion."

10. See Bustin, *Lunda under Belgian Rule,* chap. 4.

11. Territoire de Dilolo, Rapport AIMO (1957), 28–29, cited in Bustin, *Lunda under Belgian Rule*, 173.

12. See Bustin, *Lunda under Belgian Rule*, 191.

13. Ibid., 193.

14. This report, which cited no sources, appeared in the March 2, 1960, edition of the *Daily Express* in London, cited in Gerard-Libois, *Katanga Secession*, 55–56.

15. *Northern News* (Ndola, Northern Rhodesia), May 25, 1960.

16. See Bustin, *Lunda under Belgian Rule*, 277n29.

17. The Congolese National Liberation Front's own account of its political evolution and military objectives is detailed in a 1981 pamphlet, *The Question of "Zaire"/Congo*.

7. The Emergence of a New Nation-State

1. See, for example, Roberts, *History of Zambia;* and Mulford, *Zambia.*

2. See, especially, Meebelo, *Reaction to Colonialism;* Chipungu, *Guardians in Their Time;* and Rotberg, *Rise of Nationalism in Central Africa.*

3. See, for example, Berger, *Labour, Race and Colonial Rule;* and Gann, "Northern Rhodesian Copper Industry."

4. See, for example, Hooker, "Welfare Associations and Other Instruments of Accommodation"; R. Hall, *Zambia;* and Meebelo, *Reaction to Colonialism,* chap. 6.

5. See Northern Rhodesia Government, *Report of the Commission;* Roberts, *History of Zambia,* 201–23; and Powdermaker, *Copper Town,* 120–47.

6. See Northern Rhodesia Government, *Report of the Commission;* and Rotberg, *Rise of Nationalism in Central Africa,* 161–77.

7. See Epstein, *Politics in an Urban African Community,* chaps. 2 and 3; and Davidson, *Northern Rhodesia Legislative Council.*

8. Epstein, *Politics in an Urban African Community,* 90.

9. Mulford, *Zambia,* 14.

10. In addition to Mulford, *Zambia,* and Rotberg, *Rise of Nationalism in Central Africa,* more personalized accounts of the rise of UNIP can be found in Makasa, *Zambia's March to Political Freedom,* and Chitambala, *History of the United National Independence Party.*

11. Macmillan coined the phrase "winds of change" in a speech before the white South African parliament in Cape Town in February 1960.

12. The quote is attributed to an unnamed African politician addressing a mass meeting in Luapula Province, by the Monthly Intelligence Report, January 1960, S/S 123/2/01.

13. Cited in Mulford, *Northern Rhodesia General Election,* 45.

14. See Wele, *Kaunda and the Mushala Rebellion,* appendix 2.

15. See Mulford, *Northern Rhodesia General Election,* 74–75; and Kaunda, *Zambia Shall Be Free,* 93–94.

16. *Northern News,* July 9, September 6, 11, 17, 1958.

17. See Mulford, *Northern Rhodesia General Election,* 117.

18. Robert Chitambala, as cited in Wele, *Kaunda and the Mushala Rebellion,* 9.

19. See Mulford, *Northern Rhodesia General Election,* 38; and Wele, *Kaunda and the Mushala Rebellion,* 61.

20. *Lusaka Advertiser,* November 2, 1962; Mulford, *Northern Rhodesia General Election,* chap. 7.

21. Official government election results as reported in Mulford, *Northern Rhodesia General Election,* appendix 1, 189–90.

22. NAZ Mwinilunga District Notebook KSE 4/1, 45–47.

23. Ibid., 469.

24. A copy of the document is contained in Wele, *Kaunda and the Mushala Rebellion,* appendix 5, 156.

25. See Mulford, *Northern Rhodesia General Election,* 309.

26. Ibid., 324.

27. *Solwezi District Newsletter,* January 21, 1965.

28. Zambian National Archives, House of Chiefs, Box No. 82A.

29. Zambian National Archives, House of Chiefs, Box No. 82A; minutes of April 8, 1964, meeting.

30. Zambian National Archives, House of Chiefs, Box No. 82A; minutes of April 8, 1964, meeting.

31. Zambian National Archives, House of Chiefs, Box No. 82A, 5; minutes of September 28–29, 1971, meeting.

32. Zambian National Archives, House of Chiefs, Box No. 82A, 6; minutes of September 28–29, 1971, meeting.

33. *Solwezi District Newsletter,* December 20, 1965.

34. Ibid., January 13, 1966.

35. See Wele, *Kaunda and the Mushala Rebellion,* 62.

36. Ibid., 63.

37. See Tordoff, *Politics in Zambia,* 368.

38. See Wele, *Kaunda and the Mushala Rebellion,* 63.

39. The only serious research on the life of Adamson Mushala, endeavoring to sift out facts from rumors, has been undertaken by Wele in *Kaunda and the Mushala Rebellion* and *Zambia's Most Famous Dissidents.* This section draws heavily on those works to confirm and supplement innumerable stories collected in the field.

40. In many areas of Zambia, COZ funds were used to entice UNIP's opponents to defect. Local offices would frequently choose not to consider loan applications from those without up-to-date party membership cards.

41. See Kaunda, *Humanism in Zambia.*

42. See Roberts, *History of Zambia,* 243; *Solwezi District Newsletter,* September 6, 1968; and Wele, *Kaunda and the Mushala Rebellion,* 32–39.

43. Quoted in Wele, *Kaunda and the Mushala Rebellion,* 77–78.

44. Ibid., 88.

45. Ibid., 104.

46. The fact that President Kenneth Kaunda's father was from Malawi has led many to question the leader's status as a "true" Zambian.

8. Living on the Edge (of the IMF leash)

1. Father Adrian Peck spent thirty-six years in Zambia (1947–83). He provided me with a wealth of oral information about the early years of Lwawu Mission during my first visit to Mwinilunga in the summer of 1982. Brother Louis Fouquette arrived in Zambia in 1954, and Brother Joe Weissling in 1958. Both were present at Lwawu during my major period of research (1984–87), offering invaluable assistance in the form of lodging, transportation, advice, introductions, and information about Mwinilunga during the second half of the twentieth century. Although I ultimately built a house two miles from the mission, I continued to see Brother Joe and Brother Louis several times

a week. Brother Joe was still present at Lwawu during my return visits in the 1990s and still a valuable source of timely and cogent information about daily life among the Lunda-Ndembu.

2. For data on cross-border residential mobility and patterns of marriage, see Pritchett, *Lunda-Ndembu,* 341, 349.

3. These numbers are from personal communications with UNHCR field staff. The best published source for information on the status of refugees in Northwestern Zambia remains Freund and Kalumba, *Social and Economic Conditions of Refugees.*

4. See Roberts, *History of Zambia,* 181.

5. See V. W. Turner, *Schism and Continuity,* 70.

6. A frequently heard refrain from Kapala Sakaumba.

7. Personal communications from Brother Joe Weissling at Lwawu Mission, summer of 1982.

8. See Burdette, *Zambia: Between Two Worlds,* 95–132.

9. Central Statistical Office, *Monthly Digest of Statistics,* 9, 11 (Nov. 1977), table 53, p. 53.

10. See Tordoff, *Politics in Zambia,* 274–87; and Chilivumbo, *Migration and Uneven Rural Development.*

11. *Second National Development Plan: January 1972–December 1976,* Zambian Ministry of Development Planning and National Guidance, December 1971.

12. See Cheru, *Silent Revolution in Africa;* Shaw, *Dependence and Underdevelopment;* and Young and Loxley, *Zambia.*

13. See Bjornlund, Bratton, and Gibson, "Observing Multiparty Elections in Africa"; and Bratton, "Zambia Starts Over."

14. Grotpeter, Siegel, and Pletcher, *Historical Dictionary of Zambia,* 416.

15. See Pritchett, *Lunda-Ndembu,* 52–77.

16. See Ekstrand, "Conflict Diamond Trade under Pressure," *Boston Metro,* May 11, 2001; and Amnesty International, "Statement on the Clean Diamond Act," April 9, 2003, www.amnestyusa .org/news/2003/usa04092003.html (accessed August 20, 2006).

17. See Pritchett, *Lunda-Ndembu,* 177–202.

18. Ibid., 342, tables 6a and 6b.

19. V. W. Turner, *Forest of Symbols,* remains the best and most comprehensive look at the Lunda-Ndembu ritual world.

20. See Pritchett, *Lunda-Ndembu,* 352–54, tables 14, 15, 16, and 17.

Glossary

Amabwambu	friends
Banyama	vampire, or one who kidnaps and transforms Africans into zombies who mindlessly toil on European farms
chaambu	concept of physical and existential separation by gender
chibinda (*ayibinda*, pl.)	hunter
chibodi	an insulting term for a man lacking in hunting abilities
Chifunga	a famous senior headman(ship) located around Matonchi Plateau in Chief Kanongesha's territory in northwestern Zambia
chijika mukanda	inaugurator of boys' circumcision ritual
chishika	cold dry season
chitengi	colorful wrap cloth, worn at all times by most Lunda women
chituba	cane rat; a highly prized delicacy
dikwilu	hungry for meat
haloshi	yesterday
ifuku dikwawu	day after tomorrow
ifuku dina	day before yesterday
ishaku	in-laws of the same generation
Jaha mutupa	lion killer
kachayi	millet beer
kadi majilu	pure, clean; literally, without mud
kandanji	one in charge of boys' circumcision ritual
kanfunti	a person born soon after the death of another family member of the same sex; one who is the vessel of a reincarnated spirit
Kanongesha	senior chief of the Lunda in Zambia; a title that can also refer to his territory or his subjects
kanzi	younger or junior to another
kapasu	chief's retainer, messenger, enforcer
kasa wubinda	to mystically destroy (tie up) someone's hunting ability
kasolu	honey beer
kendu	marble game
kufunta	to return

kumadiki	tomorrow
Kusaloka	pot about to boil over
kutena	to mention a person or thing by its proper name
kwata	caught, physically or spiritually
lelu	today
lituku	high-proof distilled liquor from cassava
lukanu	bracelet of chiefly authority, supposedly made from the skin of human genitalia
mafwami	farm owned by an individual rather than a kinship group
mapikiniki	picnic
Mbwela	original inhabitants of Mwinilunga, northwest Zambia
mpuhu	fame, renown
mukanda	boys' circumcision ritual
mukulumpi	elder or senior to another
mukwakuheta	one who possesses many things
mukwakwashi	one who helps people
muloji	witch/sorcerer
Mulonga	council to discuss problems, try cases
muntu (*antu*, pl.)	person
Musumba	Lunda capital in Congo
Muzungu	Europeans, white people
mwani vude	greetings
Mwantiyamvwa	emperor, highest Lunda leader
mwizukulu	grandchild (*ezukulu*, pl.)
nfumu watubwiku	head teacher at boys' circumcision ritual
nganda	chief's capital village
nkaka (*ankaka*, pl.)	grandfather
non'a	hot dry season
nshima	basic staple food made of boiled cassava flour
nvula	rainy season
Nzambi	high god
taata (*ataata*, pl.)	father
tooka	pure, white; also symbolically refers to things that are open and public, not hidden and evil
wubinda	huntsmanship
wubwambu	friendship
wusensi	joking cousins; formally designated categories of individuals or groups whose interaction is characterized by good-natured public ribald behavior but also guarantees of mutual assistance

Bibliography

Abadian, Sousan. *From Wasteland to Homeland: Trauma and Renewal of Indigenous Peoples and Their Communities.* Cambridge, MA, 1999.

Allighan, Garry. *The Welensky Story.* London, 1962.

Anderson, Benedict. *Imagined Communities: Reflections on the Origin and Spread of Nationalism.* London, 1961.

Arnot, Frederick S. *Bihe and Garenganze.* London, 1893.

———. *Garenganze or Seven Years of Pioneer Mission Work in Central Africa.* London, 1969 (originally published 1889).

———. *Missionary Travels in Central Africa.* London, 1914.

Ashley, Kathleen M., ed. *Victor Turner and the Construction of Cultural Criticism: Between Literature and Anthropology.* New York, 1990.

Banda, H. K., and H. M. Nkumbula. *Federation in Central Africa.* London, 1951.

Barth, Fredrik. *Ethnic Groups and Boundaries.* Boston, 1969.

Berger, Elena L. *Labour, Race and Colonial Rule.* Oxford, 1974.

Birmingham, David, and Phyllis M. Martin, eds. *History of Central Africa.* Vol. 1. London, 1983.

Bjornlund, Eric, Michael Bratton, and Clark Gibson. "Observing Multiparty Elections in Africa: Lessons from Zambia." *African Affairs* 91 (1992): 405–32.

Bloch, Maurice. *Ritual, History and Power: Selected Papers in Anthropology.* London, 1989.

Bourdieu, Pierre. *Outline of a Theory of Practice.* Trans. Richard Nice. Cambridge, UK, 1977.

Bratton, Michael. "Zambia Starts Over." *Journal of Democracy* 3, no. 2 (1992): 81–94.

Burdette, Marcia. *Zambia: Between Two Worlds.* Boulder, CO, 1988.

Burton, Richard Francis. *Lacerda's Journey to Cazembe, and Journey of Pombeiros.* London, 1873.

———. *The Lake Regions of Central Africa.* London, 1860.

Bustin, Edouard. *Lunda under Belgian Rule: The Politics of Ethnicity.* Cambridge, MA, 1975.

Capello, Hermengildo, and Roberto Ivens. *From Benguella to the Territory of Yacca.* 2 vols. London, 1882.

Cheke Cultural Writers Association. *The History and Cultural Life of the Mbunda Speaking Peoples.* Ed. Robert Papstein. Lusaka, Zambia, 1994.

Cheru, Fantu. *The Silent Revolution in Africa: Debt, Development, and Democracy.* London, 1989.

Chibanza, S. J. "Kaonde History" (Central Bantu Historical Texts). *Rhodes-Livingstone Institute Communications*, no. 22. Lusaka, Zambia, 1961.

Chilivumbo, Alifeyo. *Migration and Uneven Rural Development in Africa: The Case of Zambia.* Lanham, MD, 1985.

Chinyama, Thomas. *The Early History of the Balove Lunda.* Lusaka, Zambia, 1945.

Chipungu, Samuel, ed. *Guardians in Their Time: Experiences of Zambians under Colonial Rule, 1890–1964.* London, 1992.

Chitambala, Frank. *History of the United National Independence Party.* Lusaka, Zambia, 1984.

Clarence-Smith, W. G. "The Myth of Uneconomic Imperialism: The Portuguese in Angola, 1836–1926." *Journal of Southern African Studies* 5, no. 2 (1979): 165–80.

———. *Slaves, Peasants, and Capitalists in Southern Angola, 1840–1926.* Cambridge, UK, 1979.

Clegg, Edward. *Race and Politics, Partnership in the Federations of Rhodesia and Nyasaland.* London, 1960.

Coad, Frederick. *A History of the Brethren Movement.* Exter, UK, 1968.

Cohen, Yuhudi. *The Transition from Childhood to Adolescence: Cross-Cultural Studies of Initiation Ceremonies, Legal Systems, and Incest Taboos.* Chicago, 1964.

Coillard, Francois. *On the Threshold of Central Africa.* London, 1897.

Coleman, James C. "Friendship and the Peer Group in Adolescence." In *Handbook of Adolescent Psychology,* ed. Joseph Adelson, 408–31. New York, 1980.

Congolese National Liberation Front. *The Question of "Zaire"/Congo: The History of the 1977–78 Uprising in the Congo.* San Francisco, 1981.

Crawford, D. *Thinking Black: 22 Years without a Break in the Long Grass of Central Africa.* London, 1912.

Crehan, Kate. *The Fractured Community: Landscapes of Power and Gender in Rural Zambia.* Berkeley, 1997.

———. "Land, Labour and Gender: Matriliny in the 1980s Rural Zambia." Paper presented at meeting of African Studies Association, Toronto, 1994.

———. "Production, Reproduction, and Gender in North-Western Zambia: A Case Study." Ph.D. diss., University of Manchester, 1987.

Cummings, Scott, and Daniel J. Monti, eds. *Gangs: The Origins and Impact of Contemporary Youth Gangs in the United States.* Albany, NY, 1993.

Davidson, J. W. *The Northern Rhodesia Legislative Council.* London, 1948.

Davison, Jean. *Voices from Mutira: Lives of Rural Gikuyu Women.* Boulder, CO, 1989.

Derricourt, R. M., and Robert J. Papstein. "Lukolwe and the Mbwela of North-Western Zambia." *Azania* 11 (1977): 169–75.

Driberg, H. H. "The 'Best Friend' among the Didanga." *Man* 35 (1935): 101–2.

DuBois, Cora. "The Gratuitous Act: An Introduction to the Comparative Study of Friendship Patterns." In *The Compact: Selected Dimensions of Friendship,* ed. Elliott Leyton, 15–32. Toronto, 1974.

Dubow, Saul. *Scientific Racism in Modern South Africa.* Cambridge, UK, 1995.

Durkheim, Emile. *The Division of Labor in Society.* Trans. W. D. Halls. New York, 1984 (originally published 1933).

――――. *The Elementary Forms of the Religious Life*. New York, 1961 (originally published 1912).

Eisenstadt, S. N. *From Generation to Generation: Age Groups and Social Structure*. Glencoe, IL, 1956.

Elder, Glen H., Jr. *Children of the Great Depression*. Chicago, 1974.

Embley, Peter. "The Early Development of the Plymouth Brethren." In *Patterns of Sectarianism: Organisation and Ideology in Social and Religious Movements*, ed. Bryan Wilson. London, 1967.

Epstein, A. L. *Politics in an Urban African Community*. Manchester, UK, 1958.

Erikson, Erik H. *Identity: Youth and Crisis*. New York 1968.

Evans-Pritchard, E. E. *The Nuer: A Description of the Modes of Livelihood and Political Institutions of a Nilotic People*. Oxford, 1940.

――――. *Social Anthropology*. New York, 1951.

Fagan, Brian, ed. *A Short History of Zambia: From the Earliest Times until A.D. 1900*. Oxford, 1966.

Ferguson, James. *Expectations of Modernity: Myths and Meanings of Urban Life on the Zambian Copperbelt*. Berkeley, 1999.

――――. "Mobile Workers, Modernist Narratives: A Critique of the Historiography of Transition on the Zambian Copperbelt." *Journal of Southern African Studies* 16, no. 3 (1990): 385–412 and no. 4 (1990): 603–621.

Firth, Raymond. "Bond Friendship in Tikopia." In *Custom Is King*, ed. L. H. D. Burton. London, 1936.

Fisher, M. K. *Lunda-Ndembu Handbook*, 4th ed. Chingola, Zambia, 1984.

Fisher, Monica. *Nswana the Heir: The Life and Times of Charles Fisher, a Surgeon in Central Africa*. Ndola, Zambia, 1991.

Fisher, W. Singleton, and Julyan Hoyte. *Africa Looks Ahead*. London, 1948.

Fraenkel, Peter. *Wayleshi*. London, 1959.

Franklin, Harry. *Report on the Development of Broadcasting to Africans in Central Africa*. Lusaka, Zambia, 1949.

Freund, Paul, and Katele Kalumba. *The Social and Economic Conditions of Refugees and Displaced Persons in Mwinilunga, Zambezi, Kabompo and Solwezi Districts of Zambia's North-Western Province*. Lusaka, Zambia, 1983.

Foucault, Michel. *The Archaeology of knowledge*. Trans. A. M. Sheridan Smith. New York, 1972.

Galbraith, J. S. *Crown and Charter: The Early Years of the British South Africa Company*. Berkeley, 1974.

Gann, Lewis. "The End of the Slave Trade in British Central Africa, 1889–1912." *Rhodes-Livingstone Journal*, no. 16 (1954).

――――. *A History of Northern Rhodesia: Early Days to 1953*. London, 1964.

――――. "The Northern Rhodesian Copper Industry and the World of Copper, 1923–62." *Rhodes-Livingstone Journal*, no. 18 (1955).

Gann, L. H., and M. Gelfand. *Huggins of Rhodesia: The Man and His Country*. London, 1964.

Gerard-Libois, Jules. *Katanga Secession*. Trans. Rebecca Young. Madison, WI, 1966.

Gertzel, C., C. Baylies, and M. Szeftel, eds. *The Dynamics of the One-Party State in Zambia.* Manchester, UK, 1984.

Giddens, Anthony. *Central Problems in Social Theory: Action, Structure and Contradiction in Social Analysis.* Berkeley, 1979.

———. *Modernity and Self-Identity: Self and Society in the Late Modern Age.* Cambridge, UK, 1991.

———. *New Rules of Sociological Method: A Positive Critique of Interpretative Sociologies.* London, 1976.

Gluckman, Max. *Custom and Conflict in Africa.* Oxford, 1956.

———. *The Judicial Process among the Barotse of Northern Rhodesia.* Manchester, UK, 1955.

Goldstein, Arnold P. *Delinquent Gangs: A Psychological Perspective.* Champaign, IL, 1991.

Grotpeter, G. J., B. V. Siegel, and J. R. Pletcher. *Historical Dictionary of Zambia.* Lanham, MD, 1998.

Hacking, Ian. *The Social Construction of What?* Cambridge, MA, 1999.

Halbwachs, Maurice. *On Collective Memory.* Ed. and trans. Lewis A. Coser. Chicago, 1992.

Hall, G. S. *Adolescence: Its Psychology and Its Relations to Physiology, Anthropology, Sociology, Sex, Crime, Religion and Education.* New York, 1904.

Hall, R. *Zambia, 1890–1964.* London, 1965.

Hammond, R. J. *Portugal and Africa, 1815–1910: A Study in Uneconomic Imperialism.* Stanford, 1966.

Hansen, Art. "When the Running Stops: The Social and Economic Incorporation of Angolan Refugees into Zambian Border Villages." Ph.D. diss., Cornell University, 1976.

Harding, Colin. *In Remotest Barotseland.* London, 1904.

Harries, Patrick. "Exclusion, Classification and Internal Colonialism: The Emergence of Ethnicity among the Tsonga-Speakers of South Africa." In *The Creation of Tribalism in Southern Africa,* ed. Leroy Vail, 82–117. Berkeley, 1991.

Henderson, L. *Angola: Five Centuries of Conflict.* Ithaca, NY, 1979.

Hobson, Dick. *Tales of Zambia.* London, 1996.

Hooker, J. R. "Welfare Associations and Other Instruments of Accommodation in the Rhodesias between the World Wars." *Comparative Studies in Society and History* 9 (1966): 51–63.

Hoppers, Wim. *Education in a Rural Society: Primary Pupils and School Leavers in Mwinilunga, Zambia.* The Hague, 1981.

International Labor Office (ILO). *Basic Needs in an Economy under Pressure: Findings and Recommendations of an ILO/JASPA Basic Needs Mission to Zambia.* Addis Ababa, 1981.

Kakoma, Benson K. "Colonial Administration in Northern Rhodesia: A Case Study of Colonial Policy in the Mwinilunga District of Zambia, 1901–1939." MA thesis, University of Auckland, New Zealand, 1971.

Kaunda, Kenneth D. *Humanism in Zambia.* Lusaka, Zambia, 1967.

———. *Humanism in Zambia II.* Lusaka, Zambia, 1974.

———. *Zambia Shall Be Free.* Lusaka, Zambia, 1962.

Leyton, Elliott, ed. *The Compact: Selected Dimensions of Friendship.* Toronto, 1974.

Linton, Ralph. "The Gratuitous Act: An Introduction to the Comparative Study of Friendship Patterns." In *The Compact: Selected Dimensions of Friendship,* ed. Elliott Leyton. Toronto, 1974.

Livingstone, David. *Missionary Travels and Researches in South Africa.* London, 1857.

Macpherson, Fergus. *Anatomy of a Conquest: The British Occupation of Zambia, 1884–1924.* London, 1981.

Makasa, Kapasa. *Zambia's March to Political Freedom.* Lusaka, Zambia, 1981.

Malinowski, Bronislaw. *Argonauts of the Western Pacific.* New York, 1922 (reissued 1984).

———. "The Group and the Individual in Functional Analysis." *American Journal of Sociology* 44 (1939): 938–64.

———. *A Scientific Theory of Culture and Other Essays.* New York, 1944.

Mannheim, Karl. "The Problem of Generations." In *Essays on the Sociology of Knowledge,* ed. P. Keckskemeti, 276–322. London, 1952.

Marter, Alan. *Cassava or Maize: A Comparative Study of the Economics of Production and Market Potential of Cassava and Maize in Zambia.* Lusaka, Zambia: Rural Development Studies Bureau, 1978.

Mauss, Marcel. *The Gift: Form and Functions of Exchange in Archaic Societies.* Trans. Ian Cunnison. New York, 1976 (originally published 1925).

McCullock, Merran. *The Southern Lunda and Related Peoples.* London, 1951.

Meebelo, Henry S. *Reaction to Colonialism: A Prelude to the Politics of Independence in Northern Zambia, 1839–1939.* Manchester, UK, 1971.

Melland, Frank. *In Witch-Bound Africa: An Account of the Primitive Kaonde Tribe and Their Beliefs.* London, 1923.

Mitchell, J. Clyde, ed. *Social Networks in Urban Situations: Analysis of Personal Relationships in Central African Towns.* Manchester, UK, 1969.

———. "Theoretical Orientations in African Urban Studies." In *The Anthropological Study of Complex Societies,* ed. Michael Banton. London, 1966.

———. *The Yao Village.* Manchester, UK, 1956.

Miller, J. C. "Chokwe Expansion, 1850–1900." MA thesis, University of Wisconsin, 1969.

———. *Kings and Kinsmen: Early Mbundu States in Angola.* Madison, WI, 1976.

———. *Way of Death: Merchant Capitalism and the Angolan Slave Trade, 1730–1830.* Madison, WI, 1988.

Miller, Stuart. *Men and Friendship.* Boston, 1983.

Miracle, Marvin P. *Agriculture in the Congo Basin.* Madison, WI, 1967.

Mulford, David. *The Northern Rhodesia General Election, 1962.* London, 1964.

———. *Zambia: the Politics of Independence, 1957–1964.* London, 1967.

Mwanza, Ilse. *Bibliography of Zambiana Theses and Dissertations, 1930s-1989.* Lusaka, Zambia, 1990.

Mwondela, W. R. *Mukanda and Makishi: Traditional Education in North Western Zambia.* Lusaka, Zambia, 1972.

Northern Rhodesia Government. *Report of the Commission Appointed to Inquire into the Disturbances in the Copperbelt, Northern Rhodesia.* Lusaka, Zambia, 1935.

Oppen, Achim von. *Terms of Trade and Terms of Trust: The History and Context of Pre-Colonial Market Production around the Upper Zambezi and Kasai.* Munster, Germany, 1993.

Paine, Robert. "Anthropological Approaches to Friendship." *Humanitas* 6, no. 2 (1970): 139–60.

Parkin, David, Lionel Caplan, and Humphrey Fisher. *The Politics of Cultural Performance*. Providence, RI, 1996.

Parpart, Jane. *Labor and Capital on the African Copperbelt*. Philadelphia, 1983.

Powdermaker, Hortense. *Copper Town*, New York, 1962.

Pritchett, James A. *The Lunda-Ndembu: Style, Change, and Social Transformation in South Central Africa*. Madison, WI, 2001.

Radcliffe-Brown, A. R. The Mother's Brother in South Africa. *South African Journal of Science* 21 (1924): 542–55.

———. *A Natural Science of Society*. Glencoe, IL, 1964 (originally published 1948).

———. *Structure and Function in Primitive Society*. London, 1971 (originally published 1952).

Radin, Paul. *Crashing Thunder: The Autobiography of a Winnebago Indian*. New York, 1926.

Reefe, Thomas Q. *The Rainbow and the Kings: A History of the Luba Empire to 1891*. Berkeley, 1981.

Report of the Committee Appointed to Investigate the Extent to Which Racial Discrimination Is Practiced in Shops and in Other Similar Business Premises. Lusaka: Government Printer, 1956.

Riesman, David. *Selected Essays from Individualism Reconsidered*. Garden City, NY, 1956.

Riley, Matilda W., Marilyn Johnson, and Anne Foner. *Aging and Society*. Vol. 3, *A Sociology of Age Stratification*. New York, 1972.

Roberts, Andrew. *A History of Zambia*. New York, 1976.

Rosaldo, Renato. *Culture and Truth: The Remaking of Social Analysis*. Boston, 1989.

Rotberg, Robert I. "Plymouth Brethren and the Occupation of Katanga." *Journal of African History* 5 (1964): 285–97.

———. *The Rise of Nationalism in Central Africa*. Cambridge, MA, 1967.

Rowdon, Harold. *The Origins of the Brethren, 1825–1850*. London, 1967.

Scapera, I., ed. *David Livingstone: Family Letters, 1841–56*. 2 vols. London, 1959.

———, ed. *Livingstone's African Journal, 1853–1856*. London, 1963.

———, ed. *Livingstone's Missionary Correspondence 1841–1856*. London, 1961.

———, ed. *Livingstone's Private Journals, 1851–1853*. London, 1960.

Schecter, Robert. "History and Historiography on a Frontier of Lunda Expansion: The Origins and Early Development of the Kanongesha." Ph.D. diss., University of Wisconsin, 1976.

Schlegel, Alice, and Herbert Barry III. *Adolescence: An Anthropological Inquiry*. New York, 1991.

Schumaker, Lyn. *Africanizing Anthropology: Fieldwork, Networks, and the Making of Cultural Knowledge in Central Africa*. Durham, NC, 2001.

Shaw, Timothy. *Dependence and Underdevelopment: The Development and Foreign Policies of Zambia*. Athens, OH, 1976.

Silva Porto, Antonio Francisco Ferreira da. "Novas Jornadas de Silva Porto nos Sertoes Africanos." *Boletim da Sociedade de Geographia e da Historia de Lisboa*, 5a serie, no. 1 (1885): 3–36, no. 3 (1885): 145–72, no. 9 (1885): 569–86, and 10, (1885): 603–42.

———. *Viagens e Apontamentos de um Portuense em Africa: Diario de Antonio Francisco Ferreira da Silva Porto.* Vol. 1, Coimbra, Portugal, 1986.

Smith, Mary F. *Baba of Karo: A Woman of the Muslim Hausa.* New Haven, CT, 1954.

Snelson, Peter. *Educational Development in Northern Rhodesia, 1883–1945.* Lusaka, Zambia, 1974.

Stabler, John B. "The British South Africa Company Proposal for Amalgamation of the Rhodesias, 1915–1917: Northern Rhodesian Reaction." *African Social Research* 7 (June 1969): 499–528.

Taylor, Don. *The Rhodesian: The Life of Sir Roy Welensky.* London, 1955.

Thornton, John. "The Chronology and Causes of Lunda Expansion to the West, c. 1700–1852." *Zambia Journal of History* 1 (1981): 1–14.

Tilsley, G. E. *Dan Crawford, Missionary and Pioneer in Central Africa.* London, 1929.

Tordoff, William. *Administration in Zambia.* Manchester, UK, 1980.

———, ed. *Politics in Zambia.* Manchester, UK, 1974.

Trapnell, C. G., and J. N. Clothier. *The Soils, Vegetation and Agricultural Systems of North Western Rhodesia: A Report of the Ecological Survey.* Lusaka, Zambia, 1936.

Turner, E. L. B., and V. W. Turner. "Money Economy among the Mwinilunga Ndembu: A Study of Some Individual Cash Budgets." *Rhodes-Livingstone Journal: Human Problems in British Central Africa,* no. 18 (1955): 19–37.

Turner, Frederick. "Hyperion to a Satyr: Criticism and Anti-structure in the Work of Victor Turner." In *Victor Turner and the Construction of Cultural Criticism,* ed. Kathleen M. Ashley. Bloomington, IN, 1990.

Turner, Victor W. "Dewey, Dilthey, and Drama: An Essay in the Anthropology of Experience." In *The Anthropology of Experience,* ed. V. W. Turner and E. M. Bruner, 33–44. Urbana, IL, 1986.

———. *The Drums of Affliction: A Study of Religious Processes among the Ndembu of Zambia.* Oxford, 1968.

———. *The Forest of Symbols.* Ithaca, NY, 1967.

———. *The Lozi People of North-Western Rhodesia.* London, 1952.

———. "A Lunda Love Song and Its Consequences." *Rhodes-Livingstone Journal,* no. 19. Lusaka, Zambia, 1955.

———. "Lunda Medicine and the Treatment of Disease." *Occasional Papers of the Rhodes-Livingstone Museum,* no. 15. Lusaka, Zambia, 1963.

———. "Lunda Rites and Ceremonies." *Occasional Papers of the Rhodes-Livingstone Museum,* no. 10. Lusaka, Zambia, 1953.

———. *Revelation and Divination in Ndembu Ritual.* Ithaca, NY, 1975.

———. *The Ritual Process.* Ithaca, NY, 1969.

———. "Ritual Symbolism, Morality, and Social Structure among the Ndembu." *Rhodes-Livingstone Journal,* no. 30. Lusaka, Zambia, 1961.

———. *Schism and Continuity in an African Society: A Study of Ndembu Village Life.* Manchester, UK, 1957.

———. "Witchcraft and Sorcery: Taxonomy versus Dynamics." *Africa* 34 (1964): 314–25.

Turner, V. W., and E. M. Bruner, eds. *The Anthropology of Experience.* Urbana, IL, 1986.

Vail, Leroy, ed. *The Creation of Tribalism in Southern Africa.* Berkeley, 1991.

Van Binsbergen, Wim M. J. *Religious Change in Zambia.* London, 1981.

———. *Tears of Rain: Ethnicity and History in Central Western Zambia.* London, 1992.

Van Binsbergen, Wim M. J., and Peter Geschierre, eds. *Old Modes of Production and Capitalist Encroachment: Anthropological Explorations in Africa.* London, 1985.

Van Binsbergen, Wim M. J., and Matthew Schoffeleers. *Theoretical Explorations in African Religion.* London, 1985.

Vansina, Jan. *Kingdoms of the Savanna.* Madison, WI, 1966.

Vellut, Jean-Luc. "Notes sur le Lunda et la Frontier Luso-Africaine, 1700–1900." *Etudes d'Histoire Africaine* 3 (1972): 61–166.

Vickery, Kenneth P. "Saving Settlers: Maize Control in Northern Rhodesia." *Journal of Southern African Studies* 2, no. 2 (April 1985): 212–34.

Watson, L. *Interpreting Life Histories.* New Brunswick, NJ, 1985.

Wele, Patrick. *Kaunda and the Mushala Rebellion.* Lusaka, Zambia, 1988.

———. *Zambia's Most Famous Dissidents.* Solwezi, Zambia, 1995.

Welensky, Sir Roy. *Welensky's 4000 Days: The Life and Death of the Federation of Rhodesia and Nyasaland.* London, 1964.

Werbner, Richard P. "The Manchester School in South-Central Africa." *Annual Review of Anthropology* 13 (1984): 157–85.

White, C. M. N. "The Balovale People and Their Historical Background." *Rhodes-Livingstone Journal* 8, Lusaka, Zambia, 1959.

———. "The Material Culture of the Lunda-Luvale People." *Occasional Papers of the Rhodes-Livingstone Museum,* no. 3. Lusaka, Zambia, 1948.

———. *An Outline of Luvale Social and Political Organization.* Manchester, UK, 1960.

White, Luise. *Speaking with Vampires: Rumor and History in Colonial Africa.* Berkeley, 2000.

Wilkin, Paul D. "To The Bottom of the Heap: Educational Deprivation and Its Social Implications in the Northwestern Province of Zambia, 1906–1945." Ph.D. diss., Syracuse University, 1983.

Wilson, Bryan, ed. *Patterns of Sectarianism: Organisation and Ideology in Social and Religious Movements.* London, 1967.

Young, R., and John Loxley. *Zambia: An Assessment of Zambia's Structural Adjustment Experience.* Ottawa, 1990.

Index

CPSIA information can be obtained
at www.ICGtesting.com
Printed in the USA
LVHW100836150722
723432LV00006B/317

9 780813 926254